THE NORTH ATLANTIC COAST

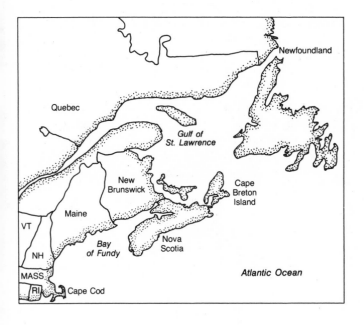

The Sierra Club Naturalist's Guides

A Sierra Club Naturalist's Guide to

THE NORTH ATLANTIC COAST
Cape Cod to Newfoundland

by Michael and Deborah Berrill
illustrations by Rob Tuckerman

SIERRA CLUB BOOKS *San Francisco*

Library of Congress Cataloging in Publication Data

Berrill, Michael.
   A Sierra Club naturalist's guide to the North Atlantic coast.
      Bibliography: p. 440
      Includes index.
      1. Natural history—New England. 2. Natural history—Atlantic coast (Canada). 3. Coastal ecology—New England. 4. Coastal ecology—Atlantic coast (Canada). I. Berrill, Deborah, 1948–   joint author. II. Sierra Club.
III. Title.
QH104.5.N4B47   574.974   80-23086
ISBN 0-87156-242-1
ISBN 0-87156-243-X (pbk.)

Book design by Drake Jordan
Illustrations by Rob Tuckerman
Printed in the United States of America on acid-free recycled paper
10   9   8   7   6   5

TABLE OF CONTENTS

Contents   vii

ACKNOWLEDGMENTS

WE FEEL EXTREMELY FORTUNATE to have coerced Rob Tuckerman to illustrate most of this book; he has captured in his drawings a spirit which we can only hope emerges in the words as well.

Several of the photographs are not ours, and we are grateful to N. J. Berrill for those of figures 32, 101, 106 and plate VII and to Robert Stewart for those of figures 121 and 122.

This book was written while we were on leave from Trent University, in Ontario. We made our headquarters near Boothbay Harbor, Maine and we appreciate our welcome there at Bigelow Laboratory for Ocean Sciences. We especially value the assistance given us by the lab's chief librarian Kimberly Douglas.

In writing this book we have drawn on the ideas and descriptions published in the professional literature by a large number of biologists, oceanographers and geologists, far too numerous for us to credit appropriately but without whom no book such as this could be attempted.

Michael and Deborah Berrill

INTRODUCTION

THERE IS SOMETHING about the sea that has captured the imagination of man, and those who are drawn to its shores inevitably seek to understand the bizarre life forms encountered there. Few places on earth have more abundant life than coasts and few are more varied than America's North Atlantic (or Boreal) coast, which extends from Cape Cod north to Newfoundland.

Though identification guides provide a vital starting point for getting to know this region, people often wish to know more than an organism's name. They are curious about the life behind the name—why a plant or animal lives where it does; how it is adapted to its environment; and what its interrelationships are with other life. We wrote this book in the hope that it will provide a basis for understanding these interrelationships on the Boreal coast.

Since all living things are adapted to specific types of environments or habitats, the book is organized according to the major marine habitats of the region.

The earth's crust provides the very tangible foundation for the habitats of the coast, and so the opening chapter deals with both the past and present geological processes which make this coast unique. The ruggedness of much of the coast is the result of the glaciations which buried a region formed initially by continents colliding with each other and then tearing themselves apart again.

The currents of the region determine the temperature and composition of the coastal waters and hence play a dominant role in influencing which organisms live here. And the tides of the region, which are among the greatest in the world, reaching amplitudes as great as 50 feet (16 m), give the region its splendid intertidal communities.

In chapters 2–4 we look at various interfaces of sea and land. Chapter 2 is given to the intertidal rocky shore; chapter 3 to beaches and sand dunes; chapter 4 to estuaries, including salt marshes and mud flats. These chapters deal first with the structure of the environment itself and with the advantages and disadvantages it offers to any plant or animal living there.

Each of these major habitats is in turn composed of sub-habitats, or zones, which are submerged for greater or lesser amounts of time by the sea. Each zone has its own community of plants and animals, and we have tried to introduce the more common members of each community and their relationships to the other plants or animals. Predation, competition and succession are recurrent themes throughout these chapters, and in fact, throughout the book.

In chapter 5 we examine the shallow subtidal world. It is subdivided into rocky and soft substrates, for very different kinds of communities exist in these two sub-habitats. The subtidal is a habitat of greater stability than the intertidal and its diversity of organisms is greater. Its space is highly competed for by the organisms found there.

Seabirds and seals, which are often seen from shore, breed on the abundant islands and ledges of the region. In chapter 6 we investigate the seabird and seal colonies, their elaborate breeding behavior and their vulnerability to human disturbances.

Finally, in chapter 7, we look at the deep offshore communities comprised of shrimp, jellyfish, whales and fish. This vast realm is subdivided into two general habitats, the upper layers of water, the pelagic environment, and the seabed and area just above it, the demersal environment. Though fishermen from many parts of the world have long depended on these offshore waters for their livelihoods, the complexities of interrelationships found there are only just beginning to be understood.

Names

To eliminate confusion, we use both common names and scientific names for organisms. An organism may well have several common names, but it has only one scientific name. For instance, the hardshell clam is also known commonly as the quahog, the round clam, the little neck clam, the cherry-stone clam and the chowder clam. However, its only scientific name is *Mercenaria mercenaria.* In addition, the same common name may be shared by different species in

2   INTRODUCTION

different areas. The common name "sole" is a good example of confusion that can possibly result. In North American Atlantic Boreal waters, winter flounder, witch flounder and hogchoker all go by the name of "sole". By using the scientific names, people are assured of talking about the same animal.

Metric Measurement

Metric equivalents are provided for all measurements used in this book. They are indicated in parentheses following the English units. The following conversions may be useful.

1 mile = 1.67 kilometers (km)
1 kilometer (km) = 0.6 miles
1 foot = 0.3 meters (m)
1 meter (m) = 40 inches
1 inch = 2.5 centimeters (cm)
1 centimeter (cm) = 0.4 inches
1 kilogram (kg) = 2.2 pounds
1 pound = .45 kilogram (kg)

To convert degrees Fahrenheit (F) to degrees Celsius (C) or vice versa, use the following equations:

$$F = 9/5 \ C + 32$$
$$C = 5/9 \ (F - 32)$$

Metric and English rulers are printed on the last page of this guide to facilitate measurements.

Appendices

The appendices at the end of the book are included especially for those who wish to pursue topics further, whether through reading, through visiting other similar habitats within this geographically extensive area, or through conservation activities.

The References have been carefully selected and annotated. The Addresses provide a starting point for parks information and for conservation groups. The Classification of

Cape Cod to Southern Maine

The southern coast of the Gulf of Maine, beginning at Cape Cod and extending north almost to Cape Elizabeth, is one of long sandy beaches, soft cliffs and bluffs, and only an occasional headland of hard bedrock jutting out beyond the beachline. The beach development is impressive, with extensive dune fields, barrier beaches, long sand spits, and even barrier islands. Salt marshes, protected from the direct impact of ocean waves and currents, thrive behind many of the beaches. Erosion by those waves and currents continues to wear back the headlands of exposed sandstone at rates up to several feet (1 m) a year, and their sediment provides further new material for the growth of the beaches. Outcroppings of older rock, much more resistant to such erosion, interrupt the coastline with increasing frequency north of Cape Cod Bay, and smaller crescent shaped beaches lie between adjacent headlands where long, dune-backed beaches lack the space and sediment they need to grow. The largest of such outcroppings forms Cape Ann, north of Boston Harbor, but even in southern Maine the harder headlands are not so frequent as to prevent the growth of some long barrier beaches and a few dune fields.

A coastline such as this, smoothed and sandy, is a relatively mature one, no matter how young in years it happens to be. All coasts eventually are eroded to such an extent by ocean waves and currents that headlands disappear. Bays and inlets are also all but eliminated as sand spits grow across their mouths and sediment fills them in and turns them into mud flats which may then support salt marshes. Glaciers did not reach south of Cape Cod and Long Island, and coastlines there have had many millions of years to become mature. But the glaciers only began to retreat from Cape Cod and the coasts north of it about 15,000 to 12,000 years ago, leaving only a short time in which to achieve maturity.

Before the glaciers came, Cape Cod and the other sand spits and barrier beaches of the southern portion of the Boreal coast simply did not exist. Wherever the melting glaciers stopped during their gradual retreat, however, different areas. The common name "sole" is a good example of confusion that can possibly result. In North American Atlantic Boreal waters, winter flounder, witch flounder and hogchoker all go by the name of "sole". By using the scientific names, people are assured of talking about the same animal.

Metric Measurement

Metric equivalents are provided for all measurements used in this book. They are indicated in parentheses following the English units. The following conversions may be useful.

> 1 mile = 1.67 kilometers (km)
> 1 kilometer (km) = 0.6 miles
> 1 foot = 0.3 meters (m)
> 1 meter (m) = 40 inches
> 1 inch = 2.5 centimeters (cm)
> 1 centimeter (cm) = 0.4 inches
> 1 kilogram (kg) = 2.2 pounds
> 1 pound = .45 kilogram (kg)

To convert degrees Fahrenheit (F) to degrees Celsius (C) or vice versa, use the following equations:

$$F = 9/5 \ C + 32$$
$$C = 5/9 \ (F - 32)$$

Metric and English rulers are printed on the last page of this guide to facilitate measurements.

Appendices

The appendices at the end of the book are included especially for those who wish to pursue topics further, whether through reading, through visiting other similar habitats within this geographically extensive area, or through conservation activities.

The References have been carefully selected and annotated. The Addresses provide a starting point for parks information and for conservation groups. The Classification of

Plants and Animals is designed to show the evolutionary relationships between organisms. And the Glossary gives brief definitions of the most important recurrent terms which might be unfamiliar.

CHAPTER I

The American Atlantic Boreal Region

The Character of the Coast

The North Atlantic or Atlantic Boreal coast begins on the north shore of Cape Cod and extends north and east to include the shores of northern New England and the Canadian Maritime Provinces. This cold-temperate, or Boreal, region is bordered on the north by the very cold Arctic region, which begins at the Strait of Belle Isle and includes the polar coastline. North of the Strait of Belle Isle, the icy Labrador Current combines with the extreme northern latitude to provide a temperature barrier to most Boreal organisms. On the south, the Boreal coast is bordered by the warmer, temperate Mid-Atlantic region, which extends from Cape Cod to Cape Hatteras.

The Boreal coast is a biogeographical region of relative climatic stability and it distinguishes itself clearly from adjacent regions. The interplay of coastal and oceanic currents keep it colder throughout even the warmest months than any region south of it, yet warmer during those same months than Arctic organisms to the north can usually tolerate.

1. Biogeographical regions of North America's coasts

The Gulf Stream swings away from the coast at Cape Cod. Warm itself, the Gulf Stream prevents warmer, more southern water from mixing with the cold currents of the Boreal region. The average annual sea temperatures on the north shore of the Cape are thus several degrees colder than those but a few miles away on the Cape's south shore.

Few Boreal organisms are common south of Cape Cod. This is especially true of those that are sedentary, and cannot walk or swim to cooler water when they need to. Boreal species that do live south of the Cape usually remain in deeper, offshore, colder water. Of the typically Arctic organisms that survive in the Boreal zone, none can tolerate the warm water south of the Cape.

The summer and autumn warming of the coastal waters south of Cape Cod allows many warm water animals, moving northward, to invade seasonally from south of Cape Hatteras. None of these passes north of Cape Cod, for they cannot tolerate the cold.

The Boreal region of the Atlantic coast of North America has some similarities with cold temperate coasts everywhere. It is remarkably similar to the corresponding region of the European Atlantic coast, where the Boreal region extends from the English Channel to the North Cape of Norway. Many plants and animals are exactly the same on both coasts; many others are closely related. And much of what we know of the American coast is derived from what northern Europeans have learned about theirs.

Relatively cold water is not the only thing that characterizes the Boreal region. Tides south of Cape Cod, including those on its own south shore, are rarely over 4 ft. (1.2 m) in amplitude. Those of the north shore of the Cape are twice as great, and increase in amplitude as one moves north in New England and into the Bay of Fundy where the world famous 50 ft (15 m) tides occur. The coastline topography shifts gradually from the beaches and salt marshes typical of most of the coast south of Cape Cod to the rugged shores which dominate the coast northward from southern Maine. This northern coastline itself is incredibly indented, in sharp contrast to coastlines to the south. Submerged offshore banks, supporting huge fisheries, extend from Georges Bank off Cape Cod to the Grand Banks off Newfoundland. Currents, tides, temperatures, fishing banks, coastal topography, glaciated past, all combine to further distinguish the Western Atlantic Boreal region from others.

Within the Boreal region, between Cape Cod and Labrador, there is considerable variation in coastal type, more in fact, than in any other biogeographical region on the Atlantic coast. Sand beaches and salt marshes dominate the coast from Cape Cod to southern Maine; rocky shores and pocket beaches dominate the rest of Maine's coast, southern New Brunswick, the seaward side of Nova Scotia, all of Newfoundland, and much of the Gulf of St. Lawrence. The Bay of Fundy, with its immense tides, has mud flats that appear endless. The beaches of Prince Edward Island and the southern Gulf of St. Lawrence are extensive, too, and remarkably comparable to areas south of the Boreal region. Tidal ledges and offshore islands are abundant along much of the coast, where large numbers of sea birds and seals breed each year.

The region then is a complex one, for each habitat presents its own set of environmental stresses, and a different community of organisms has succeeded in adapting to the stresses of each. In many places several different habitats may be so close to one another that rocky shores grade into beaches or mud flats and back again in just a matter of meters. Such local heterogeneity increases the diversity of organisms that live there.

The Coastline: Cape Cod to Newfoundland

The Gulfs of Maine and St. Lawrence, along with the Atlantic coasts of Nova Scotia and Newfoundland, make up the Boreal region. The shorelines, even within each of the gulfs, vary remarkably, however, a result of the different effects of recent glacial and preglacial events. Whether the present shores are smooth and beach-lined or indented and rock-bound depends on how hard or soft the bedrock is, and where the glaciers dumped their immense loads of rocks and sediments when they reached the ocean and later when they retreated.

8

2. The North Atlantic Boreal Coast extends from Cape Cod to the Straight of Belle Isle. Coastal National Parks, shaded black, are 1. Acadia 2. Fundy 3. Kouchibouguac 4. Prince Edward Island 5. Cape Breton Highlands 6. Forillon 7. Gros Morne 8. Terra Nova

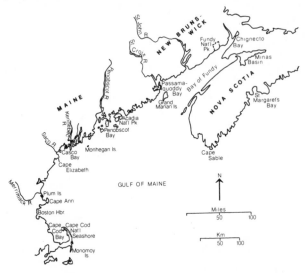

3. Detail of the Gulf of Maine

The Coastline

Cape Cod to Southern Maine

The southern coast of the Gulf of Maine, beginning at Cape Cod and extending north almost to Cape Elizabeth, is one of long sandy beaches, soft cliffs and bluffs, and only an occasional headland of hard bedrock jutting out beyond the beachline. The beach development is impressive, with extensive dune fields, barrier beaches, long sand spits, and even barrier islands. Salt marshes, protected from the direct impact of ocean waves and currents, thrive behind many of the beaches. Erosion by those waves and currents continues to wear back the headlands of exposed sandstone at rates up to several feet (1 m) a year, and their sediment provides further new material for the growth of the beaches. Outcroppings of older rock, much more resistant to such erosion, interrupt the coastline with increasing frequency north of Cape Cod Bay, and smaller crescent shaped beaches lie between adjacent headlands where long, dune-backed beaches lack the space and sediment they need to grow. The largest of such outcroppings forms Cape Ann, north of Boston Harbor, but even in southern Maine the harder headlands are not so frequent as to prevent the growth of some long barrier beaches and a few dune fields.

A coastline such as this, smoothed and sandy, is a relatively mature one, no matter how young in years it happens to be. All coasts eventually are eroded to such an extent by ocean waves and currents that headlands disappear. Bays and inlets are also all but eliminated as sand spits grow across their mouths and sediment fills them in and turns them into mud flats which may then support salt marshes. Glaciers did not reach south of Cape Cod and Long Island, and coastlines there have had many millions of years to become mature. But the glaciers only began to retreat from Cape Cod and the coasts north of it about 15,000 to 12,000 years ago, leaving only a short time in which to achieve maturity.

Before the glaciers came, Cape Cod and the other sand spits and barrier beaches of the southern portion of the Boreal coast simply did not exist. Wherever the melting glaciers stopped during their gradual retreat, however, they dumped the sediment they carried in piles or moraines at the glacier edges. The longer a glacier stopped before recommencing its retreat, the larger the moraine it left behind. The lower part of Cape Cod, along with Nantucket Island, Martha's Vineyard and Long Island are large moraines that have since been modified by erosion. The glaciers also left behind drumlins, hill-like mounds which the glaciers overrode, such as those which presently are islands in Boston Harbor. Remnants of them emerge at low tide along parts of Plum Island north of Cape Ann. Meltwater from the glaciers also carried glacial sediment far over the land tilting down to the sea, spreading the sediment in outwash plains over the underlying bedrock. When the sea level rose, the ocean waves and currents had immense amounts of easily eroded sediments to work and rework into today's mature coast.

4. The remains of this drumlin at Plum Island, Massachusetts, is a testimony to the years when glaciers covered this coast.

The Rocky Coast of Maine

In sharp contrast to the beach-lined coast of the southern Gulf of Maine is the extraordinarily rugged, indented, rockbound coast that begins at Cape Elizabeth and extends north to Passamoquoddy Bay at the mouth of the Bay of

Fundy. In the 200 miles that lie in a straight line between these two points are more than 2500 miles of shoreline, most of it rocky, including the large Casco and Penobscot Bays, an almost unlimited array of smaller bays, coves and inlets, and thousands of islands which range from the spectacular Mt. Desert and Monhegan Islands to ledges only barely exposed when the tide is high. Most of the coast lacks the sediment necessary for sandy beaches or salt marshes to develop, for the exposed bedrock is primarily granite and erodes extremely slowly. The glaciers dumped their loads of sediments on areas which now lie to the south and east, offshore.

5. The silhouette of the coast of Maine from Penobscot Bay to Machias emphasizes the rugged nature of the coastline. Mt. Desert is the larger island in the middle of this stretch of coast.

The many valleys eroded by streams in pre-glacial times generally ran north to south, the route followed by the glaciers that scoured and straightened the valleys as they too flowed to the sea. When the glaciers finally began to melt and retreat, the present coast of Maine was several hundred feet above sea level, and up to 100 miles from the sea itself. The melting of the immense ice cap soon started the sea level rising. The land rose, too, in rebound after its release from the weight of the glaciers, but the sea rose

THE ATLANTIC BOREAL REGION

faster. It flooded the basin of the Gulf of Maine first, making islands of the banks along its seaward edge. Then it flooded the banks as well, and submerged the coastal river valleys, converting them to bays and inlets. Maine's drowned indented coastline is as youthful and unmodified as any coast can be, and it is not likely to change quickly.

The Bay of Fundy

The Bay of Fundy separates most of New Brunswick from most of Nova Scotia. About 150 miles (240 km) long and 50 miles (80 km) wide at its mouth, it is famous for the tides it funnels to greater and greater heights as they surge towards Chignecto Bay and Minas Basin. The water and mud of the whole of the Bay of Fundy are tinged reddish from the erosion of the red sandstone cliffs and bluffs which stand along many parts of the shore. The tides themselves produce the currents which continue to erode back the soft headlands, providing the sediment that lines the Bay of Fundy. This sediment forms the immense mud flats in the two bays where extensive salt marshes have had a chance to grow as well.

The Bay of Fundy is a lowland trough in the northern end of the eroded remnants of the Appalachian Mountains. Glaciers during the last ice age flowed southwest along its length, eroding its escarpments in the process. When the bay emerged from beneath the retreating glaciers about 14,000 years ago, it had little if any tide. The sea level was still so low that the Gulf of Maine was mostly enclosed by land. Water entered it only through the 25 mile (40 km) wide Northeast Channel which lies between the present Georges and Browns Banks.

The rise of the sea level gradually widened and deepened the contact between the Gulf of Maine and the ocean over the continental shelf. About 4,000 years ago, the tides of the Bay of Fundy began to increase from the 6-foot (2 m) heights, which are typical of the Atlantic coast of Nova Scotia, to the 50-foot (15 m) tides which sweep the head of the Bay of Fundy today.

6. Erosion of the sandstone along the Bay of Fundy coast has left behind formations such as this flowerpot at Hopewell, New Brunswick.

THE ATLANTIC BOREAL REGION

Nova Scotia's Atlantic Coast
and Cape Breton Island

The southern and eastern coasts of Nova Scotia are rimmed offshore by large submerged banks of the northern Gulf of Maine and the Scotian Shelf. One of them, Sable Bank, emerges slightly above sea level to form Sable Island. The south and eastern shores of Nova Scotia are for the most part rocky ones. Where valleys open onto the ocean, the rising sea of post glacial times has drowned them as it drowned the valleys of Maine. But where the valleys run parallel to the sea, the rising sea could not reach them, and there the rocky coast is not indented, but smooth.

Most of Nova Scotia is part of the extremely eroded uplands of the ancient Appalachians. The heat and pressure of the mountain-building processes metamorphosed the sedimentary rocks of the region, folding and crushing them up into mountains. Those rocks less resistant to erosion were worn away long before the glaciers came and went; the remaining rocks now facing the Atlantic area are relatively hard, but they are not as hard as the Maine granites. As a result, slow erosion of the coastal headlands by ocean waves and currents continues to produce at least some sand. The seaward coast of Nova Scotia, drowned somewhat like that of Maine, is therefore not quite as raw and youthful. Its rocks are not as hard and many of its rocky headlands have trapped sandy beaches in the pockets between them.

Cape Breton Island, separated from the rest of Nova Scotia by the very narrow Canso Strait between St. Georges and Chedabucto Bays, is a complex area. It contains an almost tideless but not completely landlocked small inland sea, Bras d'Or Lake. It has low seaward shores which are further remnants of the eroded Appalachians. The Cape Breton Highlands, reaching north into the Gulf of St. Lawrence form the southern edge of Cabot Strait which separates Nova Scotia from Newfoundland. The Highlands were uplifted considerably more recently than the Appalachians, and the headlands of mostly metamorphic rock are often so steep that the rocky shores and pocket and fringing beaches are practically inaccessible.

The Southern Gulf of St. Lawrence

The entire southern crescent of the Gulf of St. Lawrence is a coast of long sandy barrier beaches, islands, and spits, sometimes backed by dune fields, and often protecting large sand and mud flats as well as extensive salt marshes. The sandy shores extend from the edge of Chaleur Bay and Miramichi Bay through Northumberland Strait, and includes Prince Edward Island as well as the Magdalen Islands farther out in the gulf. The gulf here is quite shallow, its summer temperatures relatively warm, and its coastline much like the mature ones of the Cape Cod region and southwards. In winter, however, the whole of the southern gulf usually freezes over completely, a reminder that it still lies deep in the Boreal region.

After the Appalachians were folded up, a large subsiding basin developed in their midst between the highlands of the Gaspé Peninsula and Nova Scotia. Subsequent inundations of the basin by the sea deposited thick layers of sediment, which solidified into sedimentary rock and were later uplifted to become the Maritime Plain. The Maritime Plain faces north onto the gulf, tilting gradually downward from the New Brunswick lowlands to the edge of the deep trough that runs through the middle of the gulf. During the long period of emergence of the Maritime Plain above sea level, stream erosion sculpted it into hills and valleys, washing away the less resistant rocks. When the rising sea flooded the plain after the glaciers retreated, the higher, less eroded surfaces became Prince Edward Island and the Magdalen Islands.

The soft sedimentary bedrock of the southern gulf and the ample glacial moraine on the lowlands provided the waves and currents of the gulf with abundant material to work with. Where sedimentary headlands protrude from under the glacial deposits, the sea still erodes them back, straightening the shoreline ever more, adding yet more sediment to the beaches. Like the coast of the southern Gulf of Maine, the coast of the southern Gulf of St. Lawrence has matured in a very short time (see figure 38).

The Gaspé Peninsula of Quebec

Arcing along the south shore of the St. Lawrence Estuary and extending far out into the Gulf of St. Lawrence, the Gaspé Peninsula is another eroded remnant of the northern Appalachians. Like the seaward coasts of Nova Scotia, it is smooth where its valleys run parallel to the sea, as they do along its long north shore, and it is more indented where its valleys open onto the gulf and have been drowned by the ocean's rise. Its coasts are rocky, and sandy beaches are uncommon. Though the tides of the gulf are relatively small, about 3 feet (1 m), the narrowing of the St. Lawrence Estuary funnels the tide to increasing heights, finally reaching 12 feet (4 m) or more. Some softer sedimentary rock touches the harder, metamorphic rock of the peninsula at a few places along its south and eastern shores, which erode more rapidly. Bonaventure Island is part of one such sedimentary shore; large numbers of seabirds nest on the horizontal ledges of the cliffs facing the gulf (see plate VIII).

The St. Lawrence Lowland and Trough

A deep trough lies north of the Maritime Plain and the Gaspé Peninsula, and gradually rises to the north shore of the gulf. This trough is part of the St. Lawrence Lowland which extends far to the southwest as the fertile St. Lawrence River valley and curves northeast between Newfoundland and Quebec–Labrador where it becomes the Strait of Belle Isle. In between it forms the St. Lawrence Estuary and the central and upper parts of the Gulf of St. Lawrence. Its southern margins in the Atlantic region are the uplands and lowlands of the Appalachians; its northern margin is the Canadian or Precambrian Shield. Erosion during preglacial times sculpted the emerged sedimentary rock, leaving behind more resistant rock as hills. These hills became Anticosti Island and the much smaller Mingan Islands near the north shore when the post-glacial sea flooded the gulf.

Recent glaciation filled the trough as it covered the

whole St. Lawrence Lowland. The glaciers smoothed and steepened the sides of the trough, and straightened and deepened it as well. The ice flowed seaward, deepened Cabot Strait, and poured out onto the continental shelf. The retreating glaciers as usual left their deposits deepest on the lowest lands, covering the floor of the gulf and the surface of Anticosti Island.

The North Shore of the Gulf of St. Lawrence

The Precambrian Shield dominates central and eastern Canada north of the St. Lawrence Lowland. Its Laurentian region of uplands and highlands rises abruptly above the north shores of the Gulf of St. Lawrence and the St. Lawrence Estuary. Untouched by the tectonic upheavals south of it since its Precambrian origins, the Shield was submerged at least long enough for sediments to consolidate on it. However, it has been exposed continuously since the Precambrian, and streams have eroded virtually all of the sedimentary rock off the underlying granite. The streams have cut some deep valleys into the remaining rock, and of these the most remarkable is the Saguenay River on the St. Lawrence Estuary. The Saguenay is a fjord 58 miles (92 km) long, 1-3 miles (1.5-5 km) wide, up to 800 feet (250 m) deep and with cliffs rising to similar heights above the water. It is so deep that it is really a long almost-marine inlet. The glaciers, scarcely modifying the exposed granite of the Shield, deposited their debris on the lower lands to the south and east. Except where the sedimentary rock of the St. Lawrence Lowland emerges in contact with the Shield along some parts of the north shore, erosion remains a very slow process.

Newfoundland

The highlands of western Newfoundland effectively enclose much of the eastern side of the Gulf of St. Lawrence. Central lowlands lie along much of the island-studded coast which faces northeast on to the North Atlantic. Eastern uplands cover the rest of the island, forming its southern and

THE ATLANTIC BOREAL REGION

eastern coasts. The St. Lawrence Lowland touches the highlands of western Newfoundland, forming the Port au Port Peninsula as well as a low narrow shelf between the sea and the highlands along other parts of the western coast. Beaches ranging from sand to boulders, long rocky headlands of folded and uplifted rock projecting into the gulf, and steep mountain cliffs plunging into the sea combine to make the coastline extremely varied. The post-glacial sea flooded some extremely deep valleys that streams had eroded into the coastal lowlands and highlands, forming a series of steep-sided fjords that now penetrate the western coast.

The shores of the rest of Newfoundland are mostly rocky ones with large inlets, sheltered coves, small beaches of sand, gravel or cobble, steep cliffs of folded metamorphic rock, and scattered rocky islands. The coastline is relatively youthful; its rocks erode gradually under the impact of the ocean's waves (see plate I).

To the south and southeast of Newfoundland lie the Grand Banks, the largest of the submerged, offshore banks which help to make the Boreal coast of North America unlike any other. The Grand Banks are covered with the extremely deep sediment more typical of the deeper continental shelf than the Scotian Shelf or Gulf of Maine. They are a product of the uplifting of the Avalon Platform, which occurred long after the Appalachians were folded up.

Geology of the Boreal Coastal Region

Extraordinary events during the past 600 million years have contributed to the construction of the Boreal coast as it exists now. Mountains were folded up and then eroded down again, seas intermittently inundated the lowlands, and submerged lowlands were uplifted while emerged land subsided. On top of all of this the glaciers of the Ice Age scoured the landscape, compressed the land, and dumped their immense loads of till everywhere.

Despite the tremendous impact of the recent glaciations upon the whole of the Boreal coast, of far greater impact

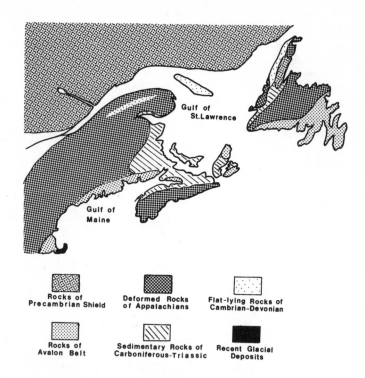

Rocks of
Precambrian Shield

Deformed Rocks
of Appalachians

Flat-lying Rocks of
Cambrian-Devonian

Rocks of
Avalon Belt

Sedimentary Rocks of
Carboniferous-Triassic

Recent Glacial
Deposits

7. Simplified geology of the Boreal coast. (The rocks of the Avalon belt probably originated from other continents.)

were the events that occurred when three of the world's continents drifted together and later wrenched themselves apart. The theory that continents are drifting in different directions relative to one another, each on its own huge tectonic plate, is now supported by many different kinds of evidence. But it is a recent theory, convincingly documented only since the 1950's, and it is a revolutionary theory, demanding the reinterpretation of much of the geological past. Understanding the evolution of the Boreal coast in the light of continental drift has been an exciting task for geologists and it is still unfinished in many of its details.

Precambrian Rock

Rocks a billion or more years old underlie the whole North American continent. They are hard and crystalline, and little is known about their origins. Over much of the continent immense seas buried them under deep layers of sedimentary rock. Later mountain-building events disrupted them and their covering layers. These Precambrian rocks are now exposed over much of eastern Canada, and line the shores of the extreme north end of the Boreal region. They were left untouched by most of the seas that inundated the land to their south, and the events that pushed up the Appalachians did not reach far enough north to affect them.

The Drifting Continents and the First Atlantic Ocean

During the Cambrian period, 600 to 500 million years ago, the massive tectonic plates upon which North America and Africa rested, drifted apart, and the first version of the Atlantic Ocean grew between them. The ocean flooded the lowlands, and great amounts of sediment were deposited. These deposits are the underlying horizontal substrates of the St. Lawrence Lowland, as well as the sedimentary rock that was later to be folded up into the Appalachians. The St. Lawrence Lowland has probably been a major river system since the time of its origin. It has gradually eroded into what is now the St. Lawrence River, Estuary and upper Gulf.

Collision of the Continents

While about 20,000 feet (6500 m) of sedimentary rock consolidated on the lowlands, the continents drifted on, somewhat erratically. Then, during the Ordovician period, about 480 million years ago, the North American and European tectonic plates drifted together. The collision resulted

was eliminated by the collision, but inland seas and large lakes continued to deposit sediment on the lowlands around the already eroding mountains.

During the Devonian period, about 390 million years ago, the two continental plates pressed even further into one another, forming a single land mass called Laurussia. The second major phase of the construction of the Appalachians had occurred, the Acadian Orogeny. The range of mountains extended from what is now Newfoundland in the north to Alabama in the south. Some parts, such as the Gaspé Peninsula, were folded up by only the first Taconic Orogeny, while others, such as the Nova Scotia uplands, were added by the second Acadian phase. Yet other regions, such as the New Brunswick highlands and the uplands of eastern Newfoundland, were folded first by the Taconic Orogeny and then refolded by the Acadian. Somewhat later, another continent, made up of what is now Australia, Antarctica, South America, Africa, India, southern Europe and Florida, called Gondwana, collided with Laurussia. A huge mass of three fused continents, known as Pangea, was created, stretching from pole to pole. A single immense ocean was left, the Panthalassic Ocean.

Filling the Appalachian Troughs

During the geological periods which followed the closing of the Atlantic Ocean, parts of the troughs of the folded Appalachians subsided even further. Streams eroded large amounts of sediment from the mountains and carried it to the water which filled the troughs. During the Permian and Carboniferous periods, from about 330 to 220 million years ago, the sedimentary rock of the Maritime Plain formed in what is now the southern part of the Gulf of St. Lawrence and the coastal lowlands of New Brunswick. Later sediments of the Triassic period (about 190 million years ago) were deposited on the trough that is now the Bay of Fundy.

Rebirth of the North Atlantic Ocean

About 150 million years ago, during the Jurassic period,

the three continents that had remained fused as a single land mass for 150 to 200 million years were torn apart from each other again as their tectonic plates separated. New fracture lines often formed only approximately where the old ones had been, and some pieces of what had once been the western edges of parts of Europe and Africa broke off and became parts of the new eastern edge of North America. The eastern coast of North America is therefore known as a collision coast with a trailing edge, a product of drifting continents.

The separation of the continents was gradual and the regions being separated were under prolonged and great tension. Eventually only the contact between Newfoundland and the Iberian Peninsula remained, and then that too broke and the northern North Atlantic and the southern North Atlantic shared their waters for the first time in 300 million years. When the continents separated, parts of western Europe and northwestern Africa remained welded to North America, forming the Avalon Belt. The rocks of the Avalon Belt are very old, and are quite different from the rocks of the Appalachians. They form eastern Newfoundland, including the Grand Banks, parts of Nova Scotia and much of the Maine coast.

Though the continents reached their present relative positions around 70 million years ago, the Atlantic Ocean continues to widen. As new molten rock emerges along the Mid-Atlantic Ridge, North America and Europe are pushed farther apart at the rate of about 2 inches (5 cm) per year.

Submergence of the Coastal Plain

While the higher land of the Appalachians remained above the reach of the ocean, the coastal lowlands subsided below sea level. What is now the Gulf of Maine and the Scotian Shelf lay submerged for over 100 million years until the Miocene epoch, 15 million years ago. Streams wore down the Appalachians ever further, washing the less resistant sediment out onto the submerged lowlands. The sea floor flattened and became a shallow, seaward sloping shelf, much like the shelf off of the present coast south of Long

Island. There were no submerged banks, gullies or ledges on the shelf, and the shoreline probably had the smoothed, beach-lined appearance of mature coasts elsewhere. Cape Cod did not exist.

Tertiary Erosion and Uplift

Early in the Tertiary period, which began 60 million years ago, various parts of the northern Appalachians uplifted. The highlands of western Newfoundland and of Cape Breton Island rose to levels that, though again eroded by streams, are now some of the highest of the Boreal region. The whole of the Maritime Plain, including the southern Gulf of St. Lawrence, emerged from below sea level as well. Streams easily eroded the soft sedimentary rocks of the plain, carving out valleys and leaving behind more resistant areas as hills.

About 15 million years ago the submerged coastal shelf also uplifted and reemerged, and its new coast came to lie up to 100 miles seaward of its present Maine and Nova Scotia limits. Still sloping seaward, its sediments eroded rapidly, and hills and valleys soon covered its landscape just as they did the Maritime Plain.

Pleistocene Glaciations

Throughout most of the past couple of million years, during the Pleistocene epoch, immense glaciers covered most of northern North America, advancing and retreating four or five times. The most recent glaciation, that of the Wisconsin Ice Age, covered all of the present Boreal coast, filling the deep trenches of the St. Lawrence Lowland, and even riding up over the highest parts of the adjacent highlands. The glaciers flowed out Cabot Strait and the Northeast Channel onto the continental shelf, and extended south over what is now Cape Cod and Long Island.

The Wisconsin glaciers did their customary work of scouring the land of its rocks and sediments, carrying immense loads of debris along as they flowed south and east.

8. The extent of the Wisconsin glaciation.

They straightened and deepened all the valleys and steepened their sides. The great weight of the glaciers also depressed the land they covered, forcing it hundreds of feet (100 m or more) lower than its preglacial levels. The sea level dropped to comparable levels as more and more of the world's water became frozen in its glaciers.

Recovery from the Glaciers

About 16,000 years ago, the glaciers of the last ice age finally started to melt back more in summer than they grew in winter. Over the next few thousand years the retreat was slow and erratic. By 13,000 to 12,000 years ago the glaciers had withdrawn from all parts of the Boreal coast with the exception of northern Newfoundland where they persisted another couple of thousand years. Where the glaciers had stopped for long before retreating, they dumped immense piles of debris, the terminal moraines. Lower Cape Cod, Nantucket Island, Martha's Vineyard and Long Island are all terminal moraines marking the southern limits to which the glaciers flowed. The glaciers left varying depths of moraine over all the lowland areas in the region, particularly on the Maritime Plain and St. Lawrence Lowland in the Gulf of St. Lawrence, and on what is now the southern coast of the Gulf of Maine and the offshore banks of the Gulf of Maine and the Scotian Shelf. They left only a thin veneer of moraine on the highlands. The meltwaters of the retreating glaciers spread the glacial debris far over the land between the glaciers and the sea, redepositing the sediment in extensive outwash plains. What is now upper Cape Cod originated this way.

As the glaciers melted, the sea level rose, and the ocean flooded over the land which the glaciers had so depressed. The sea drowned the coastal river valleys and even surged up over the present coastlines, reaching as far as 60 miles (100 km) inland of its present boundaries in Maine. Georges Bank was left as an island, and for a while around 11,000 years ago, trees grew over its surface and salt marshes developed on its protected shores. The sea flooded the Gulf of St. Lawrence, making islands of its hills. Anticosti Island, the Magdalen Islands, and finally Prince Edward Island were all cut off from the mainland. The sea flooded far eastward over the St. Lawrence Lowlands to become the large, shallow Champlain Sea, and it flooded up beyond the Saguenay fjord, creating the Laflemme Sea. Marine deposits were laid on top of the outwash plains.

After a short lag, the land that had sunk under the weight of the mile-thick glaciers also began to rise. It rose fastest where the ice had been thickest, and it rose more inland than it did along the coast itself. Soon it rose faster than the sea; the inland Champlain and Laflemme Seas were emptied, and the sea was pushed back even beyond many of its present coastlines. About 6,000 years ago, the land, in a kind of elastic rebound from the relief of glacial pressures, reached its greatest height. In many places it was higher than it had been in preglacial times.

The land began slowly to subside again while the sea still rose. The hills of the old coastal plain all submerged to become the offshore banks of the Gulf of Maine and the Scotian Shelf. Only Sable Island has not yet subsided from view. The tides of the Gulf of Maine increased and began to drive those of the Bay of Fundy to their famous heights. About 3,000 years ago, the sea level ceased to rise, for the glaciers had by then melted back to their present limits. But much of the Boreal region, especially its southern parts, continues to subside; the drowning of the coastlines continues at a rate of up to 0.3 feet (8 cm) per hundred years. Only northern Newfoundland, more recently released by the glaciers, is still rising slowly.

The changes on the Boreal coast during the past 10,000 years have been immense, despite the fact those years represent such a brief instant of geologic time. The sea has drowned the deeply sculpted coast of Maine and other somewhat similar coasts. Erosion of soft bedrock and glacial debris by waves and ocean currents has rapidly matured the coasts of the southern Gulf of Maine and the southern Gulf of St. Lawrence, and tidal erosion has worn back the soft headlands of the Bay of Fundy. Just as dramatically, an extraordinary diversity of plants and animals has covered almost all of the inhabitable surfaces and filled the waters.

Climate: Continental and Maritime Influences

The salient feature of the weather along the Boreal coast is its remarkable variability. The region experiences unpredictable alternations of sunny, cloudy and wet weather.

The climate is largely under the control of weather systems moving easterly off the continent, making the winters long and cold and the summers potentially warm. The surrounding ocean waters moderate this continental type of climate, however. The relative warmth of the sea prolongs the autumn on the coast and keeps the winter less severe than it is inland. When the air masses warm up again across the continent in spring, the now relatively colder ocean cools them along the coast and delays the coming of spring and summer. Cool ocean temperatures also help to keep the summers less hot than inland. The climate of the Boreal coast is therefore basically a continental one, moderated by maritime exposure. Those parts of the coast more exposed to the open ocean, such as parts of Newfoundland and Nova Scotia, experience greater maritime moderation than those more protected areas in the inner regions of the two Gulfs.

Though the winters along the Boreal coast may not be as cold as those of inland areas, they are amply cold for ice formation. One of the critical stresses on Boreal organisms is the impact of ice on them, at least in the intertidal regions, and intertidal ice is likely to form anywhere north of Cape Cod. In protected areas ice can be very extensive, often freezing over entire inlets, mud flats, salt marshes and estuaries. The region of the greatest freeze-up is the Gulf of St. Lawrence, where the lower gulf around Prince Edward Island freezes over completely, as does most of the St. Lawrence Estuary. Winters vary greatly of course, and severely cold winters will freeze over essentially marine bays which in other years have no ice cover at all.

Of special importance on any coastline are the winds: their strength, duration, and origin. They help drive the ocean currents. They blow sand into dunes and then move the dune fields. They blow up the waves which beat upon the shoreline, eroding headlands, tearing loose poorly attached plants and animals. Particularly strong winds drive up correspondingly large waves whose high breakers and deep surge can have especially long lasting effects. The occasional late summer hurricanes or the northeasterly gales of winter can have an influence far out of proportion to their frequency.

The summer winds along the Boreal coast are predominantly from the southwest. On most summer days local offshore winds or "seabreezes" develop and blow cooler air over the water onto the shores. During the winter, the winds are more likely to come from the west or northwest. Occasionally they come from the northeast, and it is these northeasterlies, blowing in off the north Atlantic, that are the strongest. Usually two severe north-easterly gales hit the coast each winter, and some, like the storms of January 1978, which caused extensive damage along the Maine coast, will be remembered for years.

Summer fogs are a famous feature of the Boreal coast. They are important to the intertidal plants and animals, for fogs on otherwise hot days make the intertidal a more tolerable place to live. Sometimes prolonged fogs cut out the sunlight for too long, and the photosynthesizing rockweeds suffer. Fogs occur when warm air flows out over the cooler ocean. There its temperature drops and its water vapor condenses, forming a fog bank. A high sun may warm it enough to vaporize it or it may simply disappear with a change in wind direction.

Oceanography

The Chemistry of Sea Water

Sea water is a complex medium, varying in temperature, salinity, density and dissolved salts, gases, nutrients and trace elements. Though every one of the naturally occurring elements can be detected in sea water, only a small number of them combine to form the vast majority of the dissolved salts which give sea water its most obvious characteristic. Sodium chloride (Na Cl), magnesium chloride (Mg Cl_2), sodium sulphate (Na_2SO_4), and calcium chloride (Ca Cl_2) make up about 95 percent of the salts in sea water. That doesn't mean that the less common salts are not extremely important to marine plants and animals. Some elements are so rare in sea water that they are known as the trace elements. Yet, various organisms depend upon trace elements and extract and concentrate them from the water.

The salts dissolved in sea water make the water denser so that it tends to sink when it is in contact with more dilute water. This is why it buoys up objects more easily than fresh water does. Dissolved salts also depress the freezing point of water, and fully marine sea water which contains

35 parts of salt to 1000 parts of water (35‰) freezes at about 28.5° F (−2° C) instead of 32° F (0° C). Surface temperatures of boreal seas can be very cold indeed. When ice does form on the sea surface in protected coastal areas, it is nowhere near as salty as the underlying water, however. As ice crystals form, the salts are squeezed out and concentrated in the water below the ice.

Though salts give sea water its characteristic salinity, the gases and nutrients necessary for life are also dissolved in the water. Dissolved nitrogen, oxygen and carbon dioxide all occur in sea water, originating from the atmospheric gases or from the processes of respiration and photosynthesis of the marine organisms themselves. Oxygen is relatively soluble in water. Carbon dioxide is even more soluble and as a result is almost 100 times more abundant in sea water than in air. Both dissolved oxygen and carbon dioxide are directly usable by organisms. Animals use up oxygen and eliminate carbon dioxide, while photosynthesizing plants absorb carbon dioxide and eliminate excess oxygen. Below the depths to which photosynthesis occurs oxygen levels may drop off quickly.

All animals and almost all plants get their nitrogen from nitrogen-containing compounds such as nitrates, nitrites or ammonia. In the sea, only certain bacteria and blue-green algae are able to utilize nitrogen directly, and they in turn "fix" it into the forms usable by other organisms. The other source of the nitrogen compounds is detritus, the decaying products of plants and animals. Phosphate, the other necessary nutrient, is also supplied by detritus as well as by fresh water inflow to the ocean.

Currents

Ocean temperatures determine the northern and southern limits of the Boreal coast more than any other qualities of the environment, for the distribution of marine plants and animals is generally temperature dependent. Though the temperatures of the coastal waters are products of many factors and vary with depth and season, they are influenced most by the interaction of the various major inshore cur-

THE ATLANTIC BOREAL REGION

rents. Each current has its own characteristic temperatures, salinity and density as well as other chemical and physical properties.

Despite these differences, warm currents are usually a little more saline than cold ones since more salts can dissolve in warm water. A cold marine current is a little denser than a warm one, and when the two meet, although they may mix around the edges that are in contact, the warmer current rides over the top of the colder one, pushing it deeper. To make the situation more complex, fresh water is so much less dense than marine water that it floats on the surface no matter what its temperature.

Many factors influence just how strong a current is, as well as the details of the route it follows. Especially important are winds, and where winds change in strength and direction from one season to another, currents vary correspondingly. Tides, rainfall, evaporation, cloud cover, river runoff, and bottom topography all can modify a current as well.

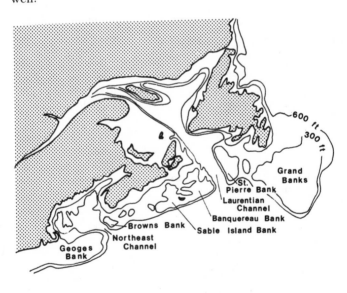

9. The fishing banks of the Boreal coast.

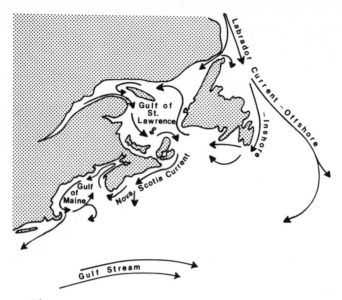

10. The major ocean currents of the Boreal coast.

THE LABRADOR CURRENT

The cold Labrador Current flows south from the Arctic along the Labrador coast. Though some of it reaches into the Strait of Belle Isle where it mixes with the water of the Gulf of St. Lawrence, most continues south along the coast of Newfoundland, where it splits into inshore and offshore branches. The offshore branch flows out around the Grand Banks where it has a cooling effect on the deeper slope water but little further direct influence on the coastal waters. Meanwhile, the inshore branch continues close to shore around the southern coast of Newfoundland, where some of it flows into the Gulf of St. Lawrence along the north shore of Cabot Strait. The rest turns south to contribute to the Nova Scotia Current.

THE GULF OF ST. LAWRENCE

The currents in the Gulf of St. Lawrence for the most part flow in a counterclockwise direction. They move north along the western coast of Newfoundland, and then are deflected west by the Quebec north shore. Around Anticosti Island, they meet and join the strong eastward-flowing Gaspé Current, slowing over the shallow regions of the southern gulf, and then continue out Cabot Strait as the Cape Breton Current. The massive discharge of the St. Lawrence River mixes with the marine water of the gulf and estuary, giving the gulf a unique set of characteristics of temperature, salinity and chemical constituents that distinguish it from all other bodies of water.

THE SCOTIAN SHELF

The Nova Scotia Current flows southwest over the Scotian Shelf, parallel to the Atlantic coast of Nova Scotia. Part of it comes from the inshore branch of the Labrador Current, part from the Cape Breton Current, and part from offshore water over the continental slope, known as slope water. The Nova Scotia Current rounds the southern tip of Nova Scotia, where some of it enters the Gulf of Maine. The rest pushes on as the Coastal Current.

THE GULF OF MAINE

As in the Gulf of St. Lawrence, the circulation of the Gulf of Maine is mainly a large counterclockwise circuit. The current within the gulf flows into the Bay of Fundy on the Nova Scotia side, flows out on the New Brunswick side, and then continues south along the coast toward Cape Cod. In the southern gulf, it turns eastward and north along Georges Bank. Some returns to the Bay of Fundy and starts the circuit again, about three months after it began, and some turns seaward around Georges Bank and leaves the gulf. The gulf waters also have several different sources, some coming from the Nova Scotia Current, some from the numerous rivers draining into the gulf, and considerable amounts from the slope water which enters the gulf via the Northeast Channel.

The circulation of the Gulf of Maine is driven by river run off and the strong tides of the gulf. Coriolis forces in conjunction with basin sides direct the circulation in a counterclockwise route, as they do in all semi-enclosed basins in the Northern Hemisphere. The strength of the counterclockwise currents varies seasonally, however, and is weakest in winter.

THE GULF STREAM

The other current whose impact may be felt along the Boreal coast is the Gulf Stream, a warm and saline mass of water which flows north along the North American coast to Cape Hatteras. The Gulf Stream begins to move offshore north of Cape Hatteras, meeting the Coastal Current which it forces into deeper water. Though the distance of the Gulf Stream from shore varies from year to year, its warming influence on coastal waters is still very significant until Cape Cod and Georges Bank deflect it eastward and it begins its journey across the Atlantic to warm northern Europe. As it is deflected eastward, it exchanges some water along its northern edge with the slope water. Small changes of temperature and salinity in the slope water are the only direct impacts the Gulf Stream has on the waters of the Boreal coast.

Temperatures

Most of the Boreal waters are cool even in summer, a result of the influence of the cold ocean currents and the lasting impact of the cold winters. Moreover, the discharge of the St. Lawrence River is so great in spring and summer that it too remains cold when smaller rivers warm up, and its cooling effects are felt far along the Scotian Shelf and the Nova Scotia Atlantic coast even into the Gulf of Maine. The immense Fundy tides continuously stir cold deep water to the surface of the bay which in midsummer rarely rises much above 50° F (10° C). The discharge of the Bay of Fundy also helps to cool the Gulf of Maine, especially its northern portions.

Summer sunshine still succeeds in warming the surface waters especially in shallow inshore areas. Temperatures along the coast of the southern Gulf of Maine may on occasion even reach 68° F (20° C), but the summer maximum decreases northwards along the Atlantic coast, perhaps reaching 60° F (15° C) on the seaward side of Nova Scotia

THE ATLANTIC BOREAL REGION

and 50° F (10° C) on the shores of the Avalon Peninsula of Newfoundland. The southern Gulf of St. Lawrence, so much shallower than the central portions of the gulf, warms to as high as 65° F (18° C) in the surface layers of the North-umberland Strait, allowing certain marine plants and animals to survive that are more typical of habitats south of Cape Cod.

In winter, these same surface waters cool almost to their freezing points even in the southern parts of the Boreal region where in especially cold winters well-protected or shallow coves may freeze over. Only the surface of the Bay of Fundy remains too warm at 36 to 37° F (2 to 3° C) along most of its length to freeze.

Though the surface waters may warm up in summer to occasionally dangerous levels for the inhabitants, then cool and perhaps freeze in winter, deeper water remains far more constant. The deep water filling the basins of the gulfs and Scotian Shelf as well as the deeper bays and inlets on the coasts is always cool, somewhere in the range of 40 to 46° F (4 to 8° C). In summer, the deep water can provide a sanctuary for cold-water animals unable to tolerate the surface warmth, and in winter a sanctuary for those which cannot withstand the extreme cold of shallow waters.

Layers of different temperatures therefore characterize the coastal sea. In summer the warm layer lies above a colder one; in winter the deeper layer is the warmer of the two. A third layer that is very cold both summer and winter lies between the surface and deep layers in the Gulf of St. Lawrence and along the Scotian Shelf. The extent to which it develops varies with season and depth, and in winter it seems not too different from the cold layer above it. It apparently forms from water cooling in place in the Gulf of St. Lawrence.

Salinity

All layers of water along the Boreal coast lack the very high concentrations of dissolved salt contained in warm, tropical waters. The Gulf Stream, with salinity of 35‰ (parts of salt per thousand parts of water, or parts per thousand) is the closest such high-salinity water comes to the Boreal coast. The Boreal sea water is less saline partly because it is colder and partly because it has been diluted by fresh-water runoff from rivers and meltwater from northern ice packs.

The most saline of the coastal water is the deep layer of relatively cool water. It originates mostly from the offshore slope water, and though it is not as saline as the Gulf Stream, its salinity is 33.5‰ or more. The surface layer, however, which ranges so greatly in temperature, is more dilute, not rising about 32‰ south of Newfoundland. The discharge of the St. Lawrence River mixes with slope water flowing west into the gulf, and forms the bulk of the surface water of the Gulf of St. Lawrence and the Scotian Shelf. Further rivers add their fresh water discharge to the Gulf of Maine surface waters.

The dilution of the surface layer depends upon the volume of fresh water discharged by local rivers and their estuaries. Such dilution is greatest in spring, when the winter's snow and ice melt, and is least in late summer. A prolonged heavy rain or winter thaw can have a profound effect at times of the year when the surface of a lower estuary might otherwise be most saline. In small estuaries, salinity may vary from relatively high concentrations when the tide is in and pushing the fresh water back, to relatively low ones when the tide is out and the fresh water is freer to flow seaward.

Plants or animals which live in shallow coastal waters therefore have not only seasonal changes in water temperature to contend with. Those which live in estuarine areas must also withstand daily and seasonal changes in salinity which may be even more stressful to them.

Tides

The coast between Cape Cod and Labrador is swept twice daily by tides that range from just several feet (1 m) to some of the world's greatest. Not only do the tides erode shores and drive currents. They also, by their ebb and flow, produce an extraordinary intertidal habitat where organisms are rhythmically submerged in sea water and then exposed to drying air.

TIDAL FORCES

The rhythmic rise and fall of the tides is controlled primarily by the gravitational pull of the moon, and to a lesser extent the sun, on the rotating earth. Opposing the gravitational pull of the moon is the centrifugal force resulting from the earth's rotation. On the side facing the moon, the gravitational pull is the greater of the two forces, and the sea bulges toward the moon, forming a high tide. On the opposite side of the earth the centrifugal force is the stronger force and a second bulge occurs, forming a second high tide that is usually a little smaller than the one facing the moon. In between the two bulges compensating low tides occur. The same forces exert an influence on the far denser land as well, but have an almost insignificant impact.

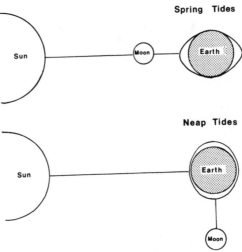

11. Spring tides occur when the sun and moon are in line and their gravitational pulls act in unison on the earth's ocean. Neap tides occur when the sun and moon pull at right angles to each other. The white area around the earth shows the bulge of tidal water.

Each day the tides occur approximately 50 minutes later than the day before, for the moon has revolved that much farther in its orbit around the earth and the tides follow the lunar cycle closely. Since the moon's orbit is elliptical, its gravitational pull varies during its monthly cycle, and there-fore the height of the tides vary as well. Only when the moon is new or full is it lined up with the sun, and the gravitational pull of the two bodies act in concert to make the tides the highest ones that month. Such tides are called spring tides, and when, on its elliptical orbit, the moon is closest to the earth at the same time it happens to be full or new, the spring tides are then the year's greatest. They in-undate areas normally out of reach of high water and expose areas normally always covered at low tide. Average or poor tides, which occur when the moon's gravitational pull on the earth is at right angles to the sun's, are called neap tides.

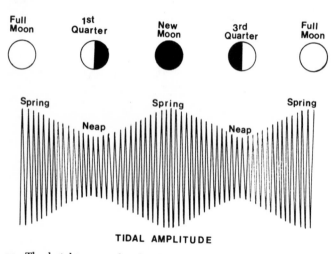

12. The height or amplitude of the tides varies according to the phase of the moon, with the highest and lowest tides (the spring tides) occurring at the times of full and new moon.

Although gravitational and centrifugal forces drive the tides, ocean basins and coastal topography drastically mod-ify them. Where the continental shelf is very narrow, tides

THE ATLANTIC BOREAL REGION

are more like open ocean ones, rising and falling only about a meter; but where the shelf is wide, as it is along the Boreal coast, tides build up to greater heights. On the other hand, where a basin is almost surrounded by land in such a way as to block and reflect the incoming tidal wave, tides may be considerably reduced, as they are in the Gulf of St. Lawrence.

The water in any enclosed basin rocks rhythmically back and forth from one end to the other, irrespective of any tides there might be. The period of this rhythm (the time between two successive high level points at one end of the basin) is related to the basin's length and depth. Every basin has its own natural rhythm, be it a bathtub full of water or the entire North Atlantic Ocean. This rhythmic movement of water, or seiche, may counteract the tidal movement of the same water, or it may augment it, depending upon the orientation of the basin and the period of its seiche. The large tides of the Bay of Fundy are at least in part a result of the two rhythms acting together.

Many bays and estuaries are funnel-shaped. Tides at the mouth of such a funnel are pushed to increasingly greater heights as they reach progressively narrower parts of the funnel. The St. Lawrence River Estuary is an excellent example, for tides that are 3 to 6 ft. (1 to 2 m) where it opens into the Gulf are driven to 12 to 15 ft. (4 to 5 m) by the time they reach the Saguenay. The Bay of Fundy is also funnel-shaped, and Chignecto Bay and Minas Basin at its head drive an already very high tide to even greater heights.

As high tides hit the very shallow regions of the coastal shoreline, their vertical displacement is converted to horizontal movement, pushing water up inlets and estuaries and creating tidal currents. Tidal currents vary from barely noticeable ones to some which are extremely treacherous, such as in Passamaquoddy Bay at the border of Maine and New Brunswick. Even weak or moderate tidal currents present yet another environmental stress which resident organisms have to cope with.

A large tide on a complex coastline may have further anomolous local effects. An incoming tide reverses the flow at the mouth of an estuary, and where it is forced into narrow rivers, as it is at St. John, New Brunswick, it may even produce rapids running up hill. Elsewhere, it produces fresh-water tides in many rivers, even forming extensive fresh-water tidal flats such as those of Merrymeeting Bay, near Brunswick, Maine. Where the slope of the shore is especially flat, and the basin funnel-shaped, water may accumulate on the advancing front of an incoming tide and form a breaking wave, or tidal bore. However, these various effects, of interest because they are uncommon, usually have little significant impact on the marine organisms in the region.

VARIATION IN TIDAL HEIGHT

Of course, the size of the intertidal zone, the region between the highest and lowest tide levels, varies not only with the vertical rise and fall of the tide, but also with the slope of the shore. Only two meters of a wharf piling may be exposed by a low tide that exposes several hundred meters of an adjacent mud flat at the same time. In determining the height, or amplitude, of a tide, however, it is the vertical distance between high and low tides that is measured.

Tidal amplitude varies predictably, depending on what phase the moon is in and where on the coast the tide is actually occurring. The height of the tide increases gradually from the 6 ft (2 m) typical of the north shore of Cape Cod to 12–15 (4–5 m) at the mouth of the Bay of Fundy, and then it escalates to the 50 ft (15 m) tides which occur at the head of the bay. The tides along the Atlantic coasts of Nova Scotia are again about 6 ft (2 m) typical of the open coast, but within the Gulf of St. Lawrence they are still smaller, rarely more than 3 ft (1 m), and they vary considerably.

Such amplitudes are averages, however, and spring tides may be surprisingly larger, neap tides smaller. The highest spring tides may cover rocks otherwise exposed to the atmosphere for months at a time, and the lowest spring tides expose organisms which are usually continually subtidal. In contrast, neap tides may not reach much of the upper intertidal shore for days at a time; the lower intertidal zone may remain continually covered by water for the same period. Since intertidal organisms differ so greatly in their ability to

13. The tides of the Bay of Fundy are among the greatest in the world, stranding lobster boats in their ebb.

withstand prolonged exposure, these variations in tidal amplitude may determine just how far up or down the intertidal shore they can survive.

The intertidal region can therefore be subdivided into zones that receive predictably different amounts of exposure to the atmosphere or submergence by seawater.

Zone 1: The area between the level of an average high tide (Mean High Water) and the level of an extremely high spring tide (Extreme High Water Spring). At least half of the high tides each month don't reach this area, and its uppermost edge may be covered by water only a few times a year. Organisms here are likely to die from drowning if submerged for too long.

Zone 2: The area between Mean High Water and the highest level reached by an extreme neap tide (Extreme High Water Neap). At least half of the high tides each month reach this level in the intertidal region.

Zone 3: The area between Extreme High Water Neap and the lower level reached by the same extreme neap tide

(Extreme Low Water Neap). Every high tide covers this area and the lower parts of it remain submerged for more than half the time.

Zone 4: The area between Extreme Low Water Neap and the level of an average low tide (Mean Low Water). Organisms living here are submerged during the days of the neap tides but are exposed by more than half of all low tides.

Zone 5: The area between Mean Low Water and the lowest level reached by the extreme spring tides (Extreme Low Water Spring). At least half of the low tides do not expose organisms living here and those living low in the area may be exposed for a short period only several times a year. The organisms of this lowest zone tend to be typically sublittoral in their distribution, with few if any adaptations for exposure to the atmosphere.

The intertidal region therefore extends from Extreme High Water Spring to Extreme Low Water Spring. In places exposed to wave action, there is a further zone above Extreme High Water Spring which is reached by the spray of the waves, extending the intertidal region even higher up the shore. The further a marine organism lives from the relatively benign realm of the subtidal region, the greater must be its adaptations for tolerating the various stresses imposed on it by exposure to the atmosphere.

THE STRESSES OF EXPOSURE

A marine organism that breathes, feeds, grows and breeds when submerged in fully marine water faces a number of problems when it is left behind by a dropping tide. Though it is surrounded by drying air, it must not dry out, or desiccate. Though the surface heat in summer, especially in the upper intertidal, may be lethal to most marine organisms, it must withstand the heat if it is to live there. Somehow it must also survive the scouring action of winter ice and the effects of freezing temperatures. A heavy rain in any season may bathe it in potentially lethal fresh water. If it lives where it may be exposed to pounding waves, it must have some way of adhering to the rock or avoiding the waves. Any marine animal which is left exposed, especially in upper zones, must have some way of breathing in an environment essentially alien to it. Because the various plants and animals of the intertidal region have evolved differing abilities to cope with these various stresses, they tend to be distributed in zones and such zonation is typical of any intertidal region.

The Mixing of the Waters

Nutrients in the surface waters tend to sink and become trapped in deeper layers. Unless in some way the bottom layers are forced back up to the surface again, the surface layer can become impoverished of life. Wherever bottom water does find its way back to the surface, however, the abundance of life is likely to increase dramatically.

The mixing of surface and bottom water layers occurs most frequently in estuarine and inshore areas and over the offshore banks. Quite a variety of forces may be involved in the process, and of these the coastal currents themselves are often the most important. Where strong counterclockwise eddies or gyres develop, deeper water is pulled to the surface in the center of the gyre. Such gyres occur in parts of the Gulf of Maine, and parts of the Gulf of St. Lawrence and St. Lawrence Estuary. When small clockwise gyres develop, as they sometimes do in both gulfs, the surface water is pushed down the center of the gyre. Since no upwelling of nutrient-rich deeper water occurs there, the area may become a small desert relative to areas nearby. Surface currents are greatly affected by the strength and direction of the prevailing winds, and since these change seasonally, gyres often develop and then deteriorate each year as well.

Deep currents are also forced to the surface when the bottom topography or seascape suddenly becomes shallow. The deep currents in the Gulf of Maine on the Scotian Shelf and over the Grand Banks are forced up the slopes of the banks and ledges, and this upwelling continues throughout the year, keeping the surface water continuously rich in nutrients.

Though the rise and fall of tides over deep water have no significant influence on forcing surface and deeper layers to mix, quite the opposite sometimes occurs in inshore, shallow waters. The greater the height of the tide, the more it mixes the layers when it reaches the coves, bays and estuaries along the coast. Tidal currents that rip back and forth through narrow passages efficiently mix the layers, usually making them treacherous at the same time. Where tides also surge daily back and forth in an estuary, they meet and mix with the fresh water runoff from the river. If the estuary is relatively shallow, temperatures and salinities may not vary too much from surface to bottom. Where estuaries are deep, however, only limited mixing occurs, and the deep layer remains largely unaffected.

The best example of the ability of strong tides to mix inshore waters is, not surprisingly, the Bay of Fundy. Its tides so thoroughly mix the deep water with the surface water that the temperatures remain fairly constant from surface to bottom, cooler than adjacent coastal waters in summers, and warmer in winters.

Where tides, winds, currents and submerged banks don't induce mixing of surface and bottom layers, the two-layered system persists. The warmth of summer air masses establishes a warm surface layer that becomes isolated from underlying cold ones. Each autumn the surface cools, and with the help of winter gales, mixes with the deeper water. In inshore or other shallow areas, such mixing restores bottom nutrients to the surface again, but in deeper areas, at depths of 300 ft. (100 m) or more, the deep water layer remains unaffected below the colder water above it. Its nutrients remain trapped within it until it is forced to the surface.

The Boreal Organisms

Endemism and Diversity

Every biogeographical region has its set of plant and animal species which are found nowhere else, or are endemic to it. Many of the attached plants of the Boreal intertidal and subtidal habitats are just not found south of Cape Cod, and are gradually replaced north of Newfoundland by the few similar species which are typically Arctic. Similarly, of all fish species which have been captured in the Gulf of Maine, 20 percent of them are endemic to the Boreal region, 23 percent are shared with the Arctic region, and the remaining species are mostly rare occurrences of warmer-water ones which have occasionally ventured north of Cape Cod in summer. The more well-defined the boundaries between regions, in the form of temperature and salinity changes, currents and physical barriers, the greater is the degree of endemism, for interchanges and overlap of species in these regions become more difficult.

The diversity of species (the total number of different species present) is least in the Arctic and greatest in the tropics. Within any one region diversity remains relatively unchanged throughout, but as the boundary at its northern edge is crossed, diversity drops. Such sudden decreases in diversity therefore occur at Capes Kennedy, Hatteras, Cod and again at northern Newfoundland. In the Arctic, physical conditions are so harsh that few organisms can survive them; those that can are often abundant and compete less with each other than in a common struggle against the elements. In contrast, the physical conditions of tropical habitats are so much more benign that large numbers of species survive them easily and are forced into intense competition with each other for limited space, food, and protective cover. The Boreal region has something in common with both extremes.

The Boreal region lacks the prolonged severity of the Arctic region. Yet few warm water intertidal organisms can withstand its winter freezing, and annual sea temperatures are too cold for most southern forms to grow and breed successfully. The diversity of Boreal organisms is therefore reduced, relative to warmer regions, due to the physical, or abiotic, stresses of its environment. However, since it is an easier place for organisms to live than the Arctic region, its species diversity is subsequently large enough that biotic factors, such as competition with other species, are often equally important in controlling the abundance and distribution of an organism in its preferred habitats.

Although most Boreal species are found from one end of the region to the other, each is usually restricted to a certain kind of habitat within it. A muddy substrate may be an excellent place for a burrower to live, but it is impossible as a habitat for those plants and animals that need something hard to cling to. Where mud, sand and rock occur close to one another, burrowers and clingers live close together as well, and species diversity there has the potential of being quite great. Of course other factors, such as exposure to desiccation, freezing, and varying temperatures and salinities also affect diversity, for the greater the degree of stress caused by any one of these factors, the fewer the species which can tolerate it. Where salinity is high and constant, temperatures stable and cool, substrates varied, and the water rich in nutrients, the greatest local diversity of Boreal organisms is likely to occur.

Plants: The Producers

Plants are autotrophs, which means that they can synthesize all the organic molecules they need for growth and reproduction from simple inorganic substances like water, carbon dioxide and ammonia. They need an energy source to do this, and they use sunlight. They are green because the pigment they use to absorb light energy absorbs violet, blue and red wavelengths but reflects green. Photosynthesis then converts the energy of sunlight to chemical energy. It is the process that makes plants producers and distinguishes them from consumers, animals that get their energy by eating plants or other animals.

During times of sunlight, at temperatures above the freezing point of the plant cells but below whatever their lethal maximum might be, plants absorb light, converting a little of its energy to that of certain high energy bonds of two complex organic molecules (NADPH and ATP), and release oxygen in the process. The converted energy is then used to change carbon dioxide into a simple organic compound that can in turn be built upon to make more complex organic compounds. The construction of the more complex compounds uses up oxygen, occurs in a somewhat similar fashion in all cells, of both plants and animals, and is called cellular respiration.

48

The producers of the Boreal coast are marine grasses, large or macroalgae, and single-celled or microalgae which include the phytoplankton.

THE MARINE GRASSES

Three basic kinds of grasses grow in the soft substrates along the shores of the Boreal coast. Eel grass beds need prolonged submergence by salt water and are rarely uncovered by low tides. The grasses of the meadows of salt marshes either tolerate or need intermittent submergence by the tide, but none can withstand prolonged tidal submergence. And marram grass, which holds the sand dunes together wherever they occur from one end of the coast to the other, tolerates extreme exposure to salt-laden winds, but grows only above the high tide level.

MACROALGAE

Macroalgae are the larger plants that grow in coastal waters, as opposed to the microscopic algae of the phytoplankton. Macroalgae are divided according to their color—brown, red or green. All three types have green chlorophyll necessary for photosynthesis, but the green pigment may be masked by additional brown and red pigments.

Brown rockweeds cover much of the rock surface exposed by low tides throughout the Boreal coastal region, often giving the rocky intertidal a dark lush covering that is lacking in all warmer-water areas. Below the low tide level, brown kelp species dominate the rocky substrates, and they too are characteristic of the Boreal coast but not coasts further to the south. Other red, green and brown macroalgae live under the canopy of the perennial rockweeds and kelp, a few surviving from year to year as perennials as well, but most regrowing each year as annuals. The macroalgae are most diverse on an open rocky coast, where water salinity is high, air temperatures in summer are not excessive, and water temperatures remain relatively low. In estuaries or in very protected areas, the stress of variable salinities and warmer summer temperatures can reduce the diversity of macroalgae considerably. North of the Boreal region, where scouring ice is often very thick along the shorelines, perennials like the brown rockweeds are scraped from the intertidal. Kelp grows only in deeper water, and fast growing annual species are more successful.

PHYTOPLANKTON AND OTHER MICROALGAE

Though macroalgae consist of immense numbers of several types of cells, microalgae are either single cells or short chains of identical cells. They live everywhere light can reach them: on the surfaces of rocks, shells, pilings, macroalgae and sand grains, and they float free in marine and estuarine water. Those that float comprise the phytoplankton, and they all have structural adaptations which help to keep them afloat. The phytoplankton live near the water surface in the photic zone where the light is sufficient for photosynthesis. At depths where insufficient light penetrates for photosynthesis to occur, the photic zone ends, and since the water of coastal regions is more turbid than open ocean water, its photic zone rarely extends to 90 ft (30 m) and is usually considerably more shallow.

Two kinds of microalgae dominate the phytoplankton, diatoms and dinoflagellates. The diatoms are especially abundant. As single cells or chains they come in many bizarre flattened shapes that make it easier for them to float. Diatoms have no way of moving themselves actively, but, encased by cell walls of silica, they drift wherever currents take them.

Not usually as abundant as diatoms, dinoflagellates may still develop very dense swarms. Most species exist as solitary cells, not chains, and they are never as small as the smallest diatoms. Their cell walls are made of cellulose instead of silica. Each cell has two flagella, one for propelling it forward, the other, wrapped around a groove, for rotating it at the same time. In many ways dinoflagellates are similar to single celled animals or protozoans. But like other plants, they have chlorophyll, they photosynthesize, and are therefore producers and not consumers.

Some dinoflagellates are bioluminescent, i.e., they produce light as a by-product of chemical processes. Each flashes intermittently, especially when it is jostled. On a dark night in summer when the populations may be dense,

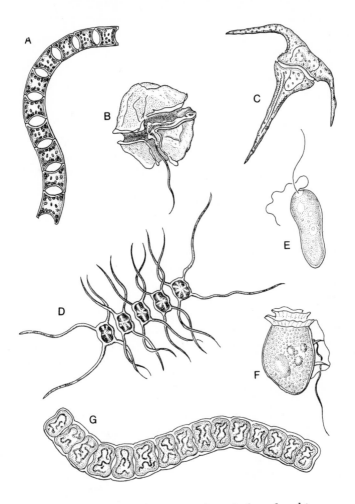

14. Common microscopic plants or phytoplankton found in surface waters include A. *Eucampia zoodiaches* B. *Gonyaulax excauta* C. *Ceratium tripos* D. *Chaetoceros laciniosus* E. *Exuviella marina* F. *Dinophysis* G. *Navicula membranacea*.

the surface water spectacularly reveals its planktonic life. Every fish, every diver, every stroke of a paddle leaves a trail of fire and a sight to be cherished.

The Boreal Organisms   51

Phytoplankton Blooms

When days are short on the Boreal coast, as they are in midwinter, the phytoplankton use up more energy in their own cellular respiration than they gain during photosynthesis. They cease to be able to reproduce themselves by dividing in half and growing again. Populations of diatoms and dinoflagellates then fall to their annual minimum sizes. The populations crash even though the surface layers of water have by then become well mixed, and nutrients from deeper water have been returned to the surface again.

With the increasingly longer daylight hours of spring, however, the cells of the phytoplankton begin to obtain more energy from photosynthesis than they use during respiration, and they begin to grow and divide. Because the diatoms in particular are so small, they can reproduce themselves rapidly, almost explosively. Huge spring blooms of phytoplankton are a dramatic feature of most temperate waters, including those along the North American Boreal coast. In warmer regions, day length remains long enough for winter photosynthesis, nutrients tend not to be recycled easily to surface waters, and the cyclic growth of the phytoplankton, so typical of colder regions, doesn't occur or is much reduced.

Actually many factors determine just how large the spring bloom of phytoplankton populations may become. Besides the amount of sunlight, the transparency or turbidity of the water determines how deep in the water the cells can survive. Spring blooms can even be delayed where estuarine runoff is so great that it makes the water too turbid for light to penetrate deeply. Spring turbidity of the St. Lawrence Estuary is such that only 1 percent of the available light penetrates as deep as 12 ft (4 m), and the phytoplankton remain impoverished until the water begins to clear in late June.

The phytoplankton illustrate just how sensitive populations are to changes in the constituents necessary for their growth. Their dramatic spring bloom is followed by an almost equally dramatic crash in midsummer. Then in fall, another bloom occurs which varies from year to year in size and duration, but never reaches the proportions of the spring-time one. Though grazing by small herbivorous animals, members of the zooplankton, removes some of the phytoplankton from the water during mid-summer, it isn't extensive enough to account for the population crashes which occur even though days are more than long enough to support photosynthesis. In autumn, when day length is rapidly shortening, another bloom occurs.

The explanation of this paradox lies in the availability of needed nutrients. The phytoplankton grow only in the surface waters, where light is sufficient. Each summer, the surface water is warmed and since warm water is less dense than cold, a permanent warm-water surface layer develops. As diatoms die, they sink into the colder water below, carrying entrapped nutrients with them. Animals that graze on them also usually leave the surface water and excrete their nutrient-laden wastes into the colder water, or they themselves die and sink to the bottom. Abundant bacteria release the nutrients from the dead plants and animals, converting them to usable forms once again, but the nutrients remain locked in the cold water. The warm surface water therefore becomes progressively depleted of nutrients which accumulate instead in the colder, deeper water. The phytoplankton no longer can grow and multiply.

In the autumn, conditions change. The surface layers cool, become denser, and sink, and vertical mixing of the water begins. Nutrients are carried to the surface where there is still enough light for photosynthesis, and phytoplankton populations bloom again. Now, however, though nutrients are abundant, the hours of daylight soon become too few to support extensive photosynthesis; the fall bloom of the phytoplankton is soon over. Throughout the winter, gales and cold temperatures continue the vertical mixing of the water. By spring the sea is of fairly uniform temperature and nutrient distribution. With the lengthening days, the spring bloom begins once again, to be cut off when summer warming once more re-establishes the thermocline.

Though this annual cycle of phytoplankton blooms is a predictable occurrence in temperate oceans, it isn't true of areas where the nutrients are continually restored to the surface by upwelling deeper water. Instead, where bottom and surface layers continue to mix, the phytoplankton bloom without crashing from early spring to late autumn. Large populations of zooplankton flourish as well, and a continual rain of plankton falls, feeding the schools of fish which accumulate. The schools of fish in turn provide food for other fish and for the sea birds that breed in colonies each summer on the islands along the Boreal coast. Areas of mixing or upwelling are therefore the most productive ones, wherever they occur in lower estuaries, over offshore banks, and elsewhere along the Boreal coast.

The Grazers

A large variety of animals in the Boreal sea are herbivores. They eat the grasses, macroalgae and microalgae. Most of the small, transparent animals that make up the zooplankton are herbivores, too. They graze on the phytoplankton. Copepods, which thoroughly dominate the zooplankton much of the year, are small crustaceans that filter the water for the phytoplankton it contains, grow rapidly to sexual maturity, have high reproductive rates and are so abundant that they are the predominant food of many fish. One copepod in particular, *Calanus finmarchius*, is so common along much of the Boreal coast that schools of herring, shad, mackerel and menhaden all selectively feed upon it in inshore well-mixed waters. Many other very small animals besides the copepods have devised ways of eating the phytoplankton. Some, like the copepods, are permanent members of the zooplankton; others are seasonally occurring larval forms of bottom dwelling, or benthic, animals. Like the phytoplankton, the zooplankton often have bizarre shapes which make it easier for them to float. They also tend to be transparent, the only way they have of hiding from the predators which seek them.

The benthic algae are also food for many herbivores. Snails and limpets scrape films of microalgae from the rock surfaces. A community of minute animals, again dominated by copepods, grazes on the microalgae growing on and among sand grains. Snails and sea urchins chew up the macroalgae, and, if they are not checked by predators or other factors, they can effectively eliminate almost all the macroalgae from an area. The grasses of the salt marshes

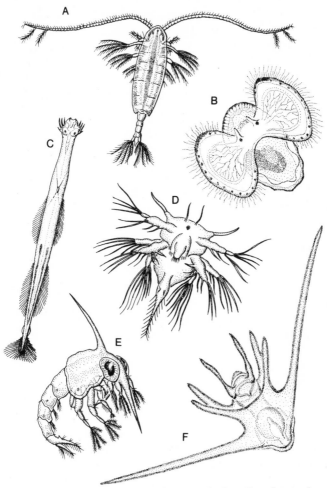

15. Common microscopic animals or zooplankton found in surface waters include A. copepod *Calanus finmarchius* B. veliger larva of a gastropod snail C. arrow worm *Sagitta elegans* D. metanauplius larva of a barnacle E. zoea larva of the green rock crab F. pluteus larva of the green sea urchin.

and eelgrass beds are food for other snails, and they may be a large part of the diet of ducks which dabble for their food, as well as for wintering Brant and Canada geese.

Filter Feeders and Deposit Feeders

Many animals are not selective of what they eat, but rather filter the water around them for any plankton and organic debris or detritus it contains. The largest filter feeders are the baleen whales which cruise through plankton-rich waters, but the vast majority are small and sessile animals that sit glued to rocks and other hard surfaces, or burrow into soft, usually sandy substrates. Sea squirts, sponges, barnacles, bryozoans, mollusks like clams and mussels, plume worms and many other animals all filter the water in some way to obtain their food; and all are common along the Boreal coast.

Where detritus settles rapidly on surfaces, especially on soft, muddy ones, the resident animals tend to be deposit feeders. Instead of filtering the water, they ingest the substrate, digest what is edible, and eliminate everything else, which is mostly mud and sand particles. Some clams concentrate on eating the surface accumulation of detritus, but most deposit feeders burrow under the surface and eat their way through it, rather like terrestrial earthworms. Sand dollars and many kinds of marine worms are deposit feeders characteristic of all coasts, including the Boreal.

Predators

In contrast to the nonselective filter and deposit feeders, predators seek out individual prey for capture. Minute predators roam around between sand and even mud grains, preying upon the equally small grazers there and being preyed upon by larger predators, including shore birds. Large crustaceans such as lobsters and various crabs forage over the substrate eating anything they can catch, as do numerous bottom-feeding or demersal fish as well as some of the diving ducks. More specialized predators, such as whelks and starfish, creep around efficiently decimating populations of their prey, while sea slugs forage on other sessile species. Many fish prey directly on the zooplankton, in turn to be preyed upon by other fish, sea birds, squid, seals and whales. All are seasonally common along the

Boreal coast, attracted there for the same reason human predators are drawn to the plankton-rich waters: prey is abundant.

Not surprisingly, some of the zooplankton are not grazers, but predators of the grazers. Large or macroplanktonic animals, such as many jellyfish and all sea gooseberries (or ctenophores), fish for smaller zooplankton as they drift along. The much smaller larval stages of benthic animals such as crabs and lobsters prey upon smaller larvae and adults of other species. Like many predators, they also cannibalize their own species. One of the most impressive of the zooplankton predators must be the arrow worm, *Sagitta elegans*. (It isn't a worm at all.) About 3/4 inch (2 cm) long, the arrow worm has two pairs of horizontal fins and a horizontal tail fin, and has remarkably powerful jaws. It is transparent but for its two black eyes. It preys mostly on copepods, but it can easily capture, crush and swallow a fish larva as long as itself.

Omnivores and Scavengers

Not all animals that select what they will or will not eat are exclusively carnivores or herbivores. Other animals are omnivores, which select either plants or animals as food depending upon what is available. The euphausiids, or krill, which are prey for pelagic fish and baleen whales of the Boreal coast, are themselves omnivores, eating both phyto- and zooplankton. In fact, many shrimp-like crustaceans can be both selective predators as well as filter feeders of detritus and diatoms. Other omnivores may be primarily scavengers, which selectively eat decaying plant and animal material. The combinations of feeding methods available to a consumer can make it difficult to label every animal species according to its feeding preferences.

Marine Food Pyramids

The energy source that the various marine ecosystems of the Boreal coast ultimately depend on is sunlight, and in that way they are no different from all but one of the other ecosystems on the planet. The one exception occurs around some recently discovered heat vents in the deep abysses near the Galapagos Islands of the Pacific Ocean where heat, instead of light, provides the driving energy.

The macroalgae, grasses and phytoplankton make up the vast majority of the bulk of living matter, or biomass, of the Boreal coast. Only about 10 percent of the biomass of the producers is converted into the biomass of the herbivores; the rest is respired or eliminated as waste. Similarly, only about 10 percent of the biomass of the herbivores is converted into the biomass of the predators. There must therefore be far fewer predators than herbivores in any ecosystem, no matter how abundant they may appear to be when they are massed in schools or colonies. A very productive system, by the sheer bulk of its plants, can support a correspondingly large biomass of herbivores and therefore predators. The combined productivity of intertidal rockweeds, salt marsh grasses, subtidal kelp beds, and phytoplankton populations of the Boreal coast is probably greater than any comparable area in the world.

Seasonal Behavior of Boreal Animals

Most Boreal marine animals respond to the annual changes in their environments almost as dramatically as the phytoplankton. The cold temperatures of winter drive mobile intertidal animals close to the low tide level, or out of the intertidal region entirely. The cold of the shallow inshore waters induces other animals to head for the deeper warmer water for the winter. Still others fly and swim southward to warmer areas that have more catchable food and fewer winter gales. Migrations therefore occur throughout the region each year with animals escaping the most rigorous aspects of the Boreal winters, but returning in spring to partake of the immense resurgence of life. The many species which don't migrate but remain in the cold shallow waters and on intertidal substrates often have remarkable adaptations that permit them to do so.

The breeding cycles of almost all the Boreal animals,

58

from seals and seabirds to crabs and periwinkles, are closely related to events in the surrounding environment. Many of the species produce their young at a time when they can take advantage of the pulse of plankton production each spring. Others make sure their young hatch where there is ample food through summer, as in estuaries and near the offshore banks. Yet others, like the seabirds, migrate from considerable distances to breed near large, predictable food supplies necessary for them to be able to raise their young successfully.

A variety of Boreal marine animals breed exclusively around the time of the new and full moons of late spring and early summer. Some of the worms leave their burrows and swarm in a kind of frenzy at the surface as they shed their eggs and sperm. Horseshoe crabs lay their eggs at the highest level the spring tides reach in the warmer waters of the estuaries, while *Loligo* squid lay their eggs just below the lowest level of the same tides elsewhere on the coast.

In contrast to those that breed in spring or summer, there are other animals that breed most actively during the winter. They are all invertebrates which live subtidally or in deep tide pools, and include some of the sea squirts, bryozoans and gastropod snails such as the nudibranchs.

The annual, seasonal, and even daily and tidal cycles bring considerable change to the Boreal coastal waters, and all the organisms living in them are attuned to those changes, often in subtle ways.

CHAPTER II

The Marine
Rocky Intertidal

The Impenetrable Substrate

The rocky shores that dominate so much of the Boreal coast distinguish it from coastal regions to the south where beaches, lagoons and salt marshes predominate instead. The intertidal expanse of rocks exposed by the receding tide is as great or greater in parts of the Boreal region than anywhere else in the world. The rocky intertidal shore is then not only the most obvious and characteristic feature of the Boreal region, it is also the most accessible for study, and its special problems and questions have intrigued generations of naturalists.

The various plants and animals that live on the intertidal rocks have evolved a wide range of ways of adhering to the hard surfaces. Most are fastened permanently in one place while others creep around with adhesive feet or just cling to the textured surface. What they all have in common is that they live on a substrate which cannot be penetrated: plants with roots and animals which burrow must live elsewhere, on soft substrates.

The rocky shores of the Boreal region often have little in common besides their hardness. The slope of the shores varies from vertical cliffs to long, gently sloping ledges. The ledges may be smooth and unadorned, penetrated by deep crevices, or covered with boulders too large for the sea to toss around. Depressions in the ledges trap water in tide pools where plants and animals that cannot tolerate exposure to air may find sanctuary so long as they can withstand whatever other stresses the pool may impose on them.

Rocky intertidal shores are not restricted to areas of high salinity, for they characterize many of the coastal estuaries as well. Estuaries, with their lower salinities, present further stresses on their inhabitants, however, and except for estuary mouths which are essentially marine, this chapter does not include the estuarine habitat (see chapter 4).

Rocky Shores of the Boreal Region

Excellent examples of the marine rocky intertidal, including protected coves and wave-beaten points, are abundant on the Boreal coast almost anywhere north of Cape Elizabeth in southern Maine. Rocky headlands certainly exist between Cape Cod and Cape Elizabeth, but with the exception of Cape Ann, none are particularly large. Cape Elizabeth itself, with its ledges and tide pools, begins the virtually unbroken rocky coast of Maine. Peninsula after peninsula then juts out into the Gulf of Maine, and some, such as Pemaquid Point, are especially fine for observing the impact of high energy waves on the intertidal organisms. The rocky shores which are most accessible for prolonged exploration are probably the varied ones of Acadia National Park, with its wave-beaten headlands and quiet, protected coves. These are just some of the more famous examples of what occurs over and over again along the full length of the coast (see plate I).

Rocky shores line parts of the Bay of Fundy, most of the Atlantic side of Nova Scotia, almost all of Newfoundland, much of the north shore of the Gulf of St. Lawrence, and most of the Gaspé Peninsula. Again, some of the national parks provide the easiest access to a variety of rocky shores, especially Fundy National Park, Gros Morne and Terra Nova National Parks in Newfoundland, and Forillon (which means "rocky") National Park at the tip of Gaspé Peninsula. But these are just convenient points of access to what often seems an unending, limitless rim of rock at land's edge.

The Stresses of Exposure

The organisms that live on the intertidal rocks face the same general environmental stresses when the tide drops below them as do the organisms of other intertidal substrates. Summer heat, winter freezing, dilution by rainwater, desiccation by the drying air, difficulties in obtaining oxygen—all are severe problems, and the higher up the intertidal the more severe they are.

Unlike soft substrates, rock surfaces don't give the plants and animals living on them much protection. The perennial macroalgae cannot survive winter by allowing their exposed parts to die back because they have no roots, and the animals cannot hide in the way those that live in soft substrates can, by burrowing a little deeper away from surface ice or rain or heat. Instead, since so many of the organisms are sessile and fixed in place on the rock surface, they either survive the full impact of the stresses of exposure or they die. Slow-moving animals migrate seasonally but must still tolerate sudden changes in their environment; a few which move more quickly easily avoid even the sudden changes. Only where the brown macroalgae grow thickly on the rocks can animals and smaller macroalgae find limited protection from the potentially extreme daily fluctuations of temperature, salinity and desiccation.

Along with their ability to tolerate the various daily and seasonal changes, the organisms of the rocky intertidal must also be able to withstand the impact of crashing waves. Unlike soft substrates, rocks absorb none of the energy of waves, and their covering organisms receive no protection. The glues which hold the macroalgae onto the rock must be strong, and the algae can grow long only if they are extremely flexible, able to bend with the waves. The animals either glue themselves on, as do the barnacles and mussels, or they have adhesive feet, as do the whelks, periwinkles, limpets and starfish. The shapes of the animals as well as their orientation to the waves may also help deflect the impact of the crashing waves.

16. Ice cakes often form on the rockweed in winter, severely stressing intertidal plants and animals.

THE MARINE ROCKY INTERTIDAL

Ice is yet another problem. The scouring effect of winter ice on any intertidal substrate cannot be underestimated, and its impact on the resident organisms of the rocky intertidal can be truly devastating. Rock cannot absorb the impact of ice any more than it can that of waves. If a winter is severe, ice can build up especially in protected areas and storm-driven waves can then churn it against the rocks. In spring the break up of the river and estuarine ice and, in the north, of the ice packs, sends blocks of ice out to sea, abrading shores along the way. Though the intertidal organisms may be adapted to withstand freezing temperatures and the thin layers of encrusting ice that often form in winter when the tide is low, none can protect themselves from the scouring action of blocks of ice: they are simply scraped away from the rock. When coastal ice is the rule rather than the exception, the ice may clean the rocky intertidal of much of the life which otherwise would cover it. More than anything else, it is ice that determines what we recognize as the northern limits of the Boreal rocky coast.

Advantages of Being There

Despite the relative hardship rocky intertidal organisms tolerate in comparison with those that live continuously submerged below the reaches of the low tide, there are some advantages to living on the intertidal rocks. Practically all the macroalgae and sessile animals of the rocky intertidal live where they do, not because they cannot survive as well or even better continuously submerged in the subtidal region, but because many of their subtidal competitors cannot tolerate intertidal exposure. Poor competitors in the subtidal, they are successful in the intertidal because they can survive there and their competitors cannot.

Though a few herbivores graze on the algae and a few predators prey on the sessile filter feeders in the intertidal, their diversity is restricted by the harshness of the environment. The algae and filter feeders therefore escape not only many of their competitors but at least some of the animals which would otherwise feast upon them as well.

The rock substrate itself, though it fails to absorb any of

the impact of waves and ice, still offers the one thing which macroalgae and many sessile filter feeders need above all else: a hard substrate. Macroalgae cannot grow on a substrate which shifts with tides, currents or waves, and neither can many filter feeders such as barnacles. The rocks provide both the surface they need to settle on and then grow.

Furthermore, since the water which ebbs and flows over the intertidal rocks is usually turbulent, as a result it usually contains ample oxygen, carbon dioxide, dissolved nutrients, and organic debris or detritus. The growth of the intertidal macroalgae in a single season is, in places, as great as any population of producers known, and local populations of barnacles or mussels can also be immense. The limiting factors for most of these organisms are ultimately the environmental stresses around them, however, and these vary considerably depending upon how exposed to waves and weather the intertidal is, and how far above the low tide level the organisms are.

Zonation

Though all plants and animals of the rocky intertidal must withstand exposure to air and the stresses it brings them, some can withstand a lot more than others. Those able to withstand most exposure are likely to live highest on the intertidal rocks. The organisms, both plants and animals, appear to be laid out in horizontal rows or zones on the intertidal rocks, one above the other. The upper and lower limits of such a zone of organisms are correlated with critical spring and neap tide levels. But just as each example of a rocky shore differs from every other example, so also the zones of organisms within the intertidal region vary from place to place. They vary for much the same reasons, for differences in slope, wave action, currents, general topography, degree of algal cover, and presence of competitors and predators all influence the distribution of the common species. As a result, a zone which may dominate one site may be virtually absent from another.

Nonetheless, distinct zones exist and are usually easily recognizable. Each is identified by the presence of one or a few dominant species of plants or sessile animals. Some motile animals may also occur in specific zones; they are more able to move into other zones when conditions become unfavorable.

Table 2: Intertidal Biotic Zones

Zone	Limits of Zone	Dominant or Indicator Species
1. Spray or Splash Zone	Above Extreme High Water Spring	*Xanthoria* (lichen)
2. Highest Inter-tidal or Black Zone	Covered only by high or highest tides	*Calothrix* (blue-green algae) *Littorina saxatilis* (rough periwinkle)
3. High Inter-tidal or Barnacle Zone	Below Black Zone but above brown algae	*Balanus balanoides* (barnacle) *Littorina littorea* (common periwinkle)
4. Mid Inter-tidal or Brown Algae Zone	Below Barnacle Zone, down to Mean Low Water	*Fucus* species (brown algae) *Ascophyllum nodosum* *Mytilus edulis* (blue mussel) *Littorina obtusata* (smooth periwinkle)
5. Low Inter-tidal or Irish Moss Zone	Below the brown algae to subtidal kelp zone	*Chondrus crispus* (Irish moss)

Within each zone the same major questions can be asked. What are the physical, or abiotic, stresses that a resident organism must withstand, and how has it adapted to them? What is the impact of competition and predation upon the diversity and abundance of organisms in the zone? How have the organisms adapted to the profound seasonal changes that occur?

The Impenetrable Substrate

17. Different zones are easy to distinguish on a rocky shore. Here, the barnacle zone ends abruptly (left) and the rockweed zone dominates the lower rocks (right).

The Spray Zone

The spray zone lies above the level reached by even the highest of the spring tides and extends high up the rocks as far as the salt spray is driven by the waves and winds. It is a transitional zone, neither truly marine nor terrestrial, and any organism that lives in it must tolerate both extreme desiccation and the impact of salt, wind and surf.

The spray zone also varies tremendously in size. Where waves crash against high cliffs, or headlands, facing the open ocean, the spray zone may be many feet or meters in height. An excellent example is the seaward side of Monhegan Island, 10 miles (16 km) off the coast of Maine, but any of the major rocky capes, from Cape Elizabeth to northern Newfoundland would serve as well. On the other hand, in a quiet, protected cove there may be no spray zone at all and terrestrial plants may grow right down to the level of the highest spring tide.

The few higher plants which are able to thrive in the spray zone are terrestrial in origin yet highly resistant to salt. Where minute amounts of soil accumulate in cracks in

68   THE MARINE ROCKY INTERTIDAL

the rocks, the hardy goosetongue or seaside plantain, *Plan-tago* species, may grow successfully. Other shore plants, such as seaside golden rod and salt spray rose may grow where there is by chance more soil, but they are also characteristic of sand dune vegetation (see chapter 3).

More typical of the spray zone on a rocky shore are several species of yellow and grey lichens which have adapted to this difficult environment. The orange-yellow species, *Xanthoria parientura,* stands out particularly well, with large patches encrusting parts of the exposed surfaces of the rocks. Every lichen is a symbiotic relationship between a particular species of alga and a particular fungus species. Neither can live without the other. The fungus is able to absorb water and survive prolonged dry periods, providing the symbiotic algal cells with a protected, moist environment. In turn the trapped algal cells produce organic carbon by-products which the fungal cells feed upon. The algal cells of the lichen also have little holdfasts that glue them to the rock surface: because of the symbiotic arrangement, the lichen has no need of the nourishing roots which higher plants depend upon, and therefore grows easily on non-nourishing surfaces. Another less obvious lichen which occurs only in the spray zone is the black *Verrucaria,* growing in tar-like patches, often in rock crevices.

Not surprisingly, the spray zone is one of very low species diversity. The species that do live there are not in competition with each other, for their numbers are not great and space is abundant. A few small, hardy terrestrial animals forage down into the spray zone, especially certain mites, spiders and ants. A small wingless insect, the springtail *Anurida maritima,* may also forage up from its lower intertidal habitat. Few species are permanent residents.

The Black Zone

The apparently barren, black, slippery zone of the highest region of the intertidal shore is covered twice daily by the tide, for only a brief period each time. Because the height to which a high tide rises varies so much from spring to neap tides, the upper edge of the zone may be difficult to define clearly as it merges gradually into a spray zone. Nonetheless, any plant or animal living in the zone must be able to tolerate if not need daily inundation by sea water, just as it must be able to withstand the greatest extremes of desiccation, heat, freezing and dilution by rain or runoff that the intertidal shore can offer. The organisms that tolerate this environment are only a little more diverse than those of the spray zone. Unlike the spray zone, the black zone is not a transitional one between the land and sea: it is truly marine, for its organisms cannot survive without the relief a high tide brings them.

The zone gets its name and color from the blue-green algae which cover it. Blue-green algae are the simplest of plants for though they photosynthesize as all plants do, they lack nuclear membranes and are therefore somewhat like bacteria. The blue-green algae of the black zone are primarily species of the genus *Calothrix*, distinguishable from each other only under a microscope. The algal cells produce mucilage sheaths which protect them from desiccation and glue them to each other and to the rock surface. Extensive thin algal mats rim every rocky intertidal shore. The mucilage isn't too slippery when the algae have dried in the sun for a couple of hours, but when the mats of *Calothrix* are wet or damp they are extremely slippery and treacherous for anyone walking on them.

Reproduction is rapid in *Calothrix*. Cell division, fragmentation and growth of filaments allow the algae to spread in all directions over the upper intertidal rocks. The algae also fix atmospheric nitrogen, taking it in its gaseous state which is unusable to most other organisms, and converting it to forms other organisms depend upon. The *Calothrix* mats therefore provide a fine food source for grazing animals, though there is only one grazing species that can withstand the severe environmental stress of the zone: the rough periwinkle snail, *Littorina saxatilis* (see *Littorina* section later in this chapter).

The Barnacle Zone

One species of barnacle, *Balanus balanoides*, lives abundantly higher in the intertidal than any other sessile animal. The upper intertidal zone below the black *Calothrix* mats belongs to this barnacle. None of its competitors can tolerate the duration and degree of exposure it survives in the upper intertidal zone, and so below the ubiquitous black zone there is often a white zone of barnacles in stark contrast. The barnacles may be sparse or crowded, depending on food availability and exposure to wave action and temperature fluctuations. Not surprisingly, the upper limits of the barnacle's distribution on the rocks is determined, once again, by abiotic factors (see plate I).

Even the lowest of the neap high tides reaches the upper edge of the barnacle zone, allowing the barnacles to feed at least briefly during every tidal cycle. During the long hours between consecutive high tides the rocks may become very warm under the summer sun, while the cold air of winter may freeze any trapped or seeping water, and may freeze the barnacles as well. The upper limit of the barnacle zone is therefore quite clearly marked, for barnacle larvae which settle higher on the rocks do not survive long.

In contrast, the lower limit of the barnacle zone is extremely variable, and depends upon the relative abundance of the dog whelk, *Thais lapillus*, which is the major predator of the barnacles, and of brown rockweeds and the blue mussel, *Mytilus edulis*, which are the barnacles' primary competitors. Where predator and competitors are abundant, the barnacle zone may be so narrow that it is difficult to find. Where predator and competitors are uncommon, the barnacle zone stretches down the intertidal even on occasion as far as the level of the low tide.

The Barnacle

With its calcium shell and sedentary nature, the barnacle was long thought to be a mollusk rather than the crustacean it really is. It wasn't until the discovery of its larval stages in 1830 that the barnacle was found to be, as Louis Agassiz the 19th century naturalist would later say, "nothing more than a little shrimp-like animal, standing on its head in a limestone house and kicking food into its mouth."

In the *Balanus* genus, the "limestone house" characteristically consists of six side plates and a pair of movable top plates which open for feeding and reproductive purposes. When the top plates of *Balanus balanoides* are closed, the animal can survive prolonged exposure to direct sun, rain and freezing. The conical shape of the shell is an adaptive feature, for this shape allows full-force waves of up to 40 lbs. per square inch to crash over the animal without dislodging it. In addition, *B. balanoides* has a membranous base to its structure, and this probably helps the animal to clamp down to the rock more tightly than others of the genus which have a calcareous base. It can thereby be more effectively sealed off from its environment, whether that consists of crashing waves or of hot sun. Populations high in the intertidal zone are able to withstand temperatures which range from 111° F (44° C) to 5° F (−15° C), an ability few, if any, other animals can duplicate. *B. balanoides* withstands low temperatures by retaining sea water which is rarely below 32° F (0° C) in winter and by being additionally warmed by the sun. In this way, it stays warmer than the surrounding air. When temperatures drop even lower, this barnacle can quickly get rid of the water in its individual cells, thus keeping ice crystals from forming within the cells and rupturing them. Instead, crystals form in between the cells, causing cellular distortion but not rupture.

The barnacle survives extreme heat by cooling itself by means of transpiration, or evaporation of its bodily water. The cooling effect of such transpiration makes it possible for a barnacle to be up to 9° F (5° C) cooler than surrounding air temperatures. That ability allows *B. balanoides* to survive heat which kills most other animals. Associated with this transpiration ability is the barnacle's ability to withstand water loss.

In addition to the above life-sustaining abilities, *B. balanoides* is also able to breathe even when not covered by sea water. When the surrounding air is humid, the barnacle retains a connection with the outside air through the micropyle, a small passage which allows air into the mantle cavity. Other species of *Balanus* which live subtidally and are always covered by water are not able to form this adaptive passageway.

If the air becomes too dry, *B. balanoides* can respire while completely closed, using oxygen it has stored inside and a special blood pigment which allows use of even a very small amount of oxygen. If this closed system goes on for too long, however, the animal will die from a combination of too little oxygen and too much accumulated lactic acid.

When covered by the tide, *B. balanoides* opens its top paired plates and uncurls its feeding appendages, called cirri, which look like delicate and graceful fans. Covered with minute sensory hairs, the cirri sweep water in and down, up to 140 times per minute, trapping planktonic food particles. The trapped particles are scraped by other cirri and transferred to the mouth. Barnacles are thus called filter feeders for they filter the water for their food.

18. Barnacles are filter feeders, sweeping the water with their cirri and trapping microscopic food particles.

The barnacle is the only large group of crustaceans that is hermaphroditic, containing both sexes in the same individual. However, with large numbers of individuals sitting glued to the rock adjacent to one another, cross-fertilization occurs easily. The ovaries are contained in the base and walls of the mantle and paired oviducts open near the base of the first pair of cirri. Each barnacle has a remarkably long penis able to reach into the mantle cavity of an adjacent barnacle where it deposits its sperm. In spring the barnacles fertilize one another, and each then broods its fertilized eggs in its mantle cavity. Retaining the eggs in this fashion protects them from predators at least until they hatch.

The Barnacle Zone

73

The eggs hatch as nauplius larvae, each with a triangular shield-shaped carapace. These larvae are swept away by local currents, molt into another larger larval form, the cypris larvae, and finally settle sometime from April to June.

Each cypris larva leaves the plankton and settles to the bottom, seeking an appropriate hard substrate where it can then metamorphose into a miniature barnacle. Before metamorphosing, the cypris larva orients its body vertically toward the light and extends its feeding apparatus into the water. Usually, then, the majority of barnacles at any site is oriented in the same direction. The larvae also have the ability to select sites where other barnacles have already settled, thereby assuring themselves of a well-tested site where there is sufficient water movement to keep food particles suspended. Once attached to a good site, the barnacles excrete a very strong cement to keep themselves firmly glued to the chosen rock, shell or piece of submerged timber.

Barnacles use two mechanisms in their growth. The shell grows larger through additional deposits of calcium carbonate at the edges and base of each plate. The body grows through molting, and body casts or molts can often be seen floating in the water during the spring and early summer months, the time of fastest barnacle growth.

Barnacles in the lower intertidal rarely live more than two years, for they are usually either eaten by the dogwhelk, *Thais lapillus*, or outcompeted for space by the mussel, *Mytilus edulis*. Barnacles higher in the intertidal are able to live longer than those in lower zones once they survive the early months in the harsh environment.

In places where the barnacles survive in large numbers and grow rapidly, problems of a new sort arise. Despite predation by the dogwhelk, far more barnacles settle and grow than the rock surfaces appear to have room for. The barnacles are forced into increasingly crowded conditions, competing now with each other for limited attachment space and access to the food carried in the water over them. Instead of growing into the typical flattened cone shape of a barnacle with ample space around it, the crowded barnacles grow, pressed against each other, into long thin cylinders. Now they are protected from dislodgement by wave action only by their attachment to one another, for they are easily broken loose if for some reason they become individually exposed.

19. The barnacles on the left show their normal tent-like shape, when there is ample growing space. In crowded conditions, as on the right, the barnacles are forced into a long cylindrical shape and are more easily dislodged.

The Brown Algae Zone

The rocky intertidal shore throughout the Boreal region is most characterized by an extensive cover of perennial brown algae, in particular by species of the Fucales family. These rockweeds may extend far up the intertidal, almost to the black zone, practically eliminating the barnacle zone. In places where there is extreme wave action, the rocks may be mostly bare of the algae and covered instead by barnacles and mussels. Usually, however, the Fucales extend from the lower edge of a barnacle zone down to approximately Mean Low Water.

Brown Algae: the Fucales

The olive-brown seaweeds of the intertidal zone have often been compared to forests. And indeed, under the luxuriant canopy of the rockweeds fish swim, crabs scuttle along, snails graze and anemones open into full bloom. It is Rachel Carson who captured the truly amazing aspect of the brown algal zone with her portrayal of the rockweeds as a mad jungle in the Lewis Carroll sense. She calls it mad, for twice every 24 hours this luxuriant tall jungle slowly sinks to the substrate, finally lying prostrate with fronds draped listlessly over the rocks.

The Fucales are often called sea wracks for when the tide is down it looks as if an angry sea has thrown the plants against the rocks. Several hours later it slowly begins to rise again with the incoming tide until it reaches its full vertical height which is often taller than most men.

Unlike terrestrial plants, marine plants do not need specialized nutrient-gathering roots, for the mineral-laden sea water continuously bathes the entire plant. Instead of roots, the algae have holdfasts that, in the intertidal Fucales, are quite simple and disc-like in shape. The holdfast glues the plant to rock, shell or wood and holds the plant in position.

The salt water also provides gentle support for the plant and that, in addition to air bladders which some of the rockweeds possess, buoys the plants up so they can get enough light for photosynthesis. The stipe or stem-like part of the plant then does not need to be nearly as firm as the stem of a terrestrial plant. The fronds, or blades, of the marine plants compare roughly to the leaves of terrestrial plants and they vary just as much in shape and size.

These intertidal seaweeds all have characteristics that enable them to survive the temperature fluctuation and desiccation stress to which they are exposed. The frost-hardiness of these plants comes from the ability of individual cells to release water quickly, thereby preventing ice from forming within the cells. In addition, when extremely cold temperatures coincide with low tides, although the uppermost layer of horizontal weed may be killed, the underlying layers are insulated. The very thick cell walls of the rockweeds also provide desiccation protection. The alginates in the cell walls are vital to the algae's survival, for not only do the alginates help the plants cope with temperature and desiccation stress, but also they help provide flexibility and strength to tolerate wave action.

In all Fucales the sperm and eggs are released separately into the water. A chemical from the egg attracts the sperm and increases the chances of fertilization. The fertilized egg attaches itself to a hard substrate with a sticky cell and once attached, a filament is extended, grows into minute crevices and secretes an adhesive.

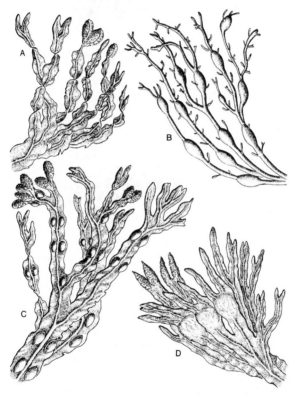

20. Common intertidal rockweeds of the Boreal coast are A. *Fucus spiralis* B. *Ascophyllum nodosum* C. *Fucus vesiculosus* D. *Fucus distichus*.

In the Boreal zone, four seaweeds of the Fucaceae family dominate the intertidal, offering protection with their fronds to literally hundreds of organisms. Two of the Fucales, *Fucus vesiculosus* and *Ascophyllum nodosum*, account for the greatest amount of weed in the rockweed zone. Two others, *Fucus spiralis* in the high intertidal and *Fucus distichus* in the low intertidal, complete the jungle. Other less common species of the same family occur less predictably along the coast.

Fucus distichus. *Fucus distichus* is often covered with water and since the plant is moderately small, growing to a maximum of about 8 inches (20 cm), the water is able to buoy up the plant without additional bladder support. Besides having no air bladders, *F. distichus* can be identified by its long flattened receptacles, or fruiting bodies, which contain the sperm and eggs.

Fucus vesiculosus. *Fucus vesiculosus*, the bladder wrack, is one of the commonest marine algae. It may blanket the mid-intertidal zone and is often found in close conjunction with *Ascophyllum nodosum*, the knotted wrack. In protected sites, *Ascophyllum* can grow more quickly and outcompete *Fucus vesiculosus*, but in more exposed areas the bladder wrack dominates. The characteristic midrib of *Fucus* gives it greater tensile strength than *Ascophyllum* and its stouter fronds are more resistant to wave action. *Ascophyllum* fronds are long and slender, unable to resist great ripping by waves. In addition, the red alga *Polysiphonia lanosa* grows epiphytically on *Ascophyllum*, increasing its weight and susceptibility to heavy surf.

The bladder wrack grows up to several feet (1 m) in length and is easily distinguished by its numerous paired bladders. These help buoy the plant up to provide maximum light for photosynthesis, but they can also become a disadvantage in very heavy surf areas where additional buoyancy can cause increased sharp tugging by the surf and possible dislodgement. Accordingly, on greatly exposed shores, *Fucus vesiculosus* has far fewer bladders than in moderately exposed areas. In marsh and estuarine conditions where the water is often turbid as well as quiet, bladder growth is greater than normal. When the bladder wrack is dried, the bladders "pop" if they are pressed sharply—a source of delight to children.

Like most of the fucoids, *F. vesiculosus* has separate sexes in different plants. The almost heart-shaped receptacles are obvious on the plant for up to six months. Generally the plants are fertile from spring through summer though further south in the range the plants are fertile earlier in the year. Sexes are easily distinguished in this species for the male receptacles are orange when opened while the female receptacles are olive-green. There is usually no receptacle formation until the plant is in its second year, and its life span varies from 3 to 5 years (see plate II).

Ascophyllum nodosum. *Ascophyllum nodosum,* the knotted wrack, is the other very common intertidal brown alga. Like *Fucus vesiculosus, Ascophyllum* has relatively constant photosynthesis in temperatures that fluctuate from 50° to 86° F (10 to 30° C). This means that there is steady growth for much of the year. The warty berry-like receptacles on the separate sexes of *Ascophyllum* generally form in the winter. Reproduction occurs in the summer. Like *F. vesiculosus, Ascophyllum* has a reproductive response to warming temperatures, fruiting in late winter in the southern end of its range and in late summer at the northern end. *Ascophyllum* lives as long as 6 or 7 years and grows to a length of 6 to 10 feet (2 to 3 m).

21. Detail of *Ascophyllum nodosum.* The fruiting bodies of *Ascophyllum nodosum* form in late winter and ripen by spring.

Fucus spiralis. High in the intertidal is the spiral wrack, *Fucus spiralis*. This bladderless twisted species spends about three-quarters of its life out of water, making the presence of bladders unnecessary. Although *F. spiralis* has both male and female receptacles on the same plant, self-fertilization is rare. The oval receptacle has an additional thick ridge of tissue, making it look almost as if the two sides of the receptacle have been glued together. *Fucus spiralis* prefers relatively quiet water and grows to 8 to 12 inches (20 to 30 cm) in its two year life span.

Competition for Space: Barnacles, Mussels and Algae

On protected shores, the growth of the Fucales, especially *Ascophyllum*, is often luxuriant. The density of the barnacle *Balanus balanoides* drops remarkably in such places, for the algae overgrow the barnacles, starving them by reducing the water circulation over them. As algae are whipped about by waves they may also prevent barnacle larvae from settling by means of a kind of whiplash effect. At the same time they provide a moist cover for the major predator of the barnacle, the dogwhelk *Thais lapillus*. Though these are of course just side effects of the algal shape and growth, the end result is successful competition by the Fucales for rock space. The barnacles are not completely eliminated, but they are likely to be scattered sparsely under the algae. A growing barnacle can in fact dislodge an algal holdfast, a slow process which indicates that the competition is not totally in favor of the algae.

The situation is quite different on shores subjected to greater intensities of wave action. Where the waves are of intermediate strength, *Ascophyllum* is far less abundant, and *Fucus vesiculosus* replaces it. The total abundance of the algae is also reduced and the barnacles then have the space to form a particularly broad barnacle zone. However, on shores that are most exposed to wave action, the blue mussel, *Mytilus edulis*, competes successfully for rock space with both the brown algae and the barnacles, and replaces both. As a result, the species that most dominates a mid-intertidal rocky shore, whether it is a rockweed, the barnacle, or the mussel, often indicates the shore's wave action.

The blue mussel is remarkably efficient at covering the rock surfaces in intertidal areas where wave action or tidal currents provide it with abundant food and where its predators are not too common. It replaces barnacles by outgrowing and smothering them. It prevents brown algae from settling simply by filter-feeding on the young algal recruits, as well as preventing them from settling on their shells. Because it can't stand the exposure to the atmosphere which the barnacles can, the blue mussel does not grow nearly as high on the intertidal rocks, and the barnacles and brown algae are left to compete with each other in the upper parts of the mid-intertidal zone. Where there are moist, protective crevices, aggregations of mussels snake higher up the intertidal, but these individuals are likely to be stunted. Because of their reduced feeding time, mussels at the upper end of their intertidal distribution do not grow nearly as quickly as mussels closer to the low tide level. They become sexually mature, nonetheless, even though they may be less than 1 inch (1 to 2 cm) long.

22. Though barnacles are generally found higher in the inter-tidal zone than are mussels, crevices can allow enough extra protection for mussels to penetrate the barnacle zone.

The brown algae, barnacles and mussels are therefore in considerable potential competition with each other on the lower half of the mid intertidal shore. Each dominates the available space under different conditions, but wherever the mussels can settle and grow easily, they replace the other competitors, establishing a lower limit to the distribution of barnacles, and eliminating the Fucales as well.

The blue mussel.   When the tide is low, extensive beds of the common blue mussel, *Mytilus edulis*, are often exposed, making the succulent mussels easy prey for man. When covered by water, though, the mussels are still vulnerable, for the green crab, *Carcinus maenus*, the dogwhelk, *Thais lapillus*, and the various starfish favor them as well. Given its attractiveness as a food source, the blue mussel ensures its survival by producing many eggs and growing quickly. Cold but increasing temperature seems to provide the initial stimulus for mussel spawning, which begins in winter and continues for six months. Eggs or sperm released in the water by the separate sexes provide a further stimulus for others of the amassed mussels to spawn. Some females may spawn as many as 12 million minute eggs, making fertilization more likely and broad distribution more probable.

Like so many marine invertebrates, the blue mussel spends its early life in planktonic larval forms being swept by currents to new locations. From June to September the larvae which have survived predation, settle to the bottom and metamorphose into miniature mussels. There each uses its agile foot to help it move upshore before attaching itself to some hard substrate with its specialized anchor lines, called byssal threads.

The strong byssal threads are spun from a special gland in the foot. Thick protein-based fluid runs along a groove in the foot and forms a rounded disc when it meets a rock or shell substrate. The flexible tough threads are put out in all directions, keeping the mussel securely in place even when pounded by surf.

In addition to the byssal threads, the shape of the blue mussel is also adaptive for living at exposed sites. Unlike most other mollusks, one end of the mussel is narrower than the other and is oriented toward breaking waves, thus minimizing their damage. If any byssal threads are broken by surf, the mussel simply spins new ones and reattaches and reorients itself. Sometimes a small blue mussel attaches

23. Mussels attach themselves to a hard substrate or to each other with their strong byssal threads.

itself to a poor site, either where food is in low supply or where the amount of silt deposit is great. It then casts off its byssal threads and, moving by means of its foot and local currents, it relocates and reattaches itself.

No other marine animal can colonize a new area as quickly or as densely as can the blue mussel. With its ability to grow quickly and to attach itself to any rough surface, the blue mussel is able to outcompete the barnacle, *Balanus balanoides*, for the same space within three months of settling at the same site. By late summer, then, rocks that had been white with barnacles often become shiny blue-black with mussels. In ideal conditions, the blue mussel grows about 1 inch (2.5 cm) per year for the first two or three years and then slows down. In natural conditions of the Boreal zone, however, it usually takes 5 to 7 years to reach 3 inches (7 to 8 cm). This lag in growth occurs mostly because all mussels can only feed when covered by water and blue mussels are usually left exposed in the intertidal unable to feed for up to half the tidal cycle.

In blue mussel culture programs, the mussels are kept totally submerged usually on ropes which hang from rafts, allowing the animals to feed constantly. When they grow to about an inch (2.5 cm) in length, the mussels are put into mesh tubes. The mussels move out through the mesh, attaching their byssal threads to the tubes and forming a rope of mussels when all are properly attached. The rope is then kept submerged in quiet water, allowing for much faster growth than neighboring intertidal mussels.

Like the barnacle, the blue mussel is a filter feeder. However, since it is a mollusk and not a crustacean able to "kick food" into its mouth, its feeding mechanism is quite different. Like almost all bivalves, the mussel inhales water and food into its mantle area with one siphon and exhales water and waste from the other. The water that is sucked in is passed over mucus-coated gills. The mucus traps fine particles of food, which are then transferred by hairlike cilia to the mouth. The cleaned water then continues on over the gills where oxygen exchange takes place. The gill area therefore serves a dual purpose: food collection and gas exchange. It is no wonder mussel gills are much larger than gills of other comparable animals.

In addition to retrieving food particles from siphoned water, the mussel is also able to find food from the detritus that settles on its shell. Mussel shells are kept clean and shiny by the extendable foot which periodically polishes the shell. This detritus is then passed over the same mucus area and into the mouth.

Occasionally a small parasite becomes lodged in the area between the mantle and the shell. To prevent infection by the parasite, the mussel surrounds it with fine layers of mother of pearl. If the parasite is moved about during this process, the resulting pearl becomes spherical or ovoid in shape; sometimes it is even embedded right in the shell of the animal. The small seed pearls of blue mussels are either white or blue-gray in color.

Since it lives in many of the same places as the barnacle, *Balanus balanoides*, the blue mussel must be able to cope with the same stresses of desiccation, heating and freezing as the barnacle does. Like the barnacle, the blue mussel is able to close its shells and resort to anaerobic breathing when exposure becomes too severe. Since anaerobiosis always yields acid (either lactic or acetic) as an end product, this means that the blue mussel can also tolerate having its body fluids at a low pH for a time.

In conditions that are less stressful, a blue mussel can breathe air by passing air over its gills, which are kept moist by water retained in the mantle cavity. Also like the barnacle, *Balanus balanoides*, the blue mussel can withstand subfreezing temperatures. At these temperatures, although tissue water freezes, the ice crystals are formed between the cells, distorting but not destroying them. A winter midday sun often thaws the mussels and, provided the tide then returns to cover them, the blue mussels can feed again within minutes of thawing.

The Predatory Dogwhelk. Where surf pounds the intertidal rocks of exposed headlands, herbivores and predators are almost entirely absent, for even those species that are best at clinging to the rocks are swept away by the waves. Barnacles and mussels cover the whole mid-intertidal zone, filling virtually all the available space as they compete with each other for it, and leaving little space for other species to colonize.

24. The dogwhelk *Thais lapillus* is a chief predator of barnacles *Balanus balanoides*.

The Brown Algae Zone 85

On protected shores where the brown rockweeds grow easily, herbivores and predators may become quite dense. Of these, the impact of the predatory dogwhelk, *Thais lapillus*, on the abundance and distribution of both mussels and barnacles can be quite extraordinary. Where the dogwhelk is abundant, it so decimates the barnacle and mussel populations that neither of the two species is able to dominate the other, and large areas of rock surfaces may even be cleared of them entirely. Space is now available for other species, especially algae and their herbivores. As a result, species diversity is usually higher on protected shores.

Unlike the barnacles and mussels, the dogwhelk has no planktonic larval stages, but spends its entire life cycle on the intertidal rocks. From winter to early spring each year large aggregations of adults form in the rock crevices as the separate sexes gather to mate with each other. The sperm are stored by the females until their eggs are ready for fertilization. Mature eggs are then fertilized as they pass the seminal receptacle where the sperm has been kept.

From 6 to 30 yellow egg capsules, each on its own stalk, are cemented to the rock as they are laid. Each capsule contains up to several hundred eggs, but most of these eggs are not fertilized and serve only as food for the other developing snails. After four months of well protected development in the egg capsules, tiny snails hatch out. At first they feed mostly on the little tubeworm, *Spirorbis*, and within a year they are about ½ inch (1 cm) in height. Since the egg laying continues for six months, young dogwhelks are continually entering the population which therefore maintains a steady size. About a year after hatching, the young migrate farther up the intertidal zone and begin to feast on barnacles and mussels.

The lifespan of the dogwhelk is about 4 years, with sexual maturity reached at 2 or 3 years of age. Once sexual maturity is reached, the overall size of the shell does not change. Rather, the shell grows thicker at the edges: a thin-lipped shell then reflects a sexually immature snail. The major predators of the whelk include crabs and birds such as sandpipers, herring gulls, and occasionally fish.

Because of its diet of barnacles and mussels, the dogwhelk must be able to withstand the stresses of the intertidal. It is not found as high on the shore as the barnacles, for it cannot tolerate quite the extremes that the barnacles can. However, it can stand prolonged exposure to the air with its ability to air breathe. It breathes by passing air over water held in its mantle cavity. If desiccation becomes too severe, it withdraws and seals the entrance to its shell with the horny plate on its foot, the operculum, and then resorts to anaerobic respiration for a short while.

Given the differences in size and shape of mussels and barnacles, it is not surprising to find that dogwhelks employ different methods of attack on each. The large strong shells of mussels are impossible for the smaller dogwhelk to force apart. Instead, it drills a hole into the shell and inserts its extendable proboscis, which contains its mouth. The tricky part of this, of course, is drilling the hole. It softens the mussel shell with a secretion, scrapes the shell with its radula, a highly developed toothed feeding organ, and gradually drills through to the soft edible underlying tissue. In addition to drilling the hole, the radula also helps break food into smaller particles.

The barnacle, on the other hand, is approached differently. Instead of drilling the shell, the dogwelk pries open the top plates of the barnacle and sticks its radula between them to feed on the animal inside. Since those plates are held tightly together, this feat also involves some special equipment. With its foot covering the barnacle, the dogwhelk secretes purpurin, a highly poisonous purple dye once used by American Indian tribes for its deep color. The barnacle is killed by the toxic secretion, its muscles relax and the dogwhelk can insert its radula and proboscis for feeding. The dogwhelk is an efficient predator, for it selects large barnacles rather than smaller ones, thereby getting more food for the same amount of work.

THE HERBIVOROUS PERIWINKLES.   Whenever there is space for algae to grow on the intertidal rocks, there are likely to be animals grazing on them, and the most successful and abundant of these are the periwinkle snails of the *Littorina* genus. The strength and shape of their shells allow them to be rolled around by wave action without damage. Even where gathered by epicureans who delight in their succulent roasted flavor, the snails persist in large

The Brown Algae Zone   87

numbers. Each of the three species of periwinkle found in the Boreal zone has adaptations which enable it to live in specific zones of the intertidal. The smooth periwinkle, *Littorina obtusata*, spends its entire life in the low intertidal area. The edible common periwinkle, *L. littorea*, roams the broad mid-intertidal zone though it lives as well in the low intertidal and parts of the subtidal zones. And the rough periwinkle, *L. saxatilis*, is able to survive in the hostile high intertidal zone.

The Smooth Periwinkle. The brightly colored smooth periwinkle, *Littorina obtusata*, ranges from brilliant yellow or orange to reddish brown, grows to about ½ inch (1 to 2 cm) in length, and looks much like a bladder of *Fucus*, the rockweed on which it lives. Because it rarely leaves the low intertidal, the smooth periwinkle is covered with water more than half the time, and therefore has many typical marine snail characteristics.

The female is fertilized internally and she then lays her eggs in gelatinous masses on the rockweed. The tough jelly surrounding the eggs gives them some protection, but further protection from the short periods of desiccation to which the eggs are exposed is provided by the rockweed itself which drapes over the rocks, trapping moisture and resisting temperature fluctuation.

Unlike most marine snails, which have a planktonic larval phase, the eggs of the smooth periwinkle develop into small bottom-dwelling stages which stay in the rockweed and therefore tend to remain in the same area as the adults. The juvenile periwinkles often chew their way into the air bladders of the rockweed where they may live for a while, protected from wave action and provided with food. The smooth periwinkle eats the rockweed, especially *Fucus vesiculosus*, most of its life, scraping off the surface cells; it rarely, if ever, leaves the rockweed.

In addition to providing food and protecting developing eggs, the blanketing seaweed also protects adult smooth periwinkles from exposure. It is not surprising, then, to find that the smooth periwinkle breathes underwater or in the high humidity air under the weed cover with its well developed gill chamber. It can also breathe in drier air for short periods of time by passing air over its moistened gills.

As an intertidal animal, the smooth periwinkle must survive some desiccation and temperature fluctuation, but its tolerance is not nearly as great as either of the other two intertidal periwinkles.

The Common Periwinkle. The common periwinkle, *Littorina littorea*, has always been a common member of the intertidal fauna of the Boreal Coast of Europe, but it was not found on the North American Boreal coast until 1860, and is probably an accidental transplant. From Nova Scotia, these periwinkles spread rapidly along the Boreal coast of North America in what must be one of the most successful introductions of an animal anywhere. Its numbers are now beyond count, more common here than in Europe perhaps in part because it has fewer limpet species to compete with in the western Atlantic.

In any case, it is remarkably well adapted to intertidal conditions. Although the smooth periwinkle can withstand temperatures of 111° F (44° C) for several hours, the common periwinkle can survive a great extreme of 115° F (46° C) for a much longer time (12 hours). It lives abundantly much higher on the intertidal rocks and algae, exposed to air for a far larger portion of its life.

25. The common periwinkle *Littorina littorea* grazes on microscopic algae.

This banded brownish-olive periwinkle is the largest of the three intertidal species, often growing to over 1 inch (2 to 3 cm) in length. It prefers the smaller tender macroalgae of the mid-intertidal zone, especially the green *Cladophora* and *Enteromorpha,* though it is quite capable of grazing on tougher brown species. The common periwinkle grazes on rocks covered with these algae, scraping the rock surfaces with its radula. The chitinous radula has many rows of minute teeth for grazing, and as old teeth are worn down, new ones are rolled up to replace them.

In order to maximize its feeding area and to maintain its position in the intertidal, the common periwinkle usually traces a circular pattern while feeding, bringing it back to its original position. It uses direction of wave movement as well as light and gravity to keep its course during feeding.

The erosional influence of rock-scraping by common periwinkles should not be underestimated, for it may have as much effect as rains, frosts and floods. In a study of a similar Californian periwinkle, it was found that 1 square mile of shoreline was grazed on by about 8.6 billion of the prolific snails and that they ground away 2,260 tons of the soft stone in a year. The erosional impact of the common

26. The small periwinkle *Littorina obtusata* (left) feeds on lower intertidal rockweed while the rough periwinkle *Littorina saxatilis* (right) grazes on microalgae of the highest intertidal rock.

THE MARINE ROCKY INTERTIDAL

periwinkles is no doubt considerable here as well.

Since desiccation at the mid intertidal is much greater than lower in the zone, the common periwinkle cannot simply lay its eggs in gelatinous masses, for the eggs would dry out long before hatching. Instead, once a female is fertilized, she spawns capsules, each containing 3 eggs, into the water, usually at night during a flood tide. Such careful timing helps to ensure that the eggs will be carried out into the ocean rather than stranded in the intertidal. The young hatch into veliger larvae, spend a short time in the plankton, and then settle on the bottom and metamorphose into miniature periwinkles. The veliger planktonic stage allows the species to disperse to other shorelines and gives it a much broader distribution than either of the other two intertidal periwinkle species. Once they have metamorphosed, young common periwinkles move up into the mid-intertidal zone and begin grazing on the various algae there.

The common periwinkle must withstand greater stresses of exposure than the smooth periwinkle. Since it is exposed to air for longer periods of time, it has to be able to air-breathe for longer periods of time as well. This is made possible by means of increased vascularization of the mantle cavity behind the gills, the extra supply of blood vessels allowing for gas exchange in the cavity without presence of water.

When temperatures are extreme, the common periwinkle moves into deep crevices where temperatures remain cooler. There it also seals its shell against the rock with mucus. Once the mucus hardens, the snail withdraws its foot and closes its operculum, providing a double seal against the environment. Large numbers of the periwinkle remain fastened in this manner throughout the time they are exposed, all with their lips facing up and the spirals of their shells hanging down. Such an orientation allows the bulk of the weight of the shell to rest on the rock while the mucus merely holds the snail in position. The light touch of the first high water causes the snail to fall into the more temperate sea once again.

In addition, when temperatures plummet to below freezing, the common periwinkle is able to survive because its cells allow water to migrate out quickly so that ice crystals are formed between the cells. In fact, it can even survive at

5° F (−15° C) with up to 59 percent of its bodily water frozen.

The Rough Periwinkle. The yellowish-gray or ash-colored rough periwinkle, *Littorina saxatilis*, is the smallest of the three species and is able to tolerate the greatest extremes of desiccation and temperature fluctuations, for it lives high in the intertidal where it often goes for days at a time without being dampened by the sea. In fact, it can survive as long as a month without being moistened by salt water. This is made possible by the high degree of vascularization of the lining of the mantle cavity. The rough periwinkle can survive by air-breathing far longer than the common periwinkle for its gill area is reduced and the abundant blood supply to the vascularized area has transformed the mantle lining to a lung-like organ not too different from the kind that true land snails possess. Because it can breathe air directly and fairly easily, it can continue to feed on *Calothrix,* the blue-green algae of the black zone, without being covered by water.

The rough periwinkle can tolerate greater extremes of exposure than the common periwinkle, though its adaptations are similar in type. It can, for example, breathe anaerobically for longer periods of time. When it seals its shell against the rock with its secreted mucus, it can survive without atmospheric contact for up to a week. In times of extreme heat or cold, when it does not have the relief that the more moderate sea water provides, it is thereby able to maintain a bodily temperature several crucial degrees more mild than its environment.

The rough periwinkle also provides extra protection for its young by brooding them within its shell. After fertilization, the female retains the eggs in a special mantle cavity, protecting them there from desiccation. The young emerge not as larvae, but as miniature versions of their parents and they immediately join their parents in grazing on the blue-green algae.

Other Grazers and Predators

Though the three periwinkle species are by far the dominant herbivores of the entire intertidal region, other herbivores do occur. In particular, the limpet *Acmaea testudinalus* may be locally common in the lower part of the mid-intertidal. Like other limpets, it can actually dislodge attached brown algae, but it is never abundant enough to completely denude rocks the way some species do on the European Boreal coast.

Similarly, other predators besides *Thais* forage on the intertidal rocks, but none are abundant enough to have anywhere near its impact. Starfish, either *Asterias vulgaris* or *A. forbesi*, may forage a short distance up from Mean Low Water when the tide is high, feeding mostly on the mussels. Starfish can withstand little exposure to the atmosphere, however, and since they move too slowly to outrun a dropping tide, they are far more abundant subtidally and in tide pools. The green crab, *Carcinus maenas*, is another predator of intertidal shores, common on the Boreal coast as far north as the mouth of the Bay of Fundy. It is abundant on almost all protected shores, not only rocky ones but also on mud flats and in salt marshes. On rocky shores, it forages on mussels when the tide is high and often seeks cover under rocks or in the collapsed rockweed when the tide is low again. These and other predators are usually more typical of the subtidal region (see chapter 5).

The mid-intertidal crabs and other animals are also prey for even larger predators. Herring gulls and crows poke in the rockweed for them when the tide is low, cormorants and common eider ducks dive for them when the tide is high, and great blue herons wade along stalking them in shallow water at any tide. Small fish often forage over the mid-intertidal rocks when the tide is high, and they are also prey for the cormorants, eider ducks, herons, as well as for terns diving into the water from a few meters above its surface.

The Rockweed: Habitats for Other Organisms

The brown rockweeds provide a canopy under which other organisms, both plants and animals, can find protective cover against desiccation and excessive predation. It allows them to forage far above Mean Low Water, too. Besides the green crabs and the more typically subtidal starfish and sea urchins, the canopy also protects an understory of other algae which could not otherwise survive the exposure of the mid-intertidal. Irish moss, *Chondrus crispus*, survives in parts of the mid-intertidal under the canopy as do a variety of annual species of red and green algae.

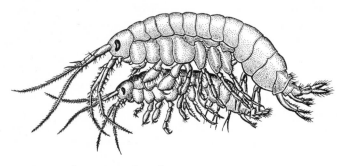

27. A pair of mating amphipods, *Gammarus oceanicus*. The larger male guards a female until she lays her eggs.

Probably commonest of all the understory organisms is an amphipod crustacean, *Gammarus oceanicus*, which lives in extraordinary numbers under the collapsed rockweed, as well as under every mid-intertidal rock. Like most of the other intertidal animals, it forages for food when the tide is high and seeks cover wherever it can when the tide drops. Pull aside any mass of rockweed at low tide, and the amphipod is sure to be there. Literally hundreds may go scurrying on their sides for cover under other rocks or weed, a habit which gives them their popular names of scuds and sideswimmers. This is a large amphipod, for the males may be about 1 inch (2 or 3 cm) long. They seem to spend most of the summer mating or waiting to mate with the smaller females. The female broods her eggs in a ventral brood pouch and when the hatched juveniles have used up their yolk, they venture from the brood pouch and begin scavenging like their parents. Measured in terms of sheer numbers, *Gammarus oceanicus* must be one of the most successful intertidal animals.

The different rockweed species are also substrates which a variety of algae and animals use to settle and grow on.

These organisms, however, are not parasites, for they don't harm the rockweed. The algae, like *Polysiphonia*, tend to be annuals and don't have to survive the extremes of winter exposure. Hydroid species, animals that may look at first a bit like algae, also often grow on the rockweeds. Among them are *Sertularia* and *Clava*. Hydroids are more typical of tidepools and the subtidal habitats.

Often practically covering the flat blades of the rockweed, especially *Fucus vesiculosus*, is a small, flat, coiled tubeworm called *Spirorbis borealis*. With its coiled shell, *Spirorbis* looks more like a minute snail than a worm, but it is in fact a segmented worm of the serpulid type which secretes a calcareous tube around itself. By closely watching the small worm, which reaches 1/5 inch (5 mm) diameter, it is possible to see the crown of tentacles which is extended for feeding and breathing purposes. The tentacles are covered with minute cilia which help filter the water for food like the cilia on the gills of a bivalve mollusk. Close inspection with a magnifying glass also reveals that one of the tentacles is modified to form an operculum, or plug, which seals the worm inside its shell. Like the operculum on a snail, this helps protect *Spirorbis* from desiccation when the tide is low.

Every first and third quarter moon between May and October eggs of *Spirorbis* are fertilized. The female holds them inside her shell where they are brooded, giving the embryos added protection. By the next quarter moon, two weeks later, the embryos have developed into larvae which are then released. Liberation of the larvae at neap tide increases the chances of keeping the young in the rockweed zone, for they are less likely to be swept away by the tide. At the same time the larvae are expelled, a new batch of eggs is fertilized and transferred to the brood pouch.

Young *Spirorbis* settle within a few hours of being liberated and they are attracted to areas that have been occupied by other *Spirorbis*. This gregariousness which is common in many sessile marine invertebrates seems to have a dual function: it assures a good settling site and it increases chances of later fertilization.

The strong protective shell of *Spirorbis* is formed quickly after a settling site has been chosen by the larvae. Within a few hours of settling, the larvae undergo a complete cataclysmic metamorphosis. A milky secretion forms the initial semitransparent tube at the same time that the head shrinks, the larval eyes approach each other closely and the operculum and tentacles are formed. Within half a day the tube worm has changed life style several times—from its brood-pouch environment to its brief free-swimming hours, and finally to its own confining but protective tube.

Succession and Recovery from Oil Spills

When a canopy of rockweed is removed, either as part of an experiment or for one of its many commercial uses, the understory algae are suddenly exposed to the atmosphere. Some of the algae are obligate understory species, unable to survive without the protective moisture of the canopy, and they soon die. Other species which had been surviving in small numbers, thoroughly outcompeted by the canopy species, suddenly have ample light and space for growth. Such fugitive species then thrive, other species settle and colonize the new space as well, and algal species diversity increases rapidly. Then, however, a new generation of the larger brown algae also resettles on the space, and soon outgrows and replaces the other colonists. Succession has occurred, much like succession in a terrestrial forest.

Succession of a more dramatic kind has followed some of the oil spills which have reached Boreal rocky shores. The oil itself, though of course harmful to the intertidal plants and animals, is not nearly as toxic as the dispersants which have on occasion been used to clean up the oil. Where dispersants have been heavily used, they have killed most of the animals, many of the plants, and left behind desert-like shores.

Bad oil spills have certainly occurred frequently enough along the American Atlantic Boreal Coast, perhaps most notably at Chedabucto Bay in Nova Scotia. But the most informative example is the spill and clean-up that followed the wreck of the *Torrey Canyon* in 1967 near the shores of Cornwall in southwest England. There, dispersants were used in massive amounts, and large stretches of rocky shoreline were effectively denuded of about every living thing.

Recolonization of the Cornwall rocky intertidal began with an extensive settling and growth of the green algae, *Enteromorpha* and *Ulva*, which are likely to grow well anywhere herbivores have been removed. Then the perennial brown algae, especially *Fucus vesiculosus*, settled, grew, and covered the intertidal rocks far more densely than they had before the oil spill. The *Fucus* growth was so thick that the few barnacles which had survived the spill were overgrown and probably starved. Herbivores now had food available to them again, and periwinkles and limpets settled, grazed and gradually eliminated most of the *Fucus*. With the loss of their major food source, the huge populations of the herbivores also dropped drastically. In the space where the algae had been, barnacles finally were able to resettle and gradually re-establish the large barnacle zone that had been typical of that shoreline before the spill. A succession of events had now occurred, each changing the community structure and setting a new stage for the next event to take place.

Recovery of a rocky shore following an oil spill can look fairly successful on a rather gross scale, although it may take 5 to 10 or 15 years to complete. However, there are other long term effects, for hydrocarbons from the oil appear to accumulate in the sediments and in plant and animal tissue.

Seasonal Changes

The changes which occur from summer to winter in the mid-intertidal community are often striking ones. The growth of rockweeds, whose productivity can exceed that of cultivated farmland, ceases in winter, and the storms and scouring ices of winter destroy plants which cannot be replaced until spring brings renewed growth. Many mussels may have settled too high on the mid intertidal rocks during the more benign conditions of summer, and large numbers of them may be decimated during the winter. The motile animals, such as the dogwhelks, crabs, limpets and periwinkles, migrate down from the overexposed intertidal zones during winter, finding greater protection in lower intertidal and even subtidal areas. Then, with spring, reproduction begins again; new generations of annual and perennial plants grow, new populations of mussels and barnacles settle on the rocks to compete for space, and herbivores and predators once again forage up over the whole mid-intertidal zone.

The Red Algae or Irish Moss Zone

Red algae dominate the rocky intertidal shores of warm water regions, but few of them can tolerate the exposure to the Boreal atmosphere to which the brown Fucales are so well adapted. However, along the low tide level, usually below Mean Low Water, several species of red algae cover the rocks in a dense mat, replacing the Fucales. One species in particular can be extremely abundant: *Chondrus crispus*, or Irish moss.

Irish moss grows especially well on flat rocks, reaching 4 to 6 inches (10 to 15 cm) in length. Though not a large species in comparison with the Fucales, it has a most tenacious holdfast which permits it to withstand the wave action of even the most exposed headlands. It forms such a dense mat that it in turn harbors small animals and other species of algae, providing them with protection from wave action and perhaps from grazers and predators.

Often growing near the Irish moss is a very similar species, *Gigartina stellata*. It grows best on vertical, fast-draining surfaces. Like *Chondrus*, it is much branched and very tough, but it doesn't grow as large, isn't nearly as common, and has small warty outgrowths which help to distinguish it. By midsummer the fronds of both species are covered with dark spots in which reproductive spores have formed.

Many other algal species occur in the low intertidal zone. Some may be locally common, like the red alga *Rhodymenia palmata*, or dulse. Most species are ephe-

28. Irish moss *Chondrus crispus* (top) and *Gigartina stellata* (bottom) are very similar in size and general shape but are easily distinguished by the wart-like structures on the *Gigartina*.

meral ones though, growing, reproducing, and dying in a short time, while others are fugitive species occurring sparsely, outcompeted for space by the Irish moss.

The Red Algae Zone   99

Competition with Irish Moss

Even though Irish moss dominates the plant community of the low intertidal, it is susceptible to invasion by ephemeral algae. When an ephemeral species dies, however, Irish moss simply reestablishes itself. On rock surfaces cleared of all algae, the brown intertidal species outcompete Irish moss because of their rapid growth, but if they are swept away or die, Irish moss replaces them and once established is not susceptible to further invasion. Irish moss maintains its space against the onslaught of other perennials at least in part because of its ability to grow vegetatively, not having to depend solely on sexual reproduction as a means of increasing its distribution as must the brown intertidal rockweeds.

Like the brown algae higher in the intertidal region, Irish moss is in competition with the intertidal mussels and barnacles for space to live on, and in fact it is competitively inferior to both. It grows abundantly only where the barnacles and mussels themselves do not survive easily. The barnacles are less likely to be common on the low intertidal rocks (mussels usually replace them there), but where barnacles are for some reason abundant, Irish moss has difficulty establishing itself. On the other hand, where Irish moss is able to grow into its typical thick mat-like cover on the rocks, it is quite safe from barnacle settlement and competition.

The competition with the blue mussel, *Mytilus edulis*, is much more intense, and is mediated by the action of various herbivores and predators. In relatively protected areas, where Irish moss dominates, the blue mussel is kept in low numbers by predation not only by the dogwhelk but also by various starfish. Where the rock surfaces have been experimentally cleared of all plants and animals and the predators then prevented from returning, blue mussels settle and grow to the exclusion of Irish moss. In fact, if the predators are removed and kept away from an established mat of Irish moss, the mussels settle and grow and eliminate the algae. On very exposed shores, wave action sweeps the predators away, and mussels dominate the low intertidal rocks instead of Irish moss.

THE MARINE ROCKY INTERTIDAL

The major herbivore in the low intertidal zone is again the common periwinkle, *Littorina littorea*. Irish moss is usually too tough for it though, and it grazes mostly on the ephemeral algal species as well as those which grow on the Irish moss itself. The common periwinkle, by keeping the rock surfaces free of ephemeral species, helps the Irish moss grow into extensive mats. Where exposed to considerable wave action, the common periwinkles are of course also swept from the rocks, and ephemeral species of algae have a chance to grow and compete with the Irish moss.

The ephemeral algae that the common periwinkles prefer to graze on and that compete so successfully with Irish moss are fast-growing green algae such as *Enteromorpha*, *Spongomorpha*, *Ulva*, and *Monostroma* and red algae such as *Porphyra* and *Ceramium* (see plate II). Other red and green species occur less commonly. Most of these annuals grow best in late winter and spring and then die back during the summer.

Other Animals of the Red Algae Zone

The common periwinkle is not the only herbivore on the low intertidal rocks. Another snail, *Lacuna vincta*, which is small and more typically subtidal, grazes in the zone. The intertidal limpet, *Acmaea testudinalis*, grazes mostly on diatoms and algal spoilings and it has little impact on the growth of Irish moss or of the ephemeral algae. In fact, the only herbivore which can actually do massive damage to Irish moss is the green sea urchin, *Strongylocentrotus droebachiensis*, which eats all parts of the algae with equal ease. The green sea urchin is abundant subtidally throughout the Boreal region but is usually quite rare intertidally. In the Bay of Fundy, though, it can be remarkably common in the low intertidal zone, and there it feeds extensively on Irish moss.

A host of other animals occur in small numbers in the red algae zone. Almost all of them are more commonly found subtidally or in low intertidal tidepools, and are considered in the discussions of those habitats. Briefly, the animals most likely to occur are the encrusting sponge, *Halichon-*

dria; hydroids such as *Obelia* and *Tubularia;* the sea anemone, *Metridium senile;* sea squirts such as the colonial *Botryllus schlosseri;* and the barnacles, *Balanus balanus* and *B. crenatus.*

The Kelp Zone

When the lowest of the spring tides occur, a band of kelp below the red algae zone may be partly exposed for a short time. Kelp such as *Laminaria* and *Alaria* are very large species of brown algae and they cannot tolerate any significant exposure to the atmosphere. The kelp tend to be entirely subtidal in the southern parts of the Boreal region, but may emerge into the low intertidal in northern parts of the region. The kelp zone, glimpsed at low tide is really a very extensive subtidal zone. It is considered in more detail in chapter 5.

Uses of Seaweeds

Seaweeds play a vital role in the general marine ecosystem, providing food and shelter for hosts of other organisms. The sea has long been a provider for man as well, and though its plants have not been exploited to the extent that certain of its animals have, the range of human uses to which seaweeds are put is impressive.

Human Food

For thousands of years the Chinese, Japanese and Hawaiians have recognized seaweeds as a good food source. Extensive use of *Porphyra* (also called nori or laver) and *Laminaria* (kombu) in the Orient resulted in early culture and marketing of these plants. In Hawaii, royal marine gardens were established, and seaweeds were transplanted and closely tended to provide delicacies for the royal families.

North Americans may know of *Porphyra* as purple laver and along with *Rhodymenia,* or dulse, are accustomed to it only as a condiment, if at all. But certain Eskimo groups have long realized the value of the plants, benefitting from the high vitamin C content of these particular species.

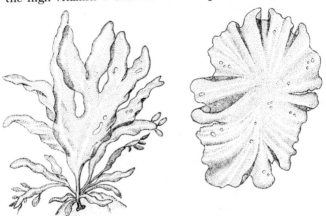

29. Dulse *Rhodymenia palmata* (left) and sea lettuce *Ulva lactuca* (right) are edible algae abundant along the coast.

As North Americans become more willing to experiment with new culinary tastes, many find dried dulse a good substitute for salt. Fresh *Porphyra* increasingly finds its way to the table as the basis for soup or as casings for rice and meat dishes. In addition to these red algae, the green sea lettuce, *Ulva lactuca,* is found both in soups and in fresh salads (see plate II).

Animal Fodder

Though the Orientals were far ahead of Europeans in realizing the value of seaweeds for human consumption, for centuries northern Europeans have driven their stock to low tide areas to let the animals browse on the intertidal plants.

With the European grain shortage of World War I, new attention was devoted to the use of seaweed for animal feed. Norway has especially taken the lead in this field and studies of dairy cows fed on meal of the brown rockweed *Ascophyllum nodosum* show superior milk production, greater fertility and greater pasture weight gain than cows not fed the meal. Farmers throughout the world who use seaweed meal as fodder for their pigs, sheep, cattle and poultry are convinced of the bonuses derived from the seaweed.

Fertilizers

The use of seaweeds as fertilizers also dates to ancient times, when the plants were usually worked directly into the soil. Today, seaweed fertilizers are available both in a pulverized form and in a liquid form. The brown rockweed, *Ascophyllum nodosum,* so plentiful along the Boreal coast, yields many of the best fertilizer results.

Though the obvious reason for using seaweeds as fertilizers is because of their content of nitrogen, phosphorus and potassium, the dramatic increase in crop yield from their use cannot be explained so easily. Rather unexpectedly, fertilizer increases germination success and uptake of plant nutrients. In addition, although the fertilizer has no direct insecticidal or fungicidal effects, use of seaweed fertilizer results in definite increase in resistance to certain pests, including aphids, red spider mites, powdery mildew botrytis and the complex of fungi that are responsible for damping off of seedlings. Also, the seaweed fertilizer gives increased shelflife to certain produce such as peaches and increased resistance to cold for tomatoes.

Therapeutic and Medicinal Uses

Recent studies show valuable medicinal aspects of seaweeds. Antibacterial activity has been seen in relation to a poultry typhoid bacterium; certain antiviral properties were apparent against an influenza virus; and evidence shows that certain seaweed products depress blood cholesterol levels.

The medicinal uses of seaweeds, however, also date back thousands of years. Dried kelp such as *Laminaria* swells gently when moisture is added to it and this property has long been used in the Orient as a surgical tool for opening wounds and for aiding in childbirth by expanding the cervix. Irish moss has a long history of use with urinary disorders and in 19th century Europe was used as a cure for consumption. Agar, extracted from red algae, was prescribed for a variety of stomach disorders long before its relatively new use as a medium for bacteria culture. As a culture medium, it is now found in virtually all hospital and pharmaceutical laboratories.

Industrial Uses

The most extensive Western use of seaweeds is of the phycocolloids or gels that are extracted from them. Agar from red algae such as *Gracilaria*, *Ahnfeltia* and *Gelidium;* algin from brown algae including *Ascophyllum*, *Fucus* and *Laminaria;* and carrageenin from *Chondrus crispus* and *Gigartina* are used in industries ranging from those involving foods to pharmaceuticals, photographics, and paints. The colloids are used for their suspending, stabilizing and antidrying properties.

The gelling property of these colloids can easily be seen by making blancmange, a vanilla pudding which depends on carrageenin to congeal. To one handful of washed Irish moss, add one quart of milk. Cook the mixture in a double boiler for about half an hour, strain to remove the Irish moss, and add vanilla and sugar or honey to taste. Then let the pudding cool until it is firm.

Harvesting the Seaweeds

Although Japan and China have well-established and sophisticated techniques for the culturing of *Porphyra* and *Laminaria*, the complex life cycles of seaweeds make complete mariculture a difficult task. Most seaweed harvested in North America is taken from wild stocks and much of this is harvested by hand.

Though certain very large seaweeds like the Pacific coast *Macrocystis* lend themselves to mechanical harvesting, the valuable Atlantic species (Irish moss, *Ascophyllum* and *Laminaria*) do not. Whether combed with long-handled rakes, gathered after being tossed ashore by storms, or collected by divers, hand-harvesting protects the holdfasts and ensures continual production by a stand.

The seaweed industry has been of continual interest along the Boreal coast. Massachusetts, Maine, southwestern Nova Scotia and Prince Edward Island have particularly good stands of Irish moss. In the Maritime Provinces, hundreds of tons of Irish moss are often washed ashore in autumn gales and then collected. Grand Manan Island, New Brunswick, is renowned for its high quality dulse and in Maine and Nova Scotia *Ascophyllum* and *Laminaria* are harvested as well. Along the Atlantic Boreal coast, the red algae are of greatest economic value. A company in Rockland, Maine presently produces the bulk of red algal colloids in North America.

Though the potential for the seaweed industry is great, very practical difficulties in culturing and harvesting retard its development. In addition to life cycle complexities, scouring of intertidal beds by winter ice adds great risk to any culturing program. Once harvested, transportation cost of the seaweed also works against establishment of a larger industry. However, as is true with many industries, if sufficient future demand is established for seaweed products, the problems of farming the plants in North America could be overcome.

Tide Pools

Tide pools occur anywhere in the rocky intertidal region where water is trapped and left behind by the receding tide. They may in fact be as high as the spray zone, not really reached by the high tide but kept saline or brackish by its spray. They may also be so low that even at a very low tide they are not totally cut off and waves continue to replenish them. Wherever they are, they vary immensely in size, shape and depth and pools at the same intertidal level may therefore greatly differ in the temperature, salinity and pH fluctuations which occur in them (see plate I).

High Tide Pools

The pools of the spray zone are usually replenished by fresh-water runoff but kept brackish by salt spray or high-tide waves. Large deep pools are likely to be permanent. Instead of drying up completely during a time of rapid evaporation and drought, they simply become more saline. Such pools aren't truly marine, of course, for though their salinities vary, they remain brackish. Moreover, their temperatures are likely to follow atmospheric temperatures rather closely, becoming warmer in summer and colder in winter than the surrounding sea. As a result, the pools of the spray zone have much in common with estuaries and some of the same organisms are found in both habitats.

The green maidenhair alga, *Enteromorpha intestinalis*, grows luxuriantly in the high tide pools, tolerating their low salinity and their temperature fluctuations more easily than most other species of algae. If the pool is large enough, the stickleback, *Gasterosteus aculeatus*, is sometimes present, feeding on the small copepod and ostracod crustaceans which are abundant in the pools, as well as on the larvae of the brackish water mosquito. Numerous flatworms occur in the high pools as well, creeping over the rocks scavenging and preying on microscopic animals.

Mid Tide Pools

The mid tide pools are saline, for they are covered for at least some portion of every tidal cycle. Salinity and temperature may still fluctuate, but not to the extent they do in the high tide pools, and no matter what size the pool is, it is still likely to be somewhat warmer in spring and summer than the adjacent sea.

Fluctuations in the acid-base balance of mid-intertidal pools probably stress the resident organisms just as much as fluctuations in salinity and temperature, particularly in pools which have large growths of algae. At night, when photosynthesis ceases, carbon dioxide accumulates in such pools, making the water acidic. During daylight, photosynthesis uses up the CO_2 and the pool water may become alkaline instead, rising to pH levels of 9 or more. Only submergence by the incoming tide stabilizes the pH at its neutral level. The organisms which live in these pools, then, may have to tolerate greater pH fluctuations than most species.

THE ORGANISMS

The green alga, *Enteromorpha*, is still likely to be a dominant species in the pools, but it is now joined by *Cladophora*, another green filamentous alga. Most of the organisms of the high tide pools are absent, however, unable to tolerate the higher salinity. Algal species that are common south of the Boreal region sometimes are able to grow in the mid tide pools because they are on the average warmer than the summer ocean. This is especially true of some of the red and green algae, but though they may grow in these Boreal pools, they are still submerged repeatedly by the colder sea, and as a result are dwarfed.

Particularly common on the surface of most mid-intertidal pools, no matter how small or high they are, are aggregations of the blue-gray wingless insect, *Anurida maritima*. Marine insects are not very common, but this species, whose name means "wingless one who goes to sea," is well adapted to intertidal life. It is about 1/5 inch (0.5 cm) long and is covered by fine hairs. When the tide drops, it leaves the crevices it has remained hidden in and forages all over the mid and upper intertidal rocks, scavenging for decomposing bits of organic matter, detritus. When the tide rises again, *Anurida* traps air bubbles in its hairs and finds a crevice to hide in, breathing from its captured bubbles until the tide falls once more. Though it forages throughout the time the rocks are uncovered by the tide, the easiest place to find it is on the surface of the pools, where it aggregates in swarms that may have hundreds of individuals in them.

Tide pools that appear to be about the same size and depth in the mid-intertidal may have some striking differences. The common periwinkle, *Littorina littorea*, is abundant in most tide pools, grazing especially on *Enteromorpha* and other ephemeral species of algae. Where the common periwinkle occurs in a pool in large numbers, it effectively eliminates *Enteromorpha* and the other ephemerals; Irish moss, *Chondrus crispus*, grows instead and covers rocky surfaces of the pool. Pools which have luxuriant growths of *Enteromorpha* usually lack many large periwinkles but instead often harbor juvenile green crabs, *Carcinus maenus*, which probably prey upon young periwinkles, keeping the herbivores away from the green algae and allowing the green algae to grow and outcompete the Irish moss. The crabs in turn are probably much safer from predation by herring gulls when they hide under the long filaments of *Enteromorpha* than when they seek cover in Irish moss.

Low Tide Pools

Tide pools low in the intertidal region have none of the physical stresses of the higher pools. They are isolated by the receding tide for a brief time at most, and often are not totally cut off. With their relatively stable, cool environments, they are like pieces of the subtidal region trapped for observation. Most of the organisms living in the pools are typically subtidal and therefore unable to tolerate exposure to the atmosphere. The pool environment is benign because of its stability, and the number of species living in it is quite high. The blades and complex holdfasts of any kelp which may be growing in the low pool provide further space and protection for a large array of juvenile and adult organisms. The smaller macroalgae are also often filled with small crustaceans seeking cover and food. The pools with greatest diversity are likely to be large, deep and very near the level reached only by the extreme low spring tides. These are also likely to be on the rocky shores of exposed capes and headlands, and since the lowest tides are often the early morning ones following a full moon, there is great beauty awaiting both within the pool itself and in the long rays of the rising sun on an awakening sea coast.

ALGAE OF THE LOW POOLS

Of the intertidal brown rockweeds, *Ascophyllum* rarely extends into a tide pool, stopping instead at the water's edge; but both *Fucus vesiculosus* and *F. distichus* can tolerate permanent submergence in a pool. Both of the tough red algae, Irish moss and *Gigartina*, that dominate the very low intertidal rocks, grow equally well in tide pools. The various leafy green and red algae such as *Monostroma, Ulva, Porphyra* and *Rhodymenia*, which grow on the low intertidal rocks as well as on shallow subtidal rocks, are also often abundant in the low pools. In amongst all these relatively large algae, tufts of the calcareous red algae, *Corallina officianalus*, stand out, hard and actually pink in contrast to the rich dark color of their leafy neighbors. And in the deep, more shaded regions of a large, low tide pool, several species of kelp fasten their complex holdfasts to the bottom rock surface and grow to the immense size typical of this family of brown algae.

HERBIVORES OF THE LOW POOLS

A pool rich in algae is likely to be rich in animals grazing on the algae as well. The intertidal common and smooth periwinkles, *Littorina littorea* and *L. obtusata*, are joined in the pools by the small snail, *Lacuna vincta*. Though *Lacuna* survives in the exposed low-intertidal algae, it is far more common on the algae of the subtidal region and of the low tide pools. It eats a wide variety of algae, but it is especially conspicuous on the blades of the kelp where it lays its eggs in small, yellow doughnut-shaped masses. *Lacuna* has a rather odd way of moving around for a snail: it has a groove down the middle of its foot and creeps along by advancing one side of the foot at a time.

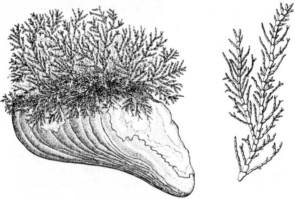

30. The calcareous algae *Corallina officianalus* grows in stiff tufts on rocks and shells.

Two other herbivores of the low tide pools, chitons and limpets, also occur on exposed intertidal rocks, but they too are more common where they can remain continuously submerged. A chiton is a primitive mollusk, with a shield-like shell made up of 8 plates held together in a row. It can withstand pounding by very large waves because of its shape and the strong contact it can make with its foot on any hard surface. Only one chiton occurs commonly intertidally in the Boreal region, a small, reddish species called *Ischnochiton ruber*, which grows to a length of about 1 inch (2.5 cm). Other species of chitons are rare in the intertidal and are more typically subtidal.

The limpet, *Acmaea testudinalis*, is the only intertidal limpet on the American Atlantic Boreal coast, unlike the Boreal coasts of Europe and the Pacific where several species occur and are the dominant intertidal herbivores. Despite its ability to withstand limited exposure to the atmosphere, *Acmaea* is most abundant in tide pools and the shallow subtidal region where, like the chiton, it scrapes microscopic and encrusting algae off the rock surfaces. Its flattened conical shell gives rise to its common name, Chinaman's hat. Like other limpets, *Acmaea* is also able to 'home,' returning unerringly to its preferred resting spot on a rock after wandering out on a foraging expedition. If it

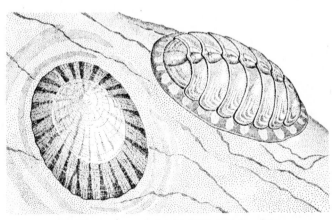

31. The limpet *Acmaea testudinalis* (left) and the chiton *Ischnochiton ruber* are common members of the low intertidal community.

lives on rock softer than granite, it erodes its home spot to fit its shell perfectly so that it is particularly well protected from dislodgement or desiccation. On granite, it usually has to erode its shell to fit the rock.

The green sea urchin, *Strongylocentrotus droebachiensis*, is also often abundant in the low tide pools, especially the large deeper ones. It is the predominant herbivore of the shallow subtidal region as well, where its large aggregations browse on practically all species of available algae (see chapter 5).

FILTER FEEDERS OF THE LOW POOLS

Any rock surface in a low tide pool not covered by algae and their herbivores is likely to be covered instead by a variety of animals which attach themselves permanently to the rock and filter the water for the detritus and microscopic organisms it contains. The intertidal barnacle, *Balanus balanoides*, may be joined in a low tide pool by two larger species, *B. balanus* and *B. crenatus*, and the intertidal blue mussel, *Mytilus edulis*, may be joined or replaced in the low pool by the larger horse mussel, *Modiolus modiolus*. The horse mussel and the larger barnacle species are even more typical of subtidal habitats, however (see chapter 5).

Sponges vary remarkably in shape, but all of them filter the water for their food. Where waves break or wave surge occurs, encrusting species are more likely to live. One species in particular is abundant in low tide pools, though, like others of the tide pool fauna, it can survive only brief exposure on low intertidal rocks and grows subtidally to considerable depths. This is *Halichondria panicea*, known as the bread crumb sponge because it crumbles easily when pried off the rocks, and as the sulphur sponge because of its odor which some find objectionable. *Halichondria* grows in relatively large patches on the rocks, thin where waves or surge may hit it, thicker on more sheltered surfaces. It is either yellow or green. The green patches get their color from the microscopic algae living within them. These algae, called zoochlorellae, probably provide nutrients for the sponge in return for the protection they get.

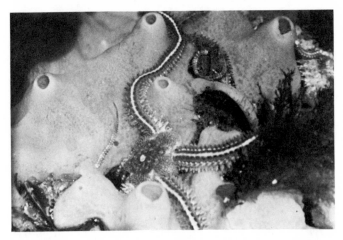

32. A brittle star *Ophiopholus aculeata* snakes between the large volcano-like pores of a breadcrumb sponge *Halichondria panicea*.

There are other filter feeders in the low pools which also occur in a wide variety of other habitats. They settle and grow on practically any hard surface, encrusting rocks, floats, pilings, moorings, skiff bottoms, large algae and they even grow on mussels and barnacles. Some are flat, crusty, colonial animals called bryozoans. The calcified skeleton of a bryozoan encloses the many individuals of the colony in small, box-like compartments. Each individual is about 1/50 inch (1/2 mm) in diameter, and it reaches out from its compartment with a crown of tentacles called a lophophore to capture detritus or passing microscopic organisms. Probably the most widespread of the Boreal species is *Electra pilosa*, which grows in lacy, white patterns that often reach several inches in diameter.

Colonial sea squirts, or ascidians, grow on almost as many kinds of hard surfaces as do the bryozoans, and they too are frequent filter feeding inhabitants of the low tide pools. Again, one species, *Botryllus*, is particularly common on the Boreal coast, and the individuals of each colony organize themselves in star-like clusters that give the sea squirt a flower-like appearance. Each individual pumps water into it by means of its own inhalant siphon, but pumps it out an exhalant siphon which it shares with the other individuals in the center of its cluster (see chapter 5).

SESSILE PREDATORS OF THE LOW TIDE POOLS: SEA ANEMONES AND HYDROIDS

Predators may be sessile and slowly moving or unattached and rapidly moving, depending upon how large their prey is and how fast it moves in turn. Sea anemones are excellent sessile predators, and the common species of the Boreal coast, *Metridium senile* and *M. dianthus*, will again settle and grow on any hard substrate where they aren't exposed to the atmosphere by a dropping tide. A low tide pool is a good place to find *Metridium*. The larger and lower the pool, the larger the anemones are likely to be. The largest individuals of all are usually in deeper, colder subtidal water (see color plate V).

Metridium comes in a variety of colors, brown, orange and cream-colored. With its many fine and sticky tentacles it captures and poisons small animals such as zooplankton, passing amphipods, even small fish, but it must wait for its prey to bump into its tentacle crown. Periodically, it withdraws its tentacles and appears to collapse completely, a kind of resting or digestive pause. When disturbed or when its environment deteriorates or becomes stressful, it will again usually withdraw its tentacles and wait for conditions to improve. Like most anemones, it can creep around slowly using its adhesive basal disk and can sometimes find a better spot to feed from.

When *Metridium* reproduces sexually, eggs develop in the parent to a larval stage known as a planula larva, which is like a small, ciliated ball. This free swimming stage then gradually develops rudimentary internal structures and settles onto a hard substrate where it adheres and grows some tentacles and begins to feed. Like many other sea anemones, *Metridium* also reproduces itself asexually, breaking off buds of tissue from its basal disk which then develop into small anemones. As a result, where one anemone thrives there will soon be many more as its buds grow and thrive as well.

Hydroids are closely related to anemones, but are much smaller. A few species, such as *Clava leptostyla* and *Sertularia*, can tolerate intertidal exposure and they grow on the brown alga, *Ascophyllum nodosum*. Most need to attach to hard surfaces and remain submerged, however, and the surfaces of the rocks and perennial algae in low tide pools are excellent places to search for them. Not unexpectedly, many also grow well subtidally on rocks, algae, pilings, under floats and on boat bottoms. All prey upon zooplankton, killing their prey with specialized cells which cover their tentacles. Each of these cells contains a stinging structure called a nematocyst which consists of a capsule with a barb coiled inside it and a fine trigger extending into the water. When a microscopic animal or other object brushes against the trigger, the nematocyst automatically ejects its coiled barb, impaling the animal and injecting it with a poison.

Some hydroids grow as clusters of relatively large individuals, or polyps, attached to each other at the base of their long stalks. *Clava* has up to 30 pink, club-shaped polyps in a cluster, each about ½ inch (1 cm) long (see plate III). Though it can be quite common on the *Ascophyllum* of the low intertidal, *Clava* grows well in tide pools. So also does *Tubularia*, probably the largest and most beautiful of the Boreal hydroids, though it is uncommon north of the Bay of Fundy. *Tubularia* grows in clusters of up to about 100 pink and red polyps, and each polyp may be 1½ inches (3 to 4 cm) long. The head region, or hydranth, of the *Tubularia* polyp has two whorls of tentacles around its mouth, and grape-like bunches of reproductive structures hang down around the stem from among the tentacles. The eggs of both *Clava* and *Tubularia* develop into sessile larvae which float away from the parent clusters to grow into new polyps which then reproduce asexually to form new clusters.

An abundant but less spectacular hydroid is the white *Sertularia pumila*. Its polyps are very small with many of them branching off from opposite sides of the 1½ inch (3 to 4 cm) stalks. *Sertularia* is common on the low intertidal rockweeds such as *Fucus* or *Ascophyllum*, but it is also abundant on kelp fronds both in tide pools and subtidally. It

33. The eggs of this cluster of the hydroid *Tubularia* look like small grapes at the head of each individual polyp.

also grows directly on the rock walls of the pools. Each stalk with its many feeding polyps is attached to other stalks by tubes or stolons fastened on the rock or algae surface between them, and a colony can become very large indeed as new stolons develop, grow and bud into new stalks. Like *Clava* and *Tubularia*, *Sertularia* eggs develop directly into sessile larvae (see plate II).

The white hydroid *Obelia* also has very small polyps, but each stalk branches into further stalks, and a wispy bush-like colony grows with many thousands of polyps, all from one original stalk (see plate III). Colonies 10 to 20 inches (25 to 50 cm) long may grow in protected pools, as well as under floats. Like many hydroids, *Obelia* produces little buds which develop not into new feeding polyps or into eggs, but instead are released as very small jellyfish. These little jellyfish, or hydromedusae, join the plankton where they feed on the zooplankton. After a few weeks, the *Obelia* medusae produce eggs and sperm and the fertilized eggs develop into sessile larvae that settle to the bottom and grow into hydroids again. The jellyfish then die. All true jellyfish, no matter what kind, are originally produced by hydroids or hydroid-like polyps. As a result, a jellyfish can be thought of as a rather elaborate way for a hydroid to reproduce itself as well as to disperse its larvae to distant habitats.

Another species that is well worth looking for is *Hydractinia echinata*, which looks like a pink fuzz occasionally covering the shell of a hermit crab. *Hydractinia* needs the continual movement a hermit crab provides, for when the hermit crab dies or abandons its shell for a larger one, the hydroid doesn't survive unless another hermit crab moves into the shell. *Hydractinia* is an extraordinary hydroid for another reason, however. The polyps which make up the large single colony on the back of a hermit crab's shell are highly specialized and have divided the various jobs a single *Tubularia* or *Clava* polyp must do. Each *Hydractinia* colony has feeding polyps that catch small animals and share their nutrients with the rest of the colony; it has defensive polyps which lack tentacles or mouths but have dense accumulations of sting cells at their free ends; and it has reproductive polyps, both male and female, that are protected and fed by the other specialists. Wherever hermit crabs occur in any number, *Hydractinia* is likely to live as well, and hermit crabs are often common in large tide pools, as well as on subtidal substrates.

CREEPING PREDATORS: SEA SLUGS OR NUDIBRANCHS

Most animals have some way of protecting themselves from predators. Sponges are made tough and unpalatable by the silica spicules they are filled with. Bryozoans are protected by calcareous skeletons. Hydroids and anemones have stinging cells that don't distinguish between prey and predator. Gastropod snails have generally been successful in evolving ways of overcoming prey defense, and outstanding among these are the shell-less sea slugs called nudibranchs, which means "naked gills." Wherever their prey are common, nudibranchs ought to be nearby. The low tide pools, as well as the appropriate subtidal habitats, are good places to look for them.

Each nudibranch is a hermaphrodite, both female and male at the same time. When two of the same species meet, they fertilize each other and together produce ribbons of eggs attached to the substrate. The eggs develop into veliger larvae with transparent shells and spend several weeks in the plankton. They then seek suitable surfaces such as hydroids or sponges to settle on and if they find them, they metamorphose into tiny, shell-less nudibranchs. Those that fail to find suitable surfaces do not survive.

There are two main kinds of nudibranchs, eolids and dorids, and both occur in tide pools. An eolid nudibranch has a large number of appendages, called cerata, all over its back. The cerata provide much increased surface area for the skin through which the nudibranch breathes since it lacks the gills of other snails. Eolids particularly distinguish themselves, though, by eating hydroids and small anemones without seeming to be stung by the sting cells. In fact, not only do they ingest the sting cells without discharging them, they pass the sting cells intact through their digestive tracts to the tips of the cerata covering their backs. There the sting cells are concentrated in batteries which then protect the nudibranchs from their own predators. Eolids are often brightly colored, perhaps to warn potential predators away from them.

Three species of nudibranchs bearing cerata are particularly common on this Boreal coast wherever their prey are also abundant. *Aeolida papillosa,* often found in the vicinity of sea anemones, is the largest, 1½ to 2 inches (4 to 5 cm) long, with a bushy covering of cerata. A species of *Coryphella,* smaller and more delicate, browses on the hydroids *Obelia* and *Tubularia* (see plate III). And *Dendronotus frondosa* is unique in having branched cerata.

The dorid nudibranchs can look quite different. A dorid lacks the cerata of the eolids, but compensates by breathing with gill-like filaments that extend in a whorl from its anus. The dorids don't eat hydroids or anemones. Each species usually specializes in preying on some other well-defended sessile animal. *Onchidorus fusca* is cream-colored, about ½ inch (1 cm) long, and preys mostly on barnacles. *O. aspera* is larger, growing to almost an inch (2 cm) in length, is mottled rose or brown, and preys on bryozoans. *Acanthodoris pilosa,* even larger at 1 inch or more (3 cm) and darker, also preys on bryozoans. *Polycera dubia,* another predator of bryozoans looks quite different, with a more delicate eolid shape, yet it still lacks the cerata of the eolids, and has prominant anal gills on the middle of its back.

OTHER PREDATORS OF THE LOW POOLS

Numerous other predators forage in the low intertidal pools. Some of them occur elsewhere on the rocky intertidal shore; others are more typical of the broad subtidal rocky habitat. Of the intertidal predators, the dogwhelk, *Thais lapillus*, and the green crab, *Carcinus maenus*, follow their prey into the pools. Most of the predators are more typically subtidal, however. They include hermit crabs, red rock crabs, spider crabs, occasional toad crabs, the starfish which occur in shallow water anywhere along the Boreal coast, the large subtidal whelks, and various fish such as the sea snail and occasional cunner. All of these are considered in more detail in chapter 5.

OTHER TIDE POOL HABITATS

The fronds of the algae, especially the kelp, provide a huge surface for plants and animals to live on, and the large intertwining kelp holdfasts provide another unique environment for a large array of juvenile and adult animals. Both habitats characterize the extensive subtidal kelp zone (see chapter 5).

The other tide pool algae, especially the Irish moss *Chondrus* and any filamentous species provide protective cover particularly for small crustaceans. Of these, various kinds of amphipods may be very common, with gammarids darting around the pool from one bit of cover to another and caprellids stalking slowly through the algae. Small true shrimp, usually *Hippolyte* or *Palaemonetes* species, which are often difficult to see or capture, also walk around on the substrate under algal cover, foraging and scavenging for small organisms.

Underneath Rocks

The Precarious Habitat

Wherever loose rocks and boulders make up the rocky intertidal shore they provide a substrate for the intertidal rockweeds to grow on their upper, exposed surfaces. They also form shaded caves and crevices between each other, and there is often a little space underneath them. The moist covering of rockweeds on top of the rocks protects these caves from desiccation and extreme temperature fluctuations, and water trapped in or on the substrate beneath the rocks helps to maintain the humidity.

Many kinds of animals live on the moist, shaded rock surfaces, while others live in the spaces between and under the rocks. The lower a rock is in the intertidal, the more likely it is to protect a diverse fauna, for rocks higher in the intertidal trap less water, dry out more quickly, and protect progressively fewer animals. Where the substrate under a rock is at all soft, burrowing animals more typical of sand and mud substrate may be abundant (see chapters 3 & 4).

An excellent way to find many kinds of animals is therefore to turn over rocks along the lower edge of the intertidal. A rock turned over suddenly exposes the animals it protected to the atmospheric conditions they are unlikely to tolerate. Those which are mobile will creep or scuttle away seeking new cover. Those which are sessile, attached to the rock, will simply die unless they are once again protected. Any rock turned over to see what lives under it should be turned back just as carefully to the way it was originally, for needless or unthinking destruction of any habitat is always a pity.

The Clingers

On the sides of the rocks, some algal growth is possible, especially of microscopic and encrusting species. Limpets, chitons, small green sea urchins and juvenile common periwinkles graze on whatever is available. Some of the hydroids, bryozoans, sponges, sea squirts and nudibranchs that inhabit the tide pools and other subtidal habitats may be quite common especially under the largest and lowest of the intertidal rocks. Barnacles, especially the species of the upper intertidal, *Balanus balanoides*, may cover a shaded rock surface, freed from competition by the rockweed which need more light and from the blue mussels which need greater water circulation. Predatory whelks, both *Thais* and young *Buccinum*, forage under the rocks after their prey as do young starfish, especially *Asterias.*

Rather strange worms, called scale worms, are usually easy to find under the low intertidal rocks, just as they are in tide pools and subtidal habitats where they forage among the byssal threads of clusters of mussels and among the complex holdfasts of kelp. Two Boreal species are particularly common, *Lepidonatus squamatus,* which grows to about an inch (3 cm) and has 12 pairs of overlapping scales covering its back, and *Harmothoë imbricata,* which has 15 pairs of scales and grows twice as long. When it is disturbed, a scale worm protects its more vulnerable side by rolling up into a scaly ball, in much the way a pill bug or an armadillo does, and quite unlike other segmented worms. Also unlike most other worms, scale worms brood their eggs instead of shedding them to be fertilized in the water.

34. Scale worms protect themselves with their armor-like scales which cover their backs.

A very different kind of worm also crawls around on the undersides of rocks, preying on other small animals. This is a primitive and unsegmented flatworm, *Notoplana atomata,* beige colored and sometimes spotted, growing to about an inch (3 cm). Like other flatworm species, it clings tightly to the rock surface by secreting sticky adhesive mucus from minute glands on its underneath side. *Notoplana* captures prey by pinning it to the substrate in the sticky slime and then engulfing it.

The Refuge Seekers

The space between the bottom of a rock and the substrate beneath it is an excellent place for animals to find refuge especially when the tide is low. The green crab *Carcinus maenus* may aggregate in fairly large numbers in such a space, surprising since they are ordinarily so aggressive toward one another. When the tide rises, the crabs disperse to forage for food. Along more northern parts of the Boreal coast, the red rock crab *Cancer irroratus* may also occur frequently under low tide rocks.

The Rock Eel. The rock eel, *Pholis gunnellus*, often hides under rocks or even in the seaweed when the tide is low. Also called the butterfish, it prefers a pebble, gravel or broken-shell substrate, avoiding mud and eelgrass as well as steep ledges. When disturbed it squirms like an eel and anyone who has tried to catch it knows just how slippery it is.

35. The rock eel *Pholis gunnellus* often hides in clumps of algae or under rocks.

The yellowish-olive butterfish grows to 6–8 inches (15 to 20 cm) and is easily identified by the 10 to 12 prominent black spots spaced along its back. It breeds from November through February and the female lays from 600 to 700 iridescent eggs in large empty mussel shells or in crevices in the rocks. Both parents loop their elongated bodies around the eggs, coiling them into balls about an inch (2 to 3 cm) in diameter. The eggs are adhesive and they remain stuck together for their month-long incubation. One or both parents are often found coiled around the eggs, giving rise to the notion that parents guard the eggs. Experiments have not corroborated this yet, however, and it may be that the shell or crevice is just a convenient place for the rock eel to be.

The eggs hatch into larvae which become part of the temporary plankton where they spend several months in the surface waters. In late summer or early autumn they sink to the bottom and work their way back to shallow water and finally to the shore where they spend the rest of their lives.

Rock eels are carnivores which eat small mollusks, amphipods, shrimp and worms. They, in turn, are eaten by cod and pollock—a fact which reveals their presence in water as deep as 265 ft. (80 m). Although they are present all year along the shore, during the winter they often migrate into slightly deeper water to avoid exposure to the cold.

Pilings: A Substitute for Rocks

Wherever pilings support wharves, buildings or bridges, they provide another hard surface as suitable for the inhabitants of the rocky intertidal habitat to settle and grow on as the rocks themselves. Horizontal zones develop on the parts of the pilings exposed by the dropping tide just as they do on the intertidal rocks. The same organisms dominate these zones as they do on the rock surfaces, and the same abiotic and biotic factors control the upper and lower limits to their distributions.

Since pilings are rarely erected where there is much wave action, the zonation typical of an exposed rocky headland is unlikely to occur on them. Pilings are almost always placed in relatively quiet water, and their zones most resemble those of protected rocky shores. The structures that pilings hold up provide shade from summer heat and protection from winter storms, so the diversity of animals may in fact be greater on a piling than on the adjacent rocks. The same shade may however inhibit any extensive growth of rockweeds. The subtidal portions of the pilings, like the tide pools and the subtidal habitat in general, are often covered by an even greater diversity of organisms, allowing another glimpse into the rocky subtidal habitat not otherwise easy to obtain. The pilings which can be the most rewarding to examine are those under narrow bridges, washed by tidal currents which keep the water temperatures cool in summer, and always rich in food.

CHAPTER III

Beaches
and Sand Dunes

A BEACH is a dynamic place, forever changing, slowly moving, and often fragile. It is made up of fragments of rock or shell that can be moved around by the unceasing action of the waves. It is in fact a product of waves, winds and ocean currents, and none of these are ever constant. Not only can a beach change in appearance from one year to the next, it also changes from one season to the next, and on a small scale, even from tide to tide.

No organism which needs a firm, solid substrate can live on a beach. None of the clinging animals or large algae which characterize a rocky intertidal can find appropriate surfaces to hang on to, and a beach looks barren of life. Though no large algae are present, certain animals have adapted to the intertidal beach habitat, however. Many are very small, and live in the spaces between the sand grains; others are larger, burrowing species which push the sand grains around.

Behind a sandy beach, sand dunes develop if there is space for them. They are created over time by the prevailing winds. Like the beaches, they too are dynamic and just as fragile. In contrast to the beaches, though, the dunes are covered with vegetation which stabilizes them. Dune plants are remarkable in their ability to grow in sand and tolerate salt-laden winds, and they in turn provide enough protection from the wind and shifting sands for shorebirds to nest successfully.

Boreal Beaches

Beach Variety

No two beaches are alike. They differ in color, slope, shape, and in the size and type of particles which form them. Most of the sandy beaches of the Boreal coast are light colored, made up primarily of grains of quartz, feldspar, and other eroded rock. Shell fragments are usually mixed in to some extent, but rarely contribute significantly in the way they do in the formation of many southern warm-water beaches.

Along the Boreal coast, especially its rockier parts, beaches are often not sandy ones but are made of gravel or

36. A cobble beach on the Avalon Peninsula in Newfoundland.

cobble instead. Even boulder beaches occur, though they then start to grade into the familiar, weed covered rocky intertidal. Where beaches flatten out and waves have little impact, particle size diminishes, and a beach can grade into sand flats, which contain clay and silt particles. Occasionally a beach is made up of unnatural particles. Beaches of saw dust occur on some of the tidal estuaries down river from the saw mills.

Table 3: Beach Particle Sizes

Beach Particle	Diameter of Particle
Boulders	8 inches (200 mm)
Cobbles	3–8 inches (76–200 mm)
Gravel (shingle, pebbles)	
Coarse	3/4–3 inches (19–76 mm)
Fine	3/16–3/4 inch (5–19 mm)
Sand	
Coarse	2–5 mm
Medium	0.4–2 mm
Fine	0.07–0.4 mm
Silt, Clay	Less than 0.07 mm

Sand from eroded granite and other hard rock tends to be coarse grained. It isn't as compact or firm as the coral sand of Florida or the dark, basaltic sand of Oregon. It therefore allows water to drain through it more easily, a feature of great importance to the animals living in it.

Formation of Beaches

POCKET AND FRINGING BEACHES

Narrow beaches, often tucked between rocky promontories, cling to the shore along the Boreal coast. Such beaches are usually small and are often shallow, having little depth between beach surface and underlying beach rock. No dunes lie behind such a beach, nor does it protect a lagoon or salt marsh behind it. The sand and gravel of a pocket beach is usually well protected from being swept irretrievably away by currents, and so the beach is a closed system that changes cyclically during the year but is fairly constant from year to year. The sand and pebbles that make up pocket and fringing beaches originate largely from glacial sediment left behind by the retreat of the glaciers.

BARRIER SPIT BEACHES

As a young coast ages, waves erode the rocky headlands, push them back, and in the process gradually straighten the coastline. As headlands are worn away into sand, the sand is picked up by the ocean and deposited downcurrent as a spit. If rivers carry glacial deposits, they similarly carry their loads to the deeper water near the headlands, and then dump their loads as their velocity drops, and add to the spits. The spits grow as long as the rivers carry sediment and as long as the headlands can be worn back.

Waves hit shorelines in the direction of the prevailing winds, provided there aren't too many obstacles such as islands, headlands and shoals in the way. Where they hit at an angle, they produce a longshore current. Longshore currents vary in strength, carrying sand parallel to the shore as a kind of river of sand, dumping sand wherever its velocity decreases. Along the Atlantic coast, sand spits grow south and west primarily, but such downdrift north of Cape Cod is small relative to the regions south of it. The Boreal coast is too young, the amount of available sediment too little and the coastal turbulence too great for long-shore currents to have the impact they do elsewhere.

Barrier spit beaches, no matter whether the source of their sediment is from rivers dumping their glacial deposit or longshore currents carrying deposits from further up the coast, extend part way across the mouth of a bay. Each spit usually has a long straight dune field and protects a tidal inlet where mud flats or salt marshes develop (see chapter 4).

BARRIER BEACHES AND ISLANDS

A barrier spit may eventually close off a bay and become attached to the mainland at both ends. There is still a tidal inlet behind it whose outlet is pushed farther down the coast and it still protects a lagoon with or without a salt marsh. Occasionally part of a lagoon may be cut off completely from tidal flow and may gradually become a fresh-water marsh.

At other places, a spit which continues to grow in size and height may become separated at both ends from the

37. The transition from beach to sand dunes is clear along this stretch of coast line in Prince Edward Island National Park.

mainland, and become a barrier island. Its dunes are usually well developed and its vegetation is often dense; but it remains essentially a large, modified sand spit. Barrier islands may originate in other ways as well, however, and it is likely that some have developed from coastal dune fields subsequently drowned by rising sea levels.

Structure of an Ocean Beach

An average of 8000 waves may break upon a beach each day, and every exposed sandy beach has several distinct parts to it which are products of the waves. Each has a foreshore or beach face which the surf washes up; a beach crest or berm which is above the high tide line and which waves therefore don't reach; and one or two sand bars parallel to the shore which are exposed only by the lowest tides.

An ocean wave breaks when it hits shallow water at a depth of about 1.3 times the height the wave had when still in deeper water. It breaks simply because there isn't enough water ahead of it to fill its crest, and it topples forward. It loses much of its energy when it breaks and as a result dumps a large portion of its load of suspended sediment. Where incoming waves first break, a sandbar therefore forms beneath them. The diminished waves move on, and if they break a second time when once again they reach a depth about equal to 1.3 times their height, they may form a second sand bar. Waves rarely have the energy to break a third time, and instead they usually just wash up the beach face, dumping more of their sand as they die. As the water then washes back down the beach face, it picks up sand grains once again as it gathers momentum.

Waves differ a little from each other in size and direction of impact. Each slightly modifies the sand substrate so that the next wave, however similar, interacts with a different bottom topography. Even when upon casual observation the beach appears to remain constant from day to day, small, subtle changes and shifts continually occur which may gradually accumulate into a major modification of the beach.

The water that surges in past the offshore bars and up the beach face may have trouble getting out past the bars again.

Currents may develop inside the bars as the water moves along the shore. Where an opening develops, the water surges out, forming a rip current out to deeper water and further modifying the bottom topography.

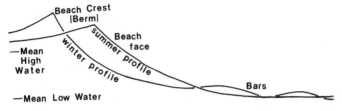

38. Comparison of summer and winter profiles of the same surf swept beach. Higher waves of winter raise the berm, steepen the beach face and produce bars.

Summer–Winter Changes

Longshore currents may cause a beach to grow or change progressively over the course of years, but even where such currents are weak or absent, a beach is likely to change dramatically in appearance from summer to winter. Each wave carries sand up the beach face and carries it back down as well. If the waves dump more than they pick up, the beach face grows; if they pick up more than they dump, the beach face diminishes.

In summer, the beach crest, or berm, is relatively low and wide. The height of the berm is a product of the height of the waves (usually about 1.3 times the height of a deep water wave), though the interaction of winds, currents and waves also modify it. The waves of summer, on the average, are low ones and the berm is correspondingly low. Such waves pick sand up off the offshore sandbars and carry it up the beach face where they dump it. During the summer, the bars are therefore gradually removed and deposited on the beach face, smoothing the underwater profile of the beach.

In winter more storms occur and with them come higher waves. The impact of the nor'easters on the beaches of the Boreal coast can be truly extraordinary, metamorphosing a beach in a matter of a couple of days. The higher waves wash up the beach face and over the crest of the berm where they dump their loads. As a result the berm grows higher. The receding waves still have high energy as they wash back down and they pick up more sand from the beach face. The berm, eaten away by the waves, is pushed back as it grows higher. When the receding waves reach the deeper water, they dump the sand they've taken from the beach face, depositing it once again on the offshore bars. The winter beach, then, is high and steep and its underwater profile is no longer smooth but dominated by the offshore bars.

Where the amount of sand that forms a beach is shallow, as it tends to be along the rocky shores north of Cape Cod, a summer sandy beach may lose most of its sand to the sandbars in winter, exposing the underlying boulders or bedrock. Where sand depth is great, as it is on the extensive beaches of Cape Cod and the southern Gulf of St. Lawrence, there isn't any possibility of bedrock exposure, but changes in beach profile can be quite surprising to anyone who is only familiar with the way beaches look in summer.

Beach Erosion

As currents shift and winds change, beaches change as well. If the sediment from glacial runoff, from erosion of headlands, and from beaches upcurrent is abundant, a beach grows. If the rivers no longer carry much sediment, if headlands are too hard to erode rapidly or have been eroded smooth, if longshore currents cease or shift, a beach may recede or cease to grow. Furthermore, as the sea level rises, which it is still doing relative to the land along most of the Boreal coast, a beach retreats, migrating slowly landward. It pushes any dune fields it might have before it over the lagoonal salt marsh that may lie behind the dunes.

A beach which erodes away or migrates inland in response to such natural forces is a commonplace occurrence, something to be expected and not to be surprised by. But beaches are also eroding as the result of human abuse and of woefully ignorant and irresponsible zoning laws. Jetties, groins and seawalls were built on the more southern populated beaches to attract sand and beat back erosion. It is now understood that these are but temporary measures, and are destructive in the long run.

Sand dunes have experienced especially severe erosion. In the most extreme cases, they have simply been built upon and destroyed. With other dunes, uncontrolled foot traffic has illustrated just how fragile they are. In addition, paved roads have been constructed through them, and in the process of keeping the roads clear, the moving dunes have been destroyed. Again a lack of understanding of both the movement and fragility of dunes has been the cause. Dunes are now being more protected where it is possible to protect them by restricting foot traffic and development, and some dunes are being reclaimed. But in other spots, people are receiving even greater access to dunes, and dune destruction proceeds unabated.

The Major Beach Areas of the Boreal Region

There are two regions of very extensive beach development on the Boreal coast. One stretches from Cape Cod to southern Maine; the other lines the southern crescent of the Gulf of St. Lawrence. Both include many fine examples of sand spits, barrier beaches, barrier islands and sand dunes, and both are accessible at a number of places to anyone wishing to explore them. Particularly outstanding are The Provincelands area and other parts of the Cape Cod National Seashore; the Parker River National Wildlife Refuge on Plum Island north of Cape Ann; Prince Edward Island National Park; and Kouchibouguac National Park on the New Brunswick coast of the Gulf of St. Lawrence. Many other beaches, often equally spectacular, extend for miles along the shores adjacent to these more public access points.

Elsewhere on the Boreal coast, the beaches are smaller, likely to be pocket and fringing beaches made up of anything from sand to boulders depending upon the availability of sediment and the slope of the beach. Even along the rockiest shores from Maine to Newfoundland, such beaches interrupt the rock.

Stresses of Living on a Beach

Grain Size and Beach Slope

The greater the slope of a beach, the larger the size of the sand grains or rock fragments that cover it. Where the slope is as much as 20 degrees or more, anything smaller than cobbles is likely to be washed away; such a beach is practically devoid of life since few organisms can withstand the crushing impact of wave tossed cobbles. Beaches with a slope of about 12 degrees are likely to be covered by gravel or shingle, a difficult habitat for animals unless there is an underlying sand matrix.

As the slope further decreases, beaches of sand develop. Ocean beaches are made up of grains of various sizes, with the larger grains accumulating on the upper parts of the beach face, and the finer and lighter grains remaining suspended in the waves until the waves lose most of their energy and drop their lighter loads on the lower, flatter parts of the beach. The flatter the beach becomes, the finer are its sand grains, and beach areas of practically no slope can become extensive sand flats which may even contain clay particles mixed in with the fine sand. Where sand just isn't available in any abundance, as on the northeast shores of Maine, gravel beaches may form on the shallow slopes instead of sand.

Slope and grain size of a beach are both related to the exposure the beach faces. The steepest beaches face the strongest winds and the highest waves. As winds and waves change seasonally, the size of grains of sand on the beach will be changed or sorted seasonally as well. In contrast, the flattest beaches are those most protected from the impact of the winds and waves.

On sandy beaches, the size of the sand grains may drastically influence which organisms are present and which aren't. Coarse quartz sand grains don't compress well, leaving spaces or pores between them in which water is trapped and through which very small animals can move. Such sand, because it doesn't compress, is easily shifted by waves and currents, and is therefore difficult for any animal to build a permanent burrow in. As sand grain size becomes

BEACHES AND SAND DUNES

39. Sand flats like this one near Jonesport, Maine, may be very extensive at low tide.

finer, the sand compacts more, shifts less easily, doesn't fall in on a burrower so easily, and burrowing animals become more common.

Oxygen and Water Drainage

On a coarse grained sandy beach, water drains through the interstitial spaces (between the grains) with ease, pulled down vertically into the beach and down the beach face by gravity. The water content at the surface of a well-drained beach may be as high as 20 percent, and the oxygen-rich, well-drained layer may be as deep as 20 inches (50 cm) as each wave brings up a new surge of water to percolate into the sand. Below the oxygen-rich surface, the sand turns dark, even black, due to accumulations of ferrous sulfides, where a lack of oxygen makes it impossible for oxygen-breathing animals to live.

As sand grain size decreases, water drains with less success. The depth of the oxygen-rich sand correspondingly

Stresses of Living on a Beach   135

decreases, and on a sand beach without high energy waves crashing on it, the black sand may begin only 4 to 6 inches (10 to 15 cm) below the surface. The depth varies during the year on any one beach, for winter storms with their higher waves increase the depth of drainage as well as grain size. Even on more sheltered beaches the oxygen-rich surface layer is usually less than 4 inches (10 cm) deep; on sand flats it is usually about 2 inches (5 cm) deep, and it decreases further as the clay content of the flat increases. In mud flats, where grain size is very small, water movement can be negligible, and the oxygen-rich layer may be as thin as half an inch (1 to 2 cm).

The animals of the beaches and sand flats must either live in the oxygen-rich surface layer, or if they burrow beneath it, they must have some way of reaching up to it with siphons or tubes in order to breathe and feed. The density of animals in the surface layer is often great, and oxygen is probably depleted from the draining water as quickly as it is replenished. Carbon dioxide can build up and be removed equally quickly. Though rapid changes in carbon dioxide ought to suggest rapid changes in pH as well in the interstitial water, there are usually enough calcareous shell fragments in the sand to buffer the carbon dioxide and keep the pH constant.

In comparison, a beach of pure cobbles or pebbles without a sand matrix below them is an exceedingly harsh environment. Water isn't trapped, but drains through rapidly. Even if the stones were not tossed percussively around by the waves, few animals would be able to live on such a beach.

Migration in Response to Other Stresses

Anyone who has walked along a sandy beach in summer sunshine knows how hot the coarse, loose sand of the upper, drier parts of the beach can become. No animal can tolerate such heat. But the temperature usually drops quickly below the surface and in a well drained beach the temperature even on a hot day is likely to equal cooler sea temperatures by a depth of 6 to 8 inches (15 to 20 cm).

BEACHES AND SAND DUNES

Many animals are able to avoid the surface heat just by burrowing deeper in the sand.

In winter the surface of a Boreal beach above the mid tide level may freeze. Most animals migrate down the beach to areas less likely to freeze when the tide is low. Few species can tolerate freezing the way barnacles of the rocky intertidal can. Still other species just burrow deeper into the sand for the winter.

Though the breaking waves bring with them more stable temperatures and a fresh supply of oxygen, they also constantly shift the surface sand grains. Small animals living in the surface layer of sand are likely to be thrown about. Small mollusks may even be moved by the waves to different places on the beach. A very few animals actually thrive in the breaking surf and follow it up and down the beach with the tide. Again, however, most species avoid the impact of the surf simply by migrating from the top half inch (1 cm) of the sand to depths of 1 to 2 inches (3 to 4 cm) and wait there for the tide to turn.

When waves are very small and when the tide is low, the surface layers of sand may dry out, and the resident animals once again migrate to damper depths. When heavy rains occur and fresh water runoff increases, the water in the surface layer of sand may become too dilute for the animals living there to tolerate. Again, they seek the more constant, saline environment of the slightly deeper sand.

Beach Zonation

Zonation on a beach isn't obvious, especially in comparison with the intertidal rocky shore, but it is there nonetheless. As on other intertidal shores, it is related to the different degrees of desiccation and temperature fluctuations experienced at different levels on the beach above the mean low tide level.

The highest is the Zone of Dry Sand above the level of Mean High Water where water is not retained by the sand but instead is lost by gravitation down the beach slope. This part of the beach is where temperature fluctuations can be the greatest, both too hot and too cold for any organisms to tolerate. In some parts of the beach, the highest zone may in fact be saturated continuously by fresh water runoff, and just as inhospitable to marine life.

The next highest is the Zone of Drying Sand. Sea water washes it irregularly for a brief time at least during every high tide, and more frequently when storm-driven waves are higher than usual. Water seeps out of the sand as it does in the highest zone, but its more frequent replenishment makes it a less stressful environment. Still, its stresses are great enough to make it impossible for all but the most hardy intertidal beach animals to survive.

The broad middle of the beach is the Zone of Water Retention. Sea water washes the zone for a considerable portion of every tidal cycle. The sand is not as loose as it is in the higher zones, but it is still loose enough for water to pass easily between its grains, and there is ample food and oxygen in the subsurface sand. When the tide drops below the zone, some water drains out, again by gravity, but most of the water remains trapped among the sand grains. The environment is now a more stable one, and large numbers of mostly small animals live in it.

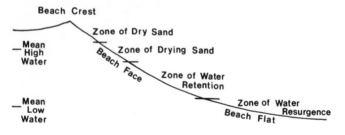

40. The zonation of an ocean beach is determined by how much water the sand retains when the tide drops.

Around the level of Mean Low Water the beach often flattens out to such an extent that breaking waves at even the lowest tides send a swash layer over the flats. Water is continually draining down from higher zones as well, so the beach flats are never stressed by desiccation problems. This is the Zone of Water Resurgence. With the flatter slope, the sand grains become finer and pack more closely together. Water circulation between the grains in fact decreases and many of the animals which live abundantly in the Zone of Water Retention are less common on the lower flat zone. On the other hand, other organisms live easily in the more compact sand of the flatter resurgence zone, and most of these are distributed without interruption on into the stable, saturated environment of the subtidal habitat.

Beaches vary so much in slope and grain size that some beach zones may be absent or they may be unusually extensive. Most sandy beaches have some form of each zone, however.

The Organisms on a Beach

Beach organisms live in a shifting world. Their major defense against the stresses all intertidal organisms face when the tide drops is to seek the wetter, more saline and stable environment of deeper sand. How deep they can migrate is usually related to the depth of the oxygen-rich sand.

A beach or flat may look devoid of life when you wander over it at low tide. But below the mid tide level, in the 2 to 4 inches (5 to 10 cm) of oxygenated sand beneath your feet, may live an extraordinary array of organisms. The smallest of these live in the interstitial spaces between the sand grains, feeding even when the tide is down. The larger animals wait until the tide covers them to feed. And yet other animals come in with the tide from deeper water to prey upon those living in the sand.

Microorganisms

A host of plants and animals small enough to pass through a sieve with mesh pores of only 0.1 mm in diameter live on the surface of the sand grains. Bacteria, diatoms and minute blue green algae are abundant, and they depend on organic molecules absorbed onto the surface of the sand grains from the water draining through the sand. The diatoms and blue green algae of course also need light, and they reach their largest populations at the surface layers of fine sand (and mud) which are richest in organic molecules as well.

These microorganisms are in turn fed upon by very small animals, the single celled protozoans. Most of the proto- zoans among the sand grains are ciliates, which scoot around on the surfaces of the grains, eating the plant cells and bacteria. The sheer mass of ciliates can be huge, and like the other micro-organisms, their diversity is also great. Because they are so small and so diverse, the micro- organisms are not well known, for they can be studied only with the aid of powerful microscopes. But they are tre- mendously important to the beach community because they are the food for a wide range of larger animals.

Beach Plants

The macroalgae which so dominate the hard substrates of other intertidal and subtidal habitats are completely absent on a beach. There just isn't any substrate both stable and hard enough on a beach for the macroalgae to attach their holdfasts to. Only on boulder beaches, where the boulders are too large to be tossed around by waves do annual species of macroalgae have a chance to grow. Winter storms are often strong enough to move those boulders, however, and any annual macroalgae are likely to be scoured off or moved into new positions where there is insufficient light. If the boulders are so large that perennial brown macro- algae are able to grow on them, the habitat can no longer be called a beach but is properly part of the rocky intertidal.

No rooted plants grow on the beach face either. Though eel grass, *Zostera marina,* may form large subtidal beds, and a variety of other higher plants may cover the dunes above the beach, none is able to withstand the rigors of breaking waves and rapidly shifting sands.

The Middle-sized Animals: the Meiofauna

The animals of the meiofauna are much larger than the microorganisms which they feed upon, but they are still small enough to move around in the spaces between coarse sand grains. Less than 1/12 to 1/15 inch (1 to 2 mm) in dia- meter (or length), they are at least big enough to see, and a

BEACHES AND SAND DUNES

hand lens is all you need to tell what kind of animal you are looking at.

These small animals are well adapted to life between the sand grains. They tend to have fewer eggs than their free-swimming or planktonic counterparts, and they protect their developing broods which usually hatch directly into bottom living forms, bypassing the planktonic larval forms which characterize most subtidal organisms. Such adaptations of the reproductive cycle keep the organisms in their preferred habitats; dispersal of eggs or larvae into the water would just result in their failing to find an intertidal beach to settle on. Life cycles tend to be short, and two to four generations within a single summer are not uncommon. These animals can produce large populations in a short time.

A meiofauna community is a relatively stable, permanent thing, a product of high diversity, large populations, complex feeding relationships, and high degree of adaptiveness of the resident species to their environment. However, when the sand grains become very fine, and the spaces between them shrink to sizes too small for most of the meiofauna to move through, diversity then drops rapidly.

NEMATODES

One group of animals, the nematodes, dominates the meiofauna, no matter how fine or coarse the sand, and in fact the finer the sand, the more common they tend to be.

Nematodes are roundworms. They are simpler in their organization than the larger and more familiar annelid worms, of which the earthworm is an example known to everyone. As a worldwide group, nematodes are about the most successful and numerous animals there are; different species have been found in practically every habitat, from deserts to poles, hot springs to ocean depths. They are slender worms, tapered at both ends and usually less than 1/16 inch (1 to 2 mm) long. Some of the marine, interstitial nematodes reach about an inch (2 to 3 cm) in length, but because they are so thin they can still easily move through the sand. They are the dominant animals of the meiofauna at all levels of the beach face. Different species occur at different levels and most of them live in the top 2 inches (5 cm) of the sand, but they are able to push their way to

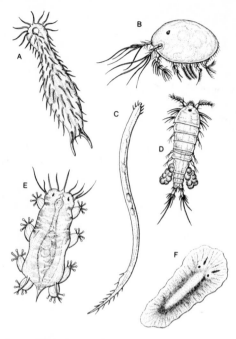

41. Members of beach meiofauna: A. gastrotrich B. ostracod C. nematode D. harpacticoid copepod carrying eggs E. tardigrade F. flatworm

depths of 3 feet (1 m) as well. Most nematodes eat the micro-organisms on the sand grains, but some species eat other nematodes, too. Not limited by the size of spaces between sand grains, they often concentrate wherever their food sources are densest.

COPEPODS

Copepods are small crustaceans that as a group are mostly marine, though some species are very successful in fresh water. Many species are parasitic, especially on fish. They are abundant in all relatively coarse grained sands. One group, the harpacticoid copepods, is benthic or bottom living. Harpacticoids are well adapted for moving between the sand grains, using their legs to crawl around instead of beating them in the oar-like motion used by swimming planktonic species. The harpacticoids are most abundant around the mid-tide level on the beach, but there is distinct zonation in their distribution with some species living higher on the beach than others, and different species preferring different sizes of sand grains. Like other copepods, the harpacticoids produce hard-shelled dormant eggs that can withstand severe environmental stress, and when conditions are good, can reproduce themselves rapidly with a more usual egg type which hatches into a simple nauplius larva. The beaches from July to September have large numbers of nauplii as well as adult copepods crawling around in them. In summer, the harpacticoids keep to the top inch (2 cm) of sand where their food is abundant and oxygen is rapidly replenished. In winter they move to depths of 1 to 2 inches (2 to 5 cm) to avoid the rigors of winter waves and temperatures. Nonetheless, they can still withstand extraordinary stress; some species have survived being frozen in sea ice at 14° F (−10° C) for as long as 9 hours.

OTHER PERMANENT MEMBERS
OF THE MEIOFAUNA

Ostracods, which are small crustaceans usually less than 1/25 inch (1 mm) in diameter and which look a little like minute clams, are common in fine sand where they use their antennae to swim or crawl between grains, eating the detritus trapped in the sand.

Gastrotrichs are flattened, elongated animals that are somewhat like nematodes in their general structure. The lower or ventral surface of a gastrotrich is ciliated and the beating of the cilia propels the animal around between the sand grains. Whenever a gastrotrich finds microorganisms, it sucks them into its mouth.

Tardigrades or water bears are short, plump animals with four pairs of stubby legs, and each leg ends in claw-like hooks. Tardigrades are rarely longer than 1/25 inch (1 mm) and crawl around between the sand grains puncturing the diatoms and blue green algal cells and sucking out their contents. Some species also treat any nematodes they bump into in much the same manner. Though tardigrades are not very common, small numbers of them occur in most beach zones, especially below the mid-tide level.

Turbellarians, or flatworms, are all carnivores. Small,

The Organisms on a Beach   143

relatively primitive species, less than 1/12 inch (2 mm) long, forage among the sand grains, eating protozoans, copepods, ostracods, and others of the micro and meiofauna.

Other groups of small animals occur less frequently, and only specialists usually search for them. They include rotifers, kinorhynchs, archiannelids, mystacocarids and halocarids.

TEMPORARY MEMBERS OF THE MEIOFAUNA

The larval and juvenile stages of many of the larger animals, the macrofauna, are for a while small enough to be meiofaunal in their habits. The young stages of snails, bivalves, crustaceans and polychaete worms may forage between sand grains in large numbers, but never for a prolonged time or over an indefinite area. They feed, grow too large for the interstitial spaces, and gradually develop the habits and needs of the larger individuals of their respective species.

The Macrofauna of an Exposed Sandy Beach

Few larger animals or macrofauna live in the intertidal sand of a surf-swept beach. Winds, waves and currents shift the sand grains to such an extent that no animal that needs to build a permanent burrow can possibly live there. A few segmented polychaete worms may forage in the sand, the flat isopod crustacean *Chirodotea caeca* may occasionally be common, and the mole crab, *Emerita talpoida,* and the surf clam, *Spisula solidissima,* have adapted to living in the sand under the surf. A group of animals that have adapted especially successfully to intertidal life on exposed sandy beaches on the Boreal coast are burrowing amphipod crustaceans known as haustoriids.

THE BURROWING AMPHIPODS. Various species of haustoriid amphipods dominate the macrofauna of exposed sandy beaches and several species are likely to occur on any one beach. The species which are most common on the beaches of the southern parts of the Boreal coast are *Amphiporeia virginiana* and *Talorchestia megalophthalma.* Like other haustoriids, they take advantage of being thrown from under the sand surface by breaking waves to scavenge detritus from the water swirling around them, and then they dive back into the protection of the sand when the waves recede. Like all amphipods the haustoriids brood their young which leave their mothers' protection looking like miniature adults and feeding the way their parents do.

Though haustoriid life cycles are much longer than those of the meiofauna, they last only about 15 months. Populations on a beach tend to be stable. *A. virginiana* is particularly well adapted to beach life in the Boreal region, for it somehow withstands the stresses of winter more easily than other species, and unlike the other haustoriids, it doesn't migrate to lower levels on the beach face for the winter.

Mole Crab. The mole crab, *Emerita talpoida*, only occurs at the very southern edge of the Boreal region, on the beaches of Cape Cod, for it is essentially a warmer water animal. It is a remarkable animal and can be quite abundant on beaches where it occurs. It is an anomuran crab, shaped rather like an egg, and is cryptically colored, the color of sand. Females grow to about 1 inch (2.5 cm) but males are only half as long and are semiparasitic on females in the summer breeding season. As a wave breaks over them, the crabs emerge from the sand and filter the water for its detrital debris with beautiful feather-like antennae. As the wave passes, they quickly reburrow and await the next one. Constantly emerging and reburrowing, they follow the tide up and down the beach, living in the turmoil of breaking waves. When winter comes, males separate from the females, and they all move into deeper subtidal water for the winter.

Surf Clam. The surf clam, *Spisula solidissima*, is a suspension or filter feeder and is the largest bivalve mollusk on the Boreal coast, growing as wide as 7 to 8 inches (17 to 20 cm). Approximately triangular in shape, it burrows upright in the sand at the lowest intertidal levels of surf-swept beaches as well as in the stretches of sand below the level of the low tide. When the surf clam is alive, the surface of its shell is covered by a light brown horny layer called the periostracum, but this layer is quickly worn off of a wave-tossed empty shell. Concentric growth lines on its shell are easy to see, for it grows rapidly in the spring and summer, and probably little if at all during the winter. On the inside of an empty shell the two large scars where the adductor

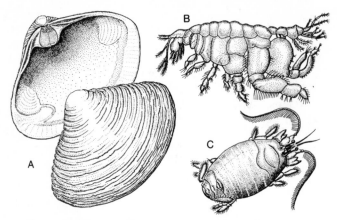

42. Some common sand burrowers. A. surf clam *Spisula solidissima* B. an haustoriid amphipod C. mole crab *Emerita talpoida.*

muscles were attached are very prominent. The adductor muscles of a living clam hold the two shells together, but they are also very sweet tasting and in recent years have made surf clams of great commercial value.

Like other bivalves the surf clam is highly adapted to living in a soft substrate. It is laterally compressed so it can be pulled easily into the sand by its foot. Its gills are large, involved in collecting food in addition to respiration, just as they are in the blue mussel. In order to remain below the sand surface, hidden from predators and protected from wave action, its siphons extend up from the buried shell to the surface of the sand. Nonetheless, relative to the soft-shelled clam, *Mya arenaria,* which has a long neck to its siphon and can burrow deep into the sand or mud, the siphons of surf clams are short, permitting the surf clam to burrow only just below the surface. The shallowness of the surf clams makes them easy to find at a very low tide and sea gulls prey upon them as eagerly as humans.

The Macrofauna of Sheltered Beaches and Sand Flats

A sheltered beach, protected from direct exposure to ocean waves, is flatter and made of finer sand than an exposed beach. It may even be sufficiently sheltered that its slope becomes almost negligible, and extensive sand flats develop. Even on the sand flats, though, tidal currents or wave action is still strong enough to prevent the finest sediments from settling out of the water, and the flats remain predominantly of fine sand rather than clay or mud. Zonation is increasingly difficult to recognize as a beach flattens and pools of water may even remain trapped on the surface at low tide. The amount of organic debris and microorganisms in the fine sand can be remarkably great, permitting a high diversity of macrofauna as well.

Burrowing amphipods no longer dominate the macrofauna, for the sand is fine enough that many other animals are able to dig or build burrows which don't easily collapse. A variety of segmented polychaete worms and bivalve mollusks as well as a few other organisms have adapted to living in the sand of sheltered beaches and sand flats. Many of them are suspension feeders, filtering the water over them for the food it contains. Others are deposit feeders, eating the detritus from the surface or eating the sediment and then eliminating whatever is indigestible.

FILTER FEEDING MOLLUSKS

One of the most abundant of filter feeding bivalve mollusks is the gem shell, *Gemma gemma,* which doesn't grow larger than 1/8 of an inch (4 mm) but reaches incredible densities of over 250,000 per square yard (0.8 m^2). It is particularly common in clean, fine sand where the spaces between sand grains remain filled with water when the tide is out. *Gemma gemma* feeds mostly at night, extending its short siphons to the sand surface to suck in, filter and exhale the water. Unlike most bivalves, *Gemma gemma* doesn't liberate planktonic veliger larvae to disperse with the water currents. Instead the veliger stage is suppressed and minute clams are liberated, settling immediately nearby their parents. They are not flushed by the tides away to substrates they cannot tolerate. Not surprisingly, *Gemma gemma* is the favored prey of predators ranging from worms and shrimp to horseshoe crabs and diving ducks.

A much larger clam lives in somewhat muddier sand but is washed up even on exposed beaches. This is the quahog, *Mercenaria mercenaria,* known also as the round or hard clam, and marketed as little neck, cherrystone or chowder clams, depending on its size. It cannot tolerate the colder summer water of parts of the Boreal coast, for its larvae are killed by cold temperatures, but it is locally common in the warmer bays on the coast of Maine and turns up in fair numbers in the Gulf of St. Lawrence. Though more oval and not as large as surf clams, quahogs still grow to 4 to 5 inches (10 to 12.5 cm) wide, and unlike the surf clam, the whole animal is eaten, not just the adductor muscles. The inside edge of the quahog is stained purple, an uncommon color that made beads cut from the shall's edge especially valuable as wampum and which in turn inspired the Latin name given to the species. The quahog's siphons are short and like the surf clam the quahog burrows only just below the surface of the sand or sandy mud near and beyond the level of the low tide.

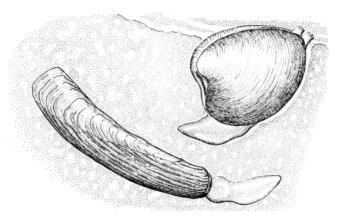

43. Common bivalves on sheltered beaches. The razor clam *Ensis directus* (left) has withdrawn below the surface. The quahog *Mercenaria mercenaria* is still feeding at the surface.

The razor clam, *Ensis directus*, is another large bivalve which burrows in sand or muddy sand in the lower intertidal flats and in the subtidal sediment beyond. Its extraordinary shape is unmistakable, for growing to 7 to 8 inches (17.5 to 20 cm) long and about an inch (2.5 cm) wide, it looks like the sheath of an old fashioned straight razor. Of all the burrowing bivalves, the razor clam must be the one best adapted to living in soft substrates. Its siphons are short and when the tide is high it sits just below the surface of the sand, filtering the water for food. However, when it is disturbed by the presence of a predator or when the tide drops past it, it burrows deeper into the sand at an extraordinary rate. Like other bivalves, it uses its foot to pull it down into the sand, but its foot is relatively larger and more agile than the feet of other species. To burrow, it extends its foot in a tapered point which shoots down into the sand. Then it expands the tip of its foot to become a kind of anchor and simply pulls the rest of its body, shell and all, down through the sand.

The other large bivalve in the muddier sands is the soft-shelled or long neck clam, *Mya arenaria*, but it is more typical of mud flats (see chapter 4).

DEPOSIT FEEDING POLYCHAETE WORMS

Polychaete worms are segmented and have paddle-like or bristle appendages called parapodia on the sides of each segment. Though a few species of polychaete worms that live in tubes or burrows in the sand of sheltered beaches and flats may filter the water for food, the commoner species are deposit feeders which have evolved a variety of methods of eating the sediment.

One of the more remarkable of these is *Pectinaria gouldii*, which lives in a cone-shaped tapered tube made up of a single layer of quartz sand grains glued together. The tube of an adult may be 2 inches (5 cm) long, and the animals may be as dense as 20 to 30 per square yard. *Pectinaria* burrows at an oblique angle upside down in the sand, its head at the larger, lower end of the conical tube. It carries sediment to its mouth on long, ciliated tentacles. The sediment is transported through the worm's gut as well as between the worm's body and tube and ejected out the hole at the upper, tapered end of the tube which opens onto the sand surface. The worm is therefore constantly excavating sand from below the surface and cleaning it of food as it passes through its gut. The small excavated caverns continually cave in and are refilled by sediment from the sides and from above. If the digestible organic material is not replaced rapidly in the sand, *Pectinaria* must move on to a new spot to burrow and feed.

44. During feeding, the polychaete worm *Pectinaria gouldii* sucks in sand and food with its ciliated tentacles.

The bamboo worm, *Clymenella torquata*, is another species which builds a tube of sand for itself and lives upside down. Its tube is vertical, not oblique, however, and can be 8 inches (20 cm) long, sticking up a little above the surface of a sandflat. The worms can also be very dense, often with as many as 500–600 per square yard (m²), and in fact a patch with 150,000 per m² has been described. The bamboo worm, so named because of the long thin segments of its body, ingests sediment at a depth of 3 to 4 inches (7.5 to 10 cm) and discharges undigested sediment at the surface. Water flows in replacing the ingested sand, and the sand itself may become saturated and porous wherever large aggregations of the worm occur.

Probably the largest and most familiar of the deposit feeding polychaete worms that burrow in sand is the lugworm, *Arenicola marina*, which grows to a length of about 8 inches (20 cm). It burrows in a wide variety of substrates which range from muddy sand to sand mixed with gravel, and its burrows are easily identified by their conical piles of defecated sediment. The lugworm digs a U-shaped burrow most of whose walls it impregnates with secretions to keep them from collapsing. The lugworm draws water down the tail shaft of the burrow and not only gets its oxygen from the current but also uses the current to soften the sand in the very loosely built head shaft of the burrow. As the water

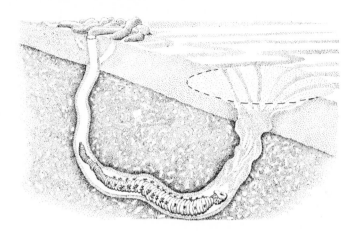

45. The lugworm *Arenicola marina* usually has a pile of castings at the tail shaft of its U-shaped burrow.

is forced up the head shaft, sand continually sinks down into it. The lugworm eats the sand at the bottom of the head shaft, and backs up the tail shaft to discharge undigested sand at the surface. It may stay where it is, working a single burrow for several weeks at a time, before moving on to a new spot. The water in a burrow stranded by low tide is likely to become stagnant, and lugworms are capable of some limited aerial respiration.

OTHER DEPOSIT FEEDERS

In many sheltered beaches and sand flats, marine relatives of the terrestrial earthworm are often abundant. These are oligochaete worms, segmented like polychaete worms but completely devoid of the segmental appendages or parapodia. The marine oligochaetes are different species of tubificids most of which are thin, under 1/16 inch (1.6 mm) in diameter and as long as 2 to 3 inches (5 to 7.5 cm). Tubifex worms are gregarious, eat sediment the way earthworms do, and can tolerate polluted and stressful conditions.

One bivalve mollusk, *Tellina agilis*, which may be common in some sandy tidal flats, differs from other intertidal bivalves in that it is a deposit feeder. It is small, growing to little over half an inch (12.5 mm) wide. Instead of sucking water in one of its siphons and filtering the water for its suspended food, it has a long, prehensile siphon which it uses to vacuum up the detrital deposit lying on the surface of the sediment.

Frequently burrowing under the surface of the sand or muddy sand is a small sea cucumber, *Synapta inhaerens*, which looks like a worm but like all sea cucumbers is closely allied to starfish and sea urchins. It may be as long as 7 inches (17.5 cm) yet only half an inch (12.5 mm) in diameter, and it feels very flimsy and breaks apart easily. Rather like *Tellina agilis*, it picks up surface detritus with its tentacles and withdraws beneath the surface when disturbed or when the tide drops past it.

Invertebrate Predators

A variety of invertebrates come in with the tide to prey upon the burrowing worms, mollusks, amphipods and other animals, and in some cases to prey upon each other. Crustaceans are particularly common, for they can move quickly and are not likely to be stranded by a dropping tide. Sand shrimp, *Crangon septemspinosus;* green crabs, *Carcinus maenus;* and where it is warm enough even horseshoe crabs, *Limulus polyphemus*, may all forage over a tide-covered sheltered beach or sand flat, but they are more typically subtidal predators (see chapters 4 and 5). However, several other predators are quite likely to remain buried on a beach when the tide drops past them, and these include several worms and the moon snails.

PREDATORY WORMS

Two relatively similar polychaete worms that burrow in Boreal sand flats and sheltered beaches as well as in subtidal sediments are quite voracious predators. *Nereis virens*, the clam worm, is the larger of the two, reaching lengths of 2 to 3 feet (60 to 90 cm), though smaller individuals are far more common, and its color is a beautiful opalescent green or pink. *Nephtys caeca*, the red-lined or sand worm doesn't grow as large and isn't as colorful, but its predatory habits are similar. Both worms prey on the other burrowing animals, including smaller individuals of their own species.

152   BEACHES AND SAND DUNES

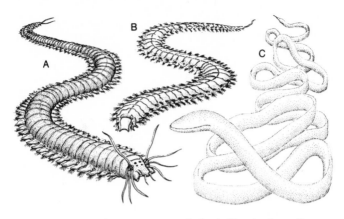

46. Voracious predatory worms include A. *Nereis virens* B. *Nephtys caeca* and C. *Cerebratulus lacteus*.

They may forage in the sand or swim over the surface in search of prey. When either of these worms detects prey, it rapidly everts its pharynx or proboscis, at the end of which is a fine pair of jaws, seizes the prey in its jaws and then retracts the proboscis again, drawing the prey to its mouth. When the tide drops the worms either remain buried in the sand or they swim out with the tide to forage elsewhere. Both species are also the prey of other predators, especially crustaceans, fish and birds, and they are avidly dug and sold by humans for fish bait.

The ribbon worm, *Cerebratulus lacteus*, also burrows in intertidal and subtidal sand and muddy sand, preying upon other burrowers and foraging over the surface when the tide is high. It may be 3 feet (1 m) or more in length, and though its habits are similar to those of the predatory polychaetes, it actually is a simpler kind of worm called a nemertean. It lacks the segments, parapodia and other features which distinguish the polychaetes, but it does have a remarkable proboscis which it can evert in order to capture prey.

THE MOON SNAILS

Moon snails are large burrowing predators which plow along just beneath the surface of the sand, preying upon small bivalve mollusks. They forage in the low intertidal as

47. The moon snail *Lunatia heros* forages for prey in the sand and lays its eggs in a fragile sand collar (background).

well as the subtidal sand, creeping along on an immense slimy foot which rather surprisingly can be fully retracted into the shell if need be. The northern moon snail, *Lunatia heros*, is especially common along the Boreal coast, its shells cast up on virtually any beach, sheltered or exposed. When it comes across a bivalve, the moon snail engulfs the bivalve in its huge foot and proceeds to bore a neat hole into one of the shells of the bivalve and then suck out the soft tissue inside.

Moon snails, including *Lunatia heros*, are also well known for the way they lay their eggs. The eggs are laid into a collar made of sand grains wrapped around the parent. As a result, each egg is surrounded by a thin layer of fine sand grains, and there are likely to be thousands of eggs in any one sand collar. The collar, which protects the eggs from predators, is left on the bottom. The embryos pass through the planktonic larval stages of most other marine snails while still in the collar, and hatch out as tiny snails. Sand collars too are cast up onto beaches by the waves, and are a familiar but transient member of the jetsam, for they dry out and crumble out of water.

Moon snails may prey so selectively on certain mollusk species that they eliminate them from the area and are forced to prey on other species instead. Because they plow up so much sediment, moon snails also destroy the tubes of tube-building polychaete worms. Where moon snails are common, mollusk and polychaete diversity decreases.

Vertebrate Predators: The Shorebirds

Shorebirds, with their long bills and long legs, are especially well adapted to finding and capturing the small animals which burrow in the soft intertidal substrates of the coastal beaches, sand flats, and mud flats.

Few shorebirds overwinter on the Boreal coast, for winter ice and cold forces much of their prey too deep into the sand or mud for the birds to reach them. Instead, the shorebirds winter along the shores of the Gulf states, the Caribbean islands, Central and South America, to the far end of Argentina and Chile. Every spring, however, the adults of the many shorebird species fly north on some of the longest migrations conceivable, heading for the arctic and subarctic tundra, meadows and bogs to breed there in the northern summer.

One of the routes the shorebirds follow north is along the Atlantic coast of North America. They first reach the southern parts of the Boreal coast in mid-April, and the last have flown north of the region by late May. For a short month or two they breed, and then in early July the first migrants turn up again on the Boreal coast, heading south once more. The southward migration is a slow one, and shorebirds are not uncommon on Boreal shores until October. Though they sometimes occur in quite large numbers during the peak times of their migrations, their populations are still but small fractions of what they once were. During the late decades of the last century they were hunted perilously close to extinction, and though they have now been protected for many years, some species such as the Eskimo Curlew which were once exceedingly common are still only rarely seen on the Atlantic coast.

The shorebirds migrate to the arctic tundra to breed because of the abundant space and food (and few competitors) they find there. Predation pressure may be less than in more temperate regions but it is still enough that the shorebirds protect themselves and their young by camouflaged coloration of nest and eggs, by cryptic plumage of young and adults, and by distracting behavior by adults to draw attention away from nest and young.

The food shorebirds rely most on in their breeding grounds is insects. Though the insects are certainly abundant during the short arctic summer, they are not unlimited. Young shorebirds are able to feed themselves within an hour or two of hatching, and they prey upon the adult insects running about on the surface of the ground. In some species of shorebirds, one parent often leaves the breeding grounds soon after the young hatch, leaving the other parent to watch over the young but also reducing the competition for the insect prey. When the young need less guarding, the other parent often leaves as well, and parents may arrive on the Boreal coast on their southward migration a month or two ahead of their offspring.

Because the southward migration is spread out over several months, the coastal habitats are not overwhelmed by the predatory shorebirds, and there is ample food for all. The various shorebird species also have preferences for different kinds of substrates, some selecting ocean beaches, others sand or mud flats, others pebble beaches. Some feed from the sand surface, others with longer bills feed at greater depths below the surface, some even feed from shallow water over the flats. As a result, though they are all shore feeders, they have evolved ways of specializing on certain subhabitats, and have reduced and sometimes eliminated competition with each other for the same food sources.

As many as 5000 shorebirds may forage daily on a single large sand flat at the height of the migration, especially along southern parts of the Boreal coast. Though a variety of species are likely to be present, four species are especially common: sanderlings, *Calidris alba;* semipalmated sandpipers, *Calidris pusilla;* short-billed dowitchers, *Limnodromus griseus;* and black-bellied plovers, *Pluvialis squatarola.* Generally, they prey most on whatever is most abundant in the sand. Few adult prey escape, and the diversity of the various prey species is considerably reduced where shorebird populations are large. Worms such as *Clymenella torquata* and *Nereis virens* are eaten, along with the bivalve *Tellina tenuis*, the sand shrimp, *Crangon sep-temspinosus*, and the abundant burrowing haustoriid amphipods. Surprisingly, the little bivalve, *Gemma gemma*, though likely to be abundant in the sand flat is not much preyed upon, and must somehow be unpalatable for the shorebirds.

The Piping Plover. The piping plover, *Charadrius melodus*, is the only shorebird that breeds along the sandy beaches of most of the Boreal coast. Other plovers nest farther north or farther south, but the piping plover alone breeds from Newfoundland and the Magdalen Islands in the Gulf of St. Lawrence south beyond the limits of the Boreal region to Virginia. During the breeding season it has a black frontal band and a black collar, but otherwise looks like its sand background. After overwintering along the shores of the southeastern and Gulf states, it migrates north in early spring, arriving on Cape Cod by early April, and on the shores of Nova Scotia and Sable Island a few weeks later. Males establish and defend territories over the belt of sand bordering the ocean where beach grass grows only sparsely. Each male advertises his territory and attracts a female with a twittering display flight. When a female joins him, they court, dig a nest depression in the sand, and mate.

Like all other shorebirds, the female piping plover lays

48. The piping plover lays its eggs in a shallow nest depression in the sand.

four eggs in the nest. The parents share the incubation of the eggs and then the guarding of the hatched young. Within several hours of hatching the young have left their nest and have begun to forage. Gradually they come to feed in the manner of their parents, bobbing a little as they run, stop, look, stab and swallow, and then run on again. And gradually they develop the soft, musical moan which gives the bird its name. Both young and adults slowly migrate south during the autumn.

The Ringed Plover. Its single dark chest band distinguishes the ringed or semipalmated plover, *Charadrius hiaticula*. Though it breeds in the Arctic, it also breeds as far south as the Magdalen Islands in the Gulf of St. Lawrence and Sable Island off Nova Scotia. It often associates with the sandpipers on the beaches and sand flats, but it also forages on mud flats and salt marshes. Some individuals still remain on the Boreal coast well into October, though they may be flying as far as Argentina for the winter.

The Black-bellied Plover. The black-bellied plover, *Pluvialis squatarola*, is the largest of the plovers to migrate along the Boreal coast, easy to recognize in spring by its truly black breast and black side of its head. Between spring and late summer migrations, nonbreeding individuals may forage along the Boreal sand flats as well as the mud flats and salt marshes. The breeding individuals continue on to the Arctic, and all migrate south during the autumn to spend the winter somewhere between the southern states and Peru.

The American Golden Plover. Almost eliminated by hunters during the last century, golden plovers, *Pluvialis dominica*, only touch down on the Boreal coast in Nova Scotia in late summer during their migration south. Astoundingly, the golden plovers then fly out of sight of land south over the Atlantic Ocean to the northeast coast of Venezuela, and continue on to Argentina. Like other shorebirds, golden plovers can swim and are able to rest en route if they need to. Their ability to navigate is impressive. Golden plovers are black-bellied in spring but molt to more cryptic colors by autumn, and are not as gray as the autumn version of the black-bellied plover.

The Ruddy Turnstone. The ruddy turnstone, *Arenaria interpres*, is a colorful plover in springtime, with its black and white breast and head, and warm brown back. In fall it is grey and cryptic, but still has a darker breast than most species. Ruddy turnstones often migrate in large flocks between breeding and wintering grounds, flying almost as far as golden plovers. Those which follow the Boreal coast north or south seek out stony and sandy beaches and sand flats, and may even forage on rocky promontories. Other shorebirds pick prey from the surface of the substrate or stab into the substrate after their prey; turnstones flip stones over, push stones or seaweed aside even with their breasts, and excavate head-sized holes in sand flats, all the while snapping up the small worms, crustaceans and mollusks they expose in the process.

49. The ruddy turnstone actually flips rocks over in its search for food.

Sanderling. Of the various sandpipers that migrate along the Boreal coast, sanderlings, *Calidris alba*, are probably the most familiar. Adults in spring plumage have a rusty brown color to them, but otherwise the birds are pale and cryptic against the sand. Sanderlings are gregarious and particularly common along ocean beaches where even in stormy weather they run along the edge of the waves, stabbing rapidly into the soft wet sand with their bills and snapping up whatever the waves leave behind. Like the other shorebirds, they move south of the Boreal region for the

winter. Some migrate as far as Chile; a few remain on the
ocean beaches not far south of Cape Cod. In parts of its
Arctic breeding range food is abundant enough that the
female sanderling has sufficient energy to lay more than one
set of eggs, and then she leaves her mate to incubate a first
brood of four eggs while she lays and incubates a second set
of four.

50. Sanderlings are a common sight at wave-pounded beaches,
darting along at the edge of the waves as they forage in the wet
sand.

The Dunlin or Red-backed Sandpiper. In spring
plumage, the reddish back and black breast patch make
dunlins, *Calidris alpina*, easy to recognize. In fall, when
they are as cryptic as the other shore birds, the long, heavy
and curved bill is the distinctive feature. Dunlins forage on
ocean beaches as well as on sand flats and mud flats of the
Boreal coast, though only during their southward fall migration. They winter just south of the Boreal region and as far
as the Gulf states. As a result, their migration is considerably shorter than that of most other shorebirds which breed
in the Arctic. Sluggish, approachable and gregarious birds,
dunlins barely survived the days of unlimited hunting of
shorebirds, and their recovery has been slow.

The Knot. Red-breasted in spring plumage and as
large as a black-bellied plover, the knot, *Calidris canutus*,
is a very striking sandpiper. Its migration rivals that of any

shorebird for length. Knots forage on sandy and pebbly beaches and on sand flats, picking prey off the surface of the sand.

The Semipalmated Sandpiper. A very cryptic bird even in spring, the semipalmated sandpiper, *Calidris pusilla*, is one of the more common shorebirds along the coast. It chases waves in and out on ocean beaches and, unlike the sanderling, it also forages on sand flats and even on mud flats. It breeds mainly in the Arctic and subarctic as far south as some of the tundra-like terrain of Newfoundland.

The Least Sandpiper. The least sandpiper, *Calidris minutilla*, looks a great deal like the semipalmated sandpiper, and though it too forages on beaches and sand flats, it is more common on mud flats and salt marshes. Like the ringed plover, its breeding range extends south to the Magdalen Islands in the Gulf of St. Lawrence and Sable Island off Nova Scotia. Its winter range is from the southern states to Brazil.

The Spotted Sandpiper. The spotted sandpiper, *Calidris macularia*, is renowned for the way it teeters up and down while foraging. It breeds all over North America provided it is somewhere near water. Like other shorebirds it can swim when necessary, and it can even dive beneath the surface to protect itself. Along the Boreal coast it regularly breeds near pebble beaches and on coastal islets. It migrates south in autumn, wintering from the southern states to Brazil.

51. Short-billed dowitchers frequent sand flats and mud flats where worms, a staple of their diet, are plentiful.

The Dowitcher.   The dowitcher, *Limnodromus griseus,* is a larger shorebird. Its long bill and chunky body are rather snipelike. Dowitchers forage in the shallow water trapped on sand flats and mud flats, often submerging their heads completely as they dig for worms in the water. Dowitchers breed north of the Boreal region as far as the Arctic, and winter from the Gulf coast to Brazil.

Other Vertebrate Predators

A number of species of fish and other birds also prey upon the worms, mollusks and crustaceans burrowing in the sand, as well as on the worms and crustaceans foraging over the sand when the tide is high. Like some invertebrate predators, a variety of fish, including the winter flounder, *Pseudopleuronectes americanus,* the little skate, *Raja erinacea,* and a few smaller species may swim in and out with the tide, but they are more typically subtidal predators (see chapter 5).

Diving ducks and a few seabirds also forage on or over the beaches and sand flats at different tides and seasons. Most of the diving ducks are more frequent predators of subtidal substrates (see chapter 5), and seabirds such as cormorants and terns feed in the intertidal waters over beaches only opportunistically (see chapter 6). Herring gulls and great black-backed gulls forage on all substrates, soft or hard, eating anything they can find and break open. Herring gulls are especially adept at eating the large bivalves for, as they do with any hard-shelled prey, they drop the bivalves from a height onto the beach face or nearby rock ledges in order to break the shells. Laughing gulls and common terns may rest on the more exposed beaches, but they forage elsewhere for their food.

The Strandline

After an onshore storm dissipates, veteran beach-combers like to search for shells and other treasures in the strandline, the row of seaweed and other jetsam left high on all sandy beaches by the retreating tide. The highest strandline shows the height of the last spring tide while any other lines reveal heights of other, lower high tides. The distance between the highest strandline and a lower one shows the amplitude difference between the spring tide and an average high tide.

BEACH-HOPPERS

Though some of the seaweeds in the strandline may still be alive, all other material of the jetsam is dead. However, by disturbing a bit of the jetsam a beachcomber is usually bombarded by life in the form of beach-hoppers or sand fleas that burrow into the moist sand under the jetsam. These semi-terrestrial talitrid amphipods include *Orchestia*, *Talitrus* and *Talorchestia* species, all of which are very closely related.

The beach-hoppers are compressed laterally and their backs are curved, giving them a shrimplike appearance. They grow to ½ inch or more (1 to 2 cm) and live for 12 to 18 months. Though they seem to be almost terrestrial, living only in the sand under the jetsam above the high tide mark, they have not made a complete transition to land, for they must have humid air for respiration. The sand in which they live is kept moist by the jetsam covering it. As another adaptation to prevent desiccation the talitrid amphipods are nocturnal: they leave their moist sand burrows to feed when the drying sun will not affect them. However, when the jetsam is disturbed in daylight hours, the small crustaceans can jump up to several feet (1 m), a remarkable distance in relation to their body length.

The beach-hoppers emerge at dusk to feed on the detritus or dead plant and animal matter of the jetsam. These amphipods breed in the spring and summer. Each female produces four broods of 12 to 18 eggs which are held in the brood pouch during development. While she has young in her brood pouch, a female remains in her burrow. The young of a summer do not reproduce until the following year and they die in the autumn or winter after one season of reproduction.

Given the fact that certain talitrid amphipods drown if they are submerged too long or suffocate if the air is not humid enough for respiration, their habitat becomes a highly restricted and narrow zone. Beach-hoppers maintain proper position on the beach by using astronomical cues and sun angle to remain at the right beach level for survival.

THE JETSAM

The jetsam is composed of both plant and animal material and gives an indication of subtidal life that is otherwise difficult for people to glimpse. Its components may come from the intertidal or from shallow areas just offshore or it may have been washed ashore from far out to sea.

The tangle of plants in the jetsam usually includes several of the rockweeds and kelps. The large kelps have often been torn off their substrate. If the kelp has recently been washed ashore it is possible to find members of the holdfast community still present, including small mussels and clams and possibly a small starfish. The salt marsh grasses, *Spartina alterniflora* and *S. patens*, and the subtidal eel grass, *Zostera marina*, are often in the jetsam as well as clumps of Irish moss, *Chondrus crispus;* sea lettuce, *Ulva lactuca;* dulse, *Rhodymenia palmata*, and in the southern part of the region, *Codium fragile*, a fleshy green seaweed which is slowly spreading northward. On Cape Cod beaches, strands of *Sargassum* weed also occur.

Distributed in the plant material are shells of both bivalves and snails. Though fragile, the small *Tellina agilis* shells can sometimes be found along with the sturdier periwinkles, *Littorina* species, and the dogwhelk, *Thais lapillus*. Translucent jingle shells, *Anomia simplex*, may be found free or still attached to a rock or another shell. Bay scallops, *Aequipecten irradians*, and the slipper limpet or boatshell limpet, *Crepidula fornicata*, are especially common in the southern end of the Boreal zone as are the triangularly shaped bivalves, the astartes. The bay scallops may often be covered with the twisted calcareous tubes of the worm *Hydroides dianthus*.

Large horse mussel shells, *Modiolus modiolus*, as well as smaller blue mussel shells, *Mytilus edulis*, are common in many strandlines and oyster shells, *Crassostrea virginia*, with their irregular shapes can be present as well. The quahog or hardshell clam, *Merceneria merceneria*, with its purple tints; the surf clam, *Spisula solidissima*, and the soft-shell or steamer clam, *Mya arenaria*, are often found, bleached and fragmented to such a degree that identification is impossible. The false angel wing, *Petricola pholadiformis*, and the razor clam, *Ensis directus*, are easier to identify, though finding any of the shells intact can be difficult.

Three large snails are often part of the jetsam—either with the presence of their shells or of their egg cases. Rarely are egg cases and shells found together. The rounded moon snail, *Lunatia heros*, shell can be up to 4 inches (10 cm) and the 2 to 3 inch (5 to 7.5 cm) high sand collar which contains its eggs becomes very fragile as it dries out. The waved whelk, *Buccinum undatum*, is between 2 and 3 inches (5 to 7.5 cm) in size and its eggs occur in masses of several hundred egg cases, each about ½ inch (1 cm) in length. Sailors formerly used these egg case masses as soap, for they produce a fine lather when scrubbed. The channeled whelk, *Busycon canaliculatum*, grows to 7 inches (17.5 cm) and is easily distinguished by its long anterior canal. Its egg cases are equally obvious. The egg capsules are disk-shaped and are about an inch (2.5 cm) in diameter.

52. The strandline on a beach is littered with many items, such as pieces of kelp, whelk and skate egg cases and a variety of bivalve and gastropod shells.

The Organisms on a Beach   165

A single string of capsules may be over 3 feet (1 m) long and may contain more than a hundred capsules, each attached at the edge. This necklace of parchment disks may rattle if any of the eggs have failed to hatch and are still inside the capsule. If the eggs are still present, they have certainly dried out as well.

Another egg case of the jetsam is the black mermaid's purse. Mermaid's purses are rectangular in shape with a tendril extending from each of the corners. These tendrils originally fastened the newly deposited egg case to seaweed or other subtidal objects. These egg cases belong to a skate, either the little skate, *Raja erinacea*, or the big skate, *Raja ocellata*, if they are 2 to 2½ inches (5 to 6 cm) in length, or to the barn door skate, *Raja laevis*, if they are 5 inches (12 cm) in length. In the extreme southern end of the Boreal zone these egg cases could also belong to the chain dogfish, *Scyliorhinus retifer*, in which case the tendrils are usually curled and the egg cases are about 2 inches (5 cm) long. Mermaid's purses are usually empty and dried by the time they reach the strandline.

Molts or carapaces of crabs are common in the jetsam with blue crab, *Callinectes sapidus*, casts being found in the extreme southern end of the Boreal zone and rock crabs, *Cancer irroratus*, and green crabs, *Carcinus maenus*, occurring farther north, though the green crab is found only to northern Maine. In addition, large casts of horseshoe crabs, *Limulus polyphemus*, are sometimes in such good condition that it is easy at first to mistake them for the live animal. These molts are particularly common during the summer and fall growing season.

Dead sponges as well as deadman's fingers, *Alcyonium digitatum*, wash up on oceanic beaches as do blobs of jelly that were recently pulsating moon jellyfish, *Aurelia aurita*, or Lion's mane jellyfish, *Cyanea capillata*. And sea urchin shells or tests, *Strongylocentrotus droebachiensis*, occur on most beaches, some with spines still intact or with the mouthparts called "Aristotle's lantern" still in place. If the spines have fallen off, the domed test shows the sea urchin's relation to the starfish as the holes for the tubefeet radiate out from the center top of the shell.

Though many of these shells, egg cases, molts and tests become drastically broken, eroded or bleached, good high

BEACHES AND SAND DUNES

tides with onshore winds often distribute specimens in al-most perfect condition. They're well worth searching for.

Sand Dunes

On the Boreal coast, the sandy beach and dune habitat is another place of extreme abiotic pressure for plants and animals. Pounding waves bring sand to the berm area of the beach where it is then transported by brisk onshore winds over the back beach area. The onshore winds are laden with salt spray as well and, as if these stresses were not enough, the constant movement of wind and sand over the dune field results in extremely dry-soil conditions. Any plant found in a dune habitat must therefore be able to tolerate sand movement, salt spray, wind abuse and low soil mois-ture conditions.

Dune Dynamics

PRIMARY DUNE FORMATION

The dunes which form on the backshore of a beach pro-tect the interior land from the onslaught of the physical forces mentioned above as well as from winter storm waves. Without some kind of stabilizing activity, however, the dunes would just continue to be swept and eroded by wind and waves. Dune vegetation, especially American beach-grass, is the primary stabilizer of dunes, encouraging dune growth and holding the sand in place.

American beachgrass, *Ammophila brevigulata,* is often washed onto the berm of a beach after severe winter storms. This true grass is amazing in its affinity to sand. It must be covered by an average of almost 3 inches (7 cm) of sand per year to survive. Even a single shoot of the beachgrass traps wind-borne beach sand around it. Con-trary to most plant reactions, this added sand stimulates the beachgrass to further growth as it responds by sending out horizontal runners, or rhizomes. Every 6 to 10 inches (15 to 25 cm) along the runners, more roots grow down into the sand and blade sprouts push up out of the sand. As more

53. Beachgrass is the great stabilizer of sand dunes, thriving only with continuous sand accumulation.

blades of grass reach the surface, they, in turn, trap more sand and are stimulated to send out even more runners.

The dune sand becomes locked in place by the mass of buried plants and rhizomes, while the live vegetation reduces sand movement of the surface. Dune building, then, is a result of interaction of waves which carry sand to the berm, wind which carries sand from the berm to the dune area, and vegetation which stabilizes the sand.

In the Boreal zone the strong onshore breezes and ferocious winter northeasterly winds shape the dunes. Usually the dunes have a steep windward (seaward) slope and a gentle leeward (landward) slope. This is often further augmented by wave erosion on the seaward side. Of course, prevailing winds change seasonally and it is easy to find dunes formed by northwest winds along this coast as well.

SECONDARY DUNE FORMATION

The stable topography of inactive secondary dunes leads to the initial impression that these are old primary foredunes on which plant succession has occurred, allowing shrubs and trees to colonize. However, the method of secondary dune formation is still subject to much controversy.

The old primary-foredune theory is usually rejected on the basis of landward migration evidence. With the rising sea level since the last glaciation, beaches and dunes have been continuously growing inland. If the secondary dunes were former primary dunes, the migration would have to be seaward, instead.

The most accepted theory of secondary dune formation suggests that the secondary dunes are formed by the primary dune-building process but much further back from the shore. In this model, as the secondary dune ridge formed, the primary dune ridge was beginning to be formed as well. Though not simultaneous in formation, the primary dune was beginning to be built before the secondary dune-building activity was complete.

PARABOLIC DUNES

Dunes occur in various forms. Sometimes they are quite regular in spacing and form a definite ridge, sometimes they are very irregularly-spaced hummocks of sand and vegetation, and sometimes they have a definite bow-shape to them. This last type, the parabolic dune, is bow or U-shaped with the prongs of the U pointing into the wind.

These well-defined parabolic dunes are formed by sand that is picked up from the flat depression in the middle of

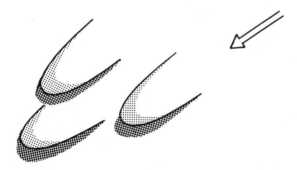

54. Parabolic dunes face U-shaped into the prevailing wind direction and migrate downwind.

Sand Dunes

the bow or U and carried to the dune crest. Because the depression is caused by blowing wind, parabolic dunes are sometimes called blowout dunes. The original blowout of a pre-existing dune may have been caused by winter storm activity or by damage to vegetation which then makes the dune vulnerable to erosion by wind.

Sand spills over the crest of the parabolic dune to a steep lee slope, called the slip face of the dune. Unless stabilized by vegetation, this slip face advances, slowly moving the whole dune leeward, often encroaching on a forest or marsh.

DUNE MIGRATION

Anyone walking along a beach on a windy day is aware that the beach and dune area is a dynamic place, with sand blowing up the beach and into the dunes. This small-scale activity is an indication of larger movement of the beach and dune field as an ecological whole. Some winter beaches, such as the one at Pemaquid Beach, Maine, reveal tree stumps and marsh peat as sand is seasonally transported offshore. This underlying peat shows that the beach and dune field have encroached upon a more inland feature, a marsh.

When sea level rises, beaches and dunes move landward. The major sand transport to back dune areas occurs during winter storms. An especially severe storm washover may deposit an inch of sand over the back dune. This inch of sand compensates for several decades of sea level rise, ensuring protection to interior land from the salt water.

In places where man has not imposed his contrivances on the shoreline, this presents no problem and dunes continue to provide protection from heavy winter storm activity. Where sea walls, houses, motels or paved roads have been built, however, man's intentions are doomed. Sand will continue to migrate, undermining buildings and covering roads. Dirt roads which run behind barrier dunes, such as the one presently at Parker River National Refuge on Plum Island, Massachusetts, can migrate with the dunes and can serve man without disturbing dune activity. Paved roads such as those in the upper Cape Cod area are unmovable.

As accumulating sand is removed by man to keep the roads passable, dunes disappear and washovers become frequent, further aggravating an already serious situation.

Cape Cod residents are acutely aware of dune migration. Much natural dune activity still occurs in the Provincelands and Monomoy Island regions. But the paving of roads and the denuding of dune vegetation have further emphasized the delicate and dynamic equilibrium that exists with dunes. Early settlers at Provincetown, Cape Cod, cut down the scrub forest which covered nearby dunes. Sand which had been stabilized began moving toward Provincetown Harbor. From 1810 to 1830 beachgrass and pitch pine were planted to stabilize the dunes: to the relief of residents, the scheme worked.

Most present-day denuding of vegetation comes not from cutting but from foot traffic of beach lovers. Although American beachgrass is an exceptionally hardy plant, if surface plants and rhizomes are broken by continuous pedestrian traffic, the plant cannot survive and dune migration accelerates. In certain parks and reserves, therefore, pathways are often periodically closed, allowing the beachgrass to revive and to maintain its role as dune stabilizer.

Zonation of Dune Plants

Once a dune has been formed, the front part of it, the foredune, is exposed to wind, sand movement and salt spray. The crest and the backdune areas become more protected from those elements. These somewhat more benign physical environments allow more species to grow. As you progress further inland in a dune field, the dunes become increasingly protected and are also able to retain greater soil moisture. The vegetation gradually diversifies to shrubs and trees, eventually becoming inland in its vegetation community.

The dune ridge and dune field can be categorized into various zones which reflect the degree of exposure to the harsh abiotic forces of salt, sand movement, and wind. Each of these zones is actually a mini-habitat in itself, supporting vegetation communities of certain tolerance levels.

Species	Primary Dune			Hollow or Swale	Secondary Dune	
	Foredune	Crest	Backdune		Foredune & Crest	Backdune & Transition
Beach-grass	X	X	X		X	
Dusty miller	X	X	X		X	
Beach pea	X	X	X		X	
Sea rocket	X					
Seaside golden-rod		X	X		X	
Salt spray rose		X	X		X	
Beach plum		X	X		X	
Beach heather			X		X	
Bayberry			X		X	
Seaside orache			X		X	
Starry false Solomon's seal			X		X	
Worm-wood			X		X	
Eastern red cedar			X		X	X
Poison ivy			X	X	X	X
Green-brier			X	X	X	X
Cran-berry				X		
Sphag-num moss				X		
High-bush blue-berry				X		
Black cherry					X	X
Pitch pine						X
Red maple						X

55. Zonation of dune plants

PRIMARY FOREDUNE

Zone 1 begins at the strandline on the beach at Mean High Water and extends to the top of the first dune. This area is called the primary foredune and is subjected to marked wind erosion, high exposure to salt spray, low soil moisture and extreme temperature fluctuation. American beachgrass overwhelmingly predominates but dusty miller, *Artemisia stelleriana;* beach pea, *Lathyrus japon-*

56. Dune plants: dusty miller is in flower in the foreground and beach pea mixed with beachgrass grows immediately behind it.

icus; sea blite, *Suaeda maritima,* and sea rocket, *Cakile edentula,* can sometimes be found, especially at more protected sites.

CREST OF THE PRIMARY DUNE

Zone 2 is found at the crest of the primary dune. There is generally somewhat less salt spray, less sand movement and less wind here. Although the beachgrass still dominates, beach pea, dusty miller and sea rocket become a definite part of the community. Beach pea is a nitrogen-fixer and as it adds usable nitrogen to the barren sand, it helps support other plants as well. Sometimes, then, seaside goldenrod, *Solidago sempervirens;* beach plum, *Prunus maritima;* salt spray rose, *Rosa rugosa;* seaside pinweed, *Lechea maritima;* and cocklebur, *Xanthium echinatum,* can be found (see plate IV). Further north on the Boreal coast, some of these primary dune species are found only on the backdune or on secondary dune formation. Also, some species may be locally absent, depending on the direction a dune faces: a dune receiving the full force of onshore winds will have less diversity than one which is oblique to them.

PRIMARY BACKDUNE

Zone 3 is the backside of the first dune, or the primary backdune. This area is further protected from heavy winds and salt spray although soil moisture level is still low. The vegetation here is not in a continuous zone like the beachgrass but rather it is in island-like groupings. This is partly due to the difference in the salt spray throughout the primary backdune. Salt spray incidence is high at the seaward edge of the zone and diminishes toward the landward edge. In addition, taller vegetation which may be more salt-resistant often provides a canopy under which low-growth-form vegetation is protected from the salt spray.

Beach heather, *Hudsonia tomentosa,* which is prolific here is a good example of a canopy-protected plant (see plate IV). At the top of the backdune, beachgrass provides a delicate but effective canopy for beach heather which is usually under a foot in height. Further down the backslope, as sand movement and salt incidence decline, the beachgrass decreases and the beach heather increases. Bayberry, *Myrica pensylvania;* starry false Solomon's seal, *Smilacina stellata;* poison ivy, *Rhus radicans;* red fescue grass, *Festuca rubra;* seaside orache, *Atriplex arenaria;* wormwood, *Artemesia caudata;* greenbrier, *Smilax rotundifolia;* and eastern red cedar, *Juniperus virginiana,* also form part of this community. Depending upon vegetation, a low impenetrable thicket can develop on the backdune, with the canopy somewhat molded by the salt spray.

THE HOLLOW OR SWALE

Zone 4 is the hollow or depression between the primary dune and the secondary dune more to the landward. This hollow, called a swale if the two dune ridges are parallel and the hollow forms a trough, is well protected from salt, sand and wind and often holds water, forming a small marsh or bog. Holly, *Ilex* species, and sea myrtle, *Baccharis halimifolia,* are found if the water is brackish.

If the water is acidic, a cranberry bog community develops. It is composed of large cranberry, *Vaccinium macrocarpon;* sphagnum moss, *Sphagnum palustre;* and sundew plants, *Drosera* species. These cranberry bogs only develop, of course, if there is sufficient water available.

If the hollow or swale is close to the water table but does not have standing water during the growing season, a highbush blueberry thicket will develop. The highbush blueberry can tolerate some salt spray but not burial by sand. Along with the blueberries, *Vaccinium corymbosum,* which dominate this community, poison ivy, sheep laurel, *Kalmia angustifolia,* and greenbrier are also found.

SECONDARY DUNE

Zone 5 is the secondary foredune and crest area. Some dune fields have only one main dune ridge and this zone would then be absent. The secondary foredune is often in the windshadow of the primary dune which reduces salt spray and sand movement. Secondary dunes are no longer active dunes and the vegetation usually progresses from the herbs and shrubs on the secondary foredune to trees on the secondary backdune. Most of the primary backdune species are found on the secondary foredune. In addition, as far north as Nova Scotia and Prince Edward Island, a high dune thicket community often develops in the salt spray shadow with black cherry, *Prunus serotina,* accounting for a large part of the vegetation. The salt spray keeps the black cherry pruned level with the primary dune wind shadow. On the tops of secondary foredunes, black cherry is joined by beach plum and Virginia creeper, *Parthenocissus quinquefolia.*

DUNE FIELD TRANSITION

Zone 6 is the dune field transition area from the secondary backdune and backdune field to upland plants, salt marsh or brackish water pools. The secondary backdune is usually covered with shrub and tree thickets, with vegetation type dependent upon soil moisture. In dry areas, the eastern red cedar dominates to the end of its range in southern Maine. In wetter areas, highbush blueberry dominates, joined by American holly, *Ilex opaca;* eastern red cedar; and pitch pine, *Pinus rigida,* as far north as Maine, and by the red maple, *Acer rubrum,* throughout the entire Boreal zone.

If the inland area is salt marsh, the transition zone can be expected to include high marsh vegetation such as *Juncus* species (see chapter 4).

Succession of Dune Plants

In more protected areas of the dune field, there is probable biotic succession of plants. American beachgrass, dusty miller, sea rocket, and beach heather are pioneer species, followed by a low thicket community of shrubs and saplings. Nitrogen fixers such as beach pea and bayberry which help support other plants also support this kind of biotic succsssion. However, in exposed areas of the dune field only those plants which can withstand the harsh abiotic pressures of salt spray, sand movement and wind action will be found. The pioneer species are very persistent in these zones.

Some plants, like the eastern red cedar, cope with these extreme abiotic factors in assuming different growth forms which are low to the ground or are burned on the seaward side but are green and growing on the leeward side. However, if salt spray is too intense, even these adaptations are not sufficient for survival and only the highly salt-resistant pioneer species remain. Plant succession in the dune field is controlled, then, by interactions between abiotic and biotic forces.

Dune Fields of the Boreal Zone

In the Boreal zone there are some excellent accessible and protected dune fields, many of which are adjacent to equivalent beach areas. One of the most outstanding is found in the Provincelands area of Cape Cod where parabolic dune belts run obliquely to the shoreline along the east coast and where the older dunes of the Mt. Ararat area are over 100 feet (33 m) in height. Also on Cape Cod, Sandy Neck at Barnstable Harbor and Monomoy Island have impressive formations. Farther north in Massachusetts at the Parker River National Wildlife Refuge on Plum Island, there is a beautifully formed six-mile-long ridge of sand dunes.

Though some of the more northern dune fields are not as extensive as those in the southern end of the Boreal region, Maine still has some good examples. Ogunquit Beach has active parabolic dunes which presently receive local protection and restricted access. Scarborough Beach State Park has a dune field which has migrated over an old marsh and which is heavily vegetated with beachgrass. Popham Beach has stabilized parabolic dunes behind its long sandy beach and Reid State Park has a primary dune ridge whose backslope leads directly into a dune field and then into a salt marsh.

In the Maritime Provinces, Kouchibouguac National Park on the Gulf of St. Lawrence coast of New Brunswick has dune fields behind its beaches, and in Prince Edward Island National Park along the northern coast of P.E.I., the dune development is magnificent and as dynamic as any on the Boreal coast. The sandstone bedrock of the Gulf-side cliffs are still being eroded at 2 to 4 feet (.6 to 1.2 m) per year, adding that sediment to beaches and to the dunes that form behind them. Blooming Point, at the far eastern end of the park, has 40 foot (12 m) high dunes which have been transported 500 feet (150 m) further inland over the last 30 years and which are still migrating.

CHAPTER IV

Estuaries

EVERY ESTUARY is the product of tidal ocean water meeting and mixing with the fresh water of a river and its tributaries. It is considered to extend seaward to a line which connects the headlands at its mouth. The seaward or lower estuary is often very similar to the adjacent marine shores, which are little affected by significant dilution of the sea water. In the other direction, an estuary is considered to extend upriver until the salinity of the water drops and remains below 0.5‰, whereupon the water is recognized as fresh. The upper estuary still experiences tidal flow, and its salinity changes as sea water flows in and out. The tidal flow in some estuaries in fact is so great that it forces the fresh water above the upper estuary to rise and fall as well, resulting in the formation of freshwater tidal flats.

An estuary is an ephemeral thing no matter where it is, and its transitional nature cannot be overemphasized. Each river carries a load of sediment that it begins to drop as its velocity decreases. Gradually the river fills itself in. Given enough time and sediment, a baymouth bar grows to enclose most of the mouth of the river, and the river behind the bar becomes so shallow that extensive intertidal mud flats develop, soon to be covered by meadows of salt marsh grasses. Finally only narrow tidal channels remain where once a deep river may have flowed.

The Boreal Estuaries

The estuaries of the Boreal coast are all young ones that have developed since the glacial ice retreated 12,000 to 10,000 years ago. The rising sea level flooded the valleys. Most of the Boreal coast has been subsiding slowly for the past several thousand years. On parts of the coast where there is little sediment available for the rivers to carry, as on the rocky coast of Maine north of Cape Elizabeth, the estuaries have remained deep, baymouth bars are poorly developed, and mud flats and salt marshes are not extensive. Where the bedrock is softer or the glaciers left a lot of till behind, as on the coasts south of Cape Elizabeth and north of Maine in the Bay of Fundy and the Gulf of St.

Lawrence, rivers have carried a great deal more sediment. Baymouth bars, sand spits and barrier beaches have partially blocked off the mouths of many of the estuaries, and shallow mud flats and large salt marshes have developed. Relative to the unglaciated coast south of Cape Cod, however, the Boreal estuaries and associated bars, mud flats and salt marshes are far less extensive, products of a still largely youthful shoreline.

Even in the deepest and most youthful of estuaries a variety of estuarine habitats exist even if some of them are very restricted in size. Intertidal mud flats and salt marshes may occur only in small protected coves, but they are still likely to be present. In shallow estuaries they may be immense. Though subtidal substrates may be hard in places, they are more likely to be soft and muddy and, in large estuaries, virtually limitless. The water flowing in and out of estuaries is of variable salinity and therefore stressful to organisms living in it, but it is also very productive and therefore attractive to those organisms which can tolerate its stresses.

The Boreal estuaries vary remarkably in size and impact. The St. Lawrence estuary is one of the world's largest, and the cold and diluting influence of its waters is felt across the Gulf of St. Lawrence, south along the Atlantic coast of Nova Scotia, and even into the Gulf of Maine. Runoff from rivers throughout the region modifies the salinity and chemistry of the waters they flow into, and the runoff also helps to drive the currents within the St. Lawrence estuary, the Gulf of St. Lawrence and the Gulf of Maine.

Besides the St. Lawrence estuary, smaller but important estuaries in the Gulf of St. Lawrence are formed by the rivers that flow into Chaleur and Miramichi bays and even smaller estuaries occur elsewhere along the shores of the southern Gulf of St. Lawrence and Prince Edward Island. The St. John River is by far the largest flowing into the Bay of Fundy, and none of the rivers to its south which flow more directly into the Gulf of Maine approach its size. Nonetheless, the St. Croix, Merrimack, Androscoggin-Kennebec, Penobscot and Saco Rivers are just the largest of a series of rivers running into the Gulf of Maine. Their estuaries, like those throughout the region, are vital for the survival of organisms that live and grow most successfully on mud flats, in salt marshes, and in the highly productive estuarine waters, and that migrate through the estuaries to breed in fresh water.

Estuarine Stresses

SALINITY

The most critical stress of an estuary as well as its most characteristic feature is its variable salinity. In the lower parts of most larger estuaries salinity is not reduced beyond the limits that most marine organisms can readily tolerate, but farther up the estuary salinity drops and fewer and fewer species can tolerate the increasing dilution. Those species that occur well into an upper estuary must be highly tolerant not only of low salinities but of rapidly changing salinities as well. Salinity at low tide may be perilously fresh, perhaps as low as 0.5‰, while 6 hours later a high tide may surge in with water of 20‰ or more.

TIDES

Tides are critical in inducing the mixing of low and high salinity waters in estuaries, breaking down the stratification caused by the seaward flow of surface fresh or brackish water and the inland flow of deeper, saline water. Since estuaries tend to be funnel shaped, wide at the mouth and narrowing upriver, an incoming tide is forced into a progressively smaller channel and its amplitude is increased. At the same time, however, the friction of its contact with the shores slows it down and eventually counteracts the funnel effect and then dampens the tide completely. Tides may remain quite strong far up the larger estuaries and their tidal currents may sculpt the shores, sort the sediment, and greatly influence the nature of the intertidal and subtidal habitats. In tidal channels where tidal currents are swiftest, the substrate is likely to be sandy or even rocky, with all finer sediment swept clean. To the sides of the channel where friction reduces current velocity, the substrate becomes increasingly soft and muddy. Intertidal mud flats develop best where current velocities are the least.

TEMPERATURE

Estuarine waters follow atmospheric temperatures more closely than do waters of the adjacent open coast. This is especially true of upper estuaries. In winter, upper estuaries in the Boreal region usually freeze over, for they are shallow and their waters are cold and dilute from the river runoff. Intertidal and shallow water organisms may be scoured by ice moving along the shore and may even be frozen into the thick ice that forms in severe winters. In summer, the estuaries are usually warmer than offshore waters, not just from the warming of surface and shallow water but from the now warmer runoff of the rivers. The warmer waters of summer act like a barrier, keeping cold water organisms in the lower estuary and in deeper water. At the same time, the relative warmth of the upper estuaries permits populations of a few warm water organisms common south of the Boreal region to survive unexpectedly far north.

In deeper and lower estuaries, the bottom remains colder than the surface throughout the summer. In autumn, the temperature of the surface water drops as days become colder, and the surface and bottom layers mix. Where estuaries are not so deep, the tidal currents may partially or completely mix surface and bottom layers even in summer, keeping the water relatively cool from top to bottom and full of nutrients.

Estuarine Productivity

Despite the temperature and salinity oscillations that make estuaries difficult for many organisms to tolerate, estuaries are exceedingly productive, more so than adjacent coastal waters are likely to be. This is so partly because the rivers carry high concentrations of nutrients into their estuaries and partly because of the upwelling of nutrient-rich deeper saline water as the estuary becomes shallower. Mixed together by the tides, the doubly enriched waters permit phytoplankton populations to remain immense throughout the spring and summer. Provided the temperature and salinity stresses are not too great, the estuary becomes an excellent nursery for the planktonic larvae of many benthic invertebrates such as worms, mollusks and crustaceans, as well as for small fish. In fact, because of the richness of their plankton throughout the summer months, Boreal estuaries are vital to about 70 percent of the fish species of commercial interest along the Boreal coast, for the fish depend upon the estuarine food for their fry, for their juveniles, and in some cases for their adults.

Salt Marshes

The grasses and other plants that form the salt marshes grow on soft, muddy, intertidal substrates mostly above the mid-tide level. They grow best in estuaries where the sediment remains protected from wave action by baymouth bars, sand spits and barrier islands, or tucked away in protected coves. The grasses are highly tolerant of inundation by water, but even the most tolerant of them needs to be exposed to air for at least half the tidal cycle. The grasses of the salt marsh are also highly tolerant of water of varying salinities. They don't grow or germinate well when exposed each tide to fully marine water and in fresh water they are quickly outcompeted by grasses and rushes of fresh water marshes. A salt marsh is strictly an estuarine phenomenon.

Salt marshes occur along many parts of the Atlantic coast as far south as Florida where they are replaced in the warm water by mangroves. They are extraordinarily extensive along the unglaciated coast between Florida and Long Island. In the Boreal region, they exist only along those parts of the coast that have matured rapidly since the glaciers retreated. The *Spartina* grasses that dominate the salt marshes from Florida to the Gulf of St. Lawrence are replaced in Labrador by shorter, tougher, more cold-resistant *Puccinellia* grasses which form the somewhat different salt marshes of the subarctic and Arctic coasts.

The Boreal Salt Marshes

The glaciers of the last ice age destroyed the salt marshes which must have been as extensive along much of the

184   ESTUARIES

Boreal coast as they are now south of it. Where all or most of the soft sediment has been scoured off the bedrock and dumped offshore by the glaciers, and where the exposed bedrock is hard and slow to erode, the estuaries have remained deep. Unprotected by baymouth bars, they lack sufficient sediment to form the shallow intertidal mud flats that precede the development of extensive salt marshes. Along the coast of Maine north of Cape Elizabeth, the Atlantic coast of Nova Scotia, the coasts of Newfoundland and the north shore of the Gulf of St. Lawrence, salt marshes are rare. In the few places where they do occur, they are products of local geological conditions, and they are usually quite small. Where erosion on some of these coastlines actually does produce considerable amounts of sediment, as on parts of the Atlantic coast of Nova Scotia, wave action, particularly in winter, is too great for the marsh grasses to survive. On much of the Boreal coast, high winter winds and waves, a lack of sediment, and the brevity of time since the glaciers left combine to prevent salt marshes from becoming established.

Other parts of the Boreal coast, however, have abundant glacial sediment and sediment eroded from soft bedrock. Estuaries there are well protected by baymouth bars, sand

57. The barrier beach at Popham State Park in Maine protects the salt marsh behind it.

spits and barrier islands, and they have become shallow. Large intertidal mud flats have formed, and on them salt marshes have had ample time to become established and grow to considerable sizes. Salt marshes lie behind the ocean beaches of southern Maine and northern Massachusetts and in several of the protected bays of Cape Cod. Excellent examples in this southern Boreal region are the Scarborough marsh in Maine, the Plum Island marsh north of Cape Ann, and the Barnstable marsh on the inner part of lower Cape Cod.

The other major beach area of the Boreal region, in the southern Gulf of St. Lawrence, also has extensive salt marshes. Particularly good examples occur in the estuaries of Prince Edward Island and Kouchibouguac National Park and in Miramichi Bay. Beaches protect the estuaries well, allowing *Spartina* grasses to grow at this very northern end of their ranges. The small salt marshes in Gros Morne National Park on the Newfoundland coast in the colder, northern part of the Gulf of St. Lawrence are formed by the sedge *Calex marina,* not *Spartina.*

Some of the largest of the Boreal salt marshes have formed not where beaches protect estuaries, but where huge tides have eroded soft bedrock to form intertidal mud flats in protected coves and bays. The tide which rushes into the Bay of Fundy is funneled and amplified to heights of about 50 feet (15 m) by the time it reaches Chignecto Bay and Minas Basin at its head. There the tides have dumped much of the fine red sediment eroded from the soft Fundy cliffs and headlands, forming particularly large mud flats. Protected from wave action, the mud flats support salt marshes that were extensive enough for very early settlers to dike and harvest. Other much smaller salt marshes occur elsewhere in the protected estuaries of the Bay of Fundy.

As the sea level has risen since the retreat of the glaciers, the salt marshes have grown inland with the encroaching sea, and have grown upward on their own peat. The salt marshes in the southern part of the Boreal region may have as much as 25 feet (7.5 m) of peat under them, indicating that the marshes were first established there about 4000 years ago when the sea was 25 feet lower relative to the land than it is now.

Stresses on Boreal Salt Marshes

Salt marshes experience most of the extremes of temperature and salinity fluctuations that occur in estuaries. Though many animals may find food and protection from predators among the blades and the roots of the *Spartina* grasses, they must be able to tolerate high temperatures and both low and high salinity levels in the tidal water as well as dilution by rain and desiccation under summer sunshine. Tidal currents do not present problems, for all but high tides are restricted to channels and creeks running through the marsh. Water washes gently over the lower marsh during each high tide, but it reaches the upper marsh areas only during high spring tides.

During an exceptionally foggy summer, the salt marsh grasses do not grow well, and the animals living in the marshes may in turn suffer and perhaps die from exposure or from easy predation. During particularly hot and dry summers, the salt marsh pools become extremely saline and even dry up, killing most of the plants and animals living in them. Less common but of potentially devastating impact are gales or hurricanes which blow up winds and waves and remove sediment and plants. The same winds may also keep the tide high far longer than usual, damaging the plants, while prolonged rain at low tide may severely harm the marsh animals.

ICE

Boreal salt marshes have a further stress they must cope with, one which more southern marshes normally lack. In the sheltered salt marshes of the Boreal region, ice covers the marshes each winter. The ice may grow to thicknesses of several feet (1 m or more) and the substrate may freeze to depths of 8 to 10 inches (20 to 25 cm); when the ice breaks up in spring it can take a lot of the marsh away with it. Severe ice scouring, something which doesn't occur south of Cape Cod, can set a salt marsh back by decades.

HUMAN DISTURBANCE

Boreal salt marshes have been rather drastically modified by human activities since the time of the early settlers.

Many of the first settlements were on the edges of large salt marshes, and the settlers gathered the *Spartina* grasses for hay for their livestock and thatch for their roofs. They also let their livestock browse upon the upper salt marsh meadows, they hunted shorebirds of the marsh, and they used the tidal creeks for navigation routes. Eventually, they cut dikes to keep the upper marshes dry, dug faster navigation channels, overcut the hay, and hunted the shorebirds almost to extinction. Parts of the salt marshes were filled in for towns to expand on and to control mosquito populations, and many marshes became badly polluted.

Most loss of salt marshes in the Boreal region is permanent. Boston, for example, has steadily built out over the salt marshes of the Charles River. Others, like the large salt marshes at East Harbor, near Provincetown at the tip of Cape Cod, and the Herring River salt marsh at Wellfleet further down the Cape, were destroyed by dikes. Wetlands, including salt marshes, are now supposedly well protected from draining and filling by the U.S. Wetlands Protection Act, but pressure to drain and fill remains great. In a few places south of the Boreal region, salt marshes are actually being replanted as a way to stabilize mud flats and increase local productivity, and perhaps an increasing recognition of the importance of salt marshes to the estuarine ecosystem will spread sufficiently to save the remaining Boreal salt marshes and to restore others.

Diversity, Productivity and Stability

Because the environment of a salt marsh fluctuates so rapidly in temperature, wetness and salinity, relatively few species can tolerate it. Those species that do survive its fluctuations may, however, be abundant. The biomass of a salt marsh is usually high. It is especially productive in grasses.

The nutrients from decaying vegetation as well as from the corpses of animals are picked up by the high tides and removed from the salt marshes, enriching the estuary. Because the salt marsh continually exports its resources, it is not a stable system.

Salt Marsh Grasses: The Two Spartinas

Cordgrass. The salt marshes of the Boreal region are dominated by two grasses, both of them *Spartina* species. Cordgrass, *Spartina alterniflora*, tolerates regular flooding and grows in the intertidal mud down to about the mid-tide level. It is the first of the *Spartinas* to colonize a mud flat, and it grows into a tall (4 to 6 ft or 1.2 to 1.8 m) stiff grass that the settlers used for thatching their roofs. It is restricted to the upper half of the intertidal, for even its roots cannot be submerged continuously.

The colonizing cordgrass plants spread by extending rhizomes. Seeds are spread over the mud flats from the colonists, and new seedlings grow where the seeds land at appropriate intertidal levels. Plants frozen into winter ice may be uprooted and rafted to new spots on the mud flat where they become new colonists. In as few as five or ten years, seedlings can cover much of a mud flat and the cover may become remarkably dense as rhizomes continue to spread and produce new plants.

The cordgrass eventually reaches upper intertidal levels and remains exposed for most of each tidal cycle. Such prolonged exposure is less than optimal for cordgrass, and the plants there become stunted and sparse. A little higher in the intertidal where only spring tides flood the sediment, cordgrass disappears completely. At this very high intertidal level, swept by high tides only every couple of weeks, salt hay, *Spartina patens*, establishes itself instead.

Salt hay. Salt hay, *Spartina patens*, is a shorter, finer grass than cordgrass, and in a mature salt marsh it forms the extensive meadows which the early settlers used for fodder and pasturage. The salt hay meadows are flat and extensive where spring tides are greatest. Though they remain dry for days at a time, the upper marsh meadows must be inundated by spring tides for the salt hay to survive. It is otherwise replaced by terrestrial and fresh water marsh plants.

SUCCESSIONAL CHANGE

The *Spartina* grasses slow the movement of tidal water and the fine sediment unloaded from it. As the years pass, the grasses grow new roots on top of layers of incompletely decomposed roots below them, and a gradually thickening layer of peat accumulates. The salt marsh grows vertically as much as 1 foot (30 cm) per year. As it grows higher, it flattens out. The cordgrass, *Spartina alterniflora,* is gradually restricted more and more to the banks of the tidal creeks, while the rest of the marsh rises to intertidal heights which only salt hay, *Spartina patens,* can tolerate. The tide is restricted increasingly to narrow creeks running through the marsh. It erodes the creek banks, producing cliffs 1 to 3 feet (30 to 90 cm) high which are densely covered by vegetation at their top but exclusively mud at their base (see plate I).

From the time *Spartina* plants first colonize a Boreal mud flat to the time a mature salt marsh has developed with its extensive, flat upper marsh meadows of salt hay, with stable tidal creeks carrying and confining tidal waters, and with cordgrass growing tall only on the banks of the tidal creeks and on the lower edge of the marsh, 500 or 600 years have probably passed. The mature salt marsh is able to grow vertically on its own peat more quickly than the sea level rises. Only when the estuary in which a salt marsh lies finally becomes silted in, or a baymouth bar completely blocks off the mouth of the estuary, do the salt marsh plants die. Then succession to fresh water and upland plants occurs.

ADAPTATIONS TO INTERTIDAL LIFE

Spartina grasses are remarkably well adapted to surviving on estuarine intertidal mud flats. The little salt that does get into the sap of a plant is actively secreted. Salt-free water is drawn to the leaves from the roots, keeping the leaves moist enough that the carbon dioxide the plants need can be absorbed from the atmosphere. The grasses avoid overheating in summer by losing heat through evaporation, and their leaves are so long and thin that rapid heat loss occurs even without evaporation. The roots of both *Spartinas* lie in mud that is rich in bacteria and poor in oxygen. So air tubes extend from the stomata openings on the leaves down to the roots, filling them with air.

The *Spartinas* survive freezing and ice scouring because

under the surface of the mud they are perennial. Their rhizomes, growing through the mud, give rise to new plants when spring returns. Above the mud surface, the plants are annuals, and they die back to the surface each autumn. Ice may scour off the annual parts, but usually some of the perennial parts remain to replace them. Each spring new leaves emerge from the mud surface, and each fall the grasses flower, though a cold, foggy Boreal summer can inhibit it. When a *Spartina* does flower, it sheds its pollen first before the female part of the flower has a chance to develop fully. It therefore cannot fertilize itself, and wind carries the pollen to fertilize other plants instead. Fertilized seeds which later fall to the mud surface need dilute salt water in order to germinate, and may have to depend upon spring rains and river runoff to dilute the tide sufficiently.

Other Plants of the Salt Marsh

Spike grass, *Distichlis spicata,* also grows on the upper marsh among the salt hay, *Spartina patens,* which it closely resembles. Spike grass can tolerate the wetter spots of the high marsh more easily than salt hay and may be the more common of the two in such places.

If there is space, black grass, *Juncus gerardii,* grows on the landward edge of Boreal salt marshes where it is inundated for only a few hours each month. *Juncus gerardii* is actually a rush with tubular leaves instead of the flat leaves of grasses.

Marsh samphire, *Salicornia* species, is a quite different plant growing on the salt marsh. It is a shrubby, swollen little green plant which projects up from the substrate and apparently makes excellent pickles. It has been called chicken-toe because of how it looks, saltwort for its taste, glasswort because it is translucent and so full of water, and pickle plant. Annual species turn red in autumn and survive as seeds. They grow slowly, can't really compete very well with the perennial grasses, and they are more common on new sand bars and trampled areas of marshes. Because *Salicornia* roots are shallow, the plants cannot grow in mud that is too soft; a strong tide can easily uproot them.

Bordering the upper *Spartina* meadow of the more southern Boreal salt marshes especially are a number of transitional plants such as swamp rose-mallow, *Hibiscus palustris;* seaside gerardia, *Gerardia maritima;* seaside goldenrod, *Solidago sempervirens;* sea lavender, *Limonium nashii;* and perennial salt-marsh aster, *Aster tenuifolius.* All are able to withstand storm-blown salt spray but not inundation of their roots by salt water.

Salt Marsh Animals

THE BURROWERS

A variety of polychaete worms, bivalve mollusks and small crustaceans burrow in the mud among the *Spartina* roots. All are more common on the mud flat below the salt marsh, and all are extremely tolerant of fluctuating temperatures and salinities. One of the few burrowers which is in fact more characteristic of salt marshes than of other habitats is the ribbed mussel, *Modiolus demissus.* It is a rough surfaced mussel and though it grows to about 4 inches (10 cm) long it isn't considered edible. Like other mussels it is a filter feeder and excretes inedible material bound in a ribbon of mucus and mud called pseudofeces. Little mounds of pseudofeces accumulate on quieter parts of the salt marsh where the ribbed mussel is most common.

GRAZING SNAILS. The salt marsh snail, *Melampus bidentatus,* is common in most salt marshes. It is a pulmonate snail, breathing air by means of a lung. Like other pulmonate snails which are almost all terrestrial or fresh water, it has lost its gills and cannot breathe directly from oxygen dissolved in water. If it is submerged in water it can breathe for an hour or two on the air in its lung and then it drowns. It climbs the *Spartina* blades a little ahead of the rising tide and descends again after the tide drops to seek protective cover from excessive heat and desiccation.

Most other pulmonate snails produce eggs from which miniature snails emerge, a necessary adaptation to terrestrial life and a not impractical one in fresh water systems. The salt marsh snail, however, produces eggs which hatch as typical snail veliger larvae which then spend several weeks in the estuarine plankton before settling on a high marsh. The veligers provide a good dispersal mechanism for the species where marshes are extensive and abundant, but are less successful where marshes are small and widely dispersed as they are along the shores of Maine and Nova Scotia. Snails one or two years old become sexually mature, and congregate on *Spartina* stems one or two days after a high spring tide in spring. They mate, lay eggs in gelatinous masses on the stems and then leave, only to do it all again with the high tides two weeks later. Like many other animals which breed in spring, the marsh snails are induced into their breeding state by the stimulation of longer daylight hours and warmer water temperatures.

Several other snails may occur on a Boreal salt marsh. The rough periwinkle, *Littorina saxatilis*, sometimes grazes in the upper meadows, while the common periwinkle, *Littorina littorea*, is often abundant over much of the marsh and on the mud flats below the marsh. Their intertidal distribution on rocky shores is similar (see chapter 2). Quite uncommon in Boreal salt marshes is the little black mud snail, *Nassarius obsoletus*, which creeps around eating diatoms from the mud surface where the *Spartina* is sparse enough for sunlight to reach the mud and allow the diatoms to become abundant. The smallest of the Boreal snails is *Hydrobia minuta* which lives primarily in the pools of water trapped on the salt marsh when the tide is low, and which is rarely larger than 1/7 inch (3 to 4 mm) in diameter.

FORAGING CRUSTACEANS. With the rising tide, larger crustaceans emerge from burrows or follow the incoming tide from the lower flats, and forage through the salt marsh. They prey on the smaller worms, crustaceans and mollusks. The almost ubiquitous shrimp, *Crangon septemspinosus*, swims in with the tide (see chapter 5). Small mud crabs such as *Panopeus herbstii* may forage around the edge of the lower and more southern Boreal marshes. Of greatest impact in the marshes south of Nova Scotia, however, is the green crab, *Carcinus maenus*, which lives in huge numbers in or near the salt marshes, either following the tide in, burrowing amongst the *Spartina* roots or retreating to tidal creeks when the tide drops. The green crab also forages over a large variety of habitats, and the southern Boreal salt marsh is just one of them (see chapter 5).

FIDDLER CRABS. Two species of fiddler crabs range north to the flats and banks of the salt marshes of Cape Cod and Cape Cod Bay. The sand fiddler crab, *Uca pugilator*, and the mud fiddler crab, *Uca minax*, both tolerate the low salinities of the marshes and they look much alike. The sand fiddler usually digs its burrows in the sandier creek banks rather than the muddier adjacent marsh flats where the mud fiddler is more common.

Fiddler crabs are highly adapted to marsh life. They have primitive lungs instead of gills and an ability to withstand prolonged submergence without oxygen. They control their internal salt balance well so that they can live in the more dilute water of the marshes, as can most estuarine animals. They can also withstand the very high salinities of the evaporating marsh pools where they sometimes forage. Both species become inactive in water that isn't really very cold by Boreal standards, and are uncommon or absent north of Cape Cod for that reason. Temperatures below about 59° F (15° C) cause them to retire to their burrows and wait for warmer times.

Fiddler crabs are justly famous for their breeding behavior. Each crab maintains a burrow where it can hide when the high tide floods the marsh. But when the tide is down and the summer breeding season is in effect, each male stands at the mouth of his burrow, waving rhythmically with his one large claw, defending his burrow from other

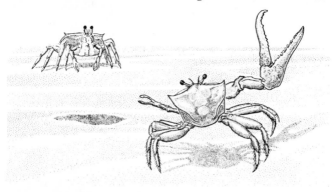

58. The male fiddler crab *Uca pugnax* beckons females to his burrow with his enlarged claw.

ESTUARIES

males and attempting to attract passing females. An attracted female is followed down into a burrow by the resident male, where the two mate. The female then leaves, and the male returns to his burrow mouth to start waving again. Each species waves with slightly different rhythms, postures and associated sounds; females are never confused by the courtship of the males of the wrong species. A mated female extrudes eggs which she carries under her tail and which, when they are fully developed, she releases into the estuarine waters. There the small larvae, dispersing with the tidal currents, develop through their planktonic stages. Those that survive metamorphose and settle to the bottom and gradually begin to forage and burrow in the salt marsh with the other fiddler crabs.

INSECTS OF THE HIGH MARSH

A fair variety of insects live in the high marsh. Marsh crickets climb around on the salt hay, *Spartina patens*. The plant hopper, *Prokelesia marginata*, sucks *Spartina* juices. Ants, beetles and springtails come down from more upland areas to forage. Dragonflies forage over the marsh after insects such as the chloropid marsh flies. The dragonflies also eat the mosquitos which can make a mid-summer high marsh extremely unpleasant for people or for their livestock.

The salt marsh mosquito, *Aedes sollicitans*, is such a nuisance to human inhabitants near a marsh that many marshes have been ditched and drained in attempts to obliterate the mosquitos' breeding habitat. The mosquitos are well adapted for surviving even such severe onslaughts as that, however. Females lay their eggs on damp mud, and there the eggs lie until heavy rains or extreme high tides form temporary pools over them. They emerge from their pools as winged adults about a week after hatching. No amount of ditching could eliminate such a transient, unpredictable habitat. In fact, ditching often produces a contrary effect, worsening the mosquito problem. This results because with the draining of a marsh, mosquito predators usually disappear. When the mosquitos do hatch, there is then no natural control of their population.

Even more bothersome to humans and the cattle and

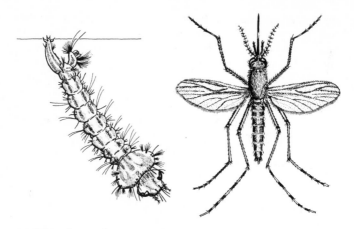

59. The salt marsh mosquito larva (left) *Aedes sollicitans* breathes at the water surface. The adult (right) can be a great nuisance to humans in a salt marsh vicinity.

horses that have been pastured on the salt hay meadows in the past are the biting flies, or greenheads, which include deerflies. As with the mosquito, only the female bites; the males suck *Spartina* juices for nourishment. A female bites by tearing a bit of skin off with her strong mandibles, and a dense population of greenheads can be torture. The females lay their eggs on *Spartina* stalks or leaves, and the larvae which hatch from them spend the next year or two foraging in the mud for prey, slowly growing to a size where they metamorphose into the winged adult stage. The adults live about 3 weeks, ample time for them to mate and for the females to lay their eggs.

Midges, which are ceratopogonids, are also very common on salt marshes. They are commonest around the sandier, drier parts of the marsh where the larvae live until they emerge in early spring as biting adults. Because they are so small, they are also widely known as no-see-ums.

FISH OF THE SALT MARSH

The salt marsh acts as a nursery for the juvenile stages of some fish species and migrant species moving up or down an estuary may stop to rest and feed in its salt marshes.

Other fish forage in with the tide, preying upon the smaller fish and the invertebrates. Several species of small fish such as the mummichog, *Fundulus heteroclitus;* the nine-spined stickleback, *Pungitius pungitius;* the three-spined stickleback, *Gasterosteus aculeatus;* the pipefish, *Syngnathus fuscus;* and the silversides, *Menidia menidia,* are all common in and around Boreal salt marshes except in winter. None of these fish are found exclusively in salt marshes, but instead occur in a variety of estuarine habitats (see Estuarine Fish section).

BIRDS NESTING IN THE MARSH

A few species of birds not only feed on the salt marshes, but nest there as well. Most also live on or near other shallow water habitats.

The sharptailed sparrow, *Ammospiza caudacuta,* nests in the salt hay, *Spartina patens,* above the high tide level, foraging for amphipod crustaceans and insects in the damp mud, leaving the Boreal salt marshes and the freshwater marshes in winter for the unfrozen salt marshes south of the Boreal coast. The seaside sparrow, *Ammospiza maritima,* nests in *Spartina* as far north as New Hampshire. It, too, winters in the more southern unfrozen marshes. Both sparrows don't fly more than a few feet when they are disturbed, and are more likely to run mouse-like among the *Spartina* plants.

The long-billed marsh wren, *Cistothorus palustris,* also nests in salt marshes, as well as in freshwater ones, as far north as the shores of the Bay of Fundy. It nests in the tall cordgrass along the edges of the tidal creeks, and must squeeze its nesting time in between successive bouts of spring tides, for inundated eggs die. Males build many sloppy nests around their territory in spring to attract females. A female then helps the male build a proper nest in the grass. The wren forages like the sparrows, after insects and crustaceans, but tends to keep to the sandier creek banks.

Black ducks, *Anas rubripes;* blue-winged teals, *A. discors;* and green-winged teals, *A. crecca,* are dabbling, surface feeding ducks which eat vegetation as well as crustaceans, mollusks, insects and fish if they can catch them.

60. Black ducks feed on surface vegetation of a salt marsh as well as on its small invertebrates.

All three favor shallow coastal waters as well as inland ponds. They nest not infrequently beside ponds near or on the Boreal salt marshes.

The willet, *Catoptrophorus semipalmatus*, is a large shorebird which nests on the upland edges of salt marshes or on high spots in the marshes. A rather gray bird when it is on the ground, its bold black and white wings distinguish it in flight. It breeds north on the Boreal coast to Nova Scotia, and like so many of the shorebirds which are known only as migrants on the Boreal coast, it feeds on both salt marshes and nearby mud flats.

Rails are usually associated with marshes, but the clapper rail, *Rallus longirostris*, which nests commonly in salt marshes south of the Boreal region, only ranges into the very southern Boreal salt marshes. More common in the Boreal salt marshes, but rarely seen, is another rail, the sora, *Porzana carolina*, which runs silently through the high marsh grass evading pursuit and foraging for prey.

Of the herons, egrets and bitterns which forage in the salt marshes, only the American bittern, *Botaurus lentiginosus*, nests there as well. Highly adapted in its cryptic coloration and habit of freezing immobile when disturbed, it can be a difficult bird to find. It, too, stalks the crustaceans, fish and insects of the marsh. In breeding season, the male gulps air, inflates his neck sack, and while displaying

ESTUARIES

his long white feathers emits a thumping mating sound which gave it its archaic name of stakedriver.

MIGRANT BIRDS

A variety of shorebirds and waterfowl stop on the Boreal salt marshes during their migrations to and from northern breeding grounds. Most of the shorebirds forage on the mud flats as well as the salt marshes (see Mud Flat section), but if the solitary sandpiper, *Tringa solitaria*, turns up on the Boreal coast at all, it is likely to be on a salt marsh during its autumn migration. The pectoral sandpiper, *Calidris melanotos*, also uncommon on the Boreal coast, is most likely to stop in the highest of the salt marsh meadows when migrating through.

Large numbers of ducks and geese settle on the salt marshes during both spring and fall migrations. Large flocks of Canada geese, *Branta canadensis*, are particularly common, and in the southern parts of the Boreal region may even overwinter, foraging on the unfrozen parts of the marshes, eating the seeds, leaves, tubers and roots of the aquatic plants. They usually feed in early morning and late afternoon, resting in midday and at night on more isolated sand bars or offshore on open water.

61. Canada geese both browse and breed on food-rich salt marshes like this one at Plum Island, Massachusetts.

Mud flats

Mud flats occur on any shore that is protected from waves or currents, where the slope of the shoreline is not great, and where there is or has been sufficient sediment available to accumulate. Mud or clay is made up, by definition, of fine particles 0.07 mm diameter or less. Because it is so fine, it is easily carried in suspension by moving water. Only when the water is moving very slowly does it dump its load of suspended fine sediment and add it to the mud it is washing over.

Mud accumulates intertidally in protected parts of estuaries that in turn are protected by baymouth bars, sand spits or barrier islands. Where the flats are shallow enough in slope for the salt marsh grasses to grow, the upper half of the intertidal mud flat is transformed into a salt marsh, but the lower half of the intertidal remains a mud flat.

Not surprisingly, Boreal mud flats are largest in estuaries where salt marshes are also large. The mud flats of the Bay of Fundy, exposed when the tide is low, are among the world's largest. In contrast, along the parts of the coast which lack much sediment and do not erode quickly, mud flats occur in protected coves and estuaries, usually in the absence of salt marshes. Though sometimes fairly large, they do not attain the size and flatness of the mud flats along the shores of the more erodable and sediment-rich estuaries.

Stresses of Mud Flats

OXYGEN

Because the sediment particles of mud flats are so fine, they compress together, and the spaces between the particles become very small. Water does not drain through the spaces easily, and the oxygen it carries can be quickly used up and only slowly replenished. In contrast to the depths to which organisms can find sufficient oxygen in sand flats and beaches, only the top 1/2 to 3/4 inch (1 to 2 cm) of a mud flat is possible to live in. Below that the mud lacks oxygen. There it is inhabited by anaerobic bacteria. It smells of hydrogen sulfide.

SALINITY

In the top thin layer of livable mud, the major stress the inhabitants face is that of salinity fluctuations. The mud flat is exposed to much more than the fluctuations of the estuarine water that covers it at high tide. At low tide, under summer sunshine, the surface can desiccate to such an extent that the salinity of the water in the surface layer may reach 50 or 60‰. A heavy rain the next night at low tide might dilute the surface layer down to 15 or 20‰ or less. The greater the likelihood of such rapid salinity change, the fewer the species that can tolerate it. The higher on the intertidal flat, the more prolonged and greater the degree of the stress is likely to be.

HEAT AND ICE

The mud flat can become hot as it desiccates in summer, enough so that temperatures might become lethal for organisms on the surface. Even more of a hazard in the Boreal mud flats is ice and its scouring action, for in a severe winter the mud surface can freeze to depths of most of the inhabitants. Ice broken and moved by the tide can simply scour the mud, with its organisms, off the surface. Recovery from such scouring occurs rapidly, often by the end of the following summer.

STORMS

Storms affecting mud flats are not particularly common, but severe storm damage can take years to recover from. The major stress comes from the wave action that gales or hurricanes can whip up. A mud flat hit by waves for any prolonged period, even just a few hours, simply loses its mud into suspension in the waves. A study of the impact of hurricane Beulah and another major storm on the intertidal mud flats of Minas Basin, at the head of the Bay of Fundy, in 1975, indicated that about the top 8 inches (20 cm) of mud was removed from the flats, and up to 90 percent of the lower intertidal burrowing organisms were killed.

STICKINESS

Mud particles tend to adhere together and though this prevents water from draining through the mud easily, it is an advantage to an organism that builds a permanent tube or digs a burrow. It is a disadvantage, however, to those organisms that depend on moving around between sediment grains or on rapidly penetrating the sediment to hide. As a result, many of the organisms that burrow in the sand of beaches and sand flats cannot survive in muddy sediments.

Diversity, Productivity and Zonation

The stresses of an intertidal mud flat restrict the diversity of organisms living there. The massively productive *Spartina* grasses are absent from the flats, along with the shade, protection and aerated substrate they provide. Nonetheless, the productivity of the mud flat is considerable, for those species that are present are often abundant. The overriding stress on the mud flat is its fluctuating salinity, and the organisms on the mud flat typically are distributed according to their abilities to withstand the fluctuations. Those most tolerant extend or occur highest up the intertidal mud flat; those that tolerate limited fluctuations extend only a short way into the intertidal from the sanctuary of the subtidal region. Even on a relatively homogeneous substrate like a muddy intertidal, zonation of organisms is just as characteristic as it is on other intertidal shores.

Microorganisms

As in other soft sediments, microorganisms are abundant in the surface layer of mud flats. Though the spaces between the particles of mud or clay are too small for larger organisms to live in, they are sufficient for diatoms, dinoflagellates and blue green algae. These survive to a depth of 1/2 inch (1 cm) where they have oxygen and where enough light penetrates for them to be able to photosynthesize. Small ciliated protozoans grazing on the algae and each other are also common. Bacteria that require oxygen live on the surfaces of the mud particles in the same top inhabitable layer of mud; anaerobic bacteria live deeper.

Bacteria species that don't use oxygen but need light for photosynthesis live at the limits to which light penetrates into the mud.

Middle-sized Animals: The Meiofauna

Most of the many kinds of animals which are larger than microorganisms but still less than about 2 mm long and which live easily among the sand grains of beaches and sand flats (see chapter 3) are uncommon in mud flats. The mud particles are too densely compacted for them. Nematodes are the major exception, for these very slender primitive worms are not limited by the size of the spaces between particles. They simply push the particles aside and burrow around preying on other small animals.

The abundance of a variety of species of nematodes on a mud flat can be staggering, for densities of as many as 2,000 per square inch (6.25 cm^2) surface area at the mid-intertidal level are not unrealistic. Species are common at different intertidal levels and in different seasons, though late summer is the time of greatest overall density. Because of their ability to burrow, nematodes can migrate down into the mud beyond the impact of severe temperature and salinity fluctuations. They can tolerate a lack of oxygen for remarkably long periods and have been found at depths of as much as 6 inches (15 cm) where certainly no other small animals can survive.

Burrowing harpacticoid copepods which dominate the meiofauna of sandy intertidal areas still occur in mud flats as well. Only the smaller species can burrow in mud successfully, however, and they are considerably less frequent, even in muds that are not too fine, than burrowing amphipods are in sand. The species burrowing in mud are most abundant in spring and are hardest to find in early winter.

Macroalgae

Though large algae are uncommon on soft substrates because of their need for a hard surface to attach their holdfasts to, some free-living species or free-living variants of attached species are able sometimes to survive on mud flats. Wave action and tidal currents there are too weak to sweep the algae away as they would be swept from sand flats or beaches.

Several species of green macroalgae, for example, grow successfully on the mud flats. The most likely species are *Chaetomorpha, Enteromorpha* and *Ulva* which are often more common on rocky shores (see chapter 2). Like all green algae, they are annuals, and they are most likely to occur on the mud flats in late winter and spring. They are able to live in the harsh environment of a mud flat because they can tolerate greater dilution by fresh water and more desiccation and freezing than can most other macroalgae.

The brown rockweeds which so thickly cover the rocky intertidal shores are not unexpectedly rare on mud flats except where they may have a precarious hold on the occasional rock sitting on the mud. One form of one of the brown rockweeds, *Ascophyllum nodosum,* may occur unattached on the mud, however. *Ascophyllum nodosum* normally grows long, is strongly attached by a holdfast to a rock surface, and has many air bladders to keep its blades floating when the tide rises (see chapter 2). The form of *Ascophyllum nodosum* which sometimes lies unattached on mud flats is much shorter, is highly branched, lacks air bladders and reproductive receptacles, and just rolls around in clumps on the surface of the mud when the tide rises.

Even when one or more of these macroalgae is present on a mud flat, the flat still appears essentially devoid of plants, for the algae are transient or ephemeral at best and are never more than locally common.

Invertebrate Macrofauna

AMPHIPODS.The burrowing haustoriid amphipod crustaceans of the sand flats and beaches are much less common in mud flats because the stickiness and fineness of the mud particles makes penetration difficult. Of the several common tube-builders on the Boreal coast, *Corophium volutator* is the one most likely to live on the estuarine mud flats as well as in the subtidal mud. It is small, up to 1/3 inch (8 mm) long, and each builds a U-shaped burrow and keeps a current of water circulating through the burrow from which it gets a fresh supply of oxygen. Populations as dense as 40,000 animals per square yard (0.8 m²) have been discovered. The amphipods eat detritus for the most part, often leaving their burrows to forage. Males also leave their burrows to find females, breeding throughout the summer months. The young leave their mothers' brood pouches looking and acting like miniature adults, and live about a year. *Corophium volutator* and related species are the dominant prey of the shorebirds.

BURROWING POLYCHAETE WORMS. A considerable number of polychaete worms live in the intertidal flats. Most of them live in the subtidal mud as well, but all of them can tolerate the usual estuarine fluctuations of temperature and salinity. Some are very similar to species living in the sand flats. The predatory species *Nephtys incisa* and *Nereis diversicolor* differ from their sand flat counterparts primarily in their ability to tolerate very low salinities and the oxygen-poor conditions of mud substrates.

Also common in the Boreal mud flats are very slender polychaete worms called thread worms which feed much in the manner of earthworms, eating the mud and eliminating all but the digestible organic material it contains. The most likely species in the Boreal mud flats are *Capitella capitata*

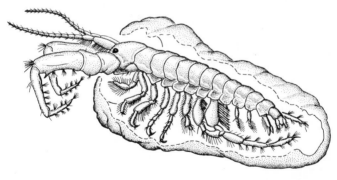

62. The tube-building amphipod *Corophium volutator* is common prey of shore birds of the mud flats.

and *Heteromastus filiformis,* both of which may grow as long as 4 inches (10 cm).

A particularly colorful polychaete is the terebellid worm. Two species, *Amphitrite ornata* and *A. johnstoni,* are fairly common in Boreal mud flats. *Amphitrite* burrows in the mud, leaving only its head exposed when it is feeding undisturbed; it can be difficult to find when it withdraws into the sediment. Under a rock, however, it constructs a partial tube around itself made of mud or sand and mucus. Like other species of terebellid worms, it has long white tentacles, and each tentacle is grooved and mucus-covered. Detritus and mud particles which touch a tentacle stick to it and are carried along the groove by beating cilia until they reach the worm's mouth. An undisturbed *Amphitrite* will extend its tentacles in all directions all over the adjacent substrate, reaching many body-lengths away. In vivid contrast to the feeding tentacles are the tentacle-like scarlet gills emerging from *Amphitrite's* head. When *Amphitrite* is disturbed, it rapidly pulls in its tentacles and gills.

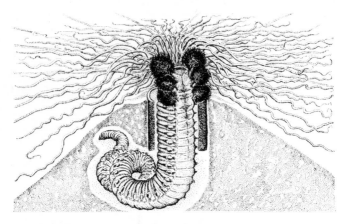

63. The ornate terebellid worm *Amphitrite* burrows in the mud leaving only its white tentacles and scarlet gills exposed.

The mud worm, *Polydora ligni,* also sweeps the mud surface for detritus. It lives in colonies in which each worm builds an upright tube and then extends its two sticky, tentacle-like palps out of the tube and over the surface of

ESTUARIES

the surrounding mud. It may even catch suspended detritus by waving its palps through the water over it. The colonies can be large ones and occur subtidally as well as low on the intertidal mud flats, and may occur on substrates of sandy mud. *Polydora ligni* is well adapted to estuarine conditions, and can tolerate very dilute seawater.

The blood worm, *Glycera dibranchiata*, is another polychaete common in mud flats and in subtidal mud, and it occurs in sandy mud as well. It is a worm remarkable in a number of ways. When it burrows, it plunges its everted proboscis into the mud, rotates its body, and screws itself rapidly out of sight. It is a predatory polychaete whose other common name is beak-thrower. It can evert its proboscis very quickly, and the four jaws at the end of the pharynx will grab and sting either prey or predator. It also is a deposit feeder, eating the diatoms and dinoflagellates in the mud around it. It is called a blood worm because instead of having proper blood vessels like most other polychaetes, the space between its gut and its skin is filled

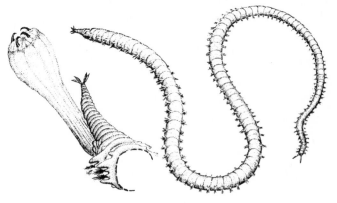

64. A favorite marine bait worm, the blood worm *Glycera* can deliver a sharp bite with the jaws of its proboscis. Detail of the everted proboscis is on the left.

with red blood. It grows to about 12 inches (30 cm) long and it is gathered from Boreal mud flats by bait fisherman and shipped in huge numbers to the coastal states south of the Boreal region. Like the other mud flat inhabitants, it also tolerates low salinity and low oxygen levels.

For a few days each spring when high water occurs in the afternoon, mature adults leave the muddy bottom and swim to the surface. Males and females swarm there, the males shedding their sperm and females swimming rapidly around the males until suddenly they rupture and liberate their eggs. A single female may release 1 to 10 million eggs. In the estuarine waters of central Maine the breeding swarms appear to be initiated by bottom temperatures reaching 55° F (13° C) or more. The females die from rupturing themselves and the males die shortly afterwards. Herring gulls and fish such as striped bass prey heavily on the swarming worms and on their remains, which litter the mud flats.

BURROWING CLAMS. Several species of bivalve mollusks are not only common on most Boreal mud flats, they are also likely to be the most familiar inhabitants. The smallest of these is the clam, *Macoma balthica*, which grows to about 1 inch (2.5 cm) in diameter, has a bluish or reddish tint to it, and can withstand very low estuarine salinities. *Macoma balthica* is a deposit feeder like the closely related *Tellina agilis* of sandier substrates (see chapter 3), and feeds in the same way by snaking its inhalant siphon over the mud surface and using it to suck up detrital debris.

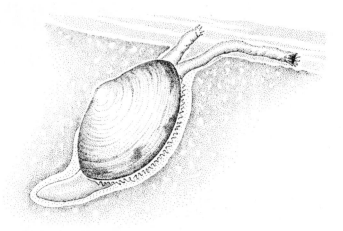

65. The small clam *Macoma balthica* feeds by sucking debris into its long, snake-like siphon.

ESTUARIES

The soft-shelled clam, *Mya arenaria*, has long been the clam most sought after by clam diggers along the Boreal coast. It lives most abundantly in sandy mud of intertidal flats and occurs subtidally as deep as 30 feet (9 m). It is known as the steamer clam after the best way of cooking it and as the long-neck clam because it can reach the substrate surface with its siphons from depths of up to 2 feet (50 cm). Because the siphon is so large, it cannot be fully retracted into the clam's shells and the shells never can close completely, giving the clam its other name: gaper.

The soft-shelled clam is a suspension feeder, sucking water down its inhalant siphon, passing it through its gills to obtain oxygen and to trap suspended phytoplankton and other food particles. The trapped particles are then transported to the mouth while the filtered water is sent back to the substrate surface thorugh the exhalant siphon. Anyone walking over a bed of clams on a tidal flat is usually squirted by exhalant water as the clams retract their siphons from underfoot.

Soft-shelled clams are able to feed and grow at salinities as low as 4 or 5‰, and they can tolerate rapid salinity change, another prerequisite of survival in upper estuaries. In reasonable environmental conditions, they may grow to about an inch (25 mm) or more by the time they are a year

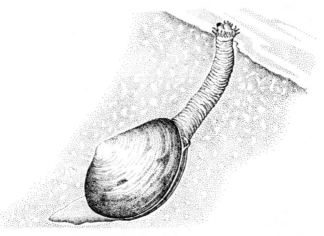

66. The soft-shelled or long-necked clam *Mya arenaria* provides the basis for the famous clam bakes of the Boreal coast.

old, and a full grown 6 inch (15 cm) clam may be as old as 10 or 15 years. Such large clams are rarely seen now on inter-tidal flats since fishing pressure is so great.

Spawning occurs when water temperatures reach 50 to 59° F (10 to 15° C) which in Boreal waters is usually in June, and the larvae disperse in the plankton for about two weeks before they metamorphose and settle to the bottom. A newly settled young clam acts much like a mussel, for it has a large foot which it uses to move around and it attaches itself to sand grains or other material in the substrate by means of a byssus thread. As the young clam grows, it loses its byssus and its foot becomes relatively smaller and increasingly useless. Gradually the clam switches to a sessile life, positioning itself vertically in the substrate and extending its siphons to the substrate surface. As it grows larger and its siphons elongate, it descends deeper into the substrate. When one is dug up it may be quite unable to rebur-row, or may take many days to do so, ample time for one of its predators to find it. Though some birds, such as the diving ducks, can dig up shallow soft-shelled clams, the most efficient predator is the green shore crab, *Carcinus maenus*. Where the green crabs are abundant, they can effectively eat all clams less than two or three years old, and can destroy a clam bed more thoroughly than can human predators.

Thick ice quickly kills many mud flat animals, and soft-shelled clams may be eliminated from some intertidal flats in particularly severe winters. The last ice age caused *Mya arenaria* to become extinct in European waters, but it has become common there again since the 17th century. Ships which accidentally or purposefully brought the common periwinkle, *Littorina littorea*, and the green crab, *Carcinus maenus*, to North America must have taken clams along on some of their return journeys.

The Blue Mussel. The blue mussel, *Mytilus edulis*, often grows in clumps on the lower intertidal parts of mud flats, and may in fact cover the lower flats. Sometimes the mussels grow in layers on each other. Mussel bars build up especially in areas where tidal current keeps them bathed in oxygen-rich water and brings them a continual supply of food. The mussels of a mussel bar in turn provide a hard substrate, free of the mud below, where animals not otherwise able to live anywhere near mud survive easily. Deposit feeding polychaete worms and small crustaceans live in between the mussels, eating the pseudofeces. Predatory polychaete worms roam around among the mussels eating the deposit feeders. The small isopod crustacean, *Jaera marina*, the limpet, *Acmaea testudinalis*, and the common periwinkle, *Littorina littorea,* graze on the microalgae growing on the mussel shells. Juvenile green crabs, *Carcinus maenus,* and gammarid amphipods scavenge for food, and larger green crabs and starfish such as the *Asterias* species prey on the mussels and other animals in the mussel bar. All of these animals are more typical of rocky substrates of the lower intertidal and subtidal habitats (see chapters 2 & 5).

The American Oyster. The American oyster, *Crassostrea virginia,* lives on very low intertidal flats and in shallow subtidal water where it often forms extensive beds. It can penetrate far up estuaries and is able to live permanently where salinities are usually as low as 12‰. Its largest and most commercially valuable populations occur in the Louisiana estuaries and in Chesapeake Bay, but it forms beds in the warm summer waters of the southern Gulf of St. Lawrence and occurs in local pockets in estuaries south along the Boreal coast. Large middens of its shells attest to its abundance on the Maine coast in precolonial times.

The American oyster tolerates siltier conditions than do most other oyster species. Like all oysters, it lies on its left shell, permanently cemented onto whatever lies beneath it. Its left shell is more bowl-shaped than is usual in oysters, however, permitting it to keep the edge of its shell higher above the substrate. Its adductor muscle is also particularly strong, and it can clap its shells closed with enough force to eject silt which may have seeped in upon its mantle.

Like other oysters, its breeding cycle is remarkable. It spawns first as a male, switches to female and liberates eggs, and continues switching back and forth throughout its adult life. In warm waters, it may switch several times in a single season; in colder, Boreal waters it is likely to switch only once a year. It ejects both sperm and eggs out its exhalent siphon, and the eggs are fertilized in the water over the oyster bed. As a female, *Crassostrea virginica* may release as many as 100 million eggs in a single season.

The eggs develop first into swimming, ciliated trochophore larvae and then into more complex veliger larvae. The veliger soon develops a foot of sorts and settles to the bottom where it crawls around in search of a suitable attachment site. Almost any kind of hard surface on the mud substrate will do, and other shells and the surface of the oyster bed itself are its most likely settling sites. Like a mussel it has a byssus gland in its foot, but the gland is capable of discharging its sticky secretion only once. When the newly settled oyster has selected an attachment site, it secretes the fluid of its byssus gland, turns to press its left shell in the secretion, and is quickly cemented permanently in place. The byssus gland soon degenerates, and a dislodged oyster is incapable of reattaching itself.

Though the American oyster grows reasonably well in Boreal waters, it doesn't necessarily spawn every year. It can feed and grow at temperatures colder than are necessary for it to produce sperm or eggs, and sometimes may spawn only during summers which are warmer than usual. In Boreal waters it grows only in summer and fall and lies dormant at temperatures below about 40° F (4 to 5° C). It has the potential to live perhaps 40 years and to grow as big as 8 inches (20 cm) in diameter with shell thickness approaching 1 inch (2.5 cm).

An oyster bed can grow quite large as successive generations settle and grow on the shells beneath them. In fact a bed can build itself out of existence by becoming too high in the low intertidal, but young oysters quickly settle new areas and start new beds. Though an oyster bed may persist in some form for thousands of years, it can be very quickly destroyed either by overfishing or by silting of the estuaries, and the disappearance of *Crassostrea virginica* from parts of the Boreal coast is likely to be due to one or both of these causes.

Oysters grow well in estuaries not just because of the relative warmth and abundant food the estuaries provide. The low salinities of estuaries prevent the more predominant oyster parasites and predators such as starfish from penetrating as far as the oysters do. The oysters grow perfectly well in high salinities, but are easy prey then to both parasites and predators. Even so, young oysters are preyed on by the green crab, *Carcinus maenus,* in estuaries where green crabs are common.

OYSTER CULTURE. The American oyster, *Crassostrea virginica,* is cultured along parts of the Boreal coast where estuarine quality and water temperatures permit. The European oyster, *Ostrea edulis,* has also been brought over to the Boreal coast for culturing, for it grows well in water somewhat cooler and more saline than the American oyster needs, and may as a result survive better in Boreal conditions.

Oysters of either species are usually grown in surface trays or in lantern nets whose mesh size depends on the size of the oysters. As they grow they are placed in trays or nets of increasing mesh diameter. Growing the oysters off the bottom keeps them free of predators and easier to service, and the oysters seem to grow more quickly near the surface. The oysters are suspended lower in the water or placed on the bottom for the winter to avoid their destruction by winter ice. American oysters are not harmed by extreme cold, and overwinter well in upper estuaries under

67. Oysters are cultured on net trays like this one in Southport, Maine, either in a laboratory or suspended in layers in the ocean.

Mud Flats

the sea ice. Young European oysters however, cannot tolerate more than a few weeks of extremely cold temperatures approaching 32° F (0° C), and sometimes need to be transplanted into deeper and more saline water for the winter.

RED TIDES

The Atlantic Boreal coast is subject to red tides whose impact on shellfisheries such as those of the soft-shelled clam, *Mya arenaria;* the blue mussel, *Mytilus edulis;* the American oyster, *Crassostrea virginica;* and the deep-sea scallop, *Plácopecten magellanicus,* can at times be quite serious. Until 1972 the Gulf of Maine had been free of red tides but the tides have been spreading south from Nova Scotia coastal water and are now reaching even beyond Cape Cod.

Red tides are the result of large concentrations of a bioluminescent dinoflagellate called *Gonyaulax,* a spherical, single-celled photosynthesizing organism. It moves itself like other dinoflagellates by means of its two flagella, one of which is wrapped in a groove around its middle and allows the cell to rotate, the other extending free and propelling the cell forward (see chapter 1). It can travel up to several feet (1 m) per hour; in summer it migrates up in the water column for photosynthesis, and down again for the more concentrated nutrients of deeper water.

When winter comes and light levels fall too low for *Gonyaulax* to photosynthesize, the cells lose their flagella and sink as cysts onto the loose flocculent layer on the surface of offshore bottom sediments. When conditions improve in spring, the cysts are triggered by a built-in annual rhythm to return to their active swimming state again. The dinoflagellates then multiply rapidly along with the other phytoplankton.

Blooms of *Gonyaulax* originate offshore but currents cause the organisms to drift inshore into the coastal bays and estuaries, and there they are fed upon by all suspension feeders, including the various bivalve mollusks which humans like to eat. *Gonyaulax* contains a toxin which doesn't effect the shellfish but which accumulates in them nonetheless. At low *Gonyaulax* densities not enough toxin accumulates in the shellfish to harm a human predator, but at higher densities the toxin becomes sufficiently concentrated to cause what is called paralytic shellfish poisoning. At even higher densities of *Gonyaulax* the water may begin to look reddish from the immense numbers of the dinoflagellates, and a true red tide occurs. Such densities are usually too great for the shellfish to handle and they are likely to stop feeding until the density drops.

The toxin of *Gonyaulax* is called saxitoxin and it acts by blocking the mechanism which normally pumps sodium out of the internal medium of nerves. (Gary Power in his famous U-2 flight had a saxitoxin suicide capsule.) Why does *Gonyaulax* contain the toxin? It appears to be a way the dinoflagellate stores the nitrogen it needs to survive the months of winter encystment. The fact that it is so toxic to vertebrates is probably accidental.

Birds of the Mud Flats

Though the ubiquitous herring gulls as well as great black-backed gulls and laughing gulls forage over the mud flats for mussels, crabs and worms, the birds most adapted for preying on the flats and along the tidal creeks are a variety of shorebirds, herons and egrets. Almost all of them also forage in any adjacent salt marshes which may be present, some forage on sand flats as frequently as they do on mud flats, and one or two species even forage on rocky shorelines as well.

SHOREBIRDS. The foraging shorebirds are for the most part migrants stopping on the Boreal coast on their way to or from their more northern breeding grounds. They include the short-billed dowitcher, *Limnodromus griseus;* the black-bellied plover, *Pluvialis squatarola;* the ringed plover, *Charadrius hiaticula;* the least sandpiper, *Calidris minutilla;* the semipalmated sandpiper, *Calidris pusilla;* and the dunlin *Calidris alpina,* all of which forage on sand flats as well (see chapter 3).

The greater yellowlegs, *Tringa melanoleucus,* and the lesser yellowlegs, *T. flavipes,* are both tall, long-legged, long-billed sandpipers that forage in salt marshes and on the mud flats of the Boreal coast during their spring and fall migration seasons. Neither species probes into the mud for its prey; instead they chase small fish and crustaceans in the shallow water. Both winter as far south as the Straits of Magellan on the southern tip of South America.

HERONS AND EGRETS.   Several herons and egrets that normally breed south of the Boreal coast wander north after the breeding season and are sometimes seen in the salt marshes and on the mud flats. The most frequent visitor is the common egret, *Casmerodius albus,* a white bird with a wing spread of 55 inches (137 cm). A smaller, less frequent visitor is the snowy egret, *Egretta thula,* which darts around in shallow water unlike other herons, chasing fish and crustaceans. Both egrets were almost completely exterminated because of the great value and popularity of their breeding plumage or aigrettes in the millinery trade and both have recovered moderately well since they became protected. The little blue heron, *Florida caerulea,* may also wander north after the breeding season, and the young of the year, which are the ones most likely to reach the Boreal coast, are white and easily confused with the egrets.

The black-crowned night heron, *Nycticorax nycticorax,* breeds as far north as Nova Scotia and the Gulf of St. Lawrence. With its thick bill and short legs (for a heron), black back and otherwise grey and white coloring, it sits with its neck contracted (unlike most other herons), and it is easily recognizable as a result. It feeds mostly at night from a variety of habitats which include salt marshes and mud flats.

68. The common egret frequently stalks its prey in salt marshes.

ESTUARIES

The Great Blue Heron. The great blue heron, *Ardea herodias*, is by far the most common heron on the Boreal coast where it hunts for food on mud flats and salt marshes as well as along other protected shores and inland fresh-water habitats. It is the largest of the herons with a wing-spread of 70 inches (1.75 m). When disturbed it jumps into the air and flies gracefully away, its huge wings beating slowly, its neck folded back so that its head rests on its shoulders, and its long legs trailing behind it.

Great blue herons eat a remarkable variety of prey, but on the coast they eat mostly crustaceans and fish. Each heron forages alone and may have a particular area along the shore to which it returns day after day. It also is an opportunistic feeder, and an extremely low tide may attract 10 or 20 birds to the same mud flat. When herring or other fish are captured in a purse seine in a quiet cove and then left unattended, great blue herons somehow find out about it, and another 10 or 20 more may balance precariously on

69. The graceful great blue heron is a common sight along mud flats as well as along rocky intertidal shores.

the floating edge of the net and stab after the passing fish.

Great blue herons leave the Boreal coast during the autumn to winter along warmer unfrozen shores. In March
they spread north again, and those that nest in the Boreal
region return to their rookeries to begin to repair and defend their nests and to court one another. Though great
blue herons sometimes nest in single pairs, they usually
nest in colonies which may have as many as 100 or more
nests. Nests are always large, about 3 feet (1 m) in diameter, and are made of sticks. A single large deciduous tree in
a dense colony may have a dozen nests on it. The early
weeks of the breeding season are raucous times in such a
colony as the birds threaten their neighbors with loud
coarse croaks and long-necked, ruffle-feathered displays;
they court their mates somewhat less violently. The guano
or excretions of the birds kill the trees over the course of 5
to 10 years and the colony slowly shifts through the available trees. When the trees have all fallen the birds are
forced to establish new colonies somewhere else. The colonies are usually in protected isolated places, not very far
from water. Along the Boreal coast some colonies are on
wooded islands, while others are on the wooded edges of
swamps or marshes.

Each pair of herons lays a clutch of four pale green eggs
and both parents share in incubating the eggs and in protecting and feeding the chicks. By midsummer the chicks
are about the size of their parents and soon after that are
able to fly and begin foraging for their own food. By autumn
they forage as proficiently as their parents along the coastal
mud flats and salt marshes.

Soft Subtidal Substrates

Much of the bottom substrate of an estuary is likely to be
mud. It is a less stressful habitat than the intertidal mud
flat, but its temperature and salinity fluctuations are still
large in comparison with those of adjacent coastal waters.

The animals that burrow in the subtidal mud, especially

in shallow areas, are for the most part the same amphipods, crustaceans, bivalve mollusks and polychaete worms that burrow in the low intertidal mud flats. Some of them are more abundant, and a few related species occur that are not able to tolerate any intertidal exposure. Quite common in the subtidal mud in the lower estuaries are the burrowing nut shells, which include the small 1/2 inch (1 cm) diameter *Nucula* species and the somewhat larger 1 to 2 inch (2.5 to 5 cm) long *Yoldia* species which are more oval and pointed at one end. All have a very strong foot for burrowing, and some of the *Yoldia* species can move quite rapidly.

Predation and Competition

Fish such as the winter flounder, *Pseudopleuronectes americanus,* and crabs such as the green crab, *Carcinus maenus,* are common predators of the shallow subtidal burrowing animals, just as they are on the mud flats when the tide is high. Where predators have been prevented from preying on the burrowing animals, the diversity of the burrowing species usually increases: no one species competitively excludes the others. This is in rather odd contrast to what happens on rocky shores (see chapter 2) and other habitats when predators are excluded, for diversity usually decreases. Competitive exclusion may be difficult in a soft, three dimensional substrate, for one species cannot crush or dislodge or smother or overgrow another as it can on hard substrates. And as any filter feeding species becomes common it is increasingly likely to eat the settling larvae of its own species. The rules of predation and competition which apply to hard substrates may not apply to soft ones.

Horseshoe Crabs. The horseshoe crab, *Limulus polyphemus,* is one of the earth's more remarkable animals. It isn't a crab or crustacean at all but is more closely related to the arachnids, which include the spiders. It has been around for a long time, essentially unchanged since Triassic times 200 million years ago. It ranges from the Gulf of Mexico to Nova Scotia, and though it is or has been abundant on the shallow soft subtidal substrates from Cape Cod south, in Maine and Nova Scotia it is restricted to the es-

70. Horseshoe crabs mate during the highest spring tides, the smaller male clasping the larger female, ready to fertilize eggs as they are laid.

tuaries where summer temperatures are warm enough for it to feed and grow.

Horseshoe crabs grow large: a mature female reaches a diameter of up to about 1 foot (30 cm) and a length of about 2 feet (60 cm). Though males grow to considerable sizes as well, they do not reach the dimensions of the females. Looking at a horseshoe crab from above, its three major body parts stand out clearly. The anterior part forms the bulk of the horseshoe shape and is the cephalothorax, covering the legs and most of the digestive and reproductive systems and all of what there is of a brain. Behind the cephalothorax is the abdomen, and the two parts are held together by flexible tissue in a kind of hinge. The five gill books lie under the abdomen. Attached to the back of the abdomen by another hinge is a spike-like tail or telson which the horseshoe crab uses for righting itself when it is tipped over. A pair of lateral eyes lie high on the sides of the cephalothorax, and a second much smaller pair of median eyes lie together on the mid-line just above the leading edge of the cephalothorax.

A horseshoe crab plows along the surface or just under the surface of soft subtidal substrates, which in Boreal estuaries is mostly mud. It preys on the abundant worms, small mollusks and crustaceans which it plows up. It lacks mouth parts but it has spines on the upper joints of its legs which it rubs together to mince its food before passing it into its mouth. Horseshoe crabs can do extensive damage to a bed of young soft-shelled clams, *Mya arenaria*.

The first pair of legs on a horseshoe crab are smaller than the rest, having small claws for grabbing and pushing prey into the spiny food grinding mill. The next five pairs of legs are walking legs as well as the chewing organ, and the last of these look like the ends of ski poles and are used to push the animal forward on a substrate it might otherwise sink into. The first pair of walking legs on a mature male have much larger and heavier claws than those of a female, and he uses them for grasping a female during the breeding season.

Each spring in the Cape Cod region and as late as June and early July in the Maine and Nova Scotia estuaries, males and females gather at the edge of the shore at high spring tides. A male grasps a female and follows her half out of the water where she scrapes a hole in the sand or mud, deposits her eggs as the male fertilizes them, covers the eggs again, and departs. The eggs develop in the damp sand or mud, diluted by rain water, baked by sunshine, inundated only by very high tides, and then hatch after a few weeks into miniature but tailless horseshoe crabs. Their tails become longer with successive molts, and like their parents they forage in the soft substrate for their food. As they get larger and older they gradually head into deeper water.

Despite its extraordinary ability to have survived essentially unchanged for such a long time, horseshoe crab populations have become severely decimated in many places in recent years.

Eel Grass.   Eel grass, *Zostera marina*, grows well in water of reduced salinity. It also grows well on shallow soft substrates in protected fully marine water, however, and since the beds are not restricted to estuaries, they are considered in more detail in chapter 5.

Soft Subtidal Substrates

Rocky Substrates

Intertidal

In the lower estuary, rocky shores are much like those of the adjacent open coast. Further up the estuary, as salinity and temperature stresses increase and water movement decreases, the diversity and abundance of the rocky intertidal plants and animals drops off sharply.

The red algae are least tolerant of estuarine conditions and are the first of the macroalgae to disappear. Of the brown rockweeds, *Ascophyllum nodosum* dominates the shore well up the estuary while the various *Fucus* species disappear. Eventually *Ascophyllum nodosum* can no longer tolerate the reduced salinity either, and only the highly tolerant annual green macroalgae such as *Enteromorpha* and *Ulva* remain.

Both the common periwinkle, *Littorina littorea*, and the blue mussel, *Mytilus edulis*, tolerate the reduced salinity far up the estuary, and the rough periwinkle, *L. saxatilis*, may even be more abundant. However, the smooth periwinkle, *L. obtusata*, and the dog whelk, *Thais lapillus*, cannot tolerate much exposure to low salinity water and are virtually absent from the upper estuary as is the barnacle, *Balanus balanoides*. The green crab, *Carcinus maenus*, abundant in the Boreal region south of New Brunswick, wanders far up the estuaries and preys on the intertidal mussels. It often remains under the rockweed when the tide drops, just as it does on marine rocky intertidal shores (see chapter 2).

Subtidal Rocky Substrates

Many of the marine animals that live on rocky substrates subtidally cannot tolerate estuarine conditions even where rocky substrates occur. None of the echinoderms, which include the starfish, sand dollars, sea urchins and sea cucumbers, or the sponges or sea squirts are able to survive significant dilution of sea water. A few other animals are very tolerant of the low salinity and high summer temperatures of the estuary, however, including crustaceans such as some of the gammarid amphipods and, in estuaries from Nova Scotia south, the estuarine barnacle, *Balanus improvisus*. Several hydroids also tolerate dilute sea water, including the wispy, branching *Obelia longissima* and especially the bushy *Cordylophora lacustris* which is really a fresh water species tolerating brackish water.

Estuarine Fish

A variety of species of fish live their whole lives in Boreal estuaries, others migrate a short distance into or out of the estuaries, and yet others migrate from offshore and from estuarine waters up into fresh water to breed. One fish species even migrates from fresh water through the estuaries to breed far offshore. Still others are neither permanent residents nor migrants but occur frequently in both estuarine and offshore waters.

Regardless of where the adult fish spawn or live, the estuary is an excellent place for their young to feed, particularly where the incoming salt water and outgoing fresh water are well mixed. There the phytoplankton and zooplankton populations remain dense throughout the warmer summer months when the juvenile fish can grow most quickly. Fish species spawn at different times and their young often prefer different habitats within the estuary, so direct competition among the fish for the available food is to some extent avoided. The salt marshes and tidal creeks are also productive places for small species of fish and juvenile stages of larger species to feed and find protective cover from their predators.

Non-migratory Estuarine Fish

A number of mostly small species of fish spend their lives in estuaries, rarely if ever venturing out onto the open coast but usually ranging far up the estuary into brackish and even fresh water.

Tomcod. Tomcod, *Microgadus tomcod*, grow to about

10 to 12 inches (25 to 30 cm), weigh up to 1 pound (0.45 kg) and look like very small cod (see chapter 7). Unlike cod, however, tomcod stay inshore in shallow water in estuaries, tolerating a very wide range in salinity. They forage on the bottom, eating shrimp, amphipods and worms. In winter they head further up the estuary into even colder water, and from about November to February they spawn. Though all fish which are permanent residents of Boreal estuaries must be able to withstand prolonged periods of cold water, tomcod are particularly cold resistant.

White Perch.   White perch, *Morone americana,* look much like the closely related striped bass, *Roccus saxatilis,* but are a great deal smaller. White perch grow to an average of 8 to 10 inches (20 to 25 cm) long and to a weight of about 1 pound (0.45 kg). They stay in estuaries behind the barrier beaches and may wander far up an estuary into brackish water. They forage in small schools after fish eggs and fry as well as shrimp and other crustaceans, staying in shallow water rarely deeper than 6 to 10 feet (2 to 3 m). Each spring white perch spawn in fresh or slightly brackish water, and as is usual with fish spawning in the rivers and estuaries, their eggs sink and stick to the bottom. White perch are so tolerant of low salinities that there are a number of land-locked populations.

Smooth Flounder.   Smooth flounder, *Liopsetta putnami,* are the smallest of the Boreal flatfish (see chapter 7). A smooth flounder lies on its right side. It grows to a maximum of about 1 foot (30 cm) and 1.5 pounds (0.7 kg) and keeps to shallow water, rarely foraging deeper than 30 feet (9 m). Like the winter flounder, *Pseudopleuronectes americanus,* it has a small mouth and preys particularly on the small crustaceans and worms burrowing in the soft subtidal sediments. Though smooth flounders do occur in sheltered bays, they are far more common in estuaries and can tolerate very low salinities. Like tomcod, they also tolerate prolonged, cold temperatures and breed in the middle of winter.

Mummichog.   Common mummichogs or killifish, *Fundulus heteroclitus,* grow only to about 4 inches (10 cm) in length and live in the very shallow water of salt marshes and the pools and tidal creeks of salt marshes, mud flats and

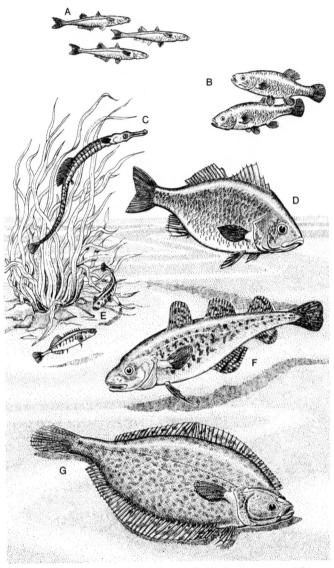

71. Small fish of the salt marsh. A. silversides B. mummichogs
C. pipefish D. white perch E. nine-spined stickleback F. tomcod
G. smooth flounder

Estuarine Fish

upper estuaries. They are remarkably resistant to highly stressful conditions of low oxygen and high carbon dioxide, for they are often trapped in small pools when the tide drops. If a pool dries up while the tide is low, a mummichog can even survive that by working its way into the damp mud. In winter time mummichogs just bury themselves in the mud at the bottom of tidal creeks. They are omnivorous little fish, eating live plants and animals and even decaying animals. During the summer breeding months, a male mummichog courts a female, clasps her and holds her against the substrate and fertilizes her eggs as she extrudes them. The eggs stick to the substrate and hatch about 2 weeks later. Partly because even their eggs are so tolerant of stressful conditions, mummichogs have been favorite research animals of embryologists for many years.

Silverside. Silversides, *Menidia menidia,* look like small smelt, growing to 4 or 5 inches (10 to 12.5 cm). They school in shallow water in the estuaries over sand and gravel substrates especially, and often follow the tide in and out as they forage for small crustaceans, worms, fish fry and eggs. In turn they are preyed upon by larger fish such as striped bass. They frequently feed in salt marshes at high tide, particularly where the *Spartina* is relatively sparse, and they often lay their sticky eggs in the salt marshes during their late spring spawning period. Though silversides can tolerate cold winter temperatures they usually move into deeper and slightly warmer water for the winter. More critical, however, is their need for temperatures to reach 68° F (20° C) for them to be able to reproduce successfully and so, though they are common in the estuaries of the southern Gulf of St. Lawrence and the coast of Maine, they are absent from the colder water of the Bay of Fundy and the estuaries of the Atlantic coast of Nova Scotia.

Pipefish. The common pipefish, *Syngnathus fuscus,* is a very slender fish which at 4 to 8 inches (10 to 20 cm) is about 30 times longer than it is wide. It is not uncommon in eel grass beds, salt marshes and under overhanging rockweed along the shores of estuaries. It eats small crustaceans such as copepods and amphipods, but itself appears to have few enemies. Pipefish breed between March and August in a manner very similar to the closely related seahorses. A female inserts her protruding oviduct into an opening in the brood pouch of a male and passes several dozen eggs into the pouch. The developing embryos get some of their nourishment from the epithelial lining of the brood pouch and hatch after about ten days. The young pipefish remain in their brood pouch until they are about ⅓ inch (8 to 9 mm) long and have used up all their yolk. They then abandon the protection of the pouch, disperse to forage on their own, and grow to sexual maturity when they are about a year old.

Stickleback. Three-spined sticklebacks, *Gasterosteus aculeatus*, distinguished by the three sharp spines they can erect along the middle of their backs, grow to about 2 to 3 inches (5 to 7.5 cm) in length. They are omnivorous, voracious little fish that live in ditches and creeks of salt marshes, brackish water ponds, protected rockpools, and around rockweed and eel grass in shallow water along estuarine shorelines. Only occasionally do any wander out of the estuaries and stray into offshore waters. In wintertime they move into slightly deeper water away from the salt marshes and tidal creeks. During the spring breeding season, males build nests which they defend against other males. Each nest is made of vegetation cemented together with mucus threads which are kidney secretions. A female approaching a nest is met by the male that possesses it; she is escorted into the nest where she lays 100 to 150 eggs and then leaves. The male stays at the nest, escorting other females into it to lay their eggs, and he guards the eggs until they hatch. Then the male tears down the nest, though he continues to guard the fry until they are a couple of weeks old. The exhausted male then often dies, but he may struggle back down the estuary from the breeding areas to more coastal waters.

Two other sticklebacks, the nine-spined *Pungitius pungitius* and the four-spined *Apeltes quadracus* are also common in Boreal estuaries, especially in the salt marshes and tidal creeks in the salt marshes. Both tend to be a little smaller than the three-spined stickleback, and they don't move around an estuary to nearly the same degree, but otherwise their breeding and feeding behavior is much the same.

Winter Flounder. A description of the winter flounder, *Pseudopleuronectes americanus*, a common resident of estuaries, coastal bays and offshore waters, is included in chapter 5.

Migrant Fish

Smelt. Smelt, *Osmerus mordax*, grow to about 10 inches (25 cm) in length and are much like small salmon to which they are closely related. They rarely are more than a mile offshore and in fact spend most of their time in schools in shallow water in or near estuaries. Soon after the ice breaks up in spring and the water warms up a little, smelt begin their spawning run. They migrate up the estuaries into the rivers, stopping just beyond tidewater. The sticky eggs hatch after a couple of weeks and the young smelt slowly move back into the estuaries. The young reach the sea by autumn, spend the next two winters along the coast and join in the spring spawning run just before they are two years old. Smelt occur everywhere along the Boreal coast, are still quite common in many estuaries, and land-locked populations exist in a number of lakes.

Salmon. Atlantic salmon, *Salmo salar*, grow to 2 to 3 feet (60 to 90 cm) or more in length, and often weigh up to 20 pounds (9 kg). They grow mostly at sea, sometimes far offshore, and then return to spawn in the rivers they were born in. Fish that migrate from sea to fresh water to spawn are called anadromous, and salmon are probably the most famous example of anadromous fish. During their spawning runs Atlantic salmon don't eat, they lose their silvery color and become a mottled reddish instead, and the lower jaw of males elongates rather unattractively. The migrating fish arrive back in their rivers during the summer and work their way upriver well above tidal water sometimes as far as 200 miles from the sea. They spawn in autumn. Many die soon after they spawn, others may overwinter in large rivers, and those that have spawned in relatively small rivers return immediately to the sea again. The physiological stress of moving from salt to fresh water can be tremendous and the salmon die as much from its effects as they do from the strain of migration and spawning.

228

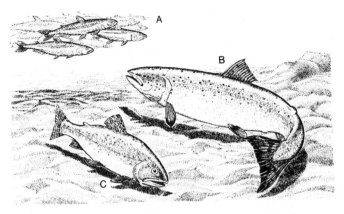

72. The salmonids: A. smelt B. Atlantic salmon C. brook trout

The eggs laid in the fall hatch the following spring, for development is very slow at the cold winter temperatures of Boreal rivers. The eggs are large at ¼ inch (6 to 7 mm) diameter. Once the fry have used up their yolk they are called parr, and the parr remain in the rivers for two or three years before swimming down to the sea, turning silver and becoming smolts. The smolts are voracious predators at sea, preying on herring, alewives, capelin, euphausiids and other pelagic fish and crustaceans. In turn, the smolts are preyed on by practically every larger predatory fish. After a year at sea, the smolts have grown into gulse and within another year or two are too big for almost all of their predators to handle, with the exception of tuna, swordfish, shark and harbor seals.

How soon an Atlantic salmon first spawns depends a great deal on how far offshore away from its home river it has wandered. Because of the fasting, physiological stress, and great amounts of energy expended by a migrating fish, it doesn't grow much after it first breeds. An individual which first migrates and breeds when it is three or four years old is likely to breed two or three more times before it dies at an age of eight or nine years. Another individual which stays at sea for five or six years may migrate and spawn only once at the end of its life, but it is likely to be a large fish, as heavy as 40 pounds (18 kg) and if a female, will produce a proportionately larger number of eggs.

Though some Atlantic salmon remain in coastal waters after they reach the sea, some travel great distances in search of food—as far as Greenland and Iceland. All adult salmon have a remarkable ability to migrate back to the river, even the tributary of the river they were born in. The distinctive chemical nature of their river, slightly different from every other river, is imprinted in the parr in some way. Years later they navigate back to their home coastline, and search for and find the river that has the chemical identity that matches their imprinted image of it. To find such a river after as many as five or six years from up to 2000 miles away, as some of the large Atlantic salmon must, is quite a feat.

Atlantic salmon were once abundant along all the coasts of the Maritime Provinces and the New England states. Until late in the 1700's rivers from Quebec and Newfoundland to Maine teemed with Atlantic salmon during the spawning migrations. Then gradually dams and mills were built on the rivers and, while the salmon were overfished, their rivers became polluted and impassable as well, and their populations plummeted. Now as the water quality of many of the rivers is improving again and dams are removed or at least made passable, Atlantic salmon are slowly returning to their old rivers. Hatcheries are raising large numbers of eggs and are stocking the rivers with parr, and though the present Atlantic salmon population can still not withstand much fishing pressure, it may recover enough to be self-sustaining along most of the Boreal coast once again.

Coho or silver salmon, *Oncorhynchus kisutch*, also occur infrequently along the more southern parts of the Boreal coast. Coho are Pacific salmon and were introduced first on the coast of Maine in the mid 1940's. Coho salmon spend one year in fresh water and about two years feeding at sea before returning to the stream they were born in (or deposited in as parr by biologists), and they die after they first spawn. The introduction of the species on the Boreal coast has met with only limited success.

Sea Sturgeon. Sea sturgeon, *Acipenser sturio*, are anadromous, growing at sea and spawning in fresh water.

There are reports from early settlers of sea sturgeon growing as long as 18 feet (5.4 m) and weighing an astounding 900 pounds (410 kg). Males are mature at about 10 feet (3 m) and 250 pounds (114 kg); in our time few sea sturgeons are larger. With its long body, shark-like tail, and bony shields or bucklers along its back and in rows along its sides, the sea sturgeon is a primitive bony fish. It lacks teeth and roots about in sand or mud after worms and mollusks.

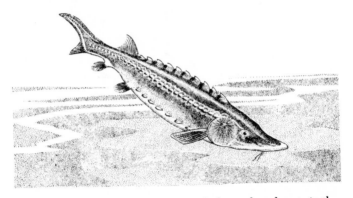

73. A primitive fish, the sea sturgeon lacks teeth and roots in the mud for its food.

Mature individuals migrate up rivers in late spring to some point beyond tidewater. They spawn and remain feeding upriver until they return to the sea in early autumn. A single female lays a few million eggs which take a week to hatch. The young fish may spend a couple of years feeding and growing near the river's mouth before moving on out of the estuaries. Once at sea the sea sturgeon grows much more quickly, and within another couple of years has few natural predators.

Sea sturgeon were overfished by the early colonists on the Boreal coast, and huge numbers were being exported back to Europe by early in the 17th century where the eggs were considered a great delicacy. River pollution and dams have further harmed the sea sturgeon just as they have Atlantic salmon, and they are now almost as scarce as they are extraordinary.

Estuarine Fish

Sea Lamprey. Sea lampreys, *Petromyzon marinus*, are anadromous, feeding and growing at sea and breeding in fresh water. Their shape is long and eel-like but they have cartilaginous rather than bony skeletons. They lack the paired fins characteristic of the more advanced bony fish. Instead of jaws they have rows of hooked teeth. Sea lampreys are blood-sucking parasites, and they prey on any fish large enough to support them, from shad and pollock to swordfish and basking sharks. Along the Boreal coast they range from immediate coastal waters out to the offshore banks.

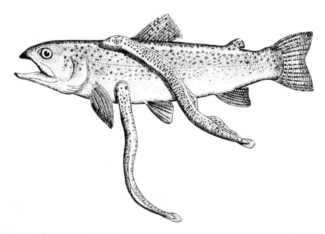

74. Sea lampreys feed by sucking blood from any fish large enough to support them, like this Atlantic salmon.

A sea lamprey reaches sexual maturity when it is 2 to 3 feet (60 to 90 cm) long and weighs about 2 pounds (0.9 kg). It migrates upriver in early spring, climbing waterfalls by latching on to rocks with its oral disk. It spawns near sandy or muddy-bottomed pools suitable for its larvae to burrow in, and then dies after spawning. The larvae, which are blind and toothless, grow slowly for three or four years in their pools and then transform into their adult form. They migrate back to sea where, growing rapidly for one or two years, they parasitize other fish. Then they migrate back into fresh water to spawn.

The dams built during the last century decimated sea lamprey populations, and though the populations seem plentiful enough during the migration runs, they are far less common now than they once were. People used to eat them, and it is said that Henry I of England died of eating too many.

Alewife. The alewife, *Pomolobus pseudoharengus,* is one of several herring-like anadromous fish common in Boreal waters. It grows to about 10 to 12 inches (25 to 30 cm). Alewives grow at sea until they are sexually mature at 3 or 4 years old, eating copepods and fish fry of the plankton, and schooling in large numbers. Spawning runs begin in Maine in late April or early May and as much as a month later further north, and they continue for about a month once they start. The St. John River in New Brunswick and the Damariscotta River in Maine have especially good runs. Alewives spawn in ponds or sluggish parts of streams and then return to the sea. They can make the transition from salt water to fresh water and back to salt water without much physiological damage. The eggs hatch after about a week and the young fish gradually move downstream. They arrive at sea at the end of the summer, 2 to 4 inches (5 to 10 cm) long. Alewives can surmount fishways built around dams more easily than some other species, and their numbers remain fairly high. Large landlocked populations also occur in the Great Lakes.

Blueback. Bluebacks, *Pomolobus aestivalis,* are hard to distinguish from alewives but their spawning runs occur later, at warmer temperatures, and their spawning rivers are much less well known.

Shad. Shad, *Alosa sapidissima,* are another of the anadromous herring-like fish, growing to about 2.5 feet (75 cm) and 6 pounds (2.7 kg) or more. Old reports suggest fish up to 12 pounds (5.4 kg) were not uncommon in Colonial days. Shad enter streams and rivers to spawn along the whole Atlantic coast when water temperatures reach 50 to 55° F (10 to 12.5° C), which on the Boreal coast occurs in May and June. The young fish work their way back to sea by the end of the summer. Shad do not handle fishways at dams very successfully and have largely disappeared from many rivers.

Estuarine Fish

75. Anadromous fish, alewives and striped bass (lower right) swim together at the New England Aquarium in Boston.

Striped Bass. Striped bass, *Roccus saxatilis*, are semi-anadromous; though they grow to maturity in the sea, they migrate only part way up estuaries to spawn in brackish water. Most of the striped bass which are caught range from about 3 to 40 pounds (1.4 to 18 kg). A 3 foot (0.9 m) fish weighs 20 pounds (9 kg). Once again there are records from over a hundred years ago indicating fish as large as 125 pounds (57 kg) once lived along the coast. Striped bass are excellent predators, eating fish, crabs, clams, worms and squid, and they are strong enough swimmers to forage in the surf zone of beaches as well as along rocky shores. At cold temperatures some populations move south out of Boreal waters, but others appear to settle sluggishly on the bottom to await the warmer waters of spring. Striped bass spawn at the heads of estuaries in summer in the Boreal region and their eggs, which are not sticky, are swept down the estuaries. The young hatch in tide water and gradually return to salt water. After about four years of foraging along the coast they become sexually mature and migrate back into the estuaries to spawn for the first time.

Brook Trout. Brook trout, *Salvelinus fontinalis*, are only occasionally migratory. They look much like small sal-

ESTUARIES

mon to which they are related but most spend their lives in fresh water. Some populations live in rivers that open onto the coast, and parts of these populations drift down their rivers to spend the winter in salt water near the river mouths. Such individuals are called salters and they spend the winter preying on small fish and crustaceans before returning back upriver to breed in the spring.

American Eel. The American eel, *Anguilla rostrata,* is the one species that reverses the migration. It grows in fresh water, breeds at sea, and is therefore a catadromous fish. An average female is 2 to 3 feet (60 to 90 cm) in length though females can grow to as much as 4 feet (1.2 m). Males are somewhat shorter, growing to about 2 feet (60 cm). Adults become sexually mature at anywhere from 5 to 20 years old. During the autumn of the year of their maturity, they migrate downstream at night, cease to feed, change in color, and their eyes grow larger. After this major physiological change, they migrate on out to sea, swimming for one to two months to the region of the Sargasso Sea where they somehow find each other, spawn and probably die.

A single female may shed as many as 20 million eggs, and those that survive predation grow into the transparent ribbon-like larvae typical of all true eels. This is called the leptocephalus stage. For the next year the larvae are carried north by the Gulf Stream. By the time a leptocephalus is a year old it is usually about 2½ inches (60 to 65 mm) long and it begins to transform into its "glass eel" stage, becoming an eel-like elver. As the elvers reach shallow water along the Atlantic shores of North America, they take on the dark coloration of the adults, settle to the bottom and begin to feed. The young eels may migrate upstream in their first spring near shore or they may remain in coastal bays and estuaries. They are able to tolerate a wide variation in salinity. Many of the young eels which stay on the coast forage in beds of eel grass, *Zostera marina,* and in salt marshes, as well as under rockweed and around rocky substrates. Juvenile and adult eels feed at night on almost anything, living or dead, and bury themselves in sand or mud by day. Those overwintering upstream bury themselves for the winter as well.

Estuarine Fish 235

76. The American eel, *Anguilla rostrata*, feeds actively at night and usually remains buried during the day.

How the American eel navigates its way to the Sargasso Sea is not known. How they find each other when they get there and what their breeding behavior is like are also unknown. The European eel, *Anguilla anguilla*, migrates to the same region from European rivers, breeds about the same time as *Anguilla rostrata* does, and produces larvae which take two or three years to return to Europe with the Gulf Stream. The two species are extremely similar, and some biologists have even suggested they are different populations of a single species. Though they are probably distinct species, there is little doubt that many questions remain to be answered about them.

Estuarine Birds and Mammals

Seabirds and Diving Ducks

Seabirds which fish by swimming underwater after their prey or by diving from the air sometimes forage in the coastal estuaries as well as in coastal bays and offshore waters. Some, such as the common tern, *Sterna hirundo*, and the double-crested cormorant, *Phalacrocorax auritus*, may

236   ESTUARIES

in fact be quite common in upper estuaries, but most of the other seabirds which fish from open water are infrequent visitors (see chapter 6).

Many diving ducks spend the winter months along the Boreal coast and often forage in the estuaries. Though some may forage as far up an estuary as it is ice-free, diving ducks are more typically winter predators of lower estuaries, coastal bays and the more exposed coastline (see chapter 5).

Birds of prey

Osprey. A familiar inhabitant of the Boreal estuaries is the osprey or seahawk, *Pandion haliaetus*. It often nests on top of a tree in a protected part of an upper or lower estuary or even on an offshore island. Since the use of DDT has been reduced, its population and distribution are increasing once again. Tall, pole-like channel markers which have been set up in recent years appear to be particularly attractive nest sites, and they are certainly safe from almost all predators but humans.

77. The female osprey incubates her clutch of eggs while the male feeds her during the incubation and brooding period.

An osprey hunts for fish in a spectacular fashion. It flies and hovers high over the water until it sights a fish near the surface, and then it dives, plunging into the water feet first to grab the fish with its talons. It immediately takes flight again, gripping the fish with both feet and carrying it head foremost to a treetop roost or to its nest where it eats it or gives the fish to its mate or offspring. Ospreys fish most successfully where the water surface is very quiet, for they can see potential prey much more clearly then. The quiet water of estuaries and protected bays is particularly suitable, and there the ospreys fish for species such as herring and alewives. In very shallow water they often dive for winter flounder.

Ospreys go north from their winter ranges in early spring. Each male establishes and advertises his breeding territory with a display flight punctuated with a high, piercing call. Both male and female of a breeding pair share in the building of their large nest, though the male does most of the stick collecting and the female gathers most of the moss and bark needed for lining material. Whenever possible they repair a nest from the previous season rather than start a new one.

During the course of the first 2 or 3 weeks they are together in the spring, they may mate a couple of hundred times, and the female then lays two or three eggs spaced over a few days. Throughout the 37 days of incubations the male fishes for his mate as well as for himself. The female incubates the eggs by herself at night but the male spells her five or six times each day when he brings her a fish to eat.

When the eggs hatch, the female broods the nestlings without help from the male who now becomes the sole provider for the entire family. The male brings fish to the female who eats some of it herself and breaks the rest of it up to feed the nestlings. The young birds grow rapidly, shielded by their mother from rain, wind and cold. By the time they are three or four weeks old, they can stand and flap their wings and the female soon moves to a nearby tree where she can watch them without being buffeted by their activity. When the young ospreys are a little over seven weeks old they try flying for the first time, but they still remain near their nest and parents for another couple of weeks until around mid-August. They gradually learn the difficult technique of diving for fish.

In the summer of their third year they breed for the first time, though rarely as successfully as older, more experienced birds. If a pair of ospreys lose their eggs to a storm or to predation, they don't re-lay eggs, but they sometimes proceed to build a number of sloppy nests in apparent frustration.

Bald Eagle. Bald eagles, *Haliaeetus leucocephalus*, which nest in summer in the estuaries of parts of the Boreal coast, used to be moderately common. Recently they appear to be re-establishing themselves especially in the Passamaquoddy region around the border between Maine and New Brunswick. They occur infrequently north to Newfoundland. The bald eagle is a magnificent animal, with its 80-inch (2-m) wingspan and distinctive white head. Bald eagles mate for life and the territory of a nesting pair is at least several square miles, large enough to provide the pair with the fish and other occasional prey they feed on. Not uncommonly they steal fish from ospreys in their territory. They usually nest high in a large living tree, building and reusing enormous nests.

Mammals

Schools of fish and squid come into the Boreal estuaries each summer; some of their mammalian predators follow them inshore. Harbor seals, *Phoca vitulina concolor*, occur throughout the summer along the Boreal coast. They are common predators of the bays and around the offshore ledges as well as in the estuaries, and they prey extensively on bottom-living fish and invertebrates (see chapter 6). Harbor porpoises, *Phocoena phocoena*, follow the fish schools into the estuaries, and though the smaller toothed whales also sometimes swim remarkably far up estuaries after their prey, they are far more common offshore (see chapter 7).

CHAPTER V

The Shallow Marine Subtidal

BELOW THE LEVEL of the lowest tides, beyond the diluting influence of rivers and upper estuaries is the shallow but fully marine subtidal environment. Just a generation ago biologists examined it almost exclusively by dragging dredges along it from boats. The present ease and relative safety of scuba diving has changed things dramatically, however. The subtidal world has now been opened to both specialized biologist and casual visitor, and the experience of exploring the diversity and complexity of the subtidal habitats by sight and touch must be one of the finest pleasures on our otherwise overcrowded, over-humanized planet. It is there for anyone qualified to scuba dive, and even snorkeling without the aid of scuba gear can be very rewarding.

The beauty and strangeness of many of the subtidal habitats cannot be overstated. Swimming among gardens of macroalgae, watching animals feed, flee, mate, fight or even sleep, a diver has the opportunity of seeing marine life in action, in contrast to what he or she might see on exposed intertidal shores where organisms are usually quiescent, waiting for the tide to rise again.

Boreal Subtidal Marine Habitats

In the Boreal region, rocky intertidal shores normally extend some distance subtidally. They are covered by macroalgae to the point where the rocks give way to gravel and sand or softer, muddier substrates. Intertidal sand beaches flatten into subtidal sand flats beyond the surf zone and then they, too, may grade into finer, muddier sediments. On parts of the Boreal coast where river runoff and coastal erosion provide fine sediments, the substrates of protected bays and offshore areas may be mostly muddy ones, interrupted by rock outcroppings and occasional stretches of shingle and sand. Where little fine sediment is available, the substrates of bays may remain exposed bedrock down to considerable depths.

Stresses of Subtidal Habitats

TEMPERATURE AND SALINITY

Inshore marine water along the Boreal coast does not warm in summer to the extent estuarine water does, but it is likely to be a little warmer than offshore water, especially in sheltered bays. Some animals migrate inshore in summer to take advantage of the food and relative warmth, and to reproduce; they move offshore into deeper water in the winter to avoid the freezing temperatures of those same shallow areas.

Similarly, though salinity fluctuations of inshore coastal waters are small and probably unimportant in comparison with the fluctuations which occur in estuaries, they are likely to be greater than those which occur in offshore, oceanic water. In spring the impact of the freshwater runoff from the Boreal rivers may be felt to considerable distances along the adjacent coastlines.

Even where summer warming and spring dilution occur, however, usually only the surface layers are affected. Below the surface layers the water is likely to be cold even in summer, saline even in spring. How deep such conditions occur also depends on the size of the tides, the strength of the currents, the degree to which the area is sheltered, and the latitude of the area. Organisms that occur just below the low tide level at the point of an exposed peninsula may live 10 feet (3 m) deeper in an adjacent warmer bay. Organisms that begin to emerge into the low intertidal in northern parts of the Boreal region may occur only well below the low tide level in the southern parts of the region.

TURBIDITY AND CURRENTS

The turbidity of the inshore marine waters varies considerably along the Boreal coast. It is related to the amount of sediment the water carries, the amount of phytoplankton-supporting nutrients, and the strength of the tidal or longshore currents. The large tides of the Bay of Fundy keep the well-mixed water cool and nutrient-rich, but also relatively turbid. The runoff from the St. Lawrence River is so great in spring that in the western Gulf of St. Lawrence only 1% of the light is able to penetrate to depths of as little as 13 feet (4 m). On the other hand, there is little fine sediment in the water along the shores of eastern Newfoundland and the clarity of the water there is unparalleled in the Boreal region. Somewhere in between the two extremes are the coasts of Maine and the Atlantic side of Nova Scotia where visibility in the water is likely to be good around exposed points and offshore islands, but considerably less in the more turbid water of protected bays. The degree of turbidity influences to what depths phytoplankton, macroalgae or eel grass may grow; as water clarity increases they are able to grow at increasingly greater depths. Their distribution in turn affects the distribution of the various animals that graze, hide, or forage for prey among them.

WAVE SURGE

The shallow subtidal plants and animals, though constantly covered by water, do not necessarily escape the effects of wave action. On exposed shores the tumult of the breaking waves may be felt as wave surge to depths of 10 feet (3 m) or more. The organisms living there must be fastened tightly to the rocks or they risk being swept away. Plants that grow on such shores during the less windy summer season may be swept away by the wave surge accompanying winter gales. Mobile animals usually seek sanctuary in the calmer, deeper water for the winter.

Stability and Diversity

The shallow marine subtidal habitats are more stable and benign than intertidal and estuarine habitats, and a greater diversity of plants and animals is able to grow there. Where the habitat is complex, with rock crevices and caves and ledges as well as patches of shingle, sand and even finer sediment, the diversity of organisms is at its greatest. Even in simple, homogeneous habitats such as mud substrates, the species diversity is relatively high. With this greater diversity comes increased competition for space, and the distribution of most species is determined more by competition and predation than by abiotic, physical factors.

The Kelp Zone: Solid Substrates

Kelp are large brown algae that grow in dense beds along temperate-water coastlines all over the world. *Nereocystis*, a species common along the western coast of North America, grows to 132 feet (40 m). The species of the Atlantic Boreal coast are smaller, but they still grow to lengths of 6.5 to 10 feet (2 to 3 m) or more. They have thick stipes and large, broad blades, which form dense beds or forests where smaller species of algae grow, animals graze and other animals seek prey and protective cover.

Kelp beds are just as characteristic of the Boreal coast as the intertidal rockweeds *Fucus* and *Ascophyllum*. The various kelp species do not grow well in the warm water south of Cape Cod, and though they extend north along the Labrador coast well beyond Newfoundland, they do not live in Arctic waters either. At the northern end of the Boreal region, the kelp are common in low tide pools; at the southern end of the region they may be restricted to cold water well below the low tide level.

Kelp along the Boreal coast may grow to depths of 65 to 100 feet (20 to 30 m) where the coastal water is very clear and the substrate rocky, and to 5 miles (8 km) from shore where the substrate has a gentle slope to it. Like all marine algae, they get their nutrients from the water. In shallow coastal regions where waves, currents and tides keep the water well-mixed, their supply of nutrients is inexhaustible. Their growth is rapid and the productivity of an area covered by kelp can be truly extraordinary. The larger the kelp bed and the faster the kelp and other algae grow, the larger are the populations of the animals which depend on the algae for food and protection.

The Kelp of the Kelp Zone

KELP DIVERSITY

A number of species of kelp grow on the subtidal rocks along the Boreal coast. The horsetail kelp, *Laminaria digitata*, and the hollow-stemmed kelp, *Laminaria longi-*

cruris, are the two species most likely to occur immediately below the low tide level. *Laminaria digitata* has a very strong but flexible stipe, a low-profile holdfast and a blade that may be divided into as many as 30 fingers, all of which allow it to withstand greater wave surge than can other species of kelp. Occasionally a low tide exposes *L. digitata* for a brief time, and though the kelp desiccates rapidly and cannot be considered an intertidal organism, its flexible stipe allows it to flatten on the exposed rocks and reduce the time of its exposure to air. It grows to 6.5 feet (2 m). The larger plants grow somewhat deeper below the low tide level than the shorter ones.

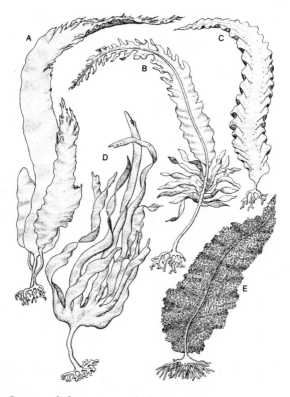

78. Common kelp species include A. *Laminaria longicruris* B. *Alaria escuelenta* C. *L. agardhii* D. *L. digitata* E. *Agarum cribosum*

Waves crashing
on the shores of
Acadia National
Park, Maine.

Salt marsh behind
sand dunes at
Parker River
National Refuge,
Massachusetts.

Tide pool on the
rocky coast of
Newfoundland.

PLATE I

Rockweed,
Fucus vesiculosus.

Kelp, *Alaria escuelenta,*
with hydroid, *Sertularia.*

Sea lettuce, *Ulva.*

Purple laver, *Porphyra.*

PLATE II

Nudibranch, *Coryphella*,
feeding on hydroid, *Obelia*.

Stalked jellyfish,
Haliclystus salpinx,
attached to eel grass,
Zostera marina.

Hydroid, *Clava
leptostyla*, growing in
clusters on rockweed,
Ascophyllum nodosum.

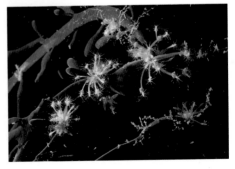

PLATE III

Dune plants

Beach rose.

Beach heather.

Beach plum.

Beach pea.

PLATE IV

Sea anemones, *Metridium senile*, and horse mussels, *Modiolus modiolus*, compete for space.

Sea peaches, *Halocynthia pyriformis*, and green sea urchins, *Strongylopentrotus droebachiensis*.

Asteriid starfish, *Asterias vulgaris*, and green sea urchins.

PLATE V

Hermit crab,
Pagurus acadianus,
in a whelk shell.

Sea anemone,
Metridium senile.

Lobster, *Homarus americanus.*

PLATE VI

Shorthorn sculpin, *Myoxocephalus scorpius.*

Embryo of the little skate, *Raja erinacea.*

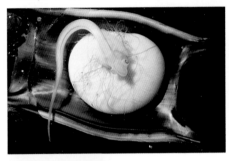

Squid,
Loligo pealei.

PLATE VII

Herring gull.

Gannets preen and court each other on their nests.

Kittiwake chick.

PLATE VIII

The hollow-stemmed kelp, *Laminaria longicruris*, grows in quieter water than *L. digitata*, and it also can survive brief exposure by a very low tide. With its long and partly hollow stipe and its equally long, broad blade, *L. longicruris* is the largest of the Boreal kelp species. In very shallow subtidal water it grows to 6.5 to 10 feet (2 to 3 m), but in deeper water it may reach lengths of 30 to 40 feet (9 to 12 m).

Two other closely related species, *L. saccharina* and *L. agardhii*, may also grow in shallow subtidal water. The two species are virtually indistinguishable and may in fact be northern and southern forms of one species. They look somewhat like a smaller version of *L. longicruris*, and they, too, grow well in quite sheltered water (see plate II). With them may be another similar kelp, *Saccorhiza dermatodea*, which is distinguished mainly by its cup-like holdfast.

The edible kelp, *Alaria escuelenta*, yet another shallow water species, grows best where the *Laminaria* species are too sparse to overshadow and outcompete it. It has a buoyant midrib running the length of its blade, a feature the *Laminaria* species lack. The blade often has a frayed appearance, and there are usually a few very small supplementary blades growing from the junction of the stipe and the primary blade. The whole plant grows to a length of about 6.5 to 10 feet (2 to 3 m).

The final species of kelp common on the Boreal coast is sea colander, *Agarum cribosum*. Like *Alaria escuelenta* it grows to a length of 6.5 to 10 feet (2 to 3 m) and has a midrib on its blade. In contrast to all other kelp species, however, its blade is perforated by many small holes, giving the plant its name and making it very easy to recognize. It grows at greater depths than any of the other kelp species and is uncommon in shallow water where the others grow best.

GROWTH OF KELP

Kelp species are perennials and they are well adapted to grow in the cold water of the Boreal region; most of them actually grow most in the winter months when sea temperatures are near the freezing point and daylight hours are short. Because the winter temperatures are so low the growing kelp have low respiration rates and their energy reserves are only slowly used up. Photosynthesis, which is necessary for building up the reserves of organic carbon compounds the kelp need for growth, is also greatly reduced since the amount of light is limited in winter. Still, the kelp continue to grow even in darkness.

Such paradoxical growth patterns in kelp are not easily explained. As in all algae, kelp cells are structurally rather simple. Yet somehow their cells store up the organic compounds before winter and later mobilize them. New growth is added at the junction of the stipe and blade. Perhaps kelp grow most in winter because it is the season of strongest storms and therefore greatest likelihood of erosion of the kelp blades, and so the growth compensates for the erosion. Perhaps winter growth permits the kelp to utilize the abundant nutrients in the water at a time when there is little phytoplankton to compete with them. We still have a lot to learn about these remarkable plants.

Annuals of the Kelp Zone

Though perennial kelp species may comprise 80 to 90 percent of the subtidal mass of macroalgae, a variety of small, annual species of green, red and brown macroalgae compete for light and space under the kelp canopy. The diversity of these annual species may be very high; over 200 species have been found along various parts of the Boreal coast.

Many annuals start as young sporophytes in late winter or spring, grow through the summer and then in autumn produce spores. The very small microscopic spores which are released have half the number of chromosomes of the parent sporophyte plants and they survive the winter's darkness as minute gametophytes while the sporophytes all die. With the increasing daylight of spring, the gametophytes produce sex cells, or gametes, which fuse, forming a new generation of sporophytes which once again have full complements of chromosomes. In higher plants, such as most flowers and trees, the gametophyte stage is represented by pollen grains and unfertilized seeds.

Most annuals are too small to be able to store the carbon reserves they would need to survive the winter; the cycle of summer growth as large sporophytes and winter survival as small gametophytes is highly adapted to the seasonal fluctuations of light and temperature. Though this cycle is typical of most of the subtidal annuals in the Boreal region, there are variations in its details. In many species the winter gametophyte generation grows as large as the sporophyte before it sheds its gametes. The two generations are virtually indistinguishable except for chromosome numbers. In a few species, the gametophyte even grows into a plant that looks radically different from the sporophyte, a confusing situation for taxonomists to unravel.

The annual species are not necessarily in direct competition with the large, brown perennial kelps. Many of the former are able to grow on less stable substrates, exploiting space the various kelp species cannot use. Because the annuals are smaller and are unlikely in summer to have to withstand the intensity of the gale-driven winter waves, they are not as restricted to very rigid substrates as are the perennial kelps.

Distribution of Subtidal Macroalgae

The marine rocky subtidal habitats vary in their degree of exposure to wave action, stability of the substrate, extent of warming in summer, and depth of penetration of light sufficient for plant photosynthesis. Macroalgae in turn vary in their ability to tolerate wave action, substrate instability and temperature stress, and some groups are able to utilize light at greater depths than others. As a result, macroalgae are distributed with some degree of predictability, both horizontally along the shore line and vertically into deeper water.

The uppermost zone is dominated by the horsetail kelp, *Laminaria digitata*, in areas exposed to wave action, and, in quieter areas, by the various other *Laminaria* species. Some of the annuals which grow on the low intertidal rocks (see chapter 2) also occur among the kelp in the subtidal fringe, species such as the leafy green algae, *Ulva* and *Monostroma;* the leafy red *Porphyra* and dulse, *Rhodymenia palmata;* and the tough branching red Irish moss, *Chondrus crispus* and *Gigartina.* The filamentous brown alga, *Chordaria*, is often common as well.

On stable rock surfaces still in shallow water but below this upper fringe, the same kelp species continue to predominate. They are joined occasionally by *Saccorhiza dermatodea*, but the smaller macroalgae are replaced by annual species more typically subtidal. Sour weeds, *Desmarestia* species, are brown and filamentous and occur very frequently. Joining them may be various filamentous red algae such as *Cystoclonium*, *Ceramium* and *Polysiphonium* along with leafy red *Phyllophora* species and species of encrusting pink coralline algae. Where the substrate is less stable, the kelp may be uncommon, but the smaller annuals may still be abundant and the wiry red *Ahnfeltia* and *Polyides* may be particularly common.

One species that is particularly distinctive is the cord weed or sea whip, *Chorda filum*, an annual deep brown alga that grows without branching into a tall thin cord up to 10 to 15 feet (3 to 4.5 m) long but less than ½ inch (1 cm) in diameter. It is hollow and therefore buoyant, and with its disk-like holdfast it is able to grow on both stable and relatively unstable substrates like many of the other annuals.

At somewhat greater depths of 30 feet (9 m) or more along a shore line where the water is cold and clear and the substrate remains rocky, algae continue to cover the rock surfaces. The *Laminaria* species become uncommon, but sea colander, *Agarum cribosum*, may predominate instead, and another deeper water kelp, *Alaria grandifolia*, may grow as well. The very bushy red fern, *Ptilota serrata*, a small perennial red alga, is likely to be abundant with the sea colander, and leafy red species such as *Phycodrys*, *Electra* and *Rhodophillus* grow well at such intermediate depths, too. Diversity is lower than in more shallow water, and none of the species which thrive in the shallow water grows with any success at such intermediate depths.

In deeper water yet, at depths approaching 100 feet (30 m), where light still penetrates and the substrate is still hard, only a few species of algae occur. None of the large kelp species persists and in fact no green or brown algae grow to such depths. A species of the leafy red *Phyllophora* may grow on the upper surfaces of boulders, a filamentous red *Polysiphonia* may lie in mats upon the rock, and the encrusting coralline algae may still be fairly extensive. These few remaining species become increasingly scarce and dwarfed as the depth increases and light diminishes, and only coralline algae of a more fleshy nature are likely to still be present. Even in the clearest of waters, however, the limits of the photic zone are reached at depths approaching 230 feet (70 m); thereafter no plants grow.

Along most shorelines of the Boreal coast the substrate has become soft long before the light diminishes enough to restrict all plant growth, and water turbidity may condense the upper, middle and deeper zones of the subtidal algae into a much shorter vertical distance.

The Grazers

GRAZING MOLLUSKS. Mollusks that graze on the algae of the low intertidal rocks and tidepools often graze on subtidal rocks as well. The limpet, *Acmaea testudinalis,* and chiton, *Ischnochiton ruber,* scrape microscopic algae from the rocks; the common periwinkle, *Littorina littorea,* scrapes algae and eats young kelp shoots and older decaying kelp; the snail *Lacuna vincta* feeds on the blades of living kelp (see chapter 2).

Green Sea Urchin. By far the most important subtidal grazer is the green sea urchin, *Strongylocentrotus droebachiensis,* which is distributed broadly in circumpolar waters. It is the only sea urchin in the Atlantic Boreal region. South of Cape Cod it occurs only in deep cold water. It is also the most common sea urchin along the coast of northern Europe and along the cold-water Pacific coast of North America. Though it forms dense aggregations on subtidal rocks, it also occurs in low tide pools and on low intertidal rocky shores along the Bay of Fundy. Elsewhere along rocky shores, low tides may leave sea urchins partially exposed in crevices and under rocks and rockweeds. The sea urchins are, however, primarily subtidal. They are able to withstand considerable wave surge and are often abundant in kelp forests.

The green sea urchin grows to 3½ inches (9 cm) in diameter, not including its spines. Its spines are bright

79. Aggregations of green sea urchins can destroy a kelp forest.

green, about ½ inch (1.3 cm) long and cover all but the
lower surface of the animal which is held against the rock.
The shell, or test, of the sea urchin is made up of a large
number of small plates which are glued together; the spines
are attached to these plates. Five pairs of longitudinal rows
of tube feet run from the sea urchin's mouth on the underneath surface to its anus on the top. The five pairs of rows of
tube feet are analogous to the five arms of a starfish. It's as if
the arms of a starfish had been pulled up over its body and
the sides of the arms sewn together (see plate V).

The spines of a sea urchin make it unpalatable to many
but not all potential predators. Its tube feet permit it to
cling to rock surfaces and in crevices, and even to cover its
upper exposed surface with bits of shells or weed to protect
it from too much exposure to sunlight in shallow water.
Scattered among the spines are much shorter, stalked, jaw-
like structures called pedicellaria whose function is to nip
small animals which might otherwise roam over the sea urchin and to keep the test clean of sediment.

Like all sea urchins, the green sea urchin feeds by scraping algae from the substrate with five teeth lying in a star
shaped pattern in the center of its underneath, or oral, surface. These teeth are held in place and moved in their
scraping actions by a remarkable apparatus inside the sea
urchin called Aristotle's lantern, a complex arrangement of

muscle and cartilage which comprises the jaws. Most of the rest of the insides of a sea urchin's test is filled by its digestive system and, in season, its ripe gonads.

The development of sea urchin eggs can be watched with a low-powered microscope. Eggs and sperm are easy to get from ripe sea urchins and once fertilized, the small transparent eggs divide repeatedly and with great precision, eventually forming a most extraordinary larval form called the pluteus larva. Sea urchins shed their eggs and sperm in the water where fertilization occurs, and the pluteus larvae that develop join the plankton and are dispersed by currents (see chapter 1). The larvae then metamorphose and settle to the bottom, select a hard substrate and become miniature sea urchins. As adults the sea urchins aggregate at least partly so that they can reproduce successfully, for a solitary urchin which sheds its sperm or eggs by itself is unlikely to have any offspring.

Green sea urchins graze on algae of many kinds, and they are also able to eat young kelp without any difficulty. Wherever green sea urchins have become over-abundant, it seems that kelp forests have diminished and in some localities have even disappeared. Along some of the shores of Newfoundland, Nova Scotia and Maine, *Laminaria* kelp species may be confined to the turbulent zone just below the low tide level; everywhere else the green sea urchins are extremely abundant.

It is possible that the extensive destruction of the Boreal kelp beds by green sea urchins is a relatively recent phenomenon. Green sea urchins are not without their predators, despite their protective spines. Herring gulls, great black-backed gulls, cod and lobsters all eat them. Where the lobsters in particular have been overfished, a major check on the populations of green sea urchins may have been removed. Considering the importance of kelp beds to many other animals, the overfishing of a single dominant predator appears to have had major repercussions through an entire community.

Though lobster populations are certainly not likely to increase again, green sea urchins do have another potentially insatiable predator. Many people like to eat the gonads of green sea urchins and there are growing markets for these so-called "sea eggs," especially in the larger cities. There has long been a market for the species in Europe, particularly in France, and as a taste for sea urchin gonads spreads, sea urchin aggregations may be reduced to sizes small enough to allow kelp beds to regrow in the places where they have disappeared.

Purple Sea Urchin. The purple sea urchin, *Arbacia punctulata*, replaces the green sea urchin from the southern shores of Cape Cod southward. It lives on rocky and shelly bottoms, in crevices and tide pools, and has a smaller test but longer spines than the green sea urchin. Its test, spines and tube feet are all a rich reddish purple. Its northern occurrence essentially marks the southern boundary of the Boreal region.

Sessile Suspension Feeders

A large diversity of animals settle and grow on hard surfaces, and rock is not the only substrate available to them. Less permanent substrates such as shells, kelp blades, pilings and the underneath sides of docks, moorings and boats may be just as suitable, especially for those able to colonize and grow rapidly. Most of such "fouling" organisms are glued permanently into place and some of them all too quickly contribute to the erosion or destruction of the substrate itself.

SPONGES. Sponges are the simplest of multicellular animals. They have no true tissues or organs and the cells behave independently of each other. Until the late 18th century, sponges were considered plants, but then their method of feeding was understood and they were recognized as simply organized animals.

Even a large sponge is structurally uncomplicated. Water is drawn in through small pores in the surface of the sponge through narrow canals lined by flagellated cells which move the water and trap the food it carries. The water is ejected from the sponge through much larger pores, or oscula, which are easily visible without the aid of a lens. Most sponges have to be small because of their relative lack of internal organization. Some species compensate by growing into flat, encrusting layers over rocks, shells and other hard objects; others grow off the substrate in folds or finger-like projections.

The skeletons of sponges support the living protective and digestive cells. The simplest sponges have minute calcium carbonate spicules supporting their cells, but more complex sponges have silicon-based spicules and often a horny framework of a substance called spongin secreted by a certain type of cell. Some warm water sponges with a great deal of spongin but few if any spicules became the sponges of the commercial trade. When washed free of its living cells, the water-absorbant spongin framework remains. Synthetic sponges have fortunately made the increasingly rare wild product almost obsolete.

Along the Boreal coast most sponge species are small and many of them grow best in deep water. Compared with the sponges of warm water regions, Boreal sponges are drab and not very diverse. Nonetheless a few species are quite common on subtidal rocks and shells and may even be quite colorful.

The smallest and most primitive are several *Leucosolenia* species. They are whitish, appear tubular and may be either encrusting or branching. Their spicules are of calcium carbonate and they lack the spongin of other common Boreal species. The breadcrumb or sulphur sponge, *Halichondria panicea*, often grows in tide pools and on low intertidal rocks as well as subtidally (see chapter 2). *Cliona celata* is a yellow, irregularly shaped species which bores into limestone or shells, eroding the rock and disintegrating the shells in the process. The reddish brown fig sponge, *Suberites ficus*, can also be fairly common, growing to about 3 inches (7.5 cm) in length above its attachment site on a rock or shell.

Probably the prettiest of the Boreal sponges is the eyed finger sponge, *Haliclona oculata*, which grows numerous forking branches from a single stalk. It is a reddish species with many large exhalent pores, or oscula, each about 1/10 inch (2.5 mm) in diameter, giving it its eyed appearance. It grows to 2 feet (60 cm) in length and like other large sponges may be broken free from its rock by storm-driven wave surge. Cast ashore, it dies and bleaches white, leaving a tough spongin skeleton filled with minute spicules.

The Kelp Zone: Solid Substrates

255

SEA SQUIRTS. Like sponges, sea squirts, or ascidians, need a hard substrate to attach themselves to and grow from. Sea squirts may be large and solitary or they may be colonial, with extremely small individuals stuck together. Colonial forms may even look a bit like an encrusting sponge until they are examined more closely.

A solitary sea squirt has a sack-like body encased in a leathery skin, or tunic, made of cellulose. It sucks water in an inhalent siphon, filters the water for the microorganisms and organic material it contains, passes the water through the gill clefts of its pharynx in order to get the oxygen it needs, and then ejects the water out its exhalent siphon. When disturbed, such a sea squirt contracts, squirts water out its siphons (hence its name), and then withdraws and closes off its siphons. It has an open, relatively unorganized circulatory system, and its heartbeat has become famous among biologists because after it beats in one direction for a while, it pauses and then beats in the opposite direction, and bloodflow through the broad blood channels is reversed.

Colonial, or compound, ascidians are structurally similar to the larger individuals of solitary species. In some colonial ascidians, the individuals are arranged in clusters, giving the colony a stellate appearance. The individuals forming a cluster usually share a single exhalant siphon in the center of the cluster but have separate inhalant siphons. Colonial ascidians are able to grow by budding asexually. The new buds grow into new individuals, and a colony may gradually spread 4 to 6 inches (10 to 15 cm) or more over the substrate.

The small and short-lived sea squirt larvae are remarkable organisms, and in terms of the question of the origin of the first vertebrate, fish-like animals they are significant. An ascidian larva looks rather like a tadpole, with the pharynx and digestive system developing in the anterior or front half of the larva while the posterior half is a muscular tail which moves the larva to a new substrate to settle on. Besides having paired muscles, the tail has a neural tube and a supporting notochord extending along its length. These along with other features have given rise to the theory that ascidian larvae are in fact the evolutionary ancestors of the most primitive of the vertebrates.

After a short planktonic larval life, an ascidian tadpole adheres to a substrate by means of adhesive organs on its anterior end. It then resorbs its tail, rotates its internal organs, and its siphons and digestive system become functional. Not all species have planktonic larvae, however, and in colonial species in particular the larvae may be brooded by their hermaphroditic parents and grow into new sea squirts on the substrate immediately next to their parents.

Among the solitary Boreal sea squirts, the sea peach, *Halocynthia pyriformis*, is certainly the most beautiful. It grows large, particularly in cold waters where it may be 4 or 5 inches (10 to 12.5 cm) long, and its color is usually vivid red or orange (see plate V). The sea potato, *Boltenia ovifera*, is also distinctive for its pinkish body, 2 to 3 inches (5 to 7.5 cm) in diameter, which grows on the end of a thin stalk that may be as long as 6 to 8 inches (15 to 20 cm). The sea vase, *Ciona intestinalis*, grows to about 2 inches (5 cm). Though the animal is light yellow, its test or tunic is quite transparent and most of its internal organs are visible. Sea grapes, *Molgula* species, are also common in Boreal waters,

80. Ascidians can be either colonial like the flowerlike star tunicate *Botryllus schlosseri* (left) or solitary like the sea grape *Molgula* (right).

smaller than the other solitary sea squirts, and rather drab and translucent in appearance.

Several compound or colonial ascidians are common especially in the southern part of the Boreal region. The star tunicate, *Botryllus schlosseri*, is abundant along warmer parts of the coast, growing over rocks, kelp blades, eel grass, pilings, moorings and boat bottoms with remarkable success by late summer. The individuals of a colony are beautifully colored in green, brown, and white, and each cluster in a colony looks like a small star-shaped flower. Several species of *Amaroucium*, or sea pork, grow in rather large pinkish lobed masses which often wash up on the coastal beaches. Another white encrusting species, *Didemnum albidum*, grows well in colder water throughout the Boreal region. Where any of these colonial ascidians occur, they are very successful competitors for space, for they easily overgrow most other organisms.

ACORN BARNACLES. The subtidal acorn barnacles, *Balanus balanus* and *B. crenatus*, are very similar to the intertidal acorn barnacle, *B. balanoides*, in structure, filter-feeding and reproduction (see chapter 2). All are generally tentlike in shape, but the two subtidal species have calcareous bases. Though they adhere strongly to their substrate, they cannot seal themselves as completely to a hard surface as can *B. balanoides* with its membranous base. In addition, neither of the subtidal barnacles can close their opercular plates as tightly as the intertidal *B. balanoides* does to withstand intertidal desiccation.

The rock barnacle, *Balanus balanus*, is a large sturdy species, reaching 2 inches (5 cm) in diameter. Where it occurs in the low intertidal it is less subject to desiccation than is the much smaller *B. balanoides* and its strongly ribbed plates help deflect the pounding surf it is exposed to at the low tide line. Subtidally it is often abundant, free of such intertidal stress.

Balanus crenatus is also large, growing to 1½ inches (4 cm) in diameter. It is found only below the low tide line where it is not subject to the wave action. As a result, its calcareous base is thinner and not nearly as strong as that of *B. balanus* and its bone white plates are smooth and much more fragile. *B. crenatus* occurs in northern waters to

81. Two closely related barnacles *Balanus balanus* (left) and *B. crenatus* (right) are adapted to withstand different amounts of wave action just by shell structure alone.

depths of 100 feet (30 m) on rocks and other hard substrates. Any bottle that has washed or been dredged up from deeper water is likely to have a spectacular array of *B. crenatus* growing on it.

SEA CUCUMBERS. Sea cucumbers, or holothurians, are closely related to starfish, sea urchins and sand dollars. Rather than being starlike or domed, these echinoderms are cylindrical, sometimes even worm-like, with a mouth at one end and an anus at the other. In many species, like *Cucumaria frondosa*, five rows of tube feet run the length of the body, showing their radial symmetry. Instead of having its mouth against the substrate as do other echinoderms, the sea cucumber lies on its side with its mouth extending forward.

Sea cucumbers always lie on the same side, showing a compromise between the radial symmetry of all echinoderms and the bilateral symmetry of most higher forms of animal life. Tube feet are sometimes lacking on the upper or dorsal side of the body. Those in contact with the substrate are used for holding the animal in place and for moving forward (at a very slow pace) over the substrate.

Sea cucumbers are suspension feeders. The tube feet surrounding the mouth area have been modified into long

The Kelp Zone: Solid Substrates   259

multi-branched hollow tentacles. These tentacles are extended by means of the water-vascular system, as are all the tube feet. The sticky tentacles capture plankton or detritus and then are retracted into the mouth area where the food particles are wiped off.

The internal skeleton of most sea cucumbers is made up of widely scattered microscopic plates. The water-vascular system helps the animals keep their cucumber size and shape, and makes the animals leathery to the touch; once out of water sea cucumbers become flaccid as the water drains out of them. The body wall of some sea cucumbers is in fact considered a gourmet delicacy in France, where it is called *bêche de mer*, and in the Orient where it is known as *trepang*. It is boiled and dried before eaten.

Sea cucumbers have separate sexes; the sperm and eggs are spawned into the sea water. The eggs develop into free swimming planktonic forms by their third day and they later metamorphose into small sea cucumbers before settling to the bottom.

The most common Boreal sea cucumber is *Cucumaria frondosa*, which is a classic cucumber shape, growing to 10 inches (25 cm) in shallow or southern areas and to 20 inches (50 cm) in Arctic waters. It is a reddish brown color and its five longitudinal rows of tube feet are often tipped in orange. It is found from low cool tide pools, where its tentacles may be spied sticking out from rock crevices or from underneath kelp, to subtidal depths of 1000 feet (300 m).

Cucumaria frondosa has tube feet on all sides, but the three most ventral rows have pneumatic suckers at their ends, which help the animal to move. The other two rows of tube feet on the upper side usually have no suckers and are involved in respiration and sensation.

Unlike *Cucumaria frondosa*, the scarlet sea cucumber, *Psolus fabricii*, has a distinct sole, or flattened side, to its body, and its bilateral symmetry is more pronounced. Though tube feet circle the margin of the sole and run down its middle, there are few tube feet on the dorsal side. *Psolus fabricii* has larger skeletal plates than many holothurians and its body wall is therefore firmer than that of other sea cucumbers.

Psolus fabricii has 10 to 15 brilliant scarlet tentacles

82. The vivid red tentacles of the scarlet sea cucumber *Psolus fabricii* capture food particles.

around its mouth which branch profusely. Though its dorsal surface is a dull reddish color, it is usually covered with detritus and only the flame red tentacles betray the animal's presence. It grows to about 8 inches (20 cm) and is found from the very low intertidal in northern areas to depths as great as 300 feet (90 m).

Slipper Limpet. The slipper limpet, *Crepidula fornicata*, is quite unlike other gastropod mollusks, for though related to periwinkles and whelks, it is a sessile animal and doesn't move about preying, scavenging or grazing like its relatives.

The slipper limpet has evolved into a suspension feeder. Larger particles, trapped by cilia and mucus, are formed into pellets which are either rejected with the outgoing current or eaten later; finer particles are collected on the mucus-coated gills and the food-laden mucus is compacted into a cylinder. Later, the radula takes bites off this food cylinder.

The slipper limpet has a shell platform that extends half-way across the underneath side. This gives the shell the appearance of a slipper or of a boat with a deck, hence its other common name: boat shell. Growing to 1½ inches (4 cm) in length, the slipper limpet is found in the Boreal zone as far north as the Gulf of St. Lawrence on any hard substrate, be it rock or another mollusk shell.

The interesting Latin name given to the slipper limpet refers to its rather uncommon sexual arrangements. Slipper limpets are often found in stacks with larger, older individuals on the bottom and smaller, young ones on top. In such a stack, the bottom animals are female, the middle ones are hermaphrodites, undergoing a sex change, and the top ones are male. The protandrous breeding cycle of slipper limpets, where the male reproductive tract degenerates and allows the female gonads to develop, is dependent on the sex of other slipper limpets around an individual. A male remains male as long as it is attached to a female. If the females of a stack die and the males are surrounded by a large number of males, some of them become female. Once a slipper limpet has become female, it remains female.

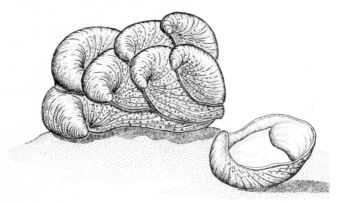

83. In a stack of slipper limpets, the larger individuals at the bottom are females and the smaller ones at the top are males.

The female slipper limpet lays a gelatinous egg mass in front of her foot, which she roofs over, giving the developing eggs protection. As long as the egg mass is under her protection, she does not spawn again. A single female spawns ten times annually, depositing 50 to 100 soft capsules each time.

Though slipper limpets compete somewhat with oysters

now at all common on the Boreal coast. 400 million years ago brachiopods were some of the sea's most successful and diverse animals.

Suspension feeding polychaete worms are not common on hard surfaces, for most species are vulnerable to predation unless they can bury themselves in soft substrates or under or among other animals. One group of polychaetes secretes hard calcareous tubes, however, and are able to glue their impregnable tubes to a variety of hard surfaces. The smallest of these serpulid worms are the minute coiled *Spirorbis* species, which grow subtidally on rock and shell surfaces just as *Spirorbis borealis* grows on the blades of intertidal rockweeds (see chapter 2). A much larger species is *Hydroides dianthus*, which grows irregularly to lengths of 3 to 4 inches (7.5 to 10 cm) on the surfaces of stones and shells. It is a southern species which extends north to Cape Cod, and is most familiar cast up attached to shells of bay scallops, *Aequipecten irradians*, in the jetsam on the beaches at the southern limits of the Boreal region (see chapter 3).

The Stinging Sessile Coelenterates

A variety of types of Boreal coelenterates sit on hard subtidal surfaces, feeding primarily on small planktonic organisms. They capture their prey and protect themselves from predators by means of their stinging cells or nematocysts. Some of them are the same species that often occur in low tide pools, particularly the hydroids and the sea anemone, *Metridium senile* (see chapter 2). Other sea anemones which may occur in more northern pools but are more typically subtidal are the northern anemone, *Tealia felina*, with its swirls of short thick tentacles, and the considerably smaller *Bunodactis stella*, which has relatively long large tentacles.

CORALS

Closely related to the solitary anemones are the colonial corals, which have many small polyps embedded in a common leathery or calcareous matrix. Most of the Boreal corals live in deep water, but two species also live in shallow

for food, as both are suspension feeders, oystermen sometimes spread stacks of limpets over an area where they want
to plant seed oysters. The oyster spat then settles on the
limpet shells. However the slipper limpet can be a pest to
oyster beds for the limpets also settle on oyster shells and
not only compete for the same food but can also smother
the oysters underneath them.

Horse Mussel. The horse mussel, *Modiolus modiolus*,
is quite similar to the intertidal blue mussel, *Mytilus edulis*
(see chapter 2). These large mussels grow to 6 inches (15
cm) in length and are easily distinguished from the blue
mussel by the fringe of fibers on the edge of the shell.
Though the shell is white, it is covered by a brownish or
bluish black coating which flakes off as the animal gets
older. The animal itself is an orange-red or gold and is easy
to see as the valves cannot close tightly.

Though the horse mussel extends upward from subtidal
depths of 480 feet (145 m) to the low intertidal, it is chiefly
subtidal as it cannot withstand desiccation. It can burrow in
gravel but it prefers a rocky bottom where it can get good
anchorage in rock crevices. The horse mussel spins especially heavy byssal threads that form a mat. This mat
catches mud and other debris and often provides a mini-
habitat ideal for small worms and brittle stars as well as for
juvenile snails and crabs.

OTHER SUSPENSION FEEDERS

Bryozoans are capable competitors for space on all types
of subtidal hard surfaces. Species such as the flat, encrusting *Membranipora* and the bushy *Bugula* are particularly
common along the Boreal coast and by late summer often
grow to considerable dimensions. Both also grow well in
low tide pools (see chapter 2).

The northern lamp shell, *Terebratulina septentrionalis*,
may occur occasionally in some abundance. It is a
brachipod, something like a large bryozoan individual encased in a thin bivalve shell which makes it at first look like
a mollusk. It feeds in the bryozoan manner, however, trapping plankton and detritus with its lophophore feeding organ. The pale shelled *Terebratulina* is the only brachiopod

The Kelp Zone: Solid Substrates   263

water especially where temperatures do not warm up too much in summer. The largest of the two is a soft coral which can look like a large finger sponge, and is known appropriately as dead man's fingers, *Alcyonium digitatum*. Calcareous spicules add strength to its leathery lobes. It grows to lengths of 8 to 10 inches (20 to 25 cm), attached to rocks or shells. Each polyp, or zooid, is connected to each of its neighbors in the colony, and the colony grows asexually by budding. The coral also reproduces sexually and, as in sea anemones, a fertilized egg develops into a creeping planula larva which grows into a single new polyp (see chapter 2). That polyp buds, secretes skeleton spicules, and a new coral colony originates.

The other common colonial Boreal species is the star coral, *Astrangia danae*. It is a scleractinian or stony coral with a hard skeleton of calcium carbonate, similar to the corals which form the coral reefs of shallow tropical waters. The star coral is delicate and beautiful, for the polyps are a translucent peach or pink, each up to ½ inch (1.3 cm) when fully extended. Each colony grows from 2 to 3 inches (5 to 7.5 cm) in diameter and may have as many as 30 to 40 polyps. In a good location in a subtidal cave or on a clean rock face in deeper water, the density of colonies of star corals may become great. Such locations are often good for scarlet sea cucumbers, *Psolus fabricii*, as well, and the combination of the two organisms covering an expanse of rock presents one of the loveliest sights a diver could hope to see.

STALKED JELLYFISH
Jellyfish are generally thought of as pulsating, free-swimming members of the plankton. One group of scyphozoan jellyfish, however, is completely sessile, and various species may be common in shallow Boreal waters in spring and early summer. These stalked jellyfish, or stauromedusae, are graceful animals, swaying and twisting gently on their stalks as they sweep the water for small organisms.

Five species of stalked jellyfish occur in Boreal waters, often attached to blades of kelp in relatively quiet water, but also growing on eel grass, *Zostera marina*, and other substrates (see color plate III). All have eight clusters of

The Kelp Zone: Solid Substrates   265

tentacles around their bell margins, and each tentacle ends in a ball of potent nematocysts, or sting cells. Of the five species, the green or brown *Haliclystus auricula* and the pink *H. salpinx* are particularly beautiful and delicate, growing to ½ to 1 inch (1.3 to 2.5 cm) in diameter. The deep rust colored *Thaumatoscyphus atlanticus* looks like a tiny wine goblet about ½ inch (1.3 cm) in diameter. *Craterolophus convolvulus* is bright green, has a remarkably short stalk and deep bell, and grows to an inch (2.5 cm) or more in length. By far the largest of the five species, though, is the brown *Lucernaria quadricornis*, particularly common on kelp blades and probably too large to hang on to eel grass. Like all stalked jellyfish it begins to grow as a very small polyp in spring, but by mid-summer when it is ready to spawn and die it may be up to 4 inches (10 cm) long from its tentacles to its adhesive basal disk, and can probably catch and eat surprisingly large prey.

Competition Among Sessile Animals

Often a shallow subtidal habitat is neither unlimited bedrock nor unlimited sand or mud, but instead consists of boulders or rock outcroppings surrounded by soft substrates. The rocks become islands in a sea of sand or mud, the only places the larvae of the sessile animals can attach themselves to. Since suspension feeders all feed in much the same way on the same food source, their competition is not really for the food itself but for space which gives them access to the food. Space becomes a limiting factor and various species have different ways of competing for it.

Which species grow successfully on such rocks, how many species share the space, and whether one or more of them actually dominate the space depend on many factors. Once the larvae find a rock surface, they select or reject it depending upon the amount of light exposure, the temperature regime, and the slope and texture of rock surface they need to grow on. They may be attracted to settle by the presence of adults of their own species, or the adults may inhibit their settling or perhaps just eat them. Even the presence of microorganisms may determine whether the larvae select the rock or move on in search of another space to settle on.

Once a species becomes established on a rock surface it may simply overgrow neighboring species, starving them to death in the process. The colonial sea squirts, *Botryllus* and *Amaroucium*, and the bread crumb sponge, *Halichondria panicea*, spread in such a manner. When two colonies of one of these species happen to grow close enough to touch each other, they usually fuse and form a single larger colony. Competition between different species may be intense, but competition between colonies of the same species is greatly reduced.

Some species can survive being overgrown, especially tube-building worms such as *Hydroides dianthus*. They need only continue building the front ends of their tubes ahead of the advancing edge of the overgrowing species. So long as their heads are exposed, the worms are able to feed, and in fact the worms derive additional protection from predation.

Another strategy in this competition for access to food is to grow upright away from the attachment surface, and a number of species grow into relatively large individuals or colonies, supported by small basal attachment disks. Branching colonial hydroids such as *Obelia*, bryozoans such as *Bugula*, the finger sponge, *Haliclona oculata*, the solitary sea squirts such as the sea potato, *Boltenia ovifera*, all escape overgrowth by flat encrusting species and feed from water unavailable to the encrusting animals. Even the large barnacles, *Balanus balanus* and *B. crenatus*, as well as the sea anemone, *Metridium senile*, despite their broad attachment surfaces, grow high enough off the substrate to escape overgrowth, and in any case sea anemones can move slowly to better sites (see plate V).

If the particular rock outcropping or boulder is large, the diversity of sessile animals inhabiting it is likely to be large as well, for larvae of many species are likely to happen upon the rock surface and settle. The longer the rock surface remains undisturbed by the wave surge of storms, the more time there is for larvae which settle at different seasons to find it. Time as well as space determines the diversity of sessile animals on a rock surface.

The Kelp Zone: Solid Substrates 267

In contrast, wave surge tosses small boulders about and colonist species may be scoured off or crushed or pushed into the substrate. Because the time of undisturbed existence is shorter, one or another of the potential colonizing species is likely to dominate the space. Some sessile species are missing from a boulder community because their larvae happened not to find it or because they settled from the plankton at a time the boulder was disturbed. Diversity on the boulder is likely to remain low, for successful colonists run a fair risk of being completely eliminated from the boulder. An individual or colony overgrown by another species may have nowhere else to go on a small boulder, and even if it does become well established, physical disturbance of the boulder prevents any species from having long term residence. Whichever species dominates a small boulder does so because it got there before its competitors and was able to monopolize the limited space before other species could establish themselves.

On rocks that are not large enough to allow space for many colonizing species to settle and grow successfully, but which are deep enough to be undisturbed by overhead wave surge, a single species such as one of the encrusting bryozoans or colonial sea squirts may actually dominate the space for years. The dominating species may be able to grow asexually over virtually all the available space. Until the boulder is eventually disturbed in some way, other species may be unable to settle.

The diversity of sessile animals is therefore greater on large boulders than on small ones. The diversity on a small boulder is low either because it is disturbed too frequently or, paradoxically, because it is disturbed too infrequently. Intermediate rates of disturbance which probably are characteristic of most moderately shallow subtidal water result in greater diversity, for colonizers then have time to find the boulders but insufficient time to monopolize them.

Other hard substrates besides boulders may be island-like in their distribution. The under sides of boats and moorings are much like small, frequently disturbed boulders. Few species should monopolize the available space and diversity should be low. The under side of a dock not cleaned for years at a time should be more like a large boulder, and diversity should be correspondingly higher.

Still other factors are involved in determining the distribution of the sessile animals. Predation by nudibranchs may restrict the growth of hydroids or sponges, and whelks may eliminate barnacles and mussels. Some species such as barnacles get a head start on others by settling in spring but they may be overgrown by bryozoans in late summer and all may be scoured off by winter ice. The holdfasts of species like the various kelp can drastically modify the texture of the substrate, making it more suitable for some animals but less so for others.

Where a rock outcropping is particularly large and the environment reasonably stable, large amounts of space may eventually be monopolized by species that cannot grow asexually to cover the available surface but instead grow large. Solitary species such as the barnacles and sea squirts are good examples, and star corals, *Astrangia danae*, and scarlet sea cucumbers, *Psolus fabricii*, may be locally abundant. Most impressive, however, are the extensive beds of horse mussels, *Modiolus modiolus*, which by virtue of their size and long life may dominate a substrate indefinitely.

Predators

Although many subtidal predators of the Boreal region forage over a wide variety of substrates, a few are generally restricted to hard substrates that they can cling on to. The most common of these are the Boreal starfish and brittle stars, some of the large whelks, and at least a couple of species of small fish.

STARFISH

The starlike shape of sea stars, or starfish, reflects the radial symmetry that is characteristic of all echinoderms, from sea urchins to sea cucumbers. A starfish has a diffuse nervous system with nerves radiating outward from a central ring into each arm. Since each arm is capable of leading the starfish, all periphery parts are equally sensitive and there is no head-type region of concentrated nerve ganglia.

The tip of each starfish arm has a red-pigmented eyespot which is especially sensitive to light. In addition to the eyespot, there are large numbers of sensory receptors in the skin which detect light, chemical and contact stimuli. These receptors are most abundant on the tube feet.

Starfish have a highly specialized water-vascular system that is unique to echinoderms. Water is continuously taken into the starfish through a large perforated plate on the upper surface called the madreporite, which means "mother of pores." The water passes into a ring which encircles the mouth area of the central disk and is then directed into each of the arms. Along the radial water canals are lateral canals, each of which ends in a single tube foot. This system keeps the body firm and provides a means of locomotion and a method for opening bivalve shells.

Each tube foot has a bulb on its internal end which forces fluid into the foot, causing it to extend by hydraulic pressure. At the tip of the tube foot is a very strong sucker. In addition to secreting a glue, the sucker adheres by vacuum pressure created by raising the central portion of the sucker. The strength of the combined tube feet can pull a large starfish up vertical surfaces or separate the shells of tightly closed mollusks. The coordination of the tube feet is equally impressive. Different arms act as the leading arm at different times and the podia, or tube feet, of the remaining arms follow the leader. Hydraulic valves open and close in step.

Starfish also have remarkable regenerative abilities, for if an arm is taken by a predator, the starfish can grow a new arm in its place. In fact, in some species if a single arm is attached to only half of the disk, new buds can form and develop into the missing arms. This ability foils man's attempts to eradicate starfish which often ravage oyster and mussel beds. People used to collect the pesty starfish, cut them in half and throw them back into the ocean where they thought the pieces would decay. Instead, more starfish were created.

Starfish sexes are usually separate. Fertilization is external as individuals spawn sperm and eggs into the water. A single spawning individual provides a stimulus for other nearby starfish to spawn, and since starfish are often found in aggregates, fertilization is usually successful. In most species, the eggs develop into planktonic larvae which are bilateral in symmetry and look radically different from the adults. The larvae metamorphose dramatically, assuming adult radial symmetry and settling to the bottom.

ASTERIID STARFISH. Some of the most common starfish of the Boreal coast are the asteriid starfish, *Asterias forbesi*, *A. vulgaris*, and *Leptasterias tenera*. These starfish differ from others in having four rows of tube feet on the underside of each arm instead of two, and in having small pincer-like appendages called pedicellariae scattered over the upper surface. These pincers can open and close and serve both to protect the starfish and to keep its surface clean by capturing and removing very small animals.

Both *Asterias forbesi* and *A. vulgaris* have five flexible arms and are highly variable in color, ranging from green or purple to pink or bright red. Both are greatly textured with tubercules and pedicellariae and grow to 6 inches (15 cm) or more in diameter. In the northern end of their ranges they reach as much as 17 inches (42.5 cm). *Asterias forbesi* becomes uncommon north of Massachusetts and has a bright orange-red madreporite. It is common intertidally from Cape Cod south. *Asterias vulgaris*, on the other hand, is common intertidally from Cape Cod north and has a light yellow madreporite (see plate V).

These two *Asterias* species eat mainly bivalve mollusks and are known for their destruction of oyster and mussel beds. The starfish literally eat the bivalves in their own shells and their method of overcoming the tightly closed shells is remarkable. The starfish wraps its five strong arms around the mollusk, gripping the shells tightly with its tube feet and placing its mouth area over the meeting line of the shells. It then pushes its stomach out through its mouth and as soon as the continual pressure of the tube feet slightly opens the mollusk's shells, a thin wall of the everted stomach slips in between the two shells. Enzymes immediately set to work digesting the mollusk while more and more of the stomach works its way inside. When the soft parts of the prey have been digested, the stomach muscles contract, pulling the stomach back inside the starfish and leaving empty oyster or mussel shells behind. The starfish are a double nuisance to the oyster beds. They breed just enough before the oysters do that the starfish larvae are settled before the oyster spat. The spat is then greedily devoured by the small starfish.

The starfish are prey to crabs, lobsters and some of the

bottom-dwelling fish. However, their time of greater susceptibility to predation is during their planktonic larval life.

Leptasterias tenera is a slender-armed asteriid and is usually light purple or pink with a very light madreporite. Though it is intertidal in the northern Boreal region, it is found only subtidally in the southern end where it sometimes lives as deep as 800 feet (240 m). *Leptasterias* differs from the other two asteriids in that it broods its young in a brood sack made partly by curling its arms under the body and partly by everting the borders of the mouth. Brooding as a reproductive strategy is more common in polar starfish and the eggs of brooding species are usually small in number but large in size with a large amount of yolk. The eggs, bypassing the planktonic larval stages, develop directly into small starfish.

BLOOD STARFISH. The blood starfish, *Henricia* species, is deep red in color and almost velvety to the touch. It is relatively small, growing to 4 inches (10 cm) in diameter in the south but up to a maximum of 8 inches (30 cm) in the polar regions. Like most starfish it has only two rows of tube feet.

The blood starfish primarily eats sponges, though it also has an auxiliary method of feeding whereby plankton and detritus that is caught in the mucous coating of its skin is

84. Common starfish of the Boreal coast. A. the sunstar *Crossaster* B. the bloodstar *Henricia* C. the asteriid *Asterias*

THE SHALLOW MARINE SUBTIDAL

swept by flagella into the mouth. Like *Leptasterias* it broods its young in a pouch formed under its mouth by its arms, and its eggs develop directly into juvenile starfish. From Maine north the blood starfish can be found in tide pools and shallow subtidal areas. In Cape Cod waters it is usually subtidal at about 15 feet (4.5 m) or more.

THE SUNSTARS. The other common starfish of the Boreal region are the multi-armed sunstars. These starfish are found in the low intertidal only north of Maine and subtidally at about 120 feet (36 m) at Cape Cod.

The purple sunstar, *Solaster endeca*, usually has 9 or 10 arms, though this can vary from 7 to 13 as well. It is a brilliant red-violet with a light yellow madreporite and it grows to 16 inches (40 cm) or more in diameter. It has no free-swimming larval stage; the eggs develop directly into juvenile sunstars. Like other starfish, the purple sunstar is a carnivore, but it concentrates mostly on holothurians.

The spiny sunstar, *Crossaster papposus*, is magnificently colored with a scarlet center surrounded by crimson bands alternating with pinkish bands radiating outward across its arms. The spiny sunstar usually has 10 to 12 arms, though again this can vary from 8 to 14. It is usually somewhat smaller in size than the purple sunstar, reaching about 14 inches (35 cm) in diameter. Its development and feeding habits are similar to those of purple sunstars, except that is apparently includes sea anemones and *Asterias* starfish in its diet as well.

BRITTLE STARS OR SERPENT STARS. The long writhing arms and strongly delineated central disk of brittle stars, or serpent stars, easily distinguishes them from starfish. The tube feet of brittle stars are greatly reduced and play little role in locomotion. Rather, brittle stars move by means of their mobile and flexible arms which often seem to be in constant motion. In contrast to starfish, the disk of brittle stars is flattened and the animals usually have only 5 arms. The madreporite is located on the underside of the disk and since brittle stars avoid light they are usually found under small rocks or in other dark places. Brittle stars feed on detritus, polychaete worms or small crustaceans (see figure 33).

The regenerative ability of brittle stars is as remarkable

as that of starfish. Though more of the central disk usually has to be present than is needed for starfish, brittle stars readily break off their fragile arms at any point, not just at the disk joint. Since the arms are constantly snaking about in search of food, the likelihood of being caught by small crustaceans and fish is great. When this happens, the brittle star simply detaches the trapped portion and leaves its predator with only part of an arm to chew on.

Most brittle stars have separate sexes, though reproduc tion in the group as a whole varies tremendously. Polar species often brood their young, as do polar starfish. Some brittle stars are hermaphroditic and certain of these are protandric, being male first and then female as they grow older.

The daisy brittle star, *Ophiopholus aculeata*, is the most common Boreal brittle star. It is found from low tide pools, where one or more of its arms can be seen snaking out from under a rock or a small cave, to depths of 5000 feet (1500 m). The disk of this colorful little brittle star reaches about 4/5 inch (20 mm) diameter and its arms grow to 3½ inches (8 cm) in length. Daisy brittle stars vary in color from a red disk with red and white banded arms to a blue disk with green or brown arms.

The dwarf brittle star, *Axiognathus squamatus*, is very common though easily overlooked. It is extremely small and delicate; its disk grows to 1/5 inch (5 mm) in diameter and its threadlike arms grow to about an inch (25 mm). The dwarf brittle star is drably colored, usually gray or brown, which adds to the difficulty of seeing it. It can be found in soft sediments under rocks, in the green algae, *Cladophora*, or in red coralline algae in tide pools, and sub- tidally to 1000 feet (300 m). The dwarf brittle star is her- maphroditic and broods its young, which emerge from the brood pouch as juvenile brittle stars.

The yellowish brown basket star, *Gorgonocephalus arcticus*, gains its common name from its basket-like ap- pearance when its branching arms are curled up. When its arms are extended its five-rayed symmetry is more obvious. The disk grows from 2¼ to 4 inches (5 to 12 cm) and its long arms, which branch from the base in V-shaped divisions, grow to 9 to 14 inches (22 to 35 cm). Individuals are often

found with sea whips, *Chorda filum*, and are sometimes en-
tangled in masses with other basket stars. When they are in
such masses, the basket stars form an inescapable net which
catches many kinds of small organisms. These beautiful
echinoderms are found at the low tide level in northern
Boreal waters, at 20 to 40 feet (6.6 to 13 m) in the Bay of
Fundy region and considerably deeper at Cape Cod. They
also occur offshore as deep as 4000 feet (1200 m).

THE WHELKS

The waved whelk, *Buccinum undatum*, is a carnivorous
tannish snail, growing to 4 inches (10 cm). It is found on
rocky substrates. Young *Buccinum* frequent tide pools and
shallow subtidal areas while the adults range to depths as
great as 600 feet (180 m). Though adults are sometimes
found foraging in the low intertidal area, the waved whelk
has no defense against desiccation. When the tide ebbs,
whelks may be left exposed, but unlike true intertidal gastropods which close their opercula and seal themselves off
from the dry air, the waved whelk invariably continues to
forage. It becomes more and more desiccated until it dies.
It is, without doubt, a subtidal species.

The waved whelk is both scavenger and predator. It
plagues lobster fishermen with its habit of stealing the fish
bait from lobster traps and can be as much of a pest to
fishermen who use fish traps. With its well developed
chemoreceptors this whelk quickly detects the presence
of fish and 10 to 20 whelks may attack a single fish caught
in a net.

As a predator the waved whelk holds the valves of
bivalve mollusks apart with the outer lip of its anterior
canal. The proboscis then consumes the soft parts of the
prey with digestive enzymes and its efficient radula. *Buccinum* is the edible whelk of Britain and other parts of
Europe but is as yet not eaten by many North Americans.
Herring gulls prey on them wherever they can catch them.
They break whelks by dropping them on rock surfaces.
Shells and empty egg capsules of *Buccinum* often wash
ashore on beaches (see chapter 3).

The other common subtidal whelk on rocky substrates is
the ten-ridged whelk or New England Neptune, *Neptunea
decemcostata*. It grows to about the same size as the waved

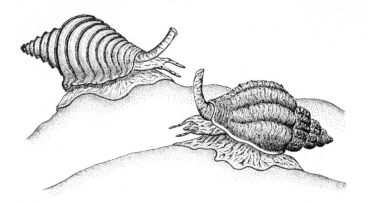

85. Two subtidal whelks, the waved whelk *Buccinum undatum* (right) and the New England Neptune *Neptunea decemcostata* (left) are both efficient carnivores.

whelk but is very easy to distinguish with its definite spiral ridges, reddish-brown color and spindle shape. It has similar habits to the waved whelk though it is more a scavenger than a predator. It occurs mostly in rocky areas, though it sometimes forages on sand patches, and it is found from shallow subtidal to deep water. Its egg capsules are laid in tower-like structures that rarely wash ashore.

FISH

A few fish are quite restricted to living on hard substrates. The rock eel, *Pholis gunnellus,* lives under rocks in the low intertidal zone along parts of the Boreal coast (see chapter 2) and, where the subtidal substrate offers the appropriate protective cover and relatively shallow slope, the rock eel occurs below the low tide level as well. Far more frequent on the rocky substrates of the kelp zone, and on the kelp itself, are the rather bizarre lumpfish and sea snails.

The Lumpfish or Lump Sucker. The lumpfish, or lump sucker, *Cyclopterus lumpus,* is an ungainly looking fish with a short head, a knobbly body, and a large sucking disk located just behind the throat. Lumpfish grow to almost 2 feet (60 cm) and 20 pounds (9 kg). With their suckers they often cling to rocks, lobster pots, the undersides of lobster cars, or even poles of fishing weirs.

Lumpfish feed on small crustaceans, including isopods,

86. The lumpfish often attaches itself to a rock or some kelp when it is not feeding on sea gooseberries or small crustaceans.

amphipods and euphausiid shrimp. In addition, they munch on moon jellyfish, *Aurelia aurita*, and are one of the few fish that include ctenophores, or sea gooseberries, as a regular part of their diet. Because they are relatively weak swimmers they are easy prey for seals and larger fish.

Most marine subtidal fish deposit and fertilize their eggs and then abandon them, but this is not the case with lumpfish. Spawning occurs from February through May, and an adult female lays around 140,000 sticky non-bouyant pink or yellow eggs in water at least a couple of fathoms (4 m) deep. The male lumpfish guards the sponge-like masses of eggs until they hatch. Incubation in the cool late-winter waters takes longer than is usual for most fish, usually lasting six to eight weeks. During this time, the male never eats nor does he leave his site except to drive off predators. He also fans the eggs, keeping them free of silt and supplied with lots of oxygen. As soon as the eggs hatch, the male departs, thin and spent from his long vigil. Females, on the other hand, leave as soon as the eggs are laid.

SEA SNAILS.   Sea snails are small tadpole-shaped fish. Two virtually indistinguishable species, *Neoliparis atlanticus* and *Liparis liparis*, occur along the Boreal coast where they hide under stones and cling to kelp stipes and blades. As in the larger lumpfish, *Cyclopterus lumpus*, the ventral fins of a sea snail are modified to form a suction disk which the fish uses to hold itself in place. Sea snails grow to only 3 or 4 inches (7.5 to 10 cm) and prey upon small crustaceans. They lay their sticky eggs in early spring, and when the subsequent larvae reach a length of about ½ inch (1.3 cm) they begin to look and act like their parents. Small individuals have been found not too uncommonly hiding in the shells of the giant scallop, *Placopecten magellanicus.*

Soft Subtidal Substrates

Along long stretches of the Boreal coast, rocky subtidal substrates are not very common. South of Maine's Cape Elizabeth, subtidal substrates are for the most part soft ones, just as they are in the southern Gulf of St. Lawrence. Even along rocky coastlines, the rocks eventually give way to sand or mud, sometimes in shallow water, sometimes at greater depths.

A number of factors influence just how extensive soft subtidal substrates are and what kind of sediment they are made of. For the most part, these are the same factors which also determine the extent and nature of soft intertidal substrates. Erosion of the sedimentary and metamorphic rock of exposed headlands contributes a continuing supply of sediment, and river runoff transports other sediment to the open coast. Such sediment is deposited on whatever other marine deposits have accumulated since the departure of the glaciers, and underlying those marine deposits there is usually a veneer of glacial debris.

Longshore currents, tidal currents and the waves of storms move the sediment along the coastlines over the course of months and years. Where little sediment is available from erosion and river runoff, soft subtidal substrates may be limited in size and depth. Where little sand is available, soft substrates are more likely to be muddy, as they are along the rocky coast of Maine.

Soft subtidal substrates have much in common with intertidal ones. The burrowing animals or infauna that dominate them push themselves into or through sandy sediments but build tubes and dig burrows in sediments that contain more mud and clay. Each soft substrate, whether it is coarse sand, fine sand, sand mixed with mud, or just mud or clay, is likely to have its own infauna community. Patches of different types of sediment often lie remarkably close to one another, and the distribution of many of the burrowers may be patchy as a result. Other species, less restricted to sediments of a certain size of particle, may be broadly distributed through the different patches. Foraging over the substrate are yet other organisms, the epifauna, which are all predators on the burrowing species and are relatively unselective in the kind of substrate they frequent.

The sediments of soft subtidal substrates shift in response to currents and wave surge and are just as unsuitable to plants and animals that need hard substrates under them as are the intertidal beaches and flats.

Only the thin upper layer of subtidal sediments contains sufficient oxygen for most animals to survive. The coarser the sediment, the deeper there is sufficient oxygen, but in fine muds animals may be restricted to the top half inch (1 cm) just as they often are on mud flats. Otherwise the soft subtidal substrates lack the large fluctuations in salinity and temperature which so characterize their intertidal counterparts and like the other marine subtidal habitats, they are relatively benign.

Subtidal Plants: Eel Grass Beds

Except where isolated rocks or clusters of mussels give them a precarious foothold, macroalgae are quite absent from subtidal soft substrates. However, along the shores of large parts of the world's protected coasts where there is extensive sand or sandy mud, several kinds of marine grasses flourish, growing, rooting, flowering and cross-pollinating while submerged. Turtle grass, *Thalassia*, is dominant in tropical and subtropical regions; eel grass, *Zostera*, in temperate ones.

The common eel grass of the North Atlantic is *Zostera marina*, a species which grows best at temperatures between 50 and 68° F (10 to 20° C), reproduces best between 59 and 68° F (15 to 20° C), but adapts well to local conditions and can tolerate temperatures as low as 32° F (0° C) and as high as 86° F (30° C). Like the other sea grasses,

87. An eel grass bed provides both food and protection for a large assortment of plants and animals. The close up on the right shows detail of the plant and roots.

Zostera marina penetrates sand or sandy mud with its roots and establishes itself where macroalgae cannot. It is unable to establish itself where there is much wave action or where tidal currents are excessive and so it occurs in sheltered bays and inlets. It can, however, tolerate quite dilute salt water and as a result grows in lower estuaries as well as in coastal bays. Like other sea grasses it has salt glands on its leaves that remove sodium and chlorine ions from the cell sap and permit the plant to survive in a salty environment.

Eel grass usually grows within a few meters below the low tide level, but in some places it may be exposed by very low tides and in others it has been found as deep as 100 feet (30 m). How deep it grows and how large its underwater meadows become depends on wave and current action, turbidity and light penetration of the water, and the extensiveness of the appropriate substrate. Where the water is murky and light penetration is low, the grass may be limited to very shallow water, perhaps no more than about 3 feet (1 m) below the low tide level.

Where conditions are good for their growth, eel grass beds may be among the world's most productive areas, for eel grass can grow as quickly as cultivated corn or hay.

The roots of a well established bed of eel grass may be so

thick and bind the sediment so well that the bed may be able to withstand the waves produced by gales or storms. The leaves of the grass also further slow the movement of even weak waves or currents, trapping sediment in and near the bed. As a result, in an estuary the formation of an eel grass bed is sometimes the first event that leads to the development of an intertidal salt marsh.

An eel grass bed therefore stabilizes the substrate it grows on. Its dense growth of grass blades gives to an otherwise uniform habitat a greatly increased structural complexity, for the blades provide surfaces for plants and animals to attach themselves to and they provide protective cover for other animals. Because the eel grass plants are so productive, there are always large amounts of detritus, particularly decaying plant material, for animals to feed on. Feeding on the detritovores are often large numbers of small fish for which an eel grass bed is an excellent nursery as it provides them with both ample cover and abundant food.

The biomass of plants growing on the eel grass blades can be almost as great as that of the eel grass itself, for they are growing in water that is rich in nutrients and is well oxygenated. Apart from birds such as black ducks and Canada geese, as well as Brants in the more southern eel grass beds, few animals actually eat the living grass. Deposit feeders predominate instead, eating what has settled on the grass blades and on the bottom substrate. In general, snails graze on the surface of the grass blades, amphipods and small shrimp on the detritus, encrusting bryozoans on suspended food particles, and attached hydroids and the occasional stalked jellyfish sting and eat small organisms that bump into them (see plate III). The eel grass permits plants and sessile animals to grow where otherwise they would find no way of attaching themselves.

Eel grass beds are not what they once were. In 1930–31 an epidemic destroyed about 90 percent of the eel grass along the Atlantic coast and all the organisms which used the beds for food or protection were seriously affected. The blue-eyed or bay scallop, *Aequipecten irradians*, depends upon eel grass for its young to settle and grow on until they are large enough to leave the beds to rest on a variety of substrates, and Brants rely heavily on eel grass for their food during the nonbreeding months. Both were never common north of Cape Cod, but their populations around Cape Cod and southward were decimated by the loss of the eel grass.

The organism which killed the eel grass was apparently a parasitic protozoan called *Labryinthula*, which elimated the grass from shorelines of high water salinity. Because the protozoan does not tolerate salinity levels as low as those tolerated by eel grass, pockets of eel grass survived in estuaries. Very gradually eel grass beds have been reestablishing themselves along the coast, but the process is slow and a major marine habitat has been severely diminished. If eel grass beds do become extensive again in marine waters, there is no real reason why the parasite may not flourish as well and push them back once more into the estuaries.

Burrowing Animals: the Infauna

The animals burrowing and digging in the soft subtidal marine substrates of the Boreal region are similar to those of intertidal substrates. Because conditions are far more stable in the subtidal, the diversity of burrowing animals there is far greater. Sediments in the shallow subtidal are exposed to colder winter temperatures and warmer summer ones than are sediments in slightly deeper water, and the deeper sediments as a result have a greater diversity of animals burrowing in them.

Many other factors also determine how many different species are present in a sediment. A sand substrate is structurally more complex than mud and there are more microhabitats available for different species to take advantage of. Time is important as well, for an environment needs to be stable for a long period before it can continue to support a high diversity of animals. The diversity of Boreal burrowing animals is greatest where water temperatures remain cool or cold, salinities remain around 35‰, oxygen is abundant, and the substrate itself is extensive and varied.

Burrowing harpacticoid copepods and nematodes are the

THE SHALLOW MARINE SUBTIDAL

dominant small organisms, or meiofauna, just as they are intertidally, though different species are likely to be present. Burrowing and tube-dwelling amphipods and polychaete worms dominate the communities of larger burrowing animals along with bivalve mollusks, again just as they do intertidally. As the proportion of mud in the substrate increases, tube-builders and deposit feeders become more common. As a substrate becomes sandier, less detritus is deposited on the surface of the sediment but more is held in suspension in the water, and suspension feeders become more common. Most of the polychaete worms that are common subtidally occur in the low intertidal as well. The predatory *Nephtys* and *Nereis* species; the burrowing lugworm, *Arenicola marina;* the trumpet worm, *Pectinaria gouldii;* and the bamboo worm, *Clymenella torquata* are as frequent on muddy sand substrates subtidally as they are on sand flats (see chapter 3). The mudworm, *Polydora ligni;* thread worm, *Capitella capitata;* and the red-gilled *Amphitrite* species also all burrow in subtidal muds just as they do in intertidal mudflats (see chapter 4).

Fanworms. Some polychaete worms are exclusively subtidal or extend into the intertidal only in the cold, northern part of their range. Among these is the lovely fanworm, *Myxicola infundibulum.* The translucent webbed tentacle crown of this segmented worm is its only visible part. This delicate 2 to 3 inch (5 to 7.5 cm) crown of feathery tentacles or radioles serves both feeding and respiratory functions. When extended, the crown forms a funnel through which beating cilia produce a current of water. Minute food particles are trapped and driven by cilia into a groove along each of the radioles. The particles descend down the funnel to the mouth area where they are sorted. The largest ones are rejected, the smallest ones ingested and the medium ones stored for future use in tube building. The continuous current of water through the crown also allows gas exchange to take place at the tentacles.

The soft leathery tube of this fanworm may be about 8 inches (20 cm) long. The tube is built by a collar just below the base of the crown. Here a mucus string is secreted while the animal rotates, causing the particle-laden mucus to coil on top of previously deposited mucus.

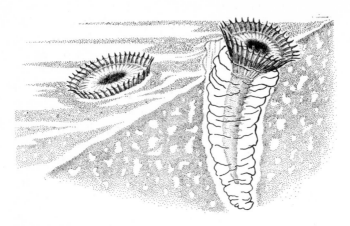

88. The fan worm *Myxicola infundibulum* burrows in soft substrates.

The body of *Myxicola* is pink and composed of 60 segments, each with bristles and hooks. Its main defense against predators is incredibly rapid contraction into its tube at the slightest shadow detected by its light-sensitive eyespots. Such rapid contraction is possible due to a single giant nerve axon running the length of the worm.

Like many other polychaete worms, the fanworm has separate sexes which deposit eggs and sperm in the sea water where external fertilization takes place. The developing young spend the first phase of their lives as free-swimming spherically-shaped larvae before metamorphosing into sedentary adult worms.

Burrowing Sea Anemone. The burrowing sea anemone, *Cerianthus borealis*, looks at first like a large champagne-colored flower. Only its tentacles and mouth surface are visible. The rest of its body is buried in the sandy or muddy substrate on which it lives, encased in a long thick tube made of mud and other materials held together by mucus. Rather than have a disk for adhering to a hard substrate like other sea anemones, the burrowing anemone's bottom end has been modified into a digging organ, allowing it to burrow into soft substrates.

Cerianthus is a suspension feeder which can sting and paralyze the small organisms which touch its tentacles. It

89. Though it feeds like other sea anemones, the flower-like *Cerianthus* burrows in soft substrates.

has two separate whorls of tentacles around the mouth area, the inner tentacles being shorter than the outer ones. In deep or northern waters *Cerianthus* grows to at least 18 inches (45 cm) in length with a tentacle span of 9 inches (22.5 cm) or more. The tentacles and anterior end of the burrowing anemone retract into the tube if the animal is disturbed or threatened by a predator. In the Cape Cod area, *Cerianthus* can be found in soft substrate patches at about 40 feet (12 m) while in northern Maine it is found just below the intertidal zone.

BURROWING BIVALVES. Like the polychaete worms, many of the bivalves which burrow in intertidal sand or mud also burrow subtidally. In mud or sandy mud, the razor clam, *Ensis directus;* the soft-shelled clam, *Mya arenaria;* and the small clam, *Macoma balthica*, are all abundant both subtidally in shallow water and intertidally (see chapter 4). The surf clam, *Spisula solidissima*, occurs subtidally in sand, and the quahog, *Mercenaria mercenaria;* the gem shell, *Gemma gemma;* and the tellin, *Tellina agilis*, occur in sand mixed with some mud, just as they do intertidally (see chapter 3).

There are a number of bivalves which, like some polychaete worms, are exclusively subtidal. All of them bury themselves in the sand or mud with their siphons barely exposed and filter the water for its suspended food particles. The chestnut astarte, *Astarte castanea,* and the waved astarte, *Astarte undata,* both live in muddy sediments, are brown on the outside, white on the inside and

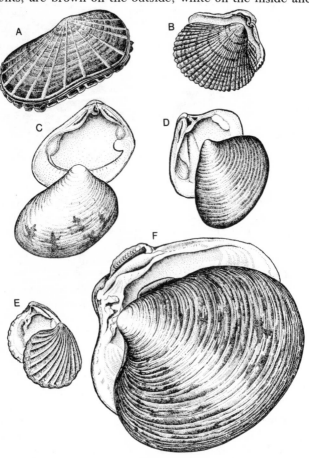

90. Subtidal burrowing bivalves: A. veiled clam, *Solemya velum* B. Iceland cockle *Clinocardium ciliatum* C. Arctic wedge clam *Mesodesma arctatum* D. Chestnut astarte *Astarte castanea* E. Northern cardita *Cyclocardia borealis* F. black clam *Arctica islandica.*

grow to about 1 inch (25 mm) or more in diameter.

Most of the subtidal bivalves live in sandier sediments, however, where suspension feeding is a more appropriate strategy. The file shell, *Yoldia limatula*, is a thin, elliptical bivalve with a row of small projections on either side of the hinge of each shell, and it grows to about 2 inches (5 cm) in length. The veiled clams, *Solemya velum* and *S. borealis*, have dark, oval fragile shells, growing to 1½ inches (4 cm) and 3 inches (7.5 cm) respectively. The Arctic wedge clam, *Mesodesma arctatum*, has a strong, thick, roughly oval shell that may be up to 2 inches (5 cm) long. The larger black clam, *Arctica islandica*, looks much like the quahog, *Mercenaria mercenaria*, but lacks the purple stain inside its shells. It grows to about 4 inches (10 cm) in diameter and is quite edible though hardly anyone eats it.

Cockles are also common in subtidal sands. The two valves of a cockle look like a heart when they are viewed from the side. Radial ribs run the length of the outer surface of the shells. Various species of cockles occur quite frequently along the Boreal coast and of these the Iceland cockle, *Clinocardium ciliatum*, with 32 to 38 radial ribs, and the northern cardita, *Cyclocardia borealis*, with 15 to 20 radial ribs, are probably the most common. Both grow to about 1½ to 2 inches (4 to 5 cm) in diameter.

Sand Dollar. The sand dollar, *Echinarchnius parma*, is a highly flattened circular echinoderm as its common name so aptly describes. Like the sea urchin, its skeletal plates are fused together making its skeleton an unmovable test. The sand dollar is covered with a multitude of very small spines, giving it a smooth texture. Although the spines on the green sea urchin are arranged in distinct rows radiating outward from the center of the upper surface, this kind of pattern is lacking in sand dollars. Each spine of the green sea urchin is attached to a separate plate of the test whereas numerous spines of the sand dollar are attached to each plate.

Sand dollars live on sandy substrates from the low intertidal in northern Boreal areas to depths of 2600 feet (800 m). They are well adapted to their burrowing existence, using their small and numerous spines to bury themselves just below the surface of the sand. Though they are not very

91. Sand dollars occur in aggregations on sandy substrates where they usually bury themselves just below the surface.

active burrowers, the burrowing serves not only as protection from wave action but also as a means for securing food. As a sand dollar burrows, sand is passed over the upper surface where minute food particles are small enough to fall in between the dense spines. These food particles are then carried by cilia to the margin of the animal and transported to the mouth on the underside. Food is also secured by the small podia, or tube feet. These modified podia extend from the five grooves on the underside and have adhesive glands and sensory cells at their tips. The sticky podia trap diatoms and other micro-organisms and move them along to the mouth.

The upper surface of the sand dollar is beautifully patterned with 5 petals radiating outward from the center. On live animals which are brownish-red to purple, these petals are often a darker color. On the bleached fragile test, the holes of the petals clearly show the position of the upper tube feet. These podia have been modified for respiration. In sand dollars, then, tube feet are not used at all for locomotion as they are in other echinoderms, but for feeding and breathing.

Sand dollars are either male or female and they reproduce like most other echinoderms, spawning eggs and sperm into the water. The planktonic phase of the developing young is followed by incredibly rapid metamorphosis, lasting about an hour, whereby the larva changes into a small sand dollar. Sand dollars grow to 3 inches (7.5 cm) in diameter and are eaten by bottom-dwelling fish such as flounders, cod and haddock.

The Wrymouth. The wrymouth, *Cryptoacanthodes maculatus,* is an eel-like fish with an oval tail fin and no ventral fins. Its dorsal fin, though long like an eel's, is spiny and helps to distinguish the wrymouth as a blenny and not a true eel. It is a brownish color with darker brown spots over much of its body and it grows to 2 or 3 feet (60 to 90 cm) in length.

Though it burrows quite commonly in the firmer subtidal mud along the Boreal coast, it is not often caught either by other fish or by fishermen. The burrow which a wrymouth digs probably protects it from all but the most persistent of predators, and when a disturbed wrymouth finally abandons its burrow, it darts off only to plunge suddenly back into the mud and disappear again. It makes its burrow by shaking itself through the mud a few inches (10 cm or more) below the surface, and often digs a small network of tunnels with four or five exits available for it.

Though little is known about this remarkable fish, it probably remains in its burrow throughout the day and preys at night on small crustaceans such as mysid shrimp and the sand shrimp, *Crangon septemspinosis,* as well as on polychaete worms and small fish.

Animals on the Surface: the Epifauna

A variety of animals occur on or near the surface of soft substrates where they feed without burying themselves. Even when they are not feeding, few of them actually burrow though they may cover themselves with a thin layer of sediment or otherwise appear well camouflaged against the surface. Most of the epifauna prey on the burrowing animals and on others of the epifauna; some are suspension feeders.

Sea Scallop. The sea scallop, *Placopecten magellanicus,* is generally thought of as a deep water species, but along much of the Boreal coast from Maine northwards small populations occur frequently in relatively shallow water. Large, deeper water populations occur from the northern Gulf of St. Lawrence to the Mid Atlantic Bight off of Virginia where they have long been gathered successfully by dredges and otter trawls. Eighty percent of the commercial catch comes from Georges Bank alone.

Sea scallops occur on a wide variety of soft substrates from mud to gravel and even boulders, but their densest aggregations are usually on coarse sand. They grow to 5 to 8 inches (12.5 to 20 cm) in diameter, and each rests on its slightly flatter right shell, which is paler in color than its reddish, more rounded upper shell. By clapping its shells together a sea scallop can move a short distance, but it usually remains fairly stationary and claps its shells mainly to clean itself of sediment. As a result, it often ends up at the bottom of a broad shallow depression which it has made in the mud or sand. A single large adductor muscle holds the shells together, and the size and taste of that particular muscle have made sea scallops a gourmet's delight.

Like most other bivalve mollusks, sea scallops are suspension feeders, inhaling water from which they filter food particles. Like other scallops but quite unlike other bivalves, they also have a ring of small bluish eyes along the edge of the mantle which are exposed when the shells gape even slightly. The eyes are simple ones, only able to detect passing shadows, but they help protect the scallop from an approaching predator.

Sea scallops have separate sexes and are able to spawn when they are about 2 inches (5 cm) in diameter. The animals spawn from August to October; the eggs are fertilized in the water over the scallop bed. The larvae spend three or four weeks in the plankton passing through the veliger larval stage to the stage known as the pediveliger, which is a veliger larva with a little foot. Pediveligers select a substrate they can crawl on for short distances. They settle on a variety of objects which range from the shells of adult sea scallops to filamentous red algae and bushy bryozoans such as *Bugula* species.

The pediveligers then metamorphose into miniature sea scallops and attach themselves to whatever they have settled on with very strong byssus threads. When they grow to

92. With its shell overgrown by algae, this feeding sea scallop *Placopecten magellanicus* reveals its rows of blue eyes along the edge of the gaping shells.

about ⅜ inch (1 cm) in diameter and are about a year old, the young sea scallops migrate to the bottom substrate, attaching themselves to stones or shells and swimming short distances by clapping their shells together. As the sea scallop grows it moves onto softer sand or mud substrates. A sea scallop 5 to 6 inches (12.5 to 15 cm) in diameter is likely to be seven to ten years old.

The larvae of sea scallops are preyed upon by zooplankton in the surface waters and by suspension-feeding predators such as the burrowing anemones, *Cerianthus borealis*. Juvenile sea scallops are probably the prey of a large number of bottom living, or demersal, fish, particularly the various flatfish (see chapter 7) as well as starfish and whelks.

A large number of animals also live on living sea scallop shells for the shells may be rare patches of hard surface on an otherwise soft substrate. Sponges, hydroids, bryozoans, barnacles, sea squirts, tube worms, and algae compete for space on limited rock surfaces and for the small space the shells provide. Juvenile sea scallops move around enough that the sessile organisms cannot settle and grow

Soft Subtidal Substrates 291

on them easily, but a large sea scallop moves little if at all and the surface of its upper shell may be entirely covered by the sessile competitors.

MYSID SHRIMP. Mysids, or opossum shrimp, are small crustaceans which in Boreal waters are usually about 1 inch (2.5 cm) or more long. Mysids are not true shrimp, but, as they swim about over the substrate, they certainly look like them. One important way mysids differ from true shrimp is the manner in which females carry their eggs and embryos. True shrimp attach their eggs to the swimmerts on the underneath sides of their abdomens or tails, just as do the closely related crabs and lobsters. A female mysid, on the other hand, has a ventral brood pouch between her legs where she deposits a relatively small number of eggs which pass through larval stages while still embryos and hatch as juvenile mysids.

Several species, extremely abundant along the Boreal coast, form large aggregations. *Mysis stenolepis* and *Neomysis americana* both swim or hover close to sandy and sandy-mud substrates, whereas the hump-backed *Praunus flexuosus* hovers under overhanging macroalgae. All are primarily suspension feeders, kicking a current of water past their mouthparts from which they filter detritus

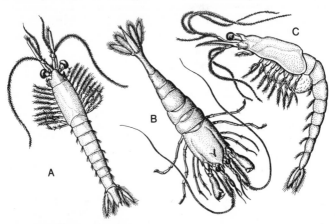

93. Mysid shrimp and sand shrimp are both cryptically colored and common near or on the substrate. A. Mysid shrimp *Praunus flexuosus* B. Sand shrimp *Crangon septemspinosus* C. Mysid shrimp *Neomysis americana.*

and small organisms. They are all also able to detect and capture larger pieces of food either as scavengers or predators.

Though mysids are generally cryptic, difficult to see in their surroundings, they are a major food item for practically all demersal fish, particularly the flatfish.

Sand Shrimp. The sand shrimp, *Crangon septemspinosus*, is larger than the mysids, growing to about 3 inches (7.5 cm), and is a true shrimp. It is just as abundant as the mysids and probably even more wide-spread over sand and sandy-mud substrates throughout the Boreal region. It is a sandy, translucent color, difficult to see when it sits motionless on sand or mud. When it isn't feeding it usually buries itself just beneath the surface of the sediment, leaving its antennae and eyes peeking out. Many sand shrimp forage in with the tide over intertidal flats, and though some bury themselves in the flats when the tide drops past them, others swim back to deeper subtidal water instead. Large numbers also remain on subtidal substrates in deeper water, attracted to any disturbance of the sand or mud where they prey on small worms and crustaceans exposed by the disturbance. In turn, they are the primary prey of flounders and other demersal fish.

Queen or Snow Crab. The queen or snow crab, *Chionectes opilio*, is a spider crab. Since the late 1960's there have been small but flourishing fisheries for queen crabs around the Maritime Provinces, particularly in the Gulf of St. Lawrence. Their meat is excellent.

Queen crabs live on soft mud or sandy-mud bottoms where they prey upon the worms and small crustaceans burrowing in the sediment. Males and females mate in late winter shortly after the females molt to become sexually mature. From that one mating, females fertilize two successive broods by mid-summer. Their eggs hatch into small nauplius larvae that grow in the plankton for a few weeks before settling to the bottom.

The juveniles become sexually mature probably during their second winter when females reach a carapace width of about 2 inches (5 cm) and males are a little larger. Once she becomes sexually mature a female doesn't molt again, but males continue to molt and grow considerably larger. Large males, which have certainly had a chance to breed, make up the commercial catch. Females remain totally protected.

Queen crabs are able to molt and breed during the coldest part of the year. They cannot tolerate warm summer temperatures and are uncommon in the waters of the Gulf of Maine.

PREDATORY GASTROPODS

The most efficient predators of the burrowing bivalves are probably the large gastropods. Moon snails plow through the surface layer of sandy sediments drilling through the shells of their bivalve prey (see chapter 3). Several large whelks also forage over sandy substrates in search of bivalves.

WHELKS. The largest Boreal whelks are *Busycon* species, which reach at least 9 inches (23 cm) in length. The channeled whelk, *Busycon canaliculatum*, and the knobbed, or giant, whelk, *B. carica*, both have a relatively short spire, a large body whorl that contains the broad foot, and a long anterior canal or channel that contains the siphon. These whelks commonly bury themselves in the sand with their long siphons extending above the substrate to keep clean water flowing in over the gill chamber. Shells

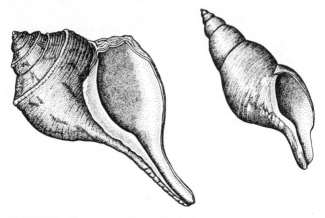

94. Though efficient predators, both the giant whelk *Busycon* (left) and the smaller *Colus* (right) spend a lot of time buried in sand.

of both whelks are yellowish gray though the knobbed whelk grows somewhat larger and has knob-like protuberances on its whorls.

The egg capsules of both *Busycon* species are disk-shaped and attached to a single string which may be 3 feet (1 m) in length. Channeled whelk capsules have a single edge to them while the giant whelk capsules are double-edged and about the size of a quarter (see chapter 3).

Busycon whelks are efficient predators, feeding primarily on bivalves and are especially unpopular with oyster farmers. The whelk inserts its long anterior canal between the shells of a bivalve mollusk and strikes the edge of the prey's shell until enough is chipped away to insert its proboscis. The long proboscis has a rasping ribbon which can be used to bore holes in mollusk shells. Once a prey's shell is penetrated, the soft parts are sucked out. Though *Busycon* may eat a couple of oysters in a day, it also remains buried for long periods of time without feeding and is not as much of an oyster pest as is the oyster drill, *Urosalpinx*, which is found south of Cape Cod. *Busycon* whelks are found in shallow subtidal waters on sandy substrates. They range south from northern Maine to Cape Hatteras but may be found in warm bays to Nova Scotia.

Colus stimpsoni is a smaller spindle-shaped whelk growing to 5 inches (12.5 cm) in length. Its bluish white shell has a more elongated spire than does *Busycon* though its anterior canal is equally elongated. It is found on soft substrates from shallow subtidal to 2500 feet (765 m) and ranges from Labrador to North Carolina. It feeds primarily on other gastropods, including moon snails.

FISH

Although most bottom-dwelling fish forage over a wide variety of substrates, some occur almost exclusively on soft sediments. These include most of the flatfish and skates which are particularly common in deeper and offshore waters (see chapter 7), but two species, the winter flounder and the little skate, occur frequently in shallow inshore waters as well. Sand launces also occur exclusively over soft substrates, often in shallow water.

Winter Flounder. The winter flounder, *Pseudo-*

pleuronectes americanus, is probably the most widespread and familiar fish in shallow water along the entire Boreal coast. It lives on all manner of soft substrates from mud to gravel. It is abundant on the offshore fishing banks, in coastal bays, on sand flats and far up coastal estuaries, and it grows to 15 to 20 inches (37.5 to 50 cm) in length and 2 to 4 pounds (4.4 to 8.8 kg) in weight.

A winter flounder lies on its pale left side on the sediment, for both of its eyes are on its right side (see chapter 7 for an account of how such an arrangement develops in flatfish). Its exposed right side has an extraordinary ability to change in color and color pattern according to the kind of bottom the animal is resting on, making it difficult to see against its background. A winter flounder often also ruffles up the sediment it settles on to so that most of its upper surface becomes covered by the sediment and only its eyes remain exposed. Finding a covered, cryptically colored flounder can be virtually impossible.

Winter flounders usually leave shallow waters that warm up too much in summer or approach the freezing point in winter. They find sanctuary in the more moderate temperatures of deeper water. They got the name of winter flounder from their habit of abandoning warm shallow water along the coast south of Cape Cod in summer, returning to the coastal bays there in winter.

Winter flounders remain active during the winter, feeding as they do most of the year on worms, small crustaceans, bivalves and fish fry. Their mouths are small and they cannot handle large prey, but they still bite chunks out of large worms and nip siphons off of buried clams.

The only time of year winter flounders cease feeding is during their breeding season in late winter and early spring, beginning when the water is at its coldest and finishing by the time it warms to about 41° F (5° C). They spawn on sandy bottoms and each season an average-sized female produces about half a million eggs that, unlike the eggs of other Boreal flatfish, sink on to the sand and stick together in dense masses. The eggs hatch into normal looking fish larvae after two or three weeks in the frigid water and then spend about two or three months as fish larvae, metamorphosing quite rapidly into small flatfish toward the end of

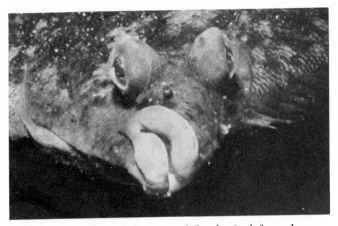

95. The winter flounder lies on its left side. Its left eye has migrated over to the right side.

that period. Once they settle on the bottom they grow quickly and by the time they are a year old are likely to be 4 to 6 inches (10 to 15 cm) long. They become sexually mature when they are three years old and eight inches (20 cm) or more in length.

Winter flounder are fished heavily wherever they are common, mostly by otter trawls by commercial fishermen, and by hook and line by sport fishermen. Large winter flounders over 3 pounds (1.3 kg) are usually marketed as sole or lemon sole; smaller individuals are marketed as blackbacks.

Little Skate. The little skate, *Raja erinacea,* is a very common brownish, blunt-nosed skate with many small dark spots on its back. It is smaller than the other Boreal skates (see chapter 7), growing only to 16 to 20 inches (40 to 50 cm) in length and 1 to 2 pounds (0.4 to 0.9 kg) in weight. Little skates occur on sandy and muddy substrates and like the winter flounders often follow the tide in and out as they forage for prey, but they appear not to tolerate brackish water and keep out of the upper estuaries where winter flounders often go. Little skates eat large numbers of crabs, sand shrimp, worms, bivalves, squid, amphipods and small demersal fish.

Soft Subtidal Substrates   297

Female little skates lay their eggs almost any time of year. They lay the eggs in pairs, each egg encased in a tough egg case about 2½ inches (6.5 cm) long not including the horns extending from each corner. The eggs are usually partly buried in sand, often in very shallow water and seem to be quite impervious to predation. Depending on when the eggs are laid the embryos take six to ten months to use up all their yolk and hatch as juvenile skates approximately 4 inches (10 cm) in length.

A skate embryo is a very beautiful sight as it rests upon its dwindling supply of yolk, its tail curled around its body. During its very long embryonic period it gets most of its oxygen from a tangle of blood vessels which act like external gills and are vivid red in contrast to the whitish body and yellow yolk (see color plate VII).

Sand Launce. The sand launce, *Ammodytes americanus*, is a toothless, sharp-nosed, slender fish which has a forked tail, no ventral fins and grows to about 5 to 6 inches (12.5 to 15 cm) in length. Because it looks like an eel and swims in the undulating manner of true eels, it is often called the sand eel. However, it is not at all related to true eels and has evolved its eel-like appearance quite independently.

Sand launces often swim in very large schools and as a result are the common prey of a wide assortment of predators including finback whales, porpoises, cod, halibut, mackerel and salmon. In turn they feed on small crustaceans and fish fry. They forage almost exclusively over sandy substrates often near the tide line of coastal beaches but also offshore around the fishing banks. When they breed, they appear to select certain areas for spawning well away from shore and their eggs adhere to the sand grains of the substrate. They are probably a year old by the time they are 3 to 4 inches (7.5 to 10 cm) long.

The most remarkable behavior of sand launces is their tendency to burrow into the sand. They seem to dive into the sand and bury themselves several inches (5 to 10 cm) below the surface. Sometimes when they are caught in shallow water on a sand flat when the tide drops past them, they bury themselves in the sand until the tide rises again. By burrowing and disappearing so quickly they are able to

96. Aggregations of sand launces are common over sandy substrates where they forage for food.

evade pursuit by some but probably not all of their predators.

Predators on Mixed Substrates

Many bottom dwelling predators are not limited to either hard or soft substrates as they search for food. Most of the large crustaceans and many of the demersal fish as well as the cormorants and diving ducks forage over a very wide variety of types of substrates.

Crustaceans

In summer, in shallow subtidal waters along the Boreal coast, crabs and lobsters are often the dominant predators on substrates ranging from rock ledges to soft mud.

Lobster. The American lobster, *Homarus americanus*, probably symbolizes the Boreal coast more than any other animal, for its inshore distribution is restricted to the Boreal region and its fine taste has made it world famous (see plate VI).

Not so long ago lobsters were far more abundant than they are now. Before 1800 the fish of the Boreal coast had long attracted fishermen from Europe and had been instrumental in settling the coast in the first place, but lobsters were considered good only as fertilizer and as poor man's food. Around 1800 a small unregulated pot fishery for lobsters developed in the Cape Cod area and gradually spread northward reaching Maine by about 1840 and Canada by about 1870. Few laws were established until around 1895 when only lobsters over 10.5 inches (26 cm) total length became legally catchable, but by then the lobster populations had already been badly overfished.

Even now when the lobster fishery is watched carefully and is highly regulated, laws vary from state to state or province, and lobstermen and fisheries biologists do not necessarily agree on what is best for the fishery. In some places lobsters may be legally sold at a size that is too small for many of them to have had a chance to breed even once, while in some of the more isolated places poaching is not unheard of. A prospect which might one day allow natural lobster populations to recover is the possibility of growing large numbers of lobsters in captivity, but it certainly is not an attractive prospect for the present lobstermen.

It is hard to believe a lobster can actually live 100 years, grow to lengths of up to 4 feet (1.2 m) and weigh as much as 45 pounds (20 kg). Though public aquaria sometimes have very large individuals, few are anywhere near that size along the coast. As many as 95% of lobsters of the inshore populations are caught when they reach the minimum legal size, and even in the more recently exploited offshore populations there are few large individuals left.

In shallow inshore water most lobsters are caught in half round parlor traps baited with fish heads or bait fish. Most are wooden traps, and the lobsters are forced to pass from an outer chamber to an inner baited one, passing through openings they are unable to find their way out of. New laws provide vents in the traps so that undersized individuals can escape. Large numbers of traps are lost every year, however, and lobsters trapped in such "ghost" traps are lost to both the natural population and the commercial market. Where lobsters are fished offshore on the more southern

97. A juvenile lobster, *Homarus americanus*.

banks and in deeper water they are either trawled or trapped from ships which set long lines of traps and haul them in with hydraulic pot haulers.

Lobsters forage at night for worms, other crustaceans, sea urchins, mollusks and virtually anything they can catch on rock ledges and pebble, shingle, sand and mud substrates. In the daytime they hide in rock caves, under kelp blades, or in burrows or depressions they may dig in mud. They are solitary, aggressive animals and threaten each other and other potential predators with their large strong claws. A large lobster has few predators. With the left claw specialized for crushing and the right for cutting or ripping, it can be quite a formidable predator itself.

A small lobster is a much more vulnerable animal. When it hatches in mid-summer from the mass of eggs its mother carries attached to the swimmerets underneath her abdomen or tail, it looks a bit like a mysid shrimp and is called a mysis larva. It joins the plankton for several weeks, molts into larger and more lobster-like stages and when it molts for the third time since hatching it looks like a small lobster, is about ¾ inch (2 cm) long, and explores the bottom for a suitable place to settle. Though it may choose one of any number of substrates to hide in, it is most likely to select a muddy bottom where it digs a U-shaped burrow and disappears from view.

Predators on Mixed Substrates

Though little is known about the early life of juvenile lobsters, they appear to remain in their burrows, molting and growing and feeding from the sediment they bulldoze around as they extend their burrows. When they are about 3½ inches (9 cm) long and one to two years old they begin to act more like the familiar image of a lobster, wandering and feeding at night, hiding by day, and aggressively fending off attackers.

Lobsters first mate when they are five to eight years old, shortly after the female molts. A male may protect the female after he mates with her until her shell is hard. The female holds the sperm which the male deposits for as long as twelve months before she extrudes her eggs, fertilizes them and attaches them to her swimmerets. She carries her slowly developing but relatively large eggs for the next ten to twelve months until they hatch. She then molts and mates again. As a result, mature females are likely to molt only once every second year whereas mature males molt once a year and grow larger more quickly than females. If they have a chance to, that is.

Many lobsters migrate seasonally from cool deeper water in winter to warmer inshore water in summer. In late autumn they move offshore again, avoiding the very cold inshore temperatures of winter. Though winter lobstering is certainly legal, most lobstermen pull their traps in for the winter since many of the lobsters have left shallow water and winter gales present major risks not only to set traps but to the lobstermen themselves. Only around Monhegan Island in Maine do lobstermen fish all winter and then pull their traps in for the summer months when the lobsters head inshore.

ROCK CRABS.   Two rock crabs are common along the Boreal coast. One is the red rock crab, *Cancer irroratus*, and the second is the very similar Jonah crab, *Cancer borealis*. Males of the red rock crab grow to about 5 inches (12.5 cm) in carapace width and male Jonah crabs grow a little larger, to about 6 inches (15 cm). Females don't grow nearly as large. Though picking the meat from either species takes some patience, the effort is certainly well rewarded, and there is a good market for the crabs, which seems to be limited only by the number of people prepared to spend their time picking.

98. The rock crab, *Cancer irroratus*, often protects itself by burrowing in sand.

Both species forage over a wide variety of substrates in search of the usual worms, small mollusks and small crustaceans that are the prey for so many animals. Red rock crabs are somewhat more common on hard substrates than Jonah crabs and are more abundant in shallow water along the southern parts of the Boreal coast. Jonah crabs are more abundant in deeper water in the southern part of the region but come into shallow water in the Gulf of St. Lawrence.

In both species, males and females mate in late summer and females carry their eggs over much of the winter. The eggs hatch in early summer, spend several weeks or more as planktonic larvae and then settle as juvenile crabs. It takes about two years for the juveniles to grow to sexual maturity and start to breed. The breeding behavior of rock crabs is in fact very similar to that of the ubiquitous green crab, *Carcinus maenus*. Unlike green crabs, rock crabs are uncommon intertidally except as newly settled juveniles, and they avoid estuarine water.

Green Shore Crab. Green crabs, *Carcinus maenus*, range from the New Jersey coast north to southern New Brunswick and Nova Scotia. They are extremely abundant in the salt marshes along the coast from Maine's Cape Elizabeth to Cape Cod and beyond. They forage far up estuaries, withstand prolonged intertidal exposure on rocky shores as well as on the salt marshes, dig in intertidal and subtidal sediments for their prey, and are likely to occur in relatively shallow water virtually anywhere that wave surge isn't too strong.

This is the same species that is so common on European shores. It probably immigrated accidentally to America with some of the earlier settlers. It was uncommon even as far north as the rocky parts of Maine's coast until a few decades ago, but now it thrives in huge numbers along the mid-coastal region of Maine, gradually becoming less frequent farther north. During years when the average temperature of the water is warmer than usual, green crabs survive more easily at the extreme north end of their present range. Several years of colder temperatures appear to push them south into Maine again.

Juvenile green crabs are especially common under intertidal rockweed and rocks and even a few adults may remain in the low intertidal when the tide drops past them. Most adults, however, forage in and out with the tide or remain exclusively subtidal except when they molt, and only then do they usually seek intertidal cover. All stages can tolerate brackish water, intertidal desiccation and heat, as well as very cold temperatures. Though all adults and large juveniles leave the rocky intertidal shores for the winter, small juveniles often remain under the low tide rocks. In salt marshes, adults and juveniles may actually spend the winter in burrows under the *Spartina* grasses, high in the intertidal.

Green crabs mate in late summer. As in many other crabs including the rock crabs, the male is much larger than the female and may be 3 inches (7.5 cm) or more in carapace width. A sexually mature female attracts a male to her shortly before she molts, probably using a chemical attractant or pheromone that she secretes with her urine. The male guards her for about a week until she molts, carrying her about with him as he continues to forage for food. When the female finally molts, she and her male spend the next couple of days in a mating embrace until her shell or exoskeleton begins to harden. The two crabs cease mating then, but the male still remains with the female, guarding her until her exoskeleton is completely hard again. Though certainly one reason the male guards the female so carefully

99. A female green crab *Carcinus* displays her bright orange eggs, held under her tail where she can easily ventilate and clean them.

is to protect her from predation while she is soft after her molt, he also protects her from other males. By guarding her before and after she molts, he ensures that he is the only one to mate with her and as a result passes his genes along successfully to a new generation.

After the male and female separate, the female doesn't extrude her eggs at once but waits until sometime during the winter, six months later. The male's sperm remain perfectly viable for that long and as the female extrudes her eggs she fertilizes them with the stored sperm and attaches them underneath her tail which is normally folded tightly under her body as it is in all true crabs.

The eggs hatch in mid-summer as small zoea larvae which molt and grow in the plankton to a larval stage called the megalops. The megalops settles to the bottom, selects an appropriate shallow-water, often intertidal substrate, and metamorphoses into a juvenile crab. As in the rock crabs, it takes about two years in Boreal waters for the juveniles to reach sexual maturity.

Green crabs are extremely successful along the southern parts of the Boreal coast. Though often scavengers, they are also voracious predators, eating large numbers of burrowing organisms in the softer substrates, preying heavily on

Predators on Mixed Substrates   305

young mussels on harder substrates. They do extensive damage to beds of the soft-shelled clam, *Mya arenaria*, removing practically all clams under two or three years old and destroying the bed as a result, along with the livelihood of any local clam diggers. In turn, green crabs are a favorite prey of herring and great black-backed gulls, great blue herons, diving ducks and shallow-water fish.

SPIDER CRABS. Spider crabs get their name from their long legs and triangular shaped shell or carapace. Several species scavenge and prey over a variety of subtidal substrates in the bays and inlets along the Boreal coast. Spider crabs are not nearly as active as rock crabs or green crabs and they rely more upon camouflage than threatening postures to protect themselves. Often bits of algae and occasional sessile animals settle and grow on their carapaces, enhancing their cryptic appearance.

The most common spider crab, *Libinia emarginata*, grows to a considerable size. Males reach a carapace width of about 4 inches (10 cm). The toad crab, *Hyas araneus*, grows almost as large but is a little more colorful and is less common in shallow water than *Libinia emarginata*. The smallest species occurring on mixed substrates in relatively

100. The spider crab is often camouflaged by the algae that grows on its shell.

THE SHALLOW MARINE SUBTIDAL

shallow water is the spider crab, *Hyas coarctatus*, which grows to little more than 1 inch (2.5 cm) carapace width but which is not uncommon even in low tide pools.

Like the queen spider crab, *Chionectes opilio*, which occurs in large numbers on the soft substrates of the Gulf of St. Lawrence, the males of these three species are bigger than their females. Females do not molt again once they reach sexual maturity and they do not need to have just recently molted in order to mate. Prolonged guarding of females by males is unnecessary, for the females are not soft and vulnerable as are the mating females of green crabs and rock crabs. Males may even court females to some degree to entice them to mate.

HERMIT CRABS. What may at first appear to be a snail moving at a rapid clip across a tide pool is usually a hermit crab using the empty mollusk shell as its own portable home. The large claws, or chelipeds, and the stalked eyes of hermit crabs reveal their relation to lobsters and crabs, but the abdomen of the hermit crab is somewhat coiled and very soft, in great contrast to the other crustaceans (see color plate VI).

The abdomen of the hermit crab is highly modified for life within a shell. It has a slight twist to it, adapted for the right-handed spirals of northern hemisphere mollusk shells. The appendage on the terminal segment is especially adapted for clinging to the spiral support of the snail shell, the columella, and the appendages of the preceding two segments act as struts for the main support. When danger threatens, the hermit crab quickly retracts itself into the shell with the same muscular reflex that causes lobsters and shrimp to flick backwards.

Though the mollusk shell is heavy, it affords protection from exposure as well as from predators. The chelipeds of the hermit crab act like the operculum of a snail when the crab is withdrawn, effectively sealing off the opening of the shell.

The chelipeds have several other important functions. Hermit crabs are omnivores, scavenging the substrate for food, scraping algae from rocks and eating any animal that can be caught and killed by the chelipeds. After prey is caught, it is held by mouthparts and torn or cut into small pieces.

The chelipeds are also used for sexual competition between males. Rather than clawing at each other with their efficient pincers, however, the males rap on each other's shells with the large chelipeds. The smaller hermit crab recognizes the dominance of the larger one and scuttles off in a different direction. Male hermit crabs also use their chelipeds to seize and drag around smaller female hermit crabs that are ready to molt. As soon as the female molts, the male fertilizes her, both animals remaining partially within their shells.

Just as the abdomen is twisted to adapt to the spiral of the mollusk shell, so too is the rest of the hermit crab abdomen adapted to its right-handed existence. Gonads of both males and females are located on the left side and the female carries the developing eggs on the left side of her pleopods. When no danger is present, the female comes far out of her shell, aerating the developing eggs. The eggs hatch into planktonic larvae, pass through typical zoea and megalops stages and then settle to the bottom where they metamorphose and seek tiny shells to carry around.

Several species of hermit crabs occur frequently in Boreal waters. *Pagurus longicarpus* is a small hermit crab, reaching 3/8 inch (1 cm) in carapace length and ranging as far north as Nova Scotia. It is a dark rose or brownish color with elongated and nearly smooth chelipeds. This pagurid inhabits shells of periwinkles, *Littorina* species; dog whelks, *Thais lapillus;* and mud snails, *Nassarius* species, and it is found in tide pools and to depths of 150 feet (45 m) on a variety of bottoms in protected water. *Hydractinia*, the fuzzy pink hydroid, often grows on its shell (see chapter 2).

Pagurus acadianus is a colder water, more truly Boreal hermit crab and is much larger, growing to 1¼ inch (3 cm) in length. Reddish brown or red-orange in color, *P. acadianus* inhabits larger mollusk shells including those of the channeled whelk, *Busycon canaliculatum;* the waved whelk, *Buccinum undatum;* and the moon snail, *Lunatia heros.* Like so many of the Boreal species, it occurs in shallow subtidal water and even in low tidal pools along northern parts of the coast but is restricted to deeper, colder water in the southern Gulf of Maine.

Other species about the same size as the large *P. acadianus* occur along parts of the Boreal coast. Of these both the very hairy *P. arcuatus* and the somewhat less hairy *P. pubescens* are uncommon in shallow water. *P. pollicaris* which is abundant south of Cape Cod, occurs infrequently north of the Cape in the Gulf of Maine.

Squid

The short-finned squid, *Ilex illecebrosus*, come into inshore water especially along northern parts of the Boreal coast during the summer to feed on herring and other fish as well as euphausiid shrimp which have moved inshore ahead of them. The long-finned squid, *Loligo pealei*, is a more southern species but it also comes inshore in summer chasing fish along the more southern parts of the Boreal coast (see chapter 7 and plate VII).

The long-finned *Loligo pealei* comes inshore not just to feed but also to breed. In late spring along the southern Boreal coast females move into shallow water when the

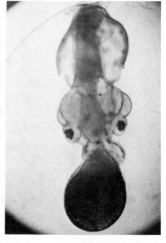

101. The mass of squid eggs on the left was deposited by several females. Each "finger" of eggs contains hundreds of embryos like the one on the right, whose yolk sac at the bottom of the picture is not yet depleted. The young embryo's complex black eyes are already well developed.

Predators on Mixed Substrates

tides are at their lowest spring tide levels. The females lay their eggs in finger-like masses of jelly with several hundred eggs in each mass, attaching the jelly fingers in clusters onto rocks or other hard objects. Egg masses are laid in deeper water as well, but females laying their eggs as high as possible up the subtidal shore remove them from the few fish predators likely to prey on them.

The embryos develop directly into juvenile squid. As they develop, their yolk sacks shrink, and an embryo ready to hatch looks as if it is holding its yolk sack between its arms, or tentacles. The squid embryo is large, about 1/10 inch (2 to 3 mm) long, and a hand lens should be enough for watching the many pigment cells in the skin of the embryo expand and contract in little flashes of spectacular color.

Fish

A large number of fish forage in inshore coastal waters over a variety of substrates, especially during the warm summer months. Some are strays from estuaries or, if not strays, at least more typical of estuaries than the open coast (see chapter 4). Others are migrant catadromous species, breeding in fresh water but growing inshore or offshore in salt water (again, see chapter 4). Still others are more typically offshore or deeper-water fish, some of which may follow their prey into inshore waters in summer (see chapter 7).

CUNNER AND TAUTOG. The cunner, *Tautogolabrus adspersus*, also called sea perch, lives close to shore and sticks close to the bottom. It is a rockfish, often resting or swimming slowly among rocks, algae, pilings or eel grass. It preys on all manner of crustaceans, mollusks, worms and small fish, but it may occasionally graze on eel grass or scavenge on animal refuse as well.

With its single dorsal fin, its rounded tail and pectoral fins and its highly variable reddish or bluish brown color, a cunner is not difficult to recognize. Most mature individuals are about 6 to 10 inches (15 to 25 cm) long and though they occur as far north as Newfoundland, they are far more common in bays along southern parts of the Boreal coast. Cunner do not wander around very much and even in winter probably go into deeper water only where inshore water is likely to freeze.

Tautoga onitis is closely related to the cunner. It grows larger, however, reaching lengths as great as 3 feet (90 cm), and it is a darker, stouter fish with a blunt nose and thick, fleshy lips. Like the cunner, the tautog rarely strays from shallow water along the immediate coast where it feeds extensively on mussels, barnacles, sand dollars and many crustaceans, including lobsters which it cracks with its strong crushing teeth. Also like the cunner, the tautog is most common along the southern parts of the Boreal coast.

SCULPINS AND SEA RAVENS. Sculpins and sea ravens have large spiny heads, broad mouths, spiny first dorsal fins, and large fan-like pectoral fins. Their ventral fins are reduced to three long rays and they are, to say the least, quite unmistakable. They are cold-water fish, found frequently throughout the Boreal region where they tend to lie rather sluggishly on sand and shingle substrates, often near ledges, sometimes among rocks, and less frequently on soft mud. They are voracious predators, eating crustaceans, worms, mollusks and fish as well as animals like sea urchins and sea squirts that are not considered particularly palatable by most predators. They are also scavengers and may be most common around wharves where a lot of fish refuse is discarded.

Three species are common in Boreal waters. Two of them, the short-horned sculpin *Myoxocephalus scorpius* and the long-horned sculpin *M. octodecimspinosus*, are extremely similar in appearance. The short-horned sculpin occurs in coastal waters over most of the north Atlantic and avoids water warmer than 60° F (15° C). It is absent from the southern Gulf of St. Lawrence in summer. The long-horned sculpin is the more common of the two species, has sharper spines, lacks the reddish tinge many short-horned sculpins have, and tolerates water as warm as 65° F (18° C). Both species can change their color somewhat to match their background and both grow to an average of 10 to 14 inches (25 to 35 cm). Though they are sluggish animals,

102. Though it is a voracious predator, the bizarre looking sea raven is a rather sluggish fish, spending much of its time lying around on the substrate.

when disturbed they fold back their winglike pectoral fins and dart ahead (see plate VII).

The third common Boreal species is the sea raven, *Hemitripterus americanus*, and it looks even more outlandish than the two sculpin species. It is a stouter fish, distinguished easily by the fleshy branched protuberances on its head and the rugged outline presented by its first dorsal fin. It is reddish purple or brown and grows larger than the two sculpins, usually reaching 18 to 20 inches (45 to 50 cm). Like others of its family, including the sculpins, it breeds in winter, laying sticky eggs that sink to the bottom. Probably unlike the others, however, it seeks out sponges such as the finger sponge, *Haliclona oculata*, and attaches its large eggs in relatively small clusters of a couple of hundred eggs each to the base of the sponges.

Goosefish. Perhaps the most bizarre demersal fish in Boreal waters is the goosefish, *Lophius americanus*, or angler as it is also called. It grows as long as 4 feet (1.2 m) and weighs up to 50 pounds (25 kg). It is incredibly flattened from top to bottom and its pectoral fins are almost armlike in appearance. In addition, its mouth is enormous and is directed upward, the lower jaw and lip extending far forward of the upper one.

Goosefish are found on all substrate types from pebbles to soft mud at depths from just below the low tide mark to over 400 fathoms (730 m). The upper surface of the fish is usually a deep mottled brown, making the goosefish almost as difficult to see as members of the flatfish tribe. Adding to its invisibility, the arm-like pectoral fins are used to push bottom sand away, allowing the fish to become almost level with the surface of the substrate.

On the top of its head, the goosefish has three stiff spines, the first two of which are movable. In addition, the most forward of the spines has a flap of skin at its tip which acts as lure for prey. Feeding by sight, the goosefish sways the flap of skin to and fro, luring fish within seizing distance. With such an enormous mouth, it is able to feed upon prey almost its own size.

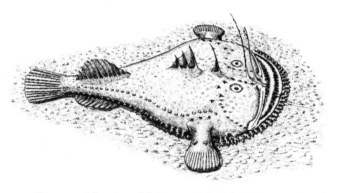

103. The goosefish or monkfish gets its food by lying on the sea bottom, its jaw agape like a large trap. When prey swims sufficiently close, the jaws snap together, engulfing the victim.

The goosefish has earned its common names both from its angling method of capturing food and from its rapacious appetite. In addition to fish of every kind from spiny dogfish, skates, mackerel and herring to flatfish and sea ravens, it also devours lobsters, crabs, squid, diving ducks and sea birds including cormorants, scoters, loons, guillemots and razor-billed auks.

Predators on Mixed Substrates 313

Goosefish spawn from spring to early summer, shedding their eggs in violet ribbonlike veils of mucus up to 36 feet (10.8 m) in length. A veil of this length contains well over a million eggs and is a conspicuous sight floating at the surface. Although the adults have few enemies, goosefish larvae are heavily preyed upon during their planktonic life.

Birds

Shorebirds, seabirds and diving ducks all prey upon whatever subtidal animals they can capture and handle. Herons, egrets and some of the sandpipers and plovers forage on very shallow subtidal flats when the tide is at its lowest, just as they do on intertidal flats (see chapters 3 and 4). Herring gulls and great black-backed gulls are able to reach a short distance into the water beyond the low tide line and will eat practically anything (see chapter 6). Cormorants and eider ducks, which also breed on the coastal islands in the Boreal region, dive from the water surface close to shore or around ledges and swim underwater in search of their prey (see chapter 6).

DIVING DUCKS

Apart from the common eider duck, *Somateria mollissima,* diving ducks of the Boreal region either breed inland, away from the sea, or migrate north, even as far as the Arctic Ocean. Throughout the non-breeding months, however, many spend their time on salt water, feeding on fish and bottom invertebrates in relatively shallow water. Most are circumpolar species, well known in winter along the coasts of western North America and western Europe as well.

Scaup. The greater scaup, *Aythya marila,* dives in 10 to 20 feet (3 to 6 m) of water, eating plants, clams and small crustaceans, kicking its feet to propel itself underwater. Males have dark greenish heads and necks and have white sides; females are brown with a white ring about their bills. Not very common north of Maine in winter, greater scaups often rest in large aggregations, or rafts, at night some distance offshore, flying in small groups to inshore feeding areas each day. They are omniverous ducks, eating clams, crustaceans and other invertebrates, along with plants like sea lettuce, *Ulva lactuca.*

BUFFLEHEADS AND GOLDENEYES. The bufflehead, *Bucephala albeola;* the common goldeneye, *B. clangula;* and the less frequent Barrow's goldeneye, *B. islandica,* all have roundish heads with puffy crests, and the males have very white necks and breasts and have white patches on their otherwise dark heads. The white patch on the common goldeneye is round and lies below the eye; the bufflehead's patch is large and stretches to the top of the head. The bufflehead is the smallest, not only of these three species but also of all the diving ducks along the Boreal coast. Like the greater scaup, all three species feed in shallow water during the day, preying on small crustaceans, mussels and snails, and sleep on open water further offshore at night.

104. A male bufflehead (right) courts a female through elaborate gestures, displaying his striking white feathers and orange feet to her.

Courtship both in buffleheads and goldeneyes is quite remarkable and uses up much of the non-feeding time males have, beginning sometime in late January or February. A courting male puffs up his head feathers, thrusts his head forward and then throws it back until it practically touches his tail. He then jerks his head forward again, darting forward on the water at the same time to reveal his orange feet. In the presence of females or competing males, he may repeat this performance over and over again for several months until weather conditions permit migration to nesting areas.

SCOTERS. The three scoters that winter along parts of most of the Boreal coast are the white-winged scoter, *Melanitta deglandi;* the surf scoter, *M. perspicillata;* and the less familiar black or common scoter, *M. nigra.* The male black scoter is all black except for a yellow protuberance on its bill; the male white-winged scoter looks quite similar except that it has white wing patches that are easy to miss when the bird is in the water; and the male surf scoter, also black bodied, has very obvious white spots on its head and an orange and white bill. All three use their inner wings to help them swim underwater over various substrates in search of small crustaceans and bivalve mollusks. The surf scoter, as its name suggests, is most frequently seen near beach surf, foraging for animals that burrow in the sand.

Oldsquaw. Oldsquaws, *Clangula hyematis,* winter along the whole of the Boreal coast, resting in sheltered bays at night. In winter both males and females appear white-headed and dark-winged, and males have long tail feathers rather like those of pintails. The male in breeding plumage has a very dark head, neck and throat, along with a large white eye patch. Oldsquaws are usually heard long before they are seen, for their loud yodel-like calls carry far across the water. As spring progresses, the flocks become increasingly noisy and an available female may receive yodelling attention from a number of males at once. Oldsquaws are able to dive to depths of 100 to 200 feet (30 to 60 m), swimming with their wings. They eat small crustaceans, including shrimp, amphipods and crabs, as well as bivalve mollusks.

Harlequin Duck. The harlequin duck, *Histrionicus histrionicus,* is an uncommon species which winters along the more exposed, rockier parts of the Boreal coast. At night it usually finds some isolated rocks to roost on, and during the day it dives in the inshore surf preying on the usual crustaceans and mollusks but also on less palatable animals such as barnacles, green sea urchins and even small sculpins. The male has patterns of white which stand out vividly against his dark body, and his flanks are brown; the female, once again, is a rather drab dark brown.

Red Breasted Merganser. The red-breasted merganser, *Mergus serrator*, is a large diving duck that winters along the Boreal coast from New Brunswick south and breeds inland in the Maritime Provinces. The male, with his green head and crest, clear white throat and spotted brownish breast patch, is distinctive. Red-breasted mergansers are able to catch fish more easily than most of the other diving ducks, but they too eat whatever small crustaceans and bivalves they can find.

105. Common mergansers (male on left) are among the most proficient of diving ducks, often catching fish on their dives.

LOONS AND GREBES

Loons are extremely fine divers but are not actually ducks. Their feet are remarkably large, webbed and set well back on the body, excellent for providing good power underwater, but virtually useless for walking on land. Two species winter along the Boreal coast; both are well adapted for swimming after capelin, herring, sand launces and other fish and adept as well at catching bottom-dwelling invertebrates, particularly crustaceans. The common loon, *Gavia immer*, is renowned for its mournful and laughing cries and is easily distinguished by its necklace. It dives to considerable depths and has been caught in fishermen's nets set 200 feet (60 m) below the surface. The red-throated loon, *G. stellata*, is smaller, quieter and is seen far less frequently.

Predators on Mixed Substrates

The red-necked grebe, *Podiceps grisegena*, is neither loon nor duck. Like other grebes it dives well in shallow water, eating small crustaceans and fish. It winters along the Boreal coast south of New Brunswick. It is smaller than the loons, and sits high in the water. In winter its long thin neck is not in fact particularly colorful, but still distinguishes it easily from ducks. Though it doesn't breed in the Boreal region, its courtship display is one of the most extraordinary known. A pair of birds may suddenly throw their heads back almost to their tails, rear up out of the water and run alongside of each other on the water surface. They then circle each other, breast to breast, kicking so hard with their feet that they are almost completely out of the water and finally they fall on to the water again to rest, feed and start the courtship display once more.

Marine Mammals

Among the marine mammals that occur along the Boreal coast, the harbor seal, *Phoca vitulina*, and the harbor porpoise, *Phocoena phocoena*, are the ones most likely to forage on bottom-dwelling fish or invertebrates, as well as on inshore populations of pelagic fish such as herring or mackerel (see chapters 6 and 7).

Planktonic and Pelagic Animals

In the water column between the substrate and the surface lies the relatively featureless world of planktonic and pelagic organisms. They are most abundant in well-mixed inshore waters, especially where tides or currents are reasonably strong and the water is quite shallow. Here nutrient levels remain high throughout the year. Plankton productivity is limited only by hours of sunlight and predation. Phytoplankton species bloom in spring and are abundant until late autumn. Zooplankton species also become increasingly abundant in spring and summer. They feed on the phytoplankton and on each other (see chapter 1).

Each summer various pelagic schooling predators swim inshore to feed on the large zooplankton populations and on each other. Herring eat the zooplankton, mackerel and squid eat the herring, and fishermen try to capture the fish and squid (see chapter 7).

Macroplankton

Some animals that are really still part of the plankton grow large and become numerous in spring and summer. Swept along with the surface waters, they prey on the zooplankton around them. A few species that are more typical of open ocean waters stray occasionally into shallow water. These include sea butterflies, or pteropods, (see chapter 7) and small, powerfully stinging, colonial jellyfish called siphonophores, a group which includes the famous warm-water Portuguese man-o'-war. Other species become extremely abundant in the shallow water and include the comb jellies, or ctenophores, and true jellyfish.

CTENOPHORES OR COMB JELLIES. Comb jellies are as gelatinous and transparent as true coelenterate jellyfish from which they have apparently evolved, but in many ways they are quite different. The eggs of comb jellies develop directly into new juveniles, without passing through bizarre larval stages. Comb jellies lack the sting cells or nematocysts which distinguish the coelenterates, and capture food with adhesive cells on tentacles or by creating currents of water moving toward their mouths. They move not in the rhythmic, pulsating fashion of jellyfish but by eight longitudinal comblike rows of beating hairs, or cilia. The combs beat in remarkable synchrony, propelling the animal mouth forward except when it bumps into something whereupon the beat of the combs is reversed, and the comb jelly backs up. Two and sometimes three species occur along the Boreal coast, often in immense numbers. They swarm in large aggregations, and the iridescence of their beating combs makes them truly beautiful to see.

The sea gooseberry, *Pleurobrachia pileus*, is most aptly named, for it has the shape and approximate size of a gooseberry. It is known in all of the world's colder oceans.

106. Comb jellies or sea gooseberries *Pleurobrachia pileus* are among the most ferocious predators of fish larvae.

It is a year-round resident of the Boreal coast but is most abundant in summer and early fall. It feeds by means of two long tentacles which it can retract into sheaths when it is disturbed. Each tentacle is covered with sticky cells and has many branches hanging from one side, rather like a fisherman's longline, and copepods, crustacean larvae, fish eggs, fish larvae and many other zooplankton are easily caught, pulled in and brushed into the mouth. Where the sea gooseberries are abundant, the water around them can soon become practically empty of potential prey, for they are voracious little predators to say the least. Their impact on populations of fish of commercial value can be considerable (see chapter 7).

The lobate comb jellies look just like sea gooseberries until they are about ¼ inch (6 mm) in diameter, and then the pattern of growth changes and the sides are drawn out into four lobes around the mouth. The species most common north of Cape Cod is *Bolinopsis infundibulum.* It grows to a length of about 6 inches (15 cm). The species characteristic of warmer waters south of Cape Cod, *Mnemiopsis leidyi,* sometimes occurs in the southern Gulf of Maine as well. Lobate comb jellies lack the long tentacles and tentacle sheaths of the sea gooseberries, but have short tentacle fringes replacing them. Very small planktonic animals are caught up in currents created by cilia and are swept in among the lobes into surface grooves leading to the mouth. Lobate comb jellies therefore do little harm to plankton of the size sea gooseberries eat.

LARGE TRUE JELLYFISH. The largest jellyfish are scyphozoan coelenterates. Though they grow to 1 foot (30 cm) or more in diameter and propel themselves through the water with a slow, rhythmic pulsing of their bodies, they are still just part of the plankton, drifting largely at the mercy of the currents. Their sting cells or nematocysts are concentrated in tentacles which may or may not be strong enough to be felt by humans.

Every large jellyfish grows from a minute jellyfish which originates as a bud of a sessile hydroid-like animal. Each spring the sessile polyp carves disks off of itself in an extraordinary process called strobilation, and each disk swims away as a tiny jellyfish perhaps ⅛ inch (3 mm) in diameter. Several months later the jellyfish have grown to their full size, whereupon sperm, shed by males, ingested by females, pass into the female digestive pouches where the gonads lie. There the eggs are fertilized, develop into planula larvae much like those of sea anemones (see chapter 2) and settle to the bottom where they grow into very small sessile polyps. The jellyfish then all die and the polyps overwinter and strobilate when spring arrives once more. In its general outline, this alternation of polyp and large jellyfish forms is similar to the alternation of hydroid and small jellyfish forms that occurs in some of the other coelenterates (see chapter 2).

The moon jelly, *Aurelia aurita*, is one of the two large jellyfish of the Boreal coast. It is shaped like a shallow umbrella and grows to about 1 foot (30 cm) by mid to late summer. It is translucent, even transparent. Its maturing gonads are distinct as four pinkish or white ovals lining the four pouches off the central stomach. The umbrella is fringed with many short tentacles which bear sting cells but which cannot be felt by humans and which curiously enough appear not to be used for capturing food. The mouth lies in the middle of the underside of the umbrella and the manubrium, or lip, extends away from the mouth, drawn out into four short arms.

Planktonic and Pelagic Animals   321

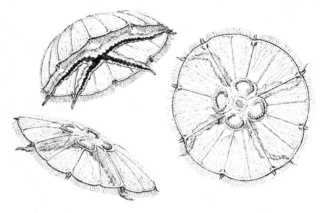

107. The moon jellyfish *Aurelia* pulsates through Boreal waters,
often in masses of hundreds of individuals.

Small moon jellies prey extensively on fish larvae, but
once the jellyfish is more than about 1 inch (2.5 cm) in
diameter, its diet shifts to small zooplankton such as
copepods and the larvae of crustaceans and worms. The
small planktonic animals stick to the surface of the jelly umbrella when they bump into it and the sticky mucus is
moved by cilia on the surface of the jellyfish toward the
manubrium. When blobs of plankton-filled mucus accumulate, an arm of the manubrium licks them up and passes
them into the mouth.

Moon jellyfish occur in practically all the world's oceans
irrespective of water temperature. They tolerate considerable dilution of sea water, drifting far up estuaries. They
form immense aggregations in coastal bays along the Boreal
coast in mid-summer as currents concentrate them and
move them along the coast. They last until September in
the colder parts of the Gulf of Maine, but they begin to be
cast ashore to evaporate into crusty films well before that.
Alive, a moon jellyfish is a thing of beauty, graceful and
fragile in its perfect symmetry.

The other large Boreal jellyfish is the lion's mane or red
jellyfish, *Cyanea capillata*. It is quite unlike the moon jelly.
The lion's mane actually can grow to 6.5 feet (2 m) in diameter (trailing tentacles 100 feet—30 m—or more) all in a

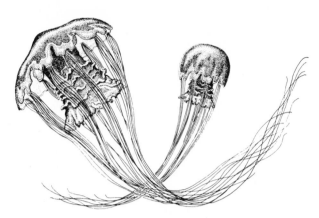

108. The lion's mane jellyfish *Cyanea* trails its long stinging tentacles behind it as it pulses through the water.

single summer after starting from a strobilated disk ⅛ inch (3 mm) in diameter in early spring. Such rapid growth depends upon a fine food supply and a low rate of energy expenditure, and not surprisingly the biggest individuals grow in the coldest, most northern waters where food is virtually infinite and metabolic rates are low.

The lion's mane is reddish-brown in color, shaped like an inverted basin with scalloped edges. The lips of its mouth hang in a long folded curtain, continually rising and lowering under the basin-like umbrella. Outside the manubrium curtain trail eight tufts of thin tentacles which can stretch extremely far behind the jellyfish as it pulses slowly through the water. The stinging cells on the tentacles are powerful enough to raise a short-lived but painful welt on human flesh and to paralyze planktonic animals with great ease. Like the sea gooseberries, a lion's mane jellyfish can have a noticeable impact upon the numbers of fish larvae of commercially valuable species.

Lion's mane jellyfish do not aggregate like moon jellyfish, but they still may occur in large numbers in coastal bays. They become sexually mature in late summer and after they spawn the giants wash ashore, their sting cells able to sting the curious for a short time until heat and desiccation kill the cells.

CHAPTER VI

Islands and Ledges:
Seabirds and Seals

Sanctuaries for Breeding

Seals and seabirds are dominant predators along most of the Boreal coast, preying on pelagic, benthic and even inter- tidal animals. They are all well adapted for feeding at sea or along seashores, but are rarely as agile on land as are their terrestrial counterparts; they are especially vulnerable to terrestrial predators during their breeding seasons. As a re- sult, seabirds breed on islands along the entire length of the Boreal coast, and seals breed on ledges and on the shores of some of the islands along the whole coast as well as on the island-like drifting ice floes of spring in the Gulf of St. Lawrence.

Many of the seals and seabirds are in fact so safe from the usual terrestrial predators on their island breeding sites that they seem very tame, unafraid and approachable. Ob- viously they evolved these characteristics without having any contact with humans. Recent predation on seals and seabirds by humans practically eliminated many of the breeding colonies or herds; and where humans have by chance allowed rats or cats to go ashore on islands, breeding populations of birds have been efficiently decimated as well. Seabirds on the Boreal coast are now protected from human predation and many of their breeding sites are protected. Seals are now protected south of the Canadian border; they are still hunted in Canadian waters.

From Newfoundland to Cape Cod, islands and ledges occur in impressive numbers; along the coast of Maine alone there are over 3000 islands and no one has counted all the ledges. The Boreal islands and ledges vary just as much in size, shape, bedrock, degree of exposure and kind of vegetation cover as do the shores of the mainland. Some are far offshore, like the flat Sable Island 200 miles east of Nova Scotia and the Magdalen Islands in the center of the Gulf of St. Lawrence. Some are large and tree-covered, like Monhegan and Matinicus Islands off the Maine coast, and Grand Manan Island at the mouth of the Bay of Fundy. Some have immense cliffs, like Bonaventure Island and Bird Rocks in the Gulf of St. Lawrence and the Bird Islands of Witless Bay in Newfoundland. Some are wooded, some exclusively sand. Some are islands only when the tide is high, like the higher elevations of salt marshes, or they are islands at low tide only, submerged by every high tide. Despite their variation, each is a potential breeding site for at least one of the species of seabirds or seals.

Seabirds

Seabird Diversity

All seabirds breed on coastal islands, but some also nest on isolated, island-like sites on the coast itself. Many, such as the shearwaters, petrels, auks and puffins, come to islands only to breed; otherwise they live at sea. The gulls, terns and cormorants remain near the coast throughout the year, gathering on particular islands to breed and then spreading out along the coast the rest of the time. They roost on dry land and do not sleep at sea. Most seabirds are exclusively marine, but cormorants forage far up estuaries and some species of terns and gulls forage and even breed around lakes across the continent.

Seabirds have evolved a remarkable diversity of feeding methods, and as a group they thoroughly exploit the food sources available to them while at the same time avoiding too extensive competition for any one particular food source. Gulls scavenge and prey along the shorelines and in the wakes of fishing boats. Terns and gannets plunge-dive from above the water for fish not far below the surface. Cormorants swim underwater after fish in inshore waters; auks, murres and puffins swim after them well offshore. Shearwaters and petrels concentrate on the fish and refuse which they mostly pick off the water surface far out to sea. And skuas and jaegers are pirates, harassing other seabirds until they disgorge whatever they have just eaten.

Slaughter of the Seabirds

Seabirds used to breed in immense colonies on many islands along the Boreal coast. The earliest explorers mentioned the astonishing sizes of the colonies they saw. The early settlers and fishermen recognized in the colonial sea-birds an excellent source of food and of bait for fishing. People found it far too easy to land on a breeding island, collect all of the eggs from accessible nests, and in many cases shoot most of the adults as well. As the millinery trade grew in the 18th century the feathers of some of the sea-birds became so valuable that by late in the 19th century whole colonies had disappeared. The populations of many of the Boreal seabirds plummeted to dangerously low levels and in fact were eliminated from parts of the coast. The one flightless seabird of the Boreal coast, the great auk, had no defense at all against the collectors and fishermen, and by 1850 the last one had been killed.

Finally at the end of the 19th century, seabirds became protected and the millinery trade lost its major con-tributors. Seabird populations have recovered slowly; pres-ent populations of most species are still but shadows of what they once were. Parts of the Boreal coast still lack even small breeding colonies of species which once were com-mon.

Several species have fared very well during the past fifty years, however. Herring gulls and great black-backed gulls are thriving. They are most abundant where human refuse is greatest, and they are outcompeting other seabirds which nest on similar habitats.

Some species that recovered early this century are de-clining in numbers again. In a few cases biologists help re-covery of the more uncommon species by establishing new breeding colonies on islands where the birds have long been absent.

Seabird Colonies

Just as seabirds have evolved divergent ways of fishing, they have evolved different preferences for nesting habitats. Most of the gulls and terns nest in open, flat areas often in or near grass. Gannets nest on broad cliff ledges, auks and murres nest on narrower ledges of the cliffs, and kittiwakes nest on some of the sheerest, most inaccessible parts of the cliffs. Puffins and storm petrels dig burrows in soft soil above the cliffs. Though many of these seabirds are

109. Several thousand pairs of breeding gannets crowd together on the cliffs of Bonaventure Island off the Gaspé Peninsula.

in fact relatively plastic in their nesting requirements, able to nest successfully in habitats other than those they usually favor, their preferences for different breeding habitats allow them to share the available space on an island without competing too much with each other.

Seabird colonies vary tremendously in size from just a few breeding pairs to thousands, perhaps hundreds of thousands, of breeding pairs. They vary just as much in density. What they all have in common, however, is that they are colonial, and the reasons for this coloniality are still the subject of debate.

Seabirds breed on islands primarily because they are safe from predators there. By breeding in colonies, close to one another, they probably increase their safety, for they can warn each other of a potential predator and perhaps join together in defense. The older, more experienced birds tend to nest in the middle of their colony, and younger, inexperienced birds are usually forced to nest near the periphery of the colony and are the most subject to predation.

Defense against predators is certainly not the only reason for colonial breeding, however. The need for social

Seabirds   329

stimulation may be equally important. The sight of courting and copulating pairs often stimulates neighboring pairs to court and copulate, and as a result, the birds in a colony tend to court, lay their eggs and have their eggs hatch in synchrony. Such synchrony means that most of the birds complete their breeding at about the same time. A restricted breeding season provides time for the newly fledged juveniles to learn how to forage before the gales and high seas of autumn make learning difficult.

Breeding Behavior

Throughout much of the animal kingdom males tend to be promiscuous and uninvolved in parental behavior. Exceptions are always noteworthy, and seabirds as a group provide a major exception. Almost all seabirds are monogamous. The sexes look very similar and the males put in about the same amount of effort into incubating the eggs and feeding the nestlings as the females do.

Because seabirds catch their food in a relatively difficult manner, young individuals have to go through a long period of growth and learning before they can feed themselves and until that time they are completely dependent upon their parents. At first a nestling needs one parent to protect it while the other forages, and later both parents must forage at once if they are to find enough food for their voracious offspring. Any male which doesn't help raise his own young leaves behind no offspring, for the job is just too great for one parent.

Every seabird therefore has to forge a strong pair-bond with another individual in order to breed, and that bond has to be reinforced constantly throughout the breeding season. Each seabird species has its own set of ritualized postures and movements which a male and female display to one another during courtship. Once they copulate and the female lays her egg or eggs, courtship displays continue in some fashion until the young are fledged. The parents can then separate and forage independently until their next breeding season.

The cost in time, effort and energy spent in raising

330   ISLANDS AND LEDGES

offspring to independence must be quite large, especially for the females who must produce such large eggs to start with. In some species the males in a sense contribute to the production of eggs by bringing food to their mates even before the eggs are laid, and the cost of reproduction may not be so much less for them than for the females. Seabirds tend to lay only a small number of eggs in a clutch. A pair of gulls or terns lay two or three eggs; gannets, auks, murres and puffins lay only one. They certainly could lay more eggs, and most years they probably could raise more than one or two offspring, but the energy cost of raising more than they do might weaken them too much to survive the winter and breed again. Seabirds are remarkably long-lived, however, and they have an opportunity to breed many times. There is no selective pressure on them to raise as many offspring as they are physiologically capable of. They can even afford to skip a year between breeding years, and some species do so regularly.

Juvenile Life

The times of heaviest mortality among seabirds occur while they are eggs, nestlings and fledglings. Once they have survived their first year, they have a good chance of living for 20 or 30 years more, but early mortality is very high. Predators, particularly herring gulls and great black-backed gulls as well as skuas and jaegers on the far northern breeding colonies, can destroy an impressive number of eggs and nestlings. Nestlings rarely die because there isn't enough food around to catch for them, but they often die because their parents are young and inexperienced, and feed and protect them inadequately. Unexpectedly cold or rainy weather in the early parts of the breeding season can also kill large numbers of young nestlings.

Seabirds rarely breed for the first time until they are three or four years old or more, and they don't grow full adult plumage until they reach breeding age. Why sexual maturity is deferred for so long is another of the questions under debate but it may relate to the experience a seabird must possess before it has a chance of feeding more than just itself, and it is a tolerable strategy because the bird is likely to live long enough to breed a few times.

Migration and Nomadism

Seabirds leave their breeding colonies as soon as they can. In most cases their young leave with them, dependent for a while longer. The coastal species such as the gulls, terns and cormorants spread along the coast while the pelagic shearwaters and petrels, and the diving gannets, puffins, auks and murres all wander farther out to sea. All spend their time closer to their food supplies, no longer tied to particular breeding sites.

As conditions along the Boreal coast deteriorate in autumn some of the coastal seabirds shift southwards, though herring gulls and great black-backed gulls remain on the Boreal coast year long. The offshore pelagic and diving species spread out wherever there is food. Large numbers winter around the various offshore fishing banks. A few species turn up on the Boreal coast only in winter. These are true northern species like some of the gulls whose northern range in winter is limited only by the southward growth of pack ice.

Not all of the seabirds remain anywhere near the Boreal coast or even the North Atlantic, however. The terns and some of the shearwaters undertake migrations of spectacular length to overwinter as far away as the food-rich waters of the subantarctic region. After spending several months there they migrate north for the spring breeding season back in the northern hemisphere.

Vulnerability of Seabird Populations

Because seabirds lay only a small number of eggs per breeding pair each year, they are slow to recover from disasters. Some are able to re-lay when they lose a brood, but second broods in a season are less successful, and a number of seabirds will not even attempt them. Though human predation of breeding seabirds has for the most part ceased, far less obvious harm continues to occur. The slightest disturbance by a human visitor can cause adults to take flight. If they are cliff nesters, a rain of eggs may be knocked to the rocks below; if they are surrounded by herring gulls or great black-backed gulls, their eggs and nestlings may be preyed upon before they dare return to their nests. It doesn't make much difference whether the visitors are picnickers or biological investigators, all with the best of intentions; their visits inevitably affect the breeding success of the birds, and the colonies should be left undisturbed until at least mid-summer.

The Gulls

Gulls are familiar along the whole of the Boreal coast. Some are dominant residents even in winter, some are summer breeders, and some are only winter or summer strays. All gulls are powerful fliers with long, pointed wings and usually square tails. They all have webbed feet, and swim easily on the water surface. Most of them are scavengers as well as predators. The larger species also prey on the eggs and young of other seabirds. Though not designed for plunge-diving from the air into the water to catch food, some of the gulls do occasionally capture fish just below the surface in that fashion.

Herring Gull. Herring gulls, *Larus argentatus*, are the most common seabirds along many parts of the Boreal coast. They are large gulls with grey wings; black wing tips; white heads, tails and breasts; yellow bills; and pink legs and feet. They are abundant along rocky shores and tidal flats, around fishing boats and harbor docks, and probably no open garbage dump is without its population of refuse eaters (see color plate VIII).

Herring gulls were almost eliminated along most of the Boreal coast by the late 19th century, for after herons and egrets became protected from those collecting plume feathers for the millinery trade, herring gulls became a popular substitute. By the 1880's only several thousand pairs remained. About that time people began to be embarrassed by hats with bird feathers in them, and laws eventually protected gulls as effectively as other species. By 1900, herring gull numbers had increased to about 10,000 pairs scattered over 17 breeding colonies, and herring gulls have been breeding farther and farther south along the Atlantic coast since then. During the 1920's they began breeding as far south as Cape Cod and Martha's Vineyard, and now they have begun to breed along the Carolina coasts.

Though populations of herring gulls south of the Boreal region continue to grow, they appear to have stabilized in the Boreal region with perhaps as many as 200,000 breeding pairs spread out over about 300 breeding sites. Populations have even begun to decline in places where inshore fisheries and their associated wastes have diminished since the 1960's. As municipal dumps increasingly become covered rather than open, herring gull populations ought to diminish further. Without doubt there will still be ample refuse as well as natural prey to continue to support herring gulls in the kinds of numbers we have come to expect.

Herring gulls have a circumpolar distribution in the Northern Hemisphere. Along the Atlantic coast they overwinter from the Gulf of St. Lawrence south into the Caribbean. In spring and summer they breed on islands along the coast as well as in inland lakes. They form the largest breeding colonies of seabirds along the southern parts of the Boreal coast, and they breed as far north as the Arctic. They usually nest in the open where they have a view of their surroundings, building shallow nests on the ground from grass and seaweed, but they have been known to nest in trees and on cliff ledges when necessary.

A breeding colony of herring gulls may consist of just a few breeding pairs or it may have thousands. One of the largest colonies is on Kent Island near Grand Manan Island at the mouth of the Bay of Fundy where about 15,000 pairs now breed each year. The distance between nests varies greatly, for in a circle with a 15 foot (4.5 m) radius there may be as many as 10 nests or as few as one. A breeding pair lays 2 or 3 eggs, at 2- or 3-day intervals, and incubates the eggs for about 4 weeks. The eggs hatch at 2- or 3-day intervals, and the last to hatch is sometimes smaller and less likely to survive than its nestmates. Breeding pairs raise an average of just one chick to fledgling age each year, for eggs and young chicks die from exposure, inattention and predation by crows and other gulls.

Herring gull chicks are born covered with down and with their eyes open. They leave the nest within a day of hatching. Though they are relatively advanced, they are still dependent on their parents for food and are therefore known as semi-precocial. A young chick is gray with dark spots, difficult to distinguish as it hides among the grass or rocks. For its first few days it is shaded from rain and excessive sun by one of its parents, but after that it controls its own body temperature well enough and is left to find its own protective cover. Still, a parent usually stays nearby for a couple of weeks to protect it from predators.

The newly born chick rapidly learns to stroke its parent's bill and strike at the red spot near the tip of the bill, stimulating the parent to regurgitate partially digested food for the chick to eat. It grows rapidly into a juvenile almost the size of its parents. When it is about six weeks old, it is able to fly, and leaves the breeding colony with its parents. It soon learns to scavenge but still begs whatever food it can get from its parents.

Juveniles come inshore with their parents usually around the middle of August along the Boreal coast. The juveniles learn to search the tidal flats and other shallow water for prey, and soon, like their parents, they begin to carry mussels, sea urchins, crabs, whelks and other animals up into the air and to drop them on to rocks below in order to crack them open. This carrying and dropping method of obtaining food is extremely characteristic of herring gulls, but it is used less frequently by other species of gulls as well.

Even when they aren't breeding, herring gulls are gregarious. They advertize food they catch, attracting others to share the find, and they roost together on ledges, islands or beaches. The juveniles are always easy to spot, for it takes them two or three years to obtain adult plumage and the red spot doesn't develop on their bills until they are three years old and ready to attempt to breed for the first time.

Herring gulls are aggressive birds. They nest on the same kind of terrain that laughing gulls and terns favor, to the detriment of the latter. Herring gulls nest near other seabirds as well, and though they don't compete for the same breeding space, they prey when they can on all the eggs and chicks they can get. The only seabirds which seem to be able to coexist easily with herring gulls are the even larger great black-backed gulls and eider ducks.

Herring gulls are intelligent. They adapt quickly to new

110. Flocks of herring gulls announce their presence with their raucous calls echoing back and forth between the birds.

food sources and breeding sites and they appear remarkably perceptive of their surroundings. They are noisy birds, and the cries of herring gulls are among the sounds most associated with the Boreal coast. Their cries have meanings to them, for herring gulls have a vocabulary of sorts, with different cries for food advertisement, territorial defense, and begging. Each has a slightly different voice and way of calling than every other and the herring gulls probably recognize each other individually at least partly by voice. Their calls also seem to mean different things to different neighbors, and in different situations, and there is a growing possibility that gulls possess the kind of awareness and intelligence that we associate with the most intelligent of birds, the crow family.

Great Black-backed Gull. Great black-backed gulls, *Larus marinus*, are the largest of gulls, with a wing spread of 65 inches (1.6 m) compared with 52 inches (1.4 m) for herring gulls. Their black wings and their size make them distinct from all other gulls. They are neither as gregarious nor abundant as herring gulls, but they roost with them, forage with them, and often breed near them.

Like herring gulls, great black-backed gulls have been increasing in numbers and breeding range throughout this century. The first record of great black-backed gulls breeding in Maine, south of the Maritime Provinces shores, was

336

111. Great black-backed gulls often prey upon eggs or chicks of other seabirds.

in 1926. They began to breed south of the Boreal region during the 1950's and have now begun to breed as far south as the Carolina coasts. Though they now breed in several hundred different colonies along the Boreal coast, their colonies tend to be small, and the total breeding population is probably on the order of about 20,000 pairs.

Great black-backed gulls nest in small numbers from

112. Great black-backed chicks and eggs are cryptically colored to blend in with their nest and with nearby vegetation.

Seabirds 337

Labrador south usually on the most elevated sites on an island, where they have a broad view of their surroundings. Each breeding female lays two or three eggs in a nest of grass and seaweeds, and the chicks and juveniles obtain their adult plumage when they are three years old and breed for the first time when they are four or five, a year or so older than their herring gull counterparts.

Like herring gulls, great black-backed gulls are omnivorous, scavenging on refuse, foraging along seashores for crustaceans and bivalves, and preying on the eggs and chicks of other seabirds. Even herring gull chicks are prey for breeding great black-backed gulls, and only eider ducks appear able to nest nearby without suffering predation.

Great black-backed gulls are common on the southern parts of the Boreal coast all winter, spreading to its northern parts each spring for the breeding season. They are relatively silent birds except on their breeding grounds, and they appear to be much shyer of human activities than herring gulls.

Ring-billed Gull. Ring-billed gulls, *Larus delawarensis*, look a great deal like herring gulls except that adults have yellowish legs and a very distinct black ring around the tip of their bills. Ring-billed gulls once bred in abundance along the Boreal coast, and Audubon found them breeding along the Maine coast and the Gulf of St. Lawrence in 1840. By 1920 none were left, for they didn't survive the egg and plume collectors. They did survive inland, however, and during the 1920's colonized the Great Lakes where about 300,000 breeding pairs now live. A few thousand pairs now also breed in the Gulf of St. Lawrence once again, but none have returned to breed on the coast of Maine. During the winter, ring-billed gulls generally move to the coast and a few winter as far north as the very southern part of the Boreal region. Ring-billed gulls forage, breed and mature much like herring gulls, and they are equally gregarious and noisy.

Laughing Gull. Laughing gulls, *Larus atricilla*, have black heads and dark wings and are considerably smaller than herring gulls. They are really warm-water gulls which range north into the southern Boreal region during the summer, breeding from islands on the coast of Maine south into the tropics. They nest on flat islands, on sand bars and among sand dunes as well as on high tide islets in salt marshes. They bred in large flourishing colonies along the southern Boreal coast until around the 1940's, but have given way to herring and great black-backed gulls since then. They are unable to compete with the larger gulls or to protect eggs and nestlings from predation by them. Only a few hundred pairs are left breeding on the coasts of Maine and Massachusetts where just a few years ago there were probably 20,000. Though their habits are generally similar to those of herring gulls, they depend less on scavenging to get their food but catch fish near the water's surface and, around their breeding colonies, prey on the eggs of the terns which often breed nearby. Their cry is a high, clear chuckle or laugh which to human ears has a touch of insanity to it.

Kittiwake. Black-legged kittiwakes, *Rissa tridactyla*, are remarkable gulls, for they have lost many of the habits of other gulls. Instead they have adapted to nesting on the sheerest cliffs and fishing at sea for months at a time as true pelagic birds. They breed on islands in the Gulf of St. Lawrence, around Newfoundland and on north to Arctic coasts. They winter at sea offshore along the Boreal coast and across the North Atlantic.

Smaller than herring gulls, black-legged kittiwakes have grey wings with black triangular tips, white heads, yellow bills and black legs. Immature juveniles have black bills and a dark neckband and are more commonly seen in winter than adults. Juveniles become sexually mature when they are three years old, but they may not breed successfully for another couple of years.

Kittiwakes build nests of seaweed on obscure promontories on the steep cliffs, gluing the weed in place with their excretions. They usually lay two eggs in their nests, and newly hatched chicks are covered with white glossy down. They have no need of cryptic coloration, for they aren't about to leave their nests, and few if any predators can reach them. The major danger they face is falling out of their nests to the distant rocks below them, and they rapidly develop the habit, perhaps learned in part from their parents, of facing into the cliff wall. They remain virtually immobile and silent as they grow, and the black patch on the back of the neck of every juvenile probably ensures that no adult mistakes it for another adult and therefore a potential competitor (see color plate VIII).

Kittiwakes are less silent when away from their nests, and their cry sounds a little like their name. They are very specialized oceanic feeders, rarely scavenging but instead fishing for small fish, euphausiid shrimp and pteropod mollusks (see chapter 6). They are able to dive from the water surface and swim underwater after their food, the only gull able to do so. With their breeding and feeding specializations, they present quite a contrast to the far less specialized gulls.

OTHER GULLS. Several gull species that breed along the Arctic occasionally stray onto the Boreal coast in winter. The ivory gull, *Pagophila eburnea*, pure white but for its black bill and legs, breeds and winters in the Arctic, following the edge of the pack ice south in winter. The glaucous gull, *Larus hyperboreous*, looks more like a herring gull but is larger and lacks black wing tips. It breeds in the Arctic as well but small colonies have been found on inaccessible parts of the west coast of Newfoundland. In winter its southern stragglers may roost with herring gulls. The Iceland gull, *Larus glaucoides*, looks and acts much like a smaller version of the glaucous gull. The Bonaparte's gull, *Larus philadelphia*, a small black-headed species which breeds inland, winters along the coast sometimes as far north as the southern Boreal coast. Quite similar to the Bonaparte's gull but a little larger is the black-headed gull, *Larus ridibundus*, which is not uncommon on the Nova Scotia coast in winter. It is a European species, but there is a possibility that it has begun to breed in North America as well.

Terns

Gulls and terns belong to the same family of birds, the Laridae, but they belong to separate sub-families. Terns' wings are more pointed, their bills thinner, their bodies more slender than gulls', and their tails are forked. They fish in a

ISLANDS AND LEDGES

spectacular fashion, hovering in the air over fish schools and plunge-diving repeatedly into the water after their prey. Each folds back its wings as it dives, easily penetrates a few feet below the water surface, rises to the surface and takes flight again, pausing to shake the water from its feathers.

Though they generally nest on sand or shingle beaches or among sand dunes or salt marsh grasses, terns do not breed as exclusively on islands as do the other seabirds. They can breed as well on beaches on the mainland and inland. Their colonies may have a thousand or more pairs, and they are extremely aggressive in their mobbing of potential predators. Anyone who has approached a colony of breeding terns is acquainted with their disconcerting habit of swooping kamikazi fashion at his or her head.

Apart from the anti-predatory advantages of colonial breeding, terns may derive other benefits as well. Because they feed in such a specialized way, they depend on food that is abundant but hard to find. There is no squabbling over a fish, for the school it came from is usually huge. As a result, terns may follow a successful forager back out to the school it has found, and by nesting in colonies they are able to share information about food discoveries. This is vital at a time when they have to feed offspring.

COMMON, ARCTIC AND ROSEATE TERNS. Common terns, *Sterna hirundo;* Arctic terns, *S. paradisaea;* and roseate terns, *S. dougallii,* may flock and breed together and can be very difficult to distinguish from each other. All three have black caps, gray wings and white forked tails, and are about the same size with wing spreads of 30 to 31 inches (75 to 77 cm). The bills of Arctic terns are bright red, those of common terns usually have black tips, while the bills of roseate terns are mostly black. Their calls are slightly different and help distinguish them as well.

Common terns are in fact the commonest of the three along the Boreal coast in summer. They breed from Labrador south to the Caribbean. Arctic terns breed from the southern edge of the Boreal region north to the Arctic. Roseate terns, infrequently seen now, breed from Nova Scotia to Venezuela. Where all three overlap on the Boreal coast, they may share a breeding site, or nest very close to

113. Common terns nest on sandy areas, hollowing out a shallow depression for their clutch of 2 to 4 eggs.

each other. In winter, all three migrate south into the Southern Hemisphere; Arctic terns travel as far as the Straits of Magellan.

These three terns were collected enthusiastically during the last century, once again on behalf of the millinery trade. The roseate tern was practically eliminated, and remains uncommon along much of its past breeding range even now. Common terns have recovered better, and Arctic terns, because of their more northern distribution, were not as severely threatened by the collectors.

When they arrive at their breeding grounds in May, the terns scoop shallow nests in the sand or gravel and usually lay two to four eggs in each nest by mid-June. They incubate the eggs for three weeks, and the chicks are born semi-precocial with a down covering and their eyes open. They don't leave their nests for two or three days and then they run about and hide in the grass or rocks. Their parents feed them with small fish which they swallow head first, and even by August, when they are fledged and able to fly, they still depend on their parents to feed them until they learn to dive successfully for fish themselves.

Terns mature more quickly than gulls, but though they may be ready to breed for the first time when they are just a

year old, many wait another year before attempting it. Because they feed exclusively by plunge-diving, they are no
threat to each other's offspring. But they also often nest
close to gulls, and laughing gulls, herring gulls and great
black-backed gulls all prey upon the eggs and chicks of
terns. Breeding terns are unable to compete adequately
with herring gulls for nesting space or to protect themselves
well enough from gull predation, and breeding tern populations are diminishing.

Least Tern. Least terns, *Sterna albifrons*, are the
smallest of the terns, with a wing spread of just 20 inches
(50 cm), and with their yellow bills and white foreheads
they are easy to distinguish from the other terns. They nest
on sandy and pebbly beaches on islands and on the mainland mostly south of the Boreal region. At the very northern edge of their breeding range, at a few sites along the
Maine coast, they nest apart from other terns and sometimes nest near piping plovers instead. Like other terns,
they winter from the Caribbean to the southern end of
South America.

Caspian Tern. Caspian terns, *Sterna caspia*, are
large, more gull-like terns with a wing spread of 53 inches
(1.3 m). They seem to associate more with ring-billed gulls
than with other species in North America and they breed in
scattered colonies on the coasts of North America, Europe,
Asia, Africa and Australia. A small number breed in the
Gulf of St. Lawrence but they are uncommon elsewhere
along the Boreal coast.

Common Eiders

Common eiders, *Somateria mollissima*, are seabirds, but
they still are diving ducks, more closely related to harle-
quins, oldsquaws and scoters (see chapter 5) than they are
to the other seabirds. As in other ducks, males and females
play very different roles in breeding and raising offspring,
for males are essentially promiscuous while females build
their nests, incubate their eggs amd raise their young.
Females are brown, difficult to see while incubating their
eggs; males are a spectacular contrast of black sides, tail,

outer wing feathers and a blazing white on the rest of the body and cap. Common eiders breed from Maine northward to Greenland and the Arctic, wintering along the same coasts south to Long Island.

Common eider females build their nests on islands, often in dense colonies, and they often nest near breeding herring and great black-backed gulls. Each female builds her nest of plant material lined thickly with her own down feathers when she starts to lay her eggs. She lays four to six eggs and then incubates them without relief for the next 25 days. At most she gets off the eggs for occasional ten minute periods, but she goes without food the whole time.

The young hatch as precocial ducklings, ready to leave the nest with their mother shortly after hatching. Females then begin the sometimes long and dangerous swim across open water to the more protected waters along the mainland. En route they form instant extended families with perhaps only two females and eight or nine ducklings or perhaps with as many as five females and sixty ducklings. The large group of ducklings are likely to remain together as a crèche for the next couple of months, protected as much as possible by the few female adults with them. In the face of predation the females can herd the ducklings together more quickly than a single female can, and reduce the chance of ducklings straying into greater danger. Ducklings begin to feed themselves as soon as their mothers guide them to shallow water where they dive and forage for bivalves and crustaceans.

The social relationships between the females with any one crèche are not simple ones. One female usually assumes leadership of the crèche, leading it, guarding it, refusing to abandon it when danger occurs, and vocalizing frequently. The other females with the crèche are subordinate, less aggressive and quieter, swim in a more peripheral position, and leave the group in the face of disturbance. The subordinate females may have such a loose association with crèches that they move from one to another even during a single day. Crèches still appear to be attractive to females, however, and the dominant super-mother rarely is left as the only adult tending a crèche of ducklings.

Common eiders, like the herring gulls and great black-

114. The brilliant white plumage of male common eiders (right foreground) contrasts greatly with the females' drab brown coloration (left foreground).

backed gulls, are increasing in numbers while other sea-birds are not. This is despite the fact that common eiders often nest among breeding predatory gulls. Because a female common eider rarely leaves her eggs unprotected, predation on eggs is low, and she is large enough herself not to be subjected to gull attack or harassment. The gulls also probably act as sentinels, by chance warning common eiders of any danger before the eiders notice it themselves. Only when people walk into a breeding colony and female common eiders are flushed from their nests before they have time to camouflage their eggs is predation by gulls more likely. The gulls return to their nests more quickly following such a disturbance than do the female common eiders, and then they have a good opportunity to notice and eat exposed, undefended eider eggs.

Cormorants

Cormorants make up one family of an order of birds, the Pelecaniformes, whose other families include the pelicans, tropic-birds, frigate-birds, gannets and boobies, and anhinga. All are large, fish-eating birds with webbed feet. The cormorants and anhinga are the only ones of the order that dive from the water surface and swim underwater in search of fish.

Two species of cormorants fish along the Boreal coast. The great cormorant, *Phalacrocorax carbo*, has a wing spread of 60 inches (1.8 m) and though it is the common cormorant of European and Asian coasts it is the less common of the two along the American Boreal coast. The double-crested cormorant, *P. auritus*, is a little smaller, with a wing spread of 50 inches (1.3 m), and is very common along the Boreal coast in summer.

Both cormorants are black, long-necked, long-tailed birds that sit low in the water and usually hit the water a number of times with their wings when they take flight. They frequently emerge from the water and stand on rocks or channel markers with their wings spread to dry. Under water they get most of their power from their large webbed feet. They hold their wings slightly open and only occasionally use them to help in the swimming, and their long tails function as rudders.

The cormorants breed in colonies which may have just a few pairs or may have many thousands. Males court females with elaborate postures, and breeding pairs then build nests of sticks and seaweed in trees or on the ground on small islands or large cliff ledges. Their excretions, called guano, are extremely rich in nitrates, excellent for fertilizer but lethal to trees and other vegetation near the nests.

Each pair lays from three to five eggs, and the purple gray young which hatch are altricial, blind, naked and helpless. They need constant brooding for about two weeks, for until then they are unable to control their body temperature and succumb easily to cold or heat exposure. The young at first sip semidigested liquid from their parents' bills, then learn to stick their heads into their parents' throats to pull out food. Finally they begin to eat solid, undigested food, and when they are about four weeks old they learn to fly and take to the water.

Double-crested cormorants breed along all of the Boreal coast as well as around inland lakes, south into the Bahamas, and in large numbers on the U.S. west coast. During the winter they shift south and are uncommon even in the most southern parts of the Boreal region. Great cormorants remain on the Boreal coast throughout the winter, breed on a few sites in the northern part of the region in summer, and are not often in the Gulf of Maine.

115. Double-crested cormorants breed in colonies of up to several thousand, their seaweed and stick nests fashioned in trees or on the ground.

Cormorants are excellent fishermen. Great cormorants were trained in Europe and China to catch but not swallow fish and return to their trainers. A sight too frequent as far as inshore fishermen along the Boreal coast are concerned is of tens or hundreds of double-crested cormorants diving time and again into a purse seine full of fish, pausing only to stand on the edge of the net to dry their wings.

Gannets

Gannets, *Morus bassana*, present quite a vivid contrast to cormorants despite their many similarities. Gannets are large white birds with black wing tips, yellowish heads, very thick, long bills, and a wing spread of 70 inches (1.8 m). They breed in 22 colonies around the north Atlantic, and four of the colonies occur along the northern parts of the American Boreal coast. The largest and most famous of these four lies on the huge, seaward-facing cliffs of Bonaventure Island in the Gulf of St. Lawrence.

When they aren't breeding, gannets spend most of their time at sea and spread out over much of the Atlantic, though they usually keep within 3 or 4 miles of land. Their most remarkable behavior is their manner of fishing. A gannet may dive from a height of 100 feet (30 m) or more if the fish school is not right at the water surface, folding its wings back as it penetrates the water. The sight of a diving gannet attracts other gannets to the fish school, and it is possible that they so disorganize the fish by their group attack that they are more successful in catching the fish than they would be if they fished independently. The sight of a hundred or so gannets diving like living arrows again and again into a fish school is memorable.

The large, heavy bill helps a gannet catch quite large fish and reach depths of up to 50 feet (15 m) on its dives. The gannet is able to swim a little underwater, scoop fish fry from the water surface, and even occasionally hunt sand launces on foot. Most of the time it plunge-dives, however, a fishing technique that is difficult to learn and keeps young birds dependent on their parents for their first few months.

Males arrive back on the breeding colonies first and establish themselves on the best nest sites they can, aggressively fending off other males. As the females arrive, the males advertize themselves and their sites and soon breeding pairs form. Males and females spend a great deal of time developing the pair bond which will hold them together as a cooperative, unselfish unit for the duration of the breeding season. They court each other with a variety of rituals that include extraordinary bouts of fencing with their bills as well as less violent periods of mutual preening. They continue to reinforce their pair bond with these rituals until they no longer need to feed their offspring (see color plate VIII).

Gannet colonies are extremely dense. Nests are spaced 32 inches (80 cm) apart, just far enough that a gannet sitting on its nest cannot quite reach the gannets sitting on adjacent ones. New breeding pairs try to squeeze into the colony but are usually forced to breed first at the periphery instead. Because nest density is so great, gannets have evolved various postures and actions which indicate their intent or mood to the birds around them in a way to reduce confusion as much as possible. A gannet standing with its head stretched upward, "sky-pointing," is indicating it is about to take flight or move on foot. A female turning her head away, "facing away," from her mate is appeasing him, inhibiting his aggressiveness. Headshaking in a particular rotary motion indicates alarm. In all, thirteen different postures and actions have been recognized, and there are probably many more subtle ones that are more difficult for non-gannets to detect and interpret.

A gannet pair lays one egg, usually in early May. Male and female take turns incubating the egg, each sitting for about 30 hours at a stint. Once the chick hatches, it is guarded by its parents which again take turns, though the stints shorten to about 20 hours. The chick is fed with fish two or three times per day, and doesn't move off of its nest until it is fledged when it is almost three months old, for only on its nest is it safe from the jabs of surrounding gannets. The parents fish opportunistically, gathering fish from nearby schools if any are present, but flying up to 200 or 300 miles away if they need to. Strong fliers, they can cover from 30 to 40 miles (48 to 64 km) in an hour.

On a rarely disturbed colony, probably 80 percent of the chicks are fledged. The eggs and chicks that die are usually the offspring of inexperienced parents. The transition to independent feeding is an extremely hazardous time for gannets, however. Those that were fed well usually have considerable fat to see them through the difficult month or two it takes to learn to catch the fish they dive for. Juveniles wander further south in winter into warmer waters than older birds, and retain their darker plumage for a couple of years. Most try to breed for the first time when they are four or five years old.

Alcids

Alcids are a family of pelagic birds which include auks, murres, guillemots and puffins. Most of them have black backs and white bellies, and swim underwater, using their wings, in search of prey. They spend their lives at sea in cold-water latitudes, coming ashore only to breed on the coastal cliffs of Greenland and other islands in the Arctic and as far south as Labrador, the Gulf of St. Lawrence and occasionally the Gulf of Maine.

Because they swim with their wings as well as fly with them, they do not fly as well as most birds, and their wing beat in air is very rapid. Several species that occur on the Boreal coast are probably as large as they could be and still be able to fly. Only one species, the great auk, gave up flight altogether as the penguins of the Southern Hemisphere have done, and it was able to grow larger. Its flightlessness gave it no defense against the fishermen and feather collectors, and the fact that it alone was hunted to extinction is no coincidence.

AUKS AND MURRES. Razor-billed auks, *Alca torda;* common murres, *Uria aalge;* and thick-billed murres, *Uria lomvia,* are large for alcids, all growing to about 14 inches (35 cm) from tail to bill. The thick bill with its white streak that stretches back to the eye on each side of the head easily distinguishes razorbills from the two murres. Murres have slimmer bills, but the bill of the thick-billed murre is the thicker of the two. Thick-billed murres have a white streak at the base of the mouth under the eye on each side of the head; common murres lack white streaks, or have a white streak extending back on the head from each eye. All three species swim underwater after fish, squid, shrimp and other invertebrates, and common murres have been caught in gill nets that were set for fish at depths as great as 180 feet (54 m).

The three species nest on the cliff ledges of their breeding sites. The murres are especially common, and north of the Boreal coast their breeding colonies are often immense. Razorbills are less common and tend to nest more under cover, concealed in crevices, than the murres. All three are well adapted to cliff-nesting. Their eggs are almost conical in shape, presumably so that when they roll, they roll in a circle and don't tumble off the ledges. They build no nests, but each pair lays its single egg on the bare rock. Like kittiwakes, both young and adults usually stand facing the cliff and don't move around very much.

The young leave the colonies with their parents when they are about six weeks old, well before they are full grown and able to fly. They glide from their ledges to the water below and swim off to sea with their parents. There are several advantages to this. The parents can feed their young right where they catch their prey and don't have to spend time and energy carrying the food back to the breeding colony. The young also have a prolonged time to learn how to

116. Common murres stand on a narrow ledge. In the foreground are two chicks and a single, typically pointed egg.

dive and fish while their parents are still nearby to feed them. Alcids become completely flightless during their post-nuptial molt, and by leaving the breeding colony early with their young, the adult auks and murres can complete the molt not long after their young become independent.

Although razorbills and the two murres do not now breed as far south as the Gulf of Maine, some apparently once bred near Grand Manan Island at the mouth of the Bay of Fundy. Small colonies still exist on islands in the Gulf of St. Lawrence and on some of the Newfoundland sites, but the large colonies occur further north along Greenland and Labrador. In winter, all three species occur in offshore waters, especially around the fishing banks as far south as Cape Cod.

Black Guillemot. Black guillemots, *Cepphus grylle*, are smaller alcids, just 10.5 inches (26 cm) long. They are black-bodied, their bills are shorter than those of murres and they have a very conspicuous white patch on each wing. They are not as pelagic as the other alcids and are frequently seen in inshore waters from the coast of Maine north. They also do not nest in colonies anywhere near the

Seabirds 351

size and density of colonies of most other alcids, and unlike other alcids they sometimes lay two eggs.

Black guillemots nest in crevices, under rocks, high on a beach or bluff, or on a cliff. They breed as far south as islands along the central coast of Maine and as far north as the other alcids along the coasts of Greenland and the islands of the Canadian Arctic. The young hide among the rocks and crevices until they grow their juvenile plumage and are able to fly. Then, like their parents, they dive along rocky shores, eating rock eels, mussels, worms, crabs and shrimp. In winter they don't move far away from where they breed, though northern populations need to shift south of the pack ice.

Common Puffin.   Common puffins, *Fratercula arctica*, are the only puffins in the North Atlantic. They are 11 inches (27.5 cm) long and are justly famous for their extraordinary, colorful parrot-like bills. Juvenile puffins have much smaller bills and even the bills of adults are somewhat smaller and much duller during their winter plumage. The colorful plates which encase the bill each breeding season are important as part of the reproductive displays of a puffin and, having no other function, are shed as soon as each breeding season ends.

Common puffins court on the water, as do most of the alcids. Their courtship displays involve throwing their heads back and flashing the brilliant yellow linings of their open mouths at each other. A mated pair usually digs a burrow in soft soil on the top of an island. A burrow is usually 2 to 3 feet (40 to 60 cm) long, curving and descending gently from its opening. The single egg is laid at the end of the burrow, and incubated for three weeks. It hatches as a semi-precocial chick. The burrow protects the growing chick from bad weather and predatory gulls, allowing both parents to fish for capelin or other small fish at the same time.

Predation and harassment by herring and great black-backed gulls is still a real problem on many of the puffin colonies. A puffin returning to its nest with several capelin dangling across its bill may be harrassed enough by the far larger gulls that it is forced to drop its fish to save itself. Hungry puffin chicks often await their parents close to their

117. A common puffin pauses a moment with its catch of capelin before entering its cliffside burrow with food for its single chick.

burrow mouths, and patrolling gulls quickly notice and eat any that stray too far into view.

When they are about five weeks old, the young puffins desert their burrows and their parents, gliding or flying down to the water under the protection of darkness. Their parents may even continue to bring fish to their empty burrows for a day or two after the fledglings have left.

The largest puffin colonies are again north of the Boreal coast, but smaller colonies occur on some of the Newfoundland seabird islands, and a few pairs have continued to breed south as far as the Gulf of Maine. Currently, small numbers of puffins are being transplanted to a small island in Muscongus Bay in Maine in hopes of re-establishing a breeding colony there.

Tubenoses

Tubenoses include the albatrosses, shearwaters, fulmars, petrels and storm petrels. They all have long tubular external nostrils and their bills are hooked. They are pelagic birds, more oceanic than the alcids, but like the alcids they come ashore only to breed. All species range over immense expanses of open ocean yet each has no more than a few square miles of breeding territory. Their abilities at migration and navigation are among the most impressive known. They are expert fliers and feed only at the water's surface. They often follow fishing boats, picking up discarded bits of fish.

Albatrosses are confined mostly to the Southern Hemisphere and none stray into the North Atlantic. Fulmars breed in the Arctic and occur on Boreal fishing banks in fall and winter. Greater and sooty shearwaters occur on the fishing banks in summer but breed in the Southern Hemisphere. Wilson's storm petrel, possibly the world's most populous bird, also breeds in the Antarctic region and comes to the Boreal fishing banks during the Northern Hemisphere's summer.

Leach's Storm Petrel. Leach's storm petrels, *Oceanodroma leucorhoa*, are the only tubenoses to breed on the islands of the Boreal coast. Like other storm petrels, they aren't much larger than swallows. They have forked tails, white rumps and they flutter over the water, skimming the surface for floating food. Sometimes they alight briefly on the water, wings held high while they pick up shrimp or large plankton, and then they spring up to flutter and glide again, sometimes pattering along the water surface with their feet.

Leach's petrels nest on coastal islands in the North Atlantic and North Pacific. On the Atlantic Boreal coast they nest south to the Gulf of Maine. They dig burrows in the soft soil above island cliffs and in amongst the trees that may cover the island. Each burrow is 1 to 3 feet (30 to 90 cm) long, and each breeding pair incubates its single small egg in a chamber at the back of the burrow. Incubation takes 40 days, about twice as long as eggs that size usually take other species to incubate. The temperature of incubation is several degrees cooler than is usual among birds, but even so, that isn't enough to account for the excessive length of incubation. Young nestlings take 63 to 70 days to fledge, which means they often do not leave their burrows until September or October.

Leach's petrels are nocturnal on their breeding colonies, very quiet in the daytime but active at night, flying and calling around the colony. Colonies are deceptively large because they are silent and hidden from view during daylight, and islands from Newfoundland to Maine may contain thousands of breeding pairs.

118. Leach's storm petrels seem to dance over the water as they search the surface for food.

Parent birds as usual share in incubating and feeding their offspring, relieving each other only every three or four days as they range hundreds of miles away on feeding trips. Predation by herring and great black-backed gulls can be heavy, one reason why the petrels are nocturnal on their breeding grounds.

Leach's petrels and other storm petrels have suffered less from human predation than other seabirds not just because they are too small to be worth shooting. They seem to become more active before storms and fishermen have long considered them lucky birds to see, for they give fair warning of deteriorating weather conditions. Storm petrels are also called Mother Carey's chickens, protected by the Virgin Mother or "Mater Cara".

Other Seabirds

There are other pelagic seabirds which are not uncommon on offshore waters along the Boreal coast but which breed north of the Boreal region and wander south only when the breeding season is over. Dovekies are the smallest of the alcids, growing to only 8 inches (20 cm). They fish offshore in the manner of the other diving auks and murres. Red and northern phalaropes are shore birds in their nesting habits, but otherwise spend their lives at sea, often in large flocks, swimming on the surface of the water, jabbing around them after planktonic animals. They are unique among shore birds in other ways as well, for sex roles are reversed. Females are larger and more colorful than males, compete with each other for the males, and then leave the males to incubate their clutches of eggs.

A group of strong, predatory pirates also roams the offshore waters, harassing terns, kittiwakes, the smaller gulls, and the shearwaters and petrels, forcing them to throw up whatever they have caught. These are the skuas, parasitic jaegers, pomarine jaegers and long-tailed jaegers. They all look rather gull-like except for their dark coloring and long tail feathers, and they are powerful, expert fliers. Around their Arctic breeding colonies they continue to rob other seabirds and they prey voraciously on unguarded eggs and nestlings.

Seals

Four species of seals occur along the Boreal coast. Harbor seals are the most familiar, for they are widespread, numerous and their curiosity will often lead them to the human observer. Gray seals are shier, but, like the harbor seals, are year-round residents of the coast. Harp seals and hooded seals are migrants, coming south as far as the Gulf of St. Lawrence to breed in late winter and early spring and then returning to more northern waters for the summer and autumn.

All four species belong to the family of seals called the Phocidae. They cannot walk on land but move themselves over sand, rocks, weed or ice by wriggling on their bellies. They have no external ears and are known as the earless or true seals. They evolved quite independently of the eared sea lions and fur seals of the family Otariidae which are much more agile on land and use their hind flippers to push themselves along.

True earless seals are cold- and temperate-water mammals and in fact only one of the world's 17 species occurs in warm water. There are no eared seals at all in the North

Atlantic though they are the dominant seals of the North Pacific and the Southern Hemisphere. Though at best they are awkward on land, all seals are beautifully adapted for swimming and diving after fish, squid and any other invertebrates they might eat. Their shape is streamlined, their hind limbs are magnificent flippers, and they have thick blubber which protects them from the cold. They are also able to dive to remarkable depths and to remain submerged for as long as 15 minutes as they search for and chase their prey.

When a seal dives, its heart rate drops from about 80 beats per minute to 10 beats per minute, and though its blood continues to carry oxygen to its brain, blood flow to the rest of the body is largely cut off, and the seal's muscles build up quite large oxygen debts. As soon as the seal resurfaces, its heart rate and circulation quickly return to normal.

Despite such adaptations, seals are still tied to land. They have evolved more recently than whales and have not had sufficient time to evolve ways of giving birth and suckling their young at sea. As a result, they must leave the water in order to breed successfully. They also often leave the water to rest and dry out and in such situations tend to be very gregarious. The combination of gregariousness and a need to breed on land or ice has resulted in the evolution of breeding colonies of varying degrees of social organization.

In some seals, such as the harbor seals, there is in fact very little social organization in breeding colonies; the animals are essentially promiscuous. In many other species, however, the bulls establish territories on breeding sites and compete with each other, often fairly violently, for possession of the best territories. When females come ashore to have their pups they select the most favorable areas, and the bulls defending those areas end up with the largest harems. The strongest bulls therefore copulate with the most females. The females in turn are likely to copulate only with males which are at their prime.

Both promiscuity and harem defense are in stark contrast to the close, long lasting pair bonds which all the seabirds establish in order to raise their offspring. But male seals cannot feed their pups since, as mammals, the pups suckle milk from the mothers. Beyond the act of copulation, the presence of male seals, and most male mammals, is unnecessary for the survival of their offspring, and can often be a hindrance. Male seals do not court females, for they are usually larger and have no need to form cooperative pair bonds. They are completely liberated from the responsibilities of parenthood, and the male which in the evolutionary sense is the most successful is the one which impregnates the most females. Promiscuity and harems are logical outcomes of such selective pressures.

After about a year of pregnancy, females haul out onto breeding sites to give birth to single pups. Once the pups are born, the females come into estrous and permit copulation. Each female establishes a close bond with her single pup, and they learn to recognize each other by voice and smell. A mother suckles only her pup, though pups may solicit milk from mothers other than their own. After a couple of weeks or more of suckling, the pups are weaned and soon learn to forage for themselves.

Harbor Seals

Harbor seals, *Phoca vitulina*, are the smallest of the seals of the Boreal coast, with males growing to about 6 feet (1.8 m) and females to about 5 feet (1.5 m). A large male probably weighs only 250 pounds (113 kg). From Labrador to Maine, harbor seals haul out on ledges to rest and to warm and dry themselves in the sun. The ledges may extend above the high tide level or they may be covered by every high tide, but the seals have favorites among them and return day after day and year after year to the same sites. A seal may even have a particular spot on a ledge to which it returns every day. Despite these preferences, a group of seals will still abandon a ledge if they are disturbed on it too frequently.

Harbor seals gather in small, gregarious herds on their ledges where, though they may be quite crowded, they do not touch one another. Because they move slowly on land they are never far from the edge of the water, and they probably favor particular ledges more than others because

119. Harbor seals sun themselves on rock ledges, splashing into the water when approached too closely.

of the quicker access they may have to deep safe water. When one seal is disturbed enough from its rest on a ledge to lurch for the safety of the water, its movements usually alert the seals around it, and a ledge covered by 20 or 30 seals one minute may be empty the next.

Though harbor seals are quick to take to the water, they usually don't flee the area but instead bob up all around their ledge and stare at whatever caused them alarm. When they leave their ledges to search for food, however, they disperse individually over considerable distances and wander far up estuaries and offshore in open water. They seem to fish most for herring and winter flounder, but as opportunistic carnivores they will eat a large diversity of fish and invertebrates.

Harbor seals occur in the North Pacific as well as the North Atlantic. Even in the North Atlantic the eastern and western populations appear to rarely meet each other or breed together and as a result there are several distinct subspecies of the harbor seal. The subspecies along the western Atlantic shores is *Phoca vitulina concolor*. Though it is concentrated most between Labrador and southern Maine, scattered individuals occur north to the Arctic and south to the Carolinas. In winter time, harbor seals tend to move to more offshore ledges and certainly away from any ice, but many also wander southward to winter in the warmer coastal bays around Cape Cod and south of the Cape.

Harbor seals have about the simplest breeding social organization of any seal. Pregnant females usually haul out apart from males and juveniles from May to June. Their pups are born on shore, and within hours or even minutes are able to swim with their mothers. Each pup remains close to its mother and gradually learns to dive with her. It suckles for perhaps as long as 4 to 6 weeks before it is weaned. Once the pups are weaned, they haul out with the juveniles, males and females for the rest of the summer, molting in August when the water is at its warmest.

Males and females mate promiscuously in September and October rather than immediately after the pups are born. Males make no attempt to defend breeding sites or harems, an impossible undertaking anyway, since many of the ledges they rest on disappear every time the tide rises. The embryos are suspended in their development until November or December, and then are implanted properly in the uterus linings of their mothers, completing their development about six months later.

About one quarter of the young seals are likely to die from accidents, exposure, predation, starvation or disease before they are a year old. Surviving females become sexually mature when they are 2 to 4 years old; males mature a little later, when they are four to six years old. Barring further accidents or disease, they are likely to breed repeatedly and live for as long as 20 to 30 years.

For many years there was a bounty on harbor seals, for they and other seals are hosts of the adult stage of a parasite that infects cod in its larval stages. Old cod in particular may be so infected by the larvae as to seriously disturb someone about to eat the fish, even though the larvae are harmless to humans and are killed by cooking the fish anyway. The larvae depend upon their host cod being eaten by a seal, whereupon the larvae infect the seal, become sexually mature adults and produce larvae which infect more cod. The bounty on harbor seals was successful at almost eliminating the seals, but did not improve the cod problem

360

to any great extent since the other Boreal seals carry the parasite as well. The bounty has been removed and the seals south of the Canadian border are now protected by the Marine Mammal Protection Act, which was passed in 1972.

Now that harbor seals are reasonably well protected, their populations are increasing again. Their gregarious herds tend to attract tourists to their ledges, but they need the ledges so briefly for breeding purposes that they can probably survive the frequent disturbances by their well meaning visitors. They are not free of problems, however, for during the winter and spring of 1980 about 1000 seals washed up dead around the Cape Cod shores, killed by an especially virulent virus whose impact on the whole Boreal population is likely to be very damaging.

Gray Seals

Gray seals, *Halichoerus grypus*, are probably more numerous than harbor seals along the Boreal coast, but they are seen less frequently in inshore waters. They prefer more remote ledges and sandbars and gather in smaller gregarious groups when they aren't breeding. Males grow to about 8 feet (2.4 m) and 800 pounds (363 kg) while females may be 7 feet (2.1 m) long and weigh 550 pounds (250 kg).

Gray seals occur only in the North Atlantic and, as with the harbor seals, several distinct populations live along the eastern and western coastlines of the Atlantic. The population on the American Boreal coast breeds from Newfoundland and the Gulf of St. Lawrence to Nova Scotia and, rarely, Maine. Non-breeding individuals have been seen north to northern Labrador and south as far as Rhode Island.

Gray seals on the Boreal coast gather in quite large colonies to breed at a relatively small number of locations, and they breed on the edge of the pack ice as well. Those breeding on the pack ice appear to form monogamous pairs, but that is probably only because the females are well dispersed. On islands such as Sable Island, 200 miles (320 km)

120. A male gray seal guards his small harem of four females.

east of Halifax, Nova Scotia, and the Magdalen Islands in the Gulf of St. Lawrence, the females gather in close proximity to one another, and the males compete with each other for the right to remain near the females.

Gray seals come ashore to breed from late December to mid-February. Each female gives birth to a light-colored pup weighing about 35 pounds (16 kg). Two and a half weeks after its birth a pup weighs as much as 80 pounds (36 kg) and is ready to be weaned. About two weeks after giving birth, a female comes into estrous and mates with the bull that has remained nearest to her. Then, as soon as her pup is weaned several days later, the female deserts the breeding colony. The bull seals remain until the females have all left, and then they desert as well to feed again for the first time in many weeks. The pups remain on the site of the breeding colony for a couple of weeks after their mothers leave in order to complete their molts, surviving at the expense of the fat they deposited while suckling. Then they too leave and scatter along the coast.

Pup mortality is relatively high because of the crowded conditions of the breeding colonies, and as many as half do not survive their first year. Females mature when they are four or five years old and are likely to live for about 35 years. Males mature when they are six to eight years old and are likely to live only about 25 years: the strains of starvation and aggression associated with their breeding behavior presumably take a heavier physiological toll.

Harp Seals

Harp seals, *Pagophilus groenlandicus,* grow to about 6 feet (1.8 m) and 400 pounds (182 kg), and the males in particular have a harp-shaped pattern on their backs, which gives the species its common name. Harp seals migrate south from Arctic waters in late fall, keeping south of the edge of the growing pack ice. In late winter they breed on the pack ice in several large herds, including a major one off the Labrador coast north of Newfoundland and another in the Gulf of St. Lawrence east of Anticosti Island.

Younger females are the first to breed in late February or early March, for they whelp, or give birth, to their pups a little earlier than more experienced females. Older females feed at sea for another two or three days and then haul out on the ice to whelp as well. The pups unfortunately are born with a lovely pure white pelt which has long been a favorite of furriers and which the pups shed about 9 days later as they grow their juvenile pelts. Hunters for a couple of hundred years have crossed ice and freezing water from the shores of northern and southern Newfoundland, killing the pups before they molt to less profitable colors. The spotted juveniles or "beaters" and "bedlamers" as well as adults are also hunted, but the major focus of the hunt is on the white pups.

Pups weigh about 22 pounds (10 kg) at birth, and gain weight at about 5 pounds (2.3 kg) per day until they are weaned when they are nine or ten days old. They lose about 20 percent of their weight in the post-weaning period before they leave the ice and begin to fish for themselves, eating euphausiids for the most part until they are large and agile enough to catch fish. The herds concentrate for several weeks on rich feeding sites where the adults feed on capelin, herring and demersal species such as cod, flounder and sculpins, and where they are further hunted by boatloads of hunters.

By mid-April the herds begin moving north to wherever the pack ice has receded and spend three or four weeks drifting with the ice as they molt, but leaving the ice to feed, particularly on sunny days. When their molt is completed, the herds migrate north to northern Greenland and

121. A female harp seal keeps a concerned eye on her white newborn pup.

the Canadian Arctic, arriving there in May or June about the time the capelin arrive.

Young seals are relatively solitary for their first year, but when they are large enough to catch pelagic schooling fish, they cease to concentrate on the pelagic crustaceans and become very sociable and gregarious.

Like other seals that have attracted hunters, the populations of harp seals are now but a small fraction of what they must have been several hundred years ago, for many thousands have been killed every year since the hunt began.

Hooded Seals

Hooded seals, *Cystophora cristata*, are the largest and least common of the seals which occur on the Boreal coast. Like harp seals they are pelagic and breed on the southern edges of the pack ice around the North Atlantic. A small part of the total population, perhaps 1000 animals, breeds

ISLANDS AND LEDGES

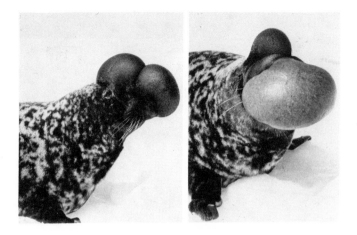

122. The overgrown nose of the male hooded seal (left) gives the
seal its common name. During aggressive displays (right) the male
inflates one of his brilliant red nasal membranes.

near the harp seals in the Gulf of St. Lawrence. Males grow
to about 10 feet (3 m) and weigh up to about 700 pounds
(318 kg) while females are not as long and weigh much less.
The pups are born with a dark pelt, and neither pups nor
adults are bothered much by the hunters.

During the breeding season, a male may have only one
female in his harem, but he vigorously defends her from
other males. A pup is weaned when it is two or three weeks
old, and its mother then comes into estrous. After mating,
the seals molt and migrate north once again, feeding much
like harp seals though usually in deeper water.

The most astounding aspect of hooded seal behavior is
the male aggressive display. Adult males have an overgrown, inflatable nose which gives them their hooded appearance. A displaying male produces a resonant snort or
growl through his inflated hood, but other seals such as the
elephant seal can do that too. What he also does during his
display is to blow one of his nasal membranes out one of his
nostrils, where it forms an impressive large red balloon on
the front of his head, which somehow indicates his strength
to other competing males.

Seals   365

CHAPTER VII

Deeper
and Offshore Waters

THE SOCIAL HISTORY of the Boreal region is intimately related to the abundant fish that live in its deeper and offshore waters. The early settlements of the Maritime Provinces and northern New England were fishing communities whose survival depended on the fish they captured and exported back across the Atlantic to their European homelands. Cod was especially vital, for it was well suited to preservation by salting and drying. At both Cape Cod and Newfoundland the cod fisheries were instrumental in the further settlement of the land. Massachusetts deemed cod so important to its heritage that the fish early became a prominent part of the state symbol.

Cod and many other species of fish of commerical interest are so abundant in the Boreal region because the waters, especially over the submerged offshore banks, are immensely productive. Herbivores are eaten by small predators, both of which serve as food for great numbers of larger fish, as well as for the seals and seabirds discussed in chapter 6. Whales are common for the same reasons. Both baleen and toothed species migrate through seasonally when food supplies are at their greatest. And joining the whales, seabirds and seals in preying upon the abundant food are fishing fleets from around the world.

The Immense Habitat

The depth of many of the bays along the Boreal coast extends far below the photic zone, the depth at which there is still enough light for plants to photosynthesize. Some of the bays, such as Somes Sound in Mt. Desert Island, Bonne Bay in western Newfoundland, and the Saguenay River in the St. Lawrence Estuary, are in fact deep, fjord-like inlets reaching depths of 800 feet (240 m) or more. Paradoxically, water depths often become relatively shallow many miles offshore, where submerged banks rise from the sea bed as they do at Georges Bank, the Grand Banks, and the many other banks and ledges in the Gulf of Maine and on the Scotian Shelf. Deep channels separate some of the banks, with the Northeast Channel opening the Gulf of Maine between Georges and Jefferies Banks, and the Laurentian Channel opening the Gulf of St. Lawrence between the Grand Banks and the Scotian Shelf.

The deeper parts of the bays and the offshore banks and channels of the Gulf of Maine, the Scotian Shelf and the Grand Banks, and the Gulf of St. Lawrence comprise a relatively continuous habitat, vastly different in many ways from the shallow subtidal inshore habitats. It extends from the water surface to wherever the bottom happens to lie, 100 to 1600 feet (30 to 500 m) below and from as close as 100 feet (30 m) from shore to as far as 100 miles (160 km) offshore.

The Sculpting and Drowning of the Coast

The outer edge of the offshore banks of the Gulf of Maine and the Scotian Shelf represents the position of the coastline in preglacial times. Before the recent glaciation, the Gulf of Maine, the Scotian Shelf, and all of the southern part of the Gulf of St. Lawrence had been a coastal terrace pushed above sea level. During the millions of years which followed, stream erosion carved valleys into the landscape, leaving more resistent rock behind as hills. Then came the glaciers, scouring, deepening and straightening the valleys. When the glaciers finally retreated just 14,000 to 10,000 years ago, dumping impressive amounts of till on the lower land especially, the sea level began to rise.

The rising sea flooded the eroded coastal lowlands, inundating the Gulf of Maine, the Scotian Shelf, and the southern Gulf of St. Lawrence. Most of the coastal hills became till-covered banks, submerged offshore, but a few have remained as islands, such as Sable Island on the Scotian Shelf, and Prince Edward Island and the Magdalen Islands in the Gulf of St. Lawrence. The deep bays which now lie along many parts of the Boreal coast are valleys eroded by the streams, scoured by the glaciers, and then drowned by the rising sea. This world of deep coastal bays and deep and shallow offshore water out to the seaward edges of the fishing banks is for the most part just as young as the rest of the Boreal coast. The huge fish populations, the migration patterns of fish and squid and whales, the rich planktonic and benthic life, all have had but a few thousand years to become established.

Variation Within the Depths

Though the immense volume of water filling the deeper bays and covering the offshore banks may at first appear homogeneous and the bottom substrates may seem obscure, both water and substrates vary in critical ways. In deep areas, the bottom layer of water is constantly cool, ranging from 40 to 46° F (4 to 8° C), and rich in nutrients. It changes little from season to season or year to year. Above it lies a surface layer of water up to several hundred feet (100 m) deep which is a little less saline and which in summer may warm to 50 to 65° F (10 to 18° C) and in winter may cool to 32° F (0° C). The nutrients of this layer are severely depleted by phytoplankton every summer and are lost to the cooler water below. An unstable, oscillating water layer therefore lies in the photic zone, overlying a stable, nutrient-rich cool water layer which is, however, below the photic zone and devoid of plants.

Wherever upwelling of the cool, nutrient-rich bottom layer occurs, the situation in the surface photic zone changes dramatically. The offshore banks force the deep water to the surface as do the circulation patterns in the two gulfs. With the upwelling comes a continual nutrient supply that from early spring to late autumn make the offshore waters over the banks some of the world's richest. The cool temperatures of the upwelling water also help, for concentrations of dissolved oxygen are higher in cold water than in warm water, and populations of both plants and animals can be greater.

Below the bottom water layer lies a variable substrate. Like inshore substrates, it may be rocky and impenetrable, suitable for clinging sessile animals that are usually filter feeders. Or it may be soft, composed of sand, mud, shingle or any combination of these, more suitable for burrowing animals that may be filter feeders or deposit feeders. Foraging over the various substrates, a host of predatory fish, crustaceans, starfish and gastropod mollusks prey upon the sessile and burrowing animals. Rained on by the by-products of the plants and animals above them, these benthic animals have virtually unlimited food, and their populations are dense.

Environmental Stresses

The seasonal and daily fluctuations that characterize the intertidal environment and still influence shallow, inshore habitats considerably are of much less impact in offshore and deeper waters. Though winds may stir up waves and disperse plankton, they have little direct effect on the organisms living any depth below the surface. The surface waters may be a little less saline in spring, particularly as a result of the runoff of the St. Lawrence River, but salinities do not drop to any stressful levels. And ice, which can abrade shorelines so severely, floats by innocuously.

Some seasonal changes are still great enough to affect the organisms profoundly, however. In particular, changes in temperature and food availability during the year are enough to cause many animals to migrate in and out of the Boreal region each year, or from one part of the region to another, and currents and winds may disturb the organisms in less predictable and more indirect ways.

FOOD AVAILABILITY

Despite the abundance of nutrients and phytoplankton in the surface water from early spring until late autumn wherever upwelling occurs, winter is a time of food scarcity. Though the surface waters everywhere are then laden with nutrients, light levels are too low to support photosynthesis. The phytoplankton populations decline and the food web loses the broad base of producers necessary to support it. Some animals move into deeper or more southern water in pursuit of other food sources. Others wait out the winter months in deeper water, feeding little and not growing. Jellyfish, which are so abundant in Boreal waters in spring and summer, all die, their fertilized eggs developing into little sessile hydroids that grow through the winter, attached to hard substrates in the cool, nutrient-rich bottom water.

TEMPERATURE CHANGES

The summer warming and winter cooling of the surface waters, though not as extreme as it is in shallow, inshore areas, is still more than many of the resident animals can tolerate. Whales, menhaden, capelin, bluefin tuna and bluefish all migrate north or south, depending on their temperature requirements. Those which just settle in deeper water for the winter, avoiding the cold, surface water, probably include swordfish, sharks (including the spiny dogfish) and the herring and mackerel. Other species cope with the cold winter temperatures by producing a special protein which acts much like an antifreeze in the blood.

Average temperatures of the surface waters can change a little over a period of several years, and even if they are only two or three degrees cooler than usual in summer, fish such as mackerel and perhaps herring will probably not migrate into the Boreal region that year. If temperatures are only two or three degrees warmer than usual, the northern shrimp, *Pandalus borealis*, stays in cooler waters further to the north. Other species, especially the predators of the mackerel and shrimp, are certainly then affected as well, and migratory species such as whales and larger fish may just follow their prey out of the region. In any case, a portion of the food web will be distorted or adjusted.

Because water temperature largely controls the time of breeding for many Boreal organisms, it can further modify the food web. Warmer or cooler temperatures than usual are likely to shift breeding times to earlier or later points in the season. Larvae may then be produced when their preferred planktonic food sources are not sufficiently abundant, and most of the larvae starve. A whole year class may be affected, and several years hence there would be a smaller than usual population of breeding individuals. Once again, repercussions would be felt through part of the food web, for predators that normally prey upon the larvae or later stages of the affected species would in turn suffer a food shortage.

CURRENTS, GYRES, WINDS, AND PLANKTON

Most of the Boreal fish breeding in deeper and offshore

waters produce buoyant eggs that may be carried out of the spawning area by surface currents even before they hatch. Even after they hatch, the larvae are too small and weak to oppose the currents. As a result, they may be swept to nutrient-rich upwelling areas where concentrations of plankton are great, assuring them of a good food supply. On the other hand, they may be swept away from that food source into relatively impoverished waters, and few may survive.

Surface currents can vary seasonally in direction and strength as well as from year to year. Such variations, even if they are small ones, can have quite an impact on the survival of a year class of plankton and on its prey and predators. Fish larvae do have some ability to avoid excessive transportation by the surface currents, however. Those of many species migrate vertically in the water, rising to the surface to feed each night and then dropping down below the surface and its currents (and predators) during daylight.

Oceanographers now know of areas of rising and falling water, referred to as gyres. In the northern hemisphere, cyclonic gyres are those of rising water which bring bottom nutrients to the surface; anti-cyclonic gyres are composed of sinking water. These gyres not only vary tremendously in size, but often they also vary seasonally, being very strong at certain times and non-existent at other times. For instance, in the summer, the central part of Georges Bank is a large anti-cyclonic gyre with sinking water. This anti-cyclonic gyre slowly deteriorates and then changes so that by March it has become a cyclonic gyre, bringing nutrients to the surface and greatly influencing the spring plankton bloom in that area. After only a couple of months this cyclonic gyre weakens and eventually becomes the anti-cyclonic gyre of summer. In addition, relatively stable cyclonic gyres exist year round in the Eastern Channel, which leads into the Gulf of Maine, and in the Laurentian Channel, which leads into the Gulf of St. Lawrence. Nutrient upwelling in these areas is correspondingly relatively great.

Since the availability of nutrients directly affects the concentrations of plankton, it is logical to associate larval fish that feed on plankton with such upwellings and cyclonic gyres. In regard to fish spawning and cyclonic gyres, it is now known that herring spawn on the northern, western and eastern slopes of Georges Bank in late summer, adjacent to and coincident with cyclonic gyres of rising water there at that time. In addition, in mid-summer, local gyres which both rise and fall exist along the southern slope of Georges Bank. Large spawning concentrations of whiting and red hake in this area at the same time have been correlated with the existence of the gyres. Greater knowledge of the gyres and their seasonal variation should give greater insight into fish larvae survival.

Though the winds have no direct effect on bottom-dwelling or demersal species, they can have an indirect effect upon all the organisms in the water below them when they disrupt normal circulation and gyre patterns, and disperse the plankton in the process. This dispersal can have devastating effects both on the larvae and adults of the many species depending on an abundant, continuous food supply, and further perturbations of the food web result.

Predation and Competition

Though many of the predators of the offshore and deeper waters often eat the same prey, they also have preferences for different prey species. By dividing up the potential food source, the predators are better able to coexist, competing less with each other than they would if they preferred the same prey species. Even the fish that eat phytoplankton may prefer some types of diatoms over others, for diatoms come in many shapes and sizes and some species of grazing fish cannot swallow the more bizarre shapes; other species can manage them easily.

The prey that a predator prefers is certain to change as the predator grows larger. A small, bottom-living or demersal fish is likely to select small crustaceans such as copepods, amphipods or mysid shrimp. The same fish as an adult may not bother with such small prey, but instead may forage after larger crustaceans such as the shrimp, *Pandalus borealis*, or the toad crab, *Hyas araneus*.

The interactions between prey and predator can become relatively complex. Juvenile fish often prey upon fish larvae; the larvae that escape may grow into adults which prey upon those same juvenile fish. Adults may even prey upon juveniles of their own species: cannibalism is frequent.

The Impact of Human Predation

The fishing pressure by human predators on the abundant pelagic and demersal species of fish of the Boreal offshore and deeper waters has been intense for over three centuries. For most of those 300 years the fish were exploited without much thought of protecting the stocks, just as whales and seals and seabirds were hunted everywhere they occurred in any abundance throughout the world. In almost all cases the largest species were the ones first searched for, and when these became uncommon, the next largest species became the target. As fishing techniques improved, pelagic schooling fish became especially susceptible to almost complete elimination, for their schools occur in predictable places, and as schools, they are conveniently packaged in catchable units. Ground-fish such as haddock and cod on the other hand are less susceptible to extinction because their aggregations are less dense and more difficult to localize.

To protect the fish species from catastrophic collapse and to keep their populations large enough to support the fishing fleets, governments established limits to which each species could be fished every year. The concept of the maximum sustainable yield (MSY) emerged. It assumes that a certain number of tons of fish must remain in a population to ensure adequate propagation of the species. This fisheries management approach was implemented to furnish a sustained, continual supply of fish. The MSY approach has certainly been a good beginning, and it has attempted to prevent catastrophic overfishing of any species. As a management approach, it is likely to work best if the fish stock concerned is a single, isolated population that has few interactions with other species.

Though a total allowable catch was established for a number of the commercially fished species of the Boreal waters, stocks still declined, and there have been large fluctuations in the sizes of the catches and of the stock populations. It appears that if the stock of a species is sustained at levels that are too low or even too high, especially great and unpredictable fluctuations can occur. To make the situation more complicated, populations have a natural tendency to fluctuate in cycles anyway, and the maximum sustained yield appropriate for one year may be inappropriate for another. Furthermore, what is an appropriate maximum sustained yield for one species may be catastrophically too large for another. It has been demonstrated that a single biomass number is not suitable for all species.

Beginning in 1973 the International Commission of North Atlantic Fisheries established a limit to the combined catch of all species, recognizing that the contribution of different species to the total biomass changes from year to year, but that the total biomass remains constant. More and more evidence has accumulated, emphasizing that in fact no species is independent of its own competitors, predators or prey, and that instead each is affected by whatever happens to the populations of the others.

The overfishing of herring and mackerel in recent years provides a good example. The best figures come from the North Sea, but they apply, in principle, to the dynamics of the Boreal ecosystem on the western side of the Atlantic as well. In 1964 there were about 6 million tons of herring and mackerel in the North Sea, and only 3 million tons of other species of fish. By 1976 after some years of high fishing pressure, only about 2 million tons of herring and mackerel remained, but now there were 7 million tons of the other fish. The biomass of fish has remained constant, but the species composition has changed dramatically. With the overfishing of the herring and mackerel, major predators of the larvae of fish such as haddock, cod and other demersal fish were simply eliminated, and the populations of these demersal fish increased enormously.

However, fish species rarely interact in a simple way and the reproductive strategies of herring reveal this. When mackerel stocks are high, the population can sustain itself with fewer offspring and so year class sizes are smaller. The herring population increases as well at this time for larval and juvenile stages have ample food. When mackerel are over-exploited, the number of reproducing individuals is less and though each female correspondingly produces more eggs, the total is still low enough that competition with young herring is not so severe as to limit the growth of herring populations. However, when herring and mackerel are both exploited at the optimal level, without over-exploiting them, both species seem to suffer in population recruitment. Management of one species therefore necessitates management of the other as well.

Many kinds of links exist between predators and prey throughout the food web. If the euphausiids or krill were to be fished for commercial purposes in the Boreal region, as there is talk of doing, the predators of the krill, which include the baleen whales as well as many of the pelagic fish, would suddenly lose their primary food source, replaced in the food web by human fishermen. In subantarctic regions the selective removal of all the largest baleen whales has resulted in far more krill surviving, and those predator species that have not been overhunted, such as the minke whale, have not only increased greatly in numbers, they have adjusted in other ways as well. The females are becoming pregnant more frequently, both males and females are becoming sexually mature at an earlier age, all in response not to a threat of extinction but to an overabundance of food around them. The same appears to be happening in some of the seals, penguins and other seabirds of the subantarctic, and points out further unexpected aspects of the complexity of the interrelationships of species. Again, there is every reason to believe similar adaptations will occur elsewhere in response to major changes in the food web, and the Boreal region is especially susceptible because of the tremendous pressure on many of its species.

The management of multispecies fisheries is fraught with problems. The relationships between species are difficult to unravel, and sometimes hard to distinguish from responses of the species to changing environmental conditions. Socioeconomic problems in administering the "whole ecosystem" approach may be even thornier than the biological ones. However, continual dependence upon maximum sustainable yields, though often successful at first, has led too often to catastrophic declines in fish stocks. Only by dealing with all the species at once, recognizing their interdependence, can catastrophes and even extinctions be prevented.

The Pelagic Realm

Many of the animals of the deeper and offshore waters never approach the bottom substrates and do not feed on benthic animals. They are truly pelagic, feeding and breeding in the water layers well above the bottom. They include the larger animals of the zooplankton, such as euphausiids, fish larvae, jellyfish and ctenophores (sea gooseberries). They include the immense schools of the herring, capelin and mackerel, as well as the squid, sharks, tuna and swordfish that prey on them. And they include the baleen whales that eat the plankton and the toothed whales and porpoises that prey upon the fish and squid.

The pelagic environment is more variable than is the bottom environment. Its changes in temperature, food abundance and currents are greater, and pelagic animals must have ways of coping with such changes that bottom-living or demersal animals need not have. Most of the pelagic animals have definite seasonal movements, as they follow their food sources elsewhere and avoid temperature extremes. These movements vary from well established migration routes to what seems to be random wandering, but all involve an ability to navigate. Many species use the direction of the sun or polarized light as navigational cues, and some are able to detect geomagnetic and electric cues in ways not yet fully understood.

Most of the smaller pelagic species move about in schools. Euphausiids, herring, menhaden and capelin all travel in particularly large schools in their search for abundant planktonic food. The schooling habit has a number of advantages, for it probably increases the foraging and reproductive efficiency of the schoolers. It probably also gives them some protection from many of their potential predators, although certainly not from human predators.

The Invertebrates

EUPHAUSIIDS (KRILL). Euphausiids get their name from the light-producing organs they possess (phausis means "a shining light" in Greek). These photophores are visible on the animals as red spots at the base of two of the pairs of legs, on the underside of the abdomen and at the base of the eye stalks. The function of luminescence for these animals is still open to debate, but the luminescent organs of euphausiids are highly developed, each having a reflecting layer of cells behind the light-producing element and a lens in front of it.

Like the copepod *Calanus finmarchius*, euphausiids migrate diurnally, rising to surface waters a few hours before sunset where they feed on the plankton. At midnight, they begin to descend again and since they are active swimmers they may descend as much as 1000 feet (300 m) or more at

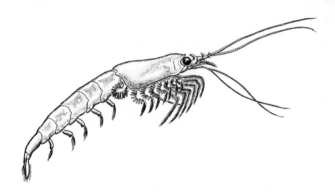

123. The eupahusiid shrimp or krill *Meganyctiphanes norvegica* provides food for many fish as well as for whales.

rates of over 300 feet (100 m) per hour. This diurnal migration has two adaptive qualities: it brings the euphausiids to the surface at a time of less predation and it enables metabolism to occur at the cooler temperatures of deeper water which is more efficient.

Two types of euphausiids occur commonly in Boreal waters, usually in very large aggregations, or schools.

Thysanoessa euphausiids breed in spring during the phytoplankton bloom, while *Meganyctiphanes* spawn from summer to early fall. The pelagic eggs and larvae circulate with surface currents, often concentrating over banks where other planktonic production is high. *Meganyctiphanes* feeds primarily on crustaceans in the plankton; *Thysanoessa* feeds on detritus and plant material. Both species reach maturity at a year and live for at least two years if not eaten by a hungry fish or whale.

CTENOPHORES AND JELLYFISH. Two other important large pelagic invertebrates are *Pleurobrachia* ctenophores, known as comb jellies or sea gooseberries and the huge jellyfish, *Cyanea capillata*. Both have been discussed in chapter 5 and will only be mentioned here in regards to their role in the pelagic habitat as a whole.

Though only the size of a gooseberry, ¾ inch (2 cm), the sea gooseberry's role has been called "sinister" by plankton specialists. Despite its fragile appearance, a transparent berry with two long tentacles, the sea gooseberry is a voracious predator, catching juvenile fish as big as itself with its numerous lasso-cells on each tentacle. It often appears to play with its prey for a while, lasso-cells springing out and back, and finally it eats the prey by bringing the victim to its mouth. The ctenophores often swarm upon fish eggs and larvae, notably those of cod, haddock and herring. They in turn are eaten by the fast-swimming mackerel, spiny dogfish and young jellyfish.

The beautifully pulsating Arctic jellyfish, the lion's mane, *Cyanea capillata*, is the largest jellyfish in the world, reaching 6 to 8 feet in diameter with 200 foot long tentacles in the coldest northern waters. *Cyanea* migrates with euphausiids, often feeding on them. Despite its stinging cells, *Cyanea* also provides refuge for certain young fish which swim in between its tentacles under its bell. Young haddock and butterfish not only gain protection but also glean a good food supply in this position. Only occasionally do they become food themselves.

PTEROPODS. Pteropods, or sea butterflies, are pelagic, free-swimming gastropod mollusks which occur in such immense numbers near the surface of cold ocean waters that they may be a major food source for some of the baleen whales. One species in particular, *Clione limacina*, may swim in schools so large that they color the water surface for miles. *Clione* grows to about 1½ inches (4 cm), completely lacks a shell, and the front of its body is drawn into two large wings which help to keep it afloat.

SQUID. The very form of the squid, a long tapered body with flexible tentacles, reveals its adaptiveness to a swimming existence. Though actually mollusks, the phylum which includes snails and clams, squid have evolved to suit their pelagic environment. The ten prehensile tentacles of this cephalopod are homologous to the foot of other mollusks, and the typical molluskan shell is highly reduced and internalized, if present at all, giving the squid the flexibility it needs for swimming (see color plate VII).

Squid are exquisite swimmers, exercising beautiful muscular control over their jet propulsion locomotion. They swim by expelling water from their mantle cavity through a highly mobile funnel which can be directed either forward or backwards. The water circulation through the mantle area provides oxygen for respiration as well as power for movement.

In the Boreal zone two squid species are common, the short-finned squid, *Ilex illecebrosus*, and the long-finned squid, *Loligo pealei*. The long-finned squid is actually a warmer-water species and it only comes into the Boreal region in summer when it comes inshore to lay its eggs (see chapter 5). The short-finned squid is a true Boreal-Arctic species, however, pursuing fish such as herring, mackerel, capelin and other squid as well as pelagic crustaceans such as euphausiids, amphipods and copepods. In true pelagic fashion, the schools of short-finned squid are highly migratory, arriving at inshore waters in the summer as they follow capelin and herring. Squid prey on surface fish at night and on crustaceans in deeper water in the day.

Two of the squid's arms, or tentacles, are twice as long as the other eight and in addition are flattened with suckers on the end. These tentacles are used to seize prey and to bring it to the mouth, located at the base of the arms, where the beak-like jaws take over. Squid beaks are used for biting and tearing. When a fish is caught, a triangular chunk is quickly bitten out of the neck, severing the nerve cord.

As well as enjoying a variety of prey types, the short-finned squid is itself preyed upon by many species including spiny dogfish, cod, hake, bluefin tuna, pilot and sperm whales, and seabirds such as shearwaters, fulmars and gannets. Just as squid follow schooling capelin, their movements are pursued by pilot whales which may remain with them throughout the year. And of course squid-jigging by man has long been a popular pastime along the Boreal coast.

In addition to changing direction rapidly, squid try to escape predation by expelling a cloud of ink in the face of a predator. This cloud can either be diffuse or it can hold quite a good squid form, depending on the species. The ink, which is a melanin pigment, acts in two ways. It distracts a predator, allowing the squid to swim off in a different direction, and since it is alkaloid in nature it is objectionable to predators, even anesthetizing some chemoreceptors.

During winter months the short-finned squid migrates to deeper offshore waters where spawning often occurs. The eggs hatch in a month and are fully mature in 18 months. Like many fast-growing pelagic species, short-finned squid are relatively short-lived and most die after their first spawning.

One other squid that is occasionally found in Boreal waters is the giant squid, *Architeuthis*, the largest invertebrate in the world, growing to 60 feet (18 m) in total length and having a body circumference of up to 12 feet (3.6 m). The giant squid is basically a deep-sea animal, found beyond the continental shelf. Occasionally, however, one washes ashore a Newfoundland beach, or even less frequently a Massachusetts beach, causing great excitement to everyone in the vicinity. Its main predator seems to be the sperm whale, but very little information is actually known about this giant of the seas.

The Fish

All fish, including sharks, have a sensing organ called the lateral line system that detects vibrations in the water. Two lines extend down each side of the fish from the head to the tail. These lines are actually made up of a series of sensor cells, each composed of a tuft of hairlike projections which extend into the water. The sensitivity of lateral line systems varies with different species. For instance, herring, which are plankton feeders, have a greatly developed lateral line system on the head. The extra sensory cells seem to help the herring better detect vibration differences set up by even the small schooling planktonic animals.

SHARKS. All members of the shark family are elasmobranchs, having cartilaginous skeletons, and are more primitive than the bony fishes. Only three sharks are common in the Boreal zone, the mackerel shark, the blue shark and the much smaller spiny dogfish. Each of these sharks is truly pelagic, haphazardly wandering in the surface waters, pursuing the fish on which they prey. This constant swimming is also necessary for the sharks to get enough oxygen from the water flowing over their gills.

Since sharks have no bone, they have no true scales, for scales are made of bony material. Instead, their bodies are covered with minute denticles which have much in common with their teeth. Their teeth wear out quickly and are constantly replaced by new ones which roll into position from a fold of skin in the mouth.

Sharks are fertilized internally and give birth to live young after 8 to 12 months of pregnancy. Generally there is no placenta-like connection and instead the developing young get their nourishment from a large yolk supply in their own eggs (spiny dogfish) or by swallowing nearby unfertilized eggs (mackerel shark). The blue shark is said to be the exception here with a well developed placenta-like organ from which the young receive their food. The small number of young (1 to 4 for larger sharks; 2 to 11 for dogfish) are born in warm summer waters and join the adults in wintering offshore in the relatively warmer deeper waters where little feeding takes place.

Though both the mackerel shark, *Lamna nasus,* and the blue shark, *Prionace glauca,* can reach a size of 10 to 12 feet (3 to 3.6 m) and up to 400 pounds (182 kg) and though they are among the most numerous of the large oceanic sharks, they do not present a danger to humans in these Boreal

The Pelagic Realm 383

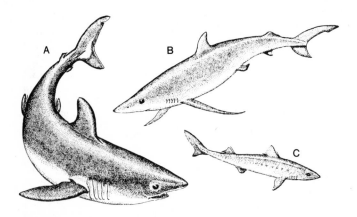

124. The common sharks of the Boreal coast are A. the mackerel shark B. the blue shark and C. the spiny dogfish.

waters. Both sharks are called the "blue dog" locally and especially pursue herring and mackerel schools as well as spiny dogfish and certain groundfish.

Fishermen have long sought a commercial use for these creatures. In the early 19th century, shark liver oil was in demand for the tanning industry. Though this market disappeared by 1825, the oil was plentiful as a single 10 foot (3 m) shark yields as much as 11 gallons of oil. More recently, a new market has developed for shark meat which is firm and delicate when cooked properly. Sharks are usually caught as by-catch in gill nets or on long lines.

The spiny dogfish, *Squalus acanthias,* is one of the most gregarious fish in the Boreal zone and in most people's sentiments, far too numerous. Most would agree with oceanographer and fisheries biologist Henry B. Bigelow who wrote in 1926 that "voracious almost beyond belief, the dogfish entirely deserves its bad reputation. Not only does it harry and drive off mackerel, herring, and even fish as large as cod and haddock, but it destroys vast numbers of them. Again and again fishermen have described [these] packs of dogs dashing among schools of mackerel, and even attacking them within the seines . . . [it] makes up for the comparative rarity of other sharks . . . by its obnoxious abundance."

Since otter trawling does not retain trapped fish in a single place, allowing the fish to be easy prey, it has lessened the impact of dogfish on the fishing industry. However, the little sharks continue to be caught far too abundantly in seine nets. Serious endeavors to utilize this species have been made, from fertilizer and oil industries to a human consumption market such as exists in northern Europe. However, none of these has been able to persist.

Herring.   Herring, *Clupea harengus,* have long held an important place in world fisheries. Their uses vary from human consumption of the young sardines and of smoked kippers to use of the fish as bait and as industrial products and fish meal. Since herring swim in schools of hundreds to thousands of fish, and since they come to inshore waters to spawn, they have been extremely susceptible to overfishing. In fact, the North American Boreal waters presently have the only healthy remaining herring stock in the world. All others have been seriously depleted or totally wiped out.

Herring are adapted for living in the upper oceanic waters. Adults swim to the surface in pursuit of plankton at night. Larval herring feed on copepod eggs and larvae, and mollusk larvae. As they grow larger, they eat larger copepod stages. Adult herring prefer adult copepods and euphausiids as well as fish under about 4 inches (10 cm) in length.

Most Boreal coast herring spawn in fall, but some stocks spawn in spring instead. The fall spawners have much greater fecundity than the spring spawners but their eggs are about half the size of the spring eggs. In addition, the spring spawners mature at a smaller size, an adaptation along with their larger egg size which helps cope with the more adverse spring conditions of heavy fresh-water runoff.

In either case, at spawning time females school inshore to locally preferred spawning grounds over rocky or gravelly bottom in 50 fathoms (300 feet or 100 m) or less of water. Such a well known highly productive area is south of Cape Elizabeth, Maine, referred to as a "breeding resort." In the fall up to 40,000 eggs are deposited by a single female. This autumn spawning is keyed to the fall bloom of the zooplankton, assuring food for the larvae. Unlike most fish eggs, herring eggs are not buoyant. Instead, they sink

to the bottom and stick to seaweed, stones, nets and an-
chors. The eggs hatch in 10 to 15 days into larvae which
then become members of the plankton. The small larvae
are extremely vulnerable to predation by ctenophores and
Sagitta arrow-worms which are especially abundant at herring spawning time.

Herring reach about 3 inches (7 to 8 cm) in length by the
end of their first year and are then called sardines. Most do
not reach reproductive size until their fourth year when
they are at least 10 inches (25 cm) in length.

The catastrophic collapse of certain herring fisheries is
not necessarily surprising, for herring schools have not
been difficult to catch. Herring are caught with trawl nets,
in fish weirs, stop seines and purse seines, the latter
methods being carried out at night when the fish are feeding inshore. Hopefully, the new understandings of multispecies interactions will help predict the status of the populations more accurately in the future, and even depleted
stocks will be able to re-establish themselves. Until that
happens, maintenance of these Boreal stocks is crucial.

Almost every fish in the sea preys upon herring. Cod
have especially high preference for them, but pollock, haddock, silver hake, mackerel, tuna and salmon take their
share as well. In addition, seals and whales feast upon the
schools whenever they find them.

Menhaden. Another member of the herring tribe is
the menhaden, *Brevoortia tyrannus*, also called pogy or
mossbunker. This toothless fish has a highly efficient filtering apparatus. Menhaden swim with their mouths open,
the mouth and throat area acting much like a tow net.
Water passes over gill rakers and out the gills, leaving behind a great abundance of micropscopic plants and some
zooplankton as well.

Like herring, menhaden swim in large schools, side by
side and layer upon layer. They are an oily fish and are
taken in large numbers by whales, porpoises and sharks and
by bluefish which kill more than they eat. The same oily
characteristic is the basis of their attraction for human
fisheries. Once they are caught by purse seines or fish
traps, the fish are used for animal feed and their oil is used
in various chemical industries. In the late 1800's menhaden

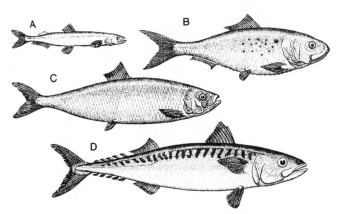

125. Commercially important small pelagic fish. A. capelin B. menhaden or pogy C. Atlantic herring D. mackerel.

fisheries made fortunes for men. Their subsequent collapse due to over-seining was followed by a similar herring boom and bust. Both fisheries seem to be recovering at present.

Little is known about menhaden breeding habits though they seem to reach maturity at four years of age and to spawn mid-summer over deep waters where their large buoyant eggs hatch in 48 hours. After spawning, menhaden head inshore to feed and it is during this fall schooling time that they are caught.

Capelin. Capelin, *Mallotus villosus*, are cold-water, truly pelagic, smelt-like fish and are even slenderer than smelt. The Canadian government now actively encourages the fisheries of this delicious small table fish so its familiarity will probably increase. Capelin eat planktonic crustaceans such as copepods, euphausiids and amphipods. They, in turn, are greedily devoured by whales, seals and almost every predaceous fish. The arrival of capelin in Newfoundland in summer is accompanied by the arrival of their predators, squid and cod.

During spawning, each female capelin is accompanied by two males, one swimming on each side of her. As in most other species of bony fish, capelin eggs are fertilized after they are deposited by the female. Spawning takes place more actively at night and the reddish sticky eggs are deposited over gravelly beds, much like herring eggs.

Since the capelin are fished when they swarm inshore to spawn, as are the herring, they are caught using the same methods of fishing weirs, purse seines and otter trawling.

Mackerel. Most species of bony fishes possess an air bladder, which evolved in Paleozoic times to assist in breathing like a lung when the oxygen content of the water was low. In many bony fish, including most Boreal species, this air bladder has evolved further into a buoyancy control mechanism. The fish produce more gas in the bladder in order to rise in the water and absorb gas back into the bloodstream in order to go deeper. This allows them to maintain a neutral buoyancy, where they float at exactly the depth they want, without swimming and wasting energy to maintain that position.

Unlike most bony fishes, the mackerel, *Scomber scombrus*, and the related bluefin tuna, *Thunnus thynnus*, do not possess a swim bladder. This means that they have to swim continuously or they will sink. In conjunction with this, these fish have a high rate of metabolism and also need to keep swimming to maintain a plentiful oxygen supply.

The mackerel is beautifully counter-shaded, dark above and silvery white underneath. It is brillantly metallic in its iridescence, with ripple bands of darker color across its upper surface. A densely schooling fish, mackerel are often found in the company of herring and like herring they feed selectively on the plankton, snapping at individual copepods, euphausiids and amphipods. As they get larger they also take small fish, including small herring and even juveniles of their own species. Mackerel also devour their own eggs if the opportunity presents itself.

Mackerel in turn fall prey to many larger predators. Cod and squid eat large numbers of small mackerel, and dogfish, tuna, bluefish, porpoises and larger whales and sharks all prey on them.

Though it is an important fisheries species, the life cycle of the mackerel is not completely known. The fish over-winter deep offshore and arrive inshore in the spring, thin from lack of food. Spawning time is prolonged, lasting from spring to mid-summer with a single female depositing about half a million eggs, 50,000 at a time. These buoyant eggs hatch in 2 to 7 days, depending on temperature, and grow to a length of 8 to 9 inches (20 cm) before they leave the coastal waters in autumn.

When mackerel leave the surface waters they concentrate in deep hollows and troughs for a few months, slowly dispersing. By February they begin to slowly work their way to surface waters for feeding and spawning. Though following north-south migratory patterns in some parts of the world, the North American mackerel appear almost simultaneously along the coast in the spring, implying migration offshore into deeper water, but not south.

Despite their unpredictability, mackerel are a very important commercial fish. They are taken by fish weirs and purse seines in the inshore phase of their yearly cycle in July. Since seining is usually done at night when the fish are feeding on plankton, they can provide a spectacular sight as they disturb luminescent plankton. Henry B. Bigelow described such a scene, tantalizing for any naturalist: "The trail of bluish light left behind by individual fish as they dart to one side or the other, while one rows or sails through a school on a moonless, overcast night when the water is firing with luminescence, is the most beautiful spectacle that our coastal waters afford and one with which every mackerel fisherman is familiar."

Bluefin Tuna. The largest sport fish of the Boreal coast is a member of the mackerel tribe. Reaching a length of 14 feet (4 m) and topping 1000 pounds (456 kg) in the more northern waters, the bluefin tuna, *Thunnus thynnus*, is an oceanic wanderer like the rest of the mackerel tribe, constantly swimming to keep oxygen levels high and in pursuit of its prey.

The bluefin tuna eats small schooling fish such as herring, mackerel and silver hake, and it also preys upon schooling squid. Since it is so fast moving, it has few predators except for killer whales and man.

The bluefin tuna is a warmer-water fish than the mackerel and wanders into Boreal waters from mid-July to September. The largest individuals are found in the Canadian Maritime waters. Bluefin tuna migrate to deeper and more southern waters in the winter. They are common as far south as Jamaica and even engage in trans-Atlantic migrations. Bluefin tuna spawn in warm Caribbean and Baha-

The Pelagic Realm

126. The bluefin tuna is a fast-swimming fish, often seen porpoising at the surface.

mian waters in spring before working their way north to feed in the productive summer waters of the Boreal region.

In Massachusetts waters, bluefin tuna are taken in fish traps. Most fish weigh under 200 pounds (91 kg). The larger bluefin tuna of 500 to 800 pounds (227 to 364 kg) of Maine, Nova Scotia and Newfoundland are too large for traps and are generally taken by hook and line or by harpoon. Like the mackerel fisheries, the tuna fisheries are somewhat unpredictable due to the wandering migratory movements of the fish.

Swordfish. Next to the bluefin tuna, the swordfish, *Xiphias gladius*, is the largest bony fish to frequent Boreal waters. Growing to over 1100 pounds (500 kg) and 16 feet (5 m) in length, this well-armed animal is prized as a game fish. Like the tuna, the swordfish is a truly oceanic and warm-water fish, visiting the Boreal coast only in the summer as it pursues its prey. At other times it is found as far south as Brazil. Whether or not a specific individual wanders the whole range is unknown, but it is probable that individuals travel at least to the Bahamas for the winter.

Though toothless, the adult swordfish is a successful predator as it swims through a school of fish, striking in all directions with its smooth sword and then turning to devour the dead or mangled fish. Mackerel, menhaden, herring, bluefish and silver hake commonly fall prey to them as do squid which seem to be their main food source at times. In fact, even the beak of a giant squid has been found in the stomach of a swordfish.

127. The swordfish slashes through a school of fish and then turns to eat the fish it has killed.

When swordfish arrive off the Boreal coast in early summer they are spent from lack of food and recent spawning but they fatten quickly in these food-rich waters. Though spawning probably occurs in the subtropics in spring, little else is known about early development.

Swordfish juveniles have equally lengthened jaws and teeth until they are about half a pound (.2 kg) in weight. The upper jaw then elongates into the sword, which is one-third the whole body length, and the teeth disappear. Apparently the fish is large enough at this size to be an effective predator with sword alone.

Swordfish is now appreciated greatly as a food fish though 100 years ago it was unsalable at fish markets along the eastern seaboard. The fish are most common on the offshore banks where they often bask at the surface, easy targets for harpooning which is the main method used for commercial purposes. Some fish are taken on long lines and hand lines as well, and many sport fishermen consider this to be the most fighting of the game fish. Their great swimming power and formidable sword enable swordfish to escape most other predators, falling prey only to larger sharks and possibly to sperm and killer whales.

Bluefish. The bluefish or snapper, *Pomatomus saltatrix*, has a reputation for outdoing even the spiny dogfish

128. The bluefish is a rapacious predator, ravaging schools of small fish.

in its rapacious menacing of other fish. These warm water oceanic fish work their way north in schools of thousands, appearing off Florida in March and reaching Boreal waters in late May to early June. This sea-green fish with a deeply forked tail reaches a maximum size of about 3½ feet (1 m) and 25 pounds (11 kg), though 10 to 12 pounds (5.5 kg) is more common.

Though bluefish are an excellent table fish, fishermen never can decide if their unpredictable appearance is a good or bad sign. Though they demand a good market and are felt by some to have superior taste to salmon, they also destroy or drive away mackerel, menhaden and herring. These strong-toothed fish, known locally as sea pirates, can be seen at the surface late in the season, harrying schools of other fish. When in abundance, they are caught by trolling and seining and in fish traps.

Marine Mammals

Though at first whales may appear to be larger versions of fish, these mammals of the sea are very different in their behavior, evolutionary history and life-cycle. Whales have fascinated the human imagination for eons and work in the last thirty years has been expecially exciting as evidence of

DEEPER AND OFFSHORE WATER

considerable cetacean intelligence has become indisputable. Not only do whales have large brains—the sperm whale's brain is the largest on earth, weighing almost 20 pounds (9 kg)—but the complexity of the brain cortex also points to high intelligence. In addition, whales indulge in much play behavior and display a marked capacity for mutual aid, characteristics which suggest superior intelligence.

The fact that sounds are produced by whales was forcefully brought to human attention in World War II when the U.S. Navy was listening underwater for German submarines. The Navy was frustrated by the hours and hours of mysterious noises their microphones picked up, noises that were termed interference. These, as it turned out, were the first recordings of the songs of the humpback whale.

Although the method of sound production is still disputed, whale sounds seem to be involved in communicating information about migration, mating, and food location. The most well-publicized sounds are the songs which humpback whales sing in warm waters. However, sound production, though not humpback songs, still occurs in Boreal waters.

The function of the sounds produced in northern waters is still not fully understood but various species use echolocation for finding schooling prey. Different kinds of sounds from "click trains" to "moans", "belches" and distinctive pulses have been described for different species of baleen whales. The different frequencies correlate well with the different sizes of food items preferred, and various frequencies seem to locate prey of specific sizes.

Orientation and migrational information seems to be transferred in the same way for toothed whales as it is for baleen whales, though no prolonged singing has been noted for the toothed whales. However in the last two decades there has been much discussion about the use of echolocation in odontocete feeding, especially in reference to two types of sounds emitted: click sequences and pure tones or modulated whistles. Some dolphins, like the bottlenose dolphin, appear to be able to control different frequencies of these "click train" sounds wherein low frequency clicks give a more generalized profile of the underwater environment and high frequency clicks allow for more subtle discrimination. These dolphins can carry out complicated behavior in total darkness in conjunction with the intense trains of click sounds produced, leaving little doubt that the environment is being scanned acoustically.

Toothed whales have varying amounts of tissue in the area between the top of the head and the upper jaw. When this tissue is abundant, it is called melon, from its firm rounded shape. The melon seems to be intimately involved in echo-location as it focuses sound pulses, apparently through the unusual triglycerides and wax esters found there. Though baleen whales do not have any melon, all whale hearing is very acute. The mechanisms are not yet fully understood, but skull bones seem to be very involved in whale hearing, giving whales more acute hearing than any mammal except bats.

All cetaceans, including whales, porpoises and dolphins, are mammals which evolved from four-legged terrestrial ancestors. Though hind limbs are invisible outside the animals, vestigal thigh and pubic bones still exist. The forelimbs have become modified into flippers which are used only for steering purposes. The foetal development of the whale forelimb reveals its evolution, for a five-finger appendage is apparent in early stages. This appendage develops into a flipper, with digital bones still intact, by the time the young whale is born.

Though whales swim in the manner of fish, with tail propulsion, they kick their tails up and down instead of from side to side. Unlike fish, tails or flukes of cetaceans are horizontal rather than vertical. The general symmetry of fish and whale shape is a result of convergent evolution, for the same streamlined shape has evolved from two very different sources. This streamlined shape is highly adaptive for rapid movement in an aquatic environment.

Unlike fish and like other mammals, whales cannot breathe under water. They are lung-breathers with the position of the nostrils moved to the top of the head where they form the blowhole. This adaptive change allows the animals to breathe with only a minimum amount of the body out of water.

The spout of a whale is not a stream of water, although a bit of water may be blown off the top of the blowhole.

Rather, the spout is a combination of moist lung air and droplets of an oily emulsion that is discharged with the breath. This oil serves a very important function, especially for whales that are deep divers. Unlike scuba divers who breathe continuously even at great depths and pressures, whales take only one breath for a whole dive and are therefore not afflicted by the possible caisson sickness, or bends, of which human divers must be aware. This sickness is caused by atmospheric nitrogen which is forced, under pressure, to dissolve in the blood stream. The greater the depth, or pressure, the more nitrogen is dissolved. On surfacing, this nitrogen can come out of solution as tiny bubbles in the blood and can be extremely dangerous.

Though whales do not breathe additional air, they still have a lungful of original air when they dive. What happens to its nitrogen? It seems that there is a fatty emulsion which is formed and which absorbs the nitrogen more readily than the bloodstream does. This emulsion, which is fluid at body temperatures, is expelled with each exhalation. The tiny droplets add to the naturally moist vapor of lung air, making the spout more apparent than it would otherwise be.

Every pregnant whale has a well developed placenta and gives birth to a live calf which is born tail first, a positioning that aids its progress to the surface for its first breath and prevents it from drowning before reaching the surface. Usually another female, referred to as a midwife whale, accompanies the mother-to-be, assisting in the birth if necessary and helping the newborn calf to the surface. This midwife often remains with the mother and calf, caring for the calf whenever the mother feeds.

To keep the mother's body streamlined, the teats are only exposed after stimulation from a calf nuzzling for food. The milk, which is ten times richer than cow's milk, is actually squirted into the calf's mouth by the muscles around the mammary glands. This helps the calf to nurse more quickly than it would otherwise and is of vital importance as the calf nurses underwater and still has a relatively small lung capacity. The nursing period, which is one of great dependence, lasts from 7 to 24 months, depending on the cetacean species.

Whales are broadly divided into two groups, Mysticetes, which have baleen, or whalebone, instead of teeth, and

Odontocetes, or toothed whales. For information on whale-watching activities, please see appendix.

Baleen or Whalebone Whales

The baleen, or whalebone, whales are named after the horny plates which are set in the roof of the mouth instead of teeth. This baleen, or whalebone, is made up of from 100 to 500 individual plates, each of which is frayed on the inner edge and which overlaps the next plate, forming a highly efficient mat for straining large amounts of plankton or small fish.

Since baleen whales evolved from toothed land animals, the baleen represents a long evolutionary process in the suppression of normal dentition. In addition, the whole front end of baleen whales has been modified into a large buccal cavity to allow the huge amounts of water into the mouth that are necessary for this type of feeding.

The baleen whales are highly migratory, wintering in southern waters where seas are calm and temperatures are warm enough for calving. At tropical latitudes, however, there is not as much vertical mixing of the water, and food availability is greatly reduced, allowing the whales to maintain themselves but not to grow. In the spring, then, whales and offspring migrate poleward to richer feeding grounds, spending the summer and early autumn feeding on the plankton and pelagic fish of the Boreal waters.

The stimulus that prompts migration is uncertain but most information points to change in length of daylight, or photoperiod. Since the baleen whales cover huge distances in migration, their orientation mechanisms are of tantalizing interest. They seem to use currents for some of their directional information, but they also travel across currents as well. Temperature does not seem to be involved, as it is with fish, and the general consensus is that a high degree of learned behavior is involved, based on information passed from one whale generation to another.

Two of the four distinct families of baleen whales migrate into the Boreal zone: the right whales which graze on plankton and have long, finely fringed whalebone plates,

396 DEEPER AND OFFSHORE WATER

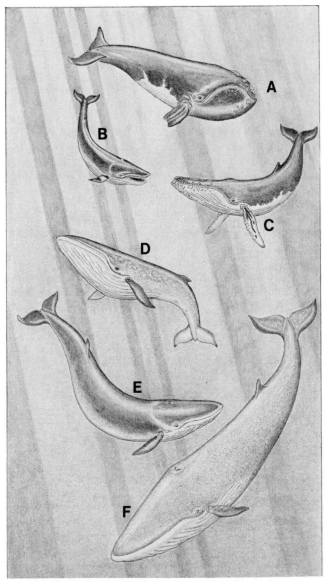

129. The baleen or whalebone whales of the Boreal coast.
A. right whale B. minke whale C. humpback whale D. sei whale
E. fin whale F. great blue whale

and the rorquals, or finner whales, which eat fish in addition to planktonic krill.

THE RIGHT WHALES

The right whale, *Eubalaena glacialis,* gained its common name because it was the best whale to catch for commercial purposes, the right whale rather than the wrong one. It is a slow swimming, moderately large whale, 35 to 50 feet (10 to 16 m) long, which floats when dead, making capture and recovery easy. Having the most elastic and longest baleen, up to 12 feet (3 to 4 m) in length, and yielding good quantities of oil, its economic value was assured. In fact, evidence shows that right whales were hunted by the Basques in Spain and France and by Britons earlier than A.D. 1000. Given this history it is no surprise that this mammal was hunted almost to its extinction. Though in the last century right whales were commonly seen in large herds, now they are only seen singly or in very small numbers. It is hoped that the International Whaling Commission laws enacted in 1967 will allow their recovery.

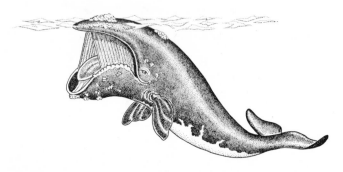

130. The right whale feeds by letting water flow through its baleen which traps planktonic animals.

To feed, the right whale swims along the surface, its mouth open, straining *Calanus* copepods, or meadows of brit as early whalers called them, from the surface. The tongue then presses against the roof of the mouth, forcing the water out through the baleen filtering system. The stranded prey is then swallowed. When the whale is not

398

feeding, the jaws are closed and the elastic baleen curves backward in the direction of the throat. When the jaws open, the baleen springs forward, completely filling all available space, no matter how wide the jaw is opened. The lower lip is actually a flap of blubber that allows the mouth to close tightly, covering the long baleen when the animal is not feeding.

Calving by right whale females occurs from January to March after 9 to 10 months of pregnancy. The 13 to 18 foot (4 to 5.5 m) calves are usually born singly, and like all other baleen whales, they are born without whalebone, an adaptation which allows the calves to nurse properly.

RORQUAL OR FINNER WHALES

The other main type of baleen whales migrating into the Boreal region are the rorquals, which gain their name from the structure of their lower jaw. Early Norwegian whalers noted the grooves or tubes ("ror" is Norwegian for "tube") stretching along the throat and upper chest of these whales. These grooves stretch to impressive widths, allowing the

131. The rorqual or finner whales feed by engulfing water in their expandable mouths and then forcing the trapped water out through the baleen.

whale to actually engulf tons of water in its mouth. The blue whale, for instance, can hold at least 70 tons of water for a moment inside the expanded mouth. The pouch is then contracted, squeezing the water out through the baleen and leaving the food to be swallowed by the relatively small throat. Except for the sei whales, which utilize straining as well as engulfment methods, all other rorquals (finbacks, minkes, humpbacks, and blue whales) use only engulfment to catch their prey.

Sei Whale. The sei whales (pronounced "say"), *Balaenoptera borealis*, is a planktonic feeder, filtering *Calanus* copepods, *Thysanoessa* euphausiids and pelagic amphipods through its fine black and white baleen. It also takes small schooling fish at certain times of the year.

Sei whales calve in the winter after 10 to 12 months of pregnancy. The newborn calves are about 15 feet (5 m) at birth and grow an inch (2 to 3 cm) a day in the early nursing months. They mature when they are about 40 to 45 feet (12 to 13.5 m) long and have a lifespan of 70 years.

These whales have a high vertical spout and can be seen in large groups, especially off Nova Scotia. Though seis were one of the most heavily hunted whales, they often escaped capture due to their swift swimming ability.

Finback or Fin Whale. Formerly the most abundant of the rorquals, the fin whale, *Balaenoptera physalus*, is a relatively large whale, reaching 70 feet (21 m) in length and weighing up to 50 to 60 tons. Its large slender baleen indicates a preference for fish, though it also takes the large euphausiids *Meganyctiphanes* when they are plentiful in the summer.

The lower right lip of the fin whale is white and this coloration may be used to help concentrate its prey. In the spring and summer, fins migrate northward along the Boreal coast. They have been seen repeatedly in the Bay of Fundy and Nova Scotia areas taking unique advantage of the tidal flow. At these places *Meganyctiphanes* euphausiids are harassed by large schools of mackerel preying on them. The planktonic shrimp are concentrated by this pursuit in the upper 6 to 7 feet (2 m) of the water, especially over or adjacent to offshore ledges and banks as the tide ebbs out. After the tide begins its ebb, finback whales gather in the vicinity of these ledges and, doing a "racing turn" by rolling on one side and turning quickly, they sweep through the krill, engulfing extraordinary numbers with each mouthful. In the winter, finbacks feed more exclusively on fish, especially herring and mackerel.

Finback calving occurs from December to April after a

year of pregnancy. The 20 foot (6 m) newborn calves nurse for seven months and have usually grown to about 36 feet (11 m) by the time they are weaned. The young then feed on *Calanus* copepods and other smaller planktonic crustaceans. As their baleen becomes larger they progressively take larger prey.

Minke Whale. The minke (minkee), *Balaenoptera acutorostrata,* is the smallest of the baleen whales that enter Boreal waters, growing to a maximum of 30 feet (9 m) and 11 tons. Minkes can be very acrobatic, breaching or jumping out of the water and swimming close to shore or to ships. Their white flippers or white dorsal crescents which stretch from the blowhole to each flipper easily distinguish them from other whales.

The minke seems especially attracted to cold, turbulent, summer waters and is more dependent on a fish diet than the other baleen whales. In the Boreal region minke whales are often seen swimming solitarily about a mile (1 to 2 km) apart, apparently dispersed to feed from tidal currents close to shore. With increased whale watching activities, minkes are now known to return to the same places with one individual working a single tidal streak or passage for several successive days or weeks. In New Brunswick and Nova Scotia waters, herring are usually taken; in coastal Newfoundland and the Saguenay River of Quebec the minkes chase capelin instead.

Minke migrations are not well understood but these extremely social whales seem to winter offshore as far south as Florida. In the spring and summer they work their way north, arriving in Nova Scotia by May, Newfoundland by June and travelling as far as northern Labrador by August.

Female minkes in the North Atlantic mature at 23 feet (7 m) and calve from December to May, producing a 9 foot (2.7 m) calf every second year. Like most other whales and schooling fish, there is apparent sexual segregation of groups as well as segregation by age classes.

In the Southern Ocean around Antarctica the minke populations have established a new equilibrium as a result of the overhunting of the other rorquals. With reduced competition for food due to decimated populations of the blue and humpback whales, reproductive capacity of other rorquals has increased dramatically. Not only have pregnancy rates increased for minkes as well as for finbacks and seis, but in addition minkes become sexually mature at 6 years of age rather than at 14 years. The plasticity of this Southern Ocean whale equilibrium has amazed those studying the situation. Unfortunately for the minke, it is now the most heavily harvested baleen whale in the world. The Japanese take the largest portion of the catch.

Humpback Whale. Growing to a length of about 50 feet (15 m) the humpback whale, *Megaptera novaeangliae*, is easily distinguished by its very long white flippers and the knob-like swellings on its head and snout. Unlike most baleens which have high vertical spouts, the humpback spout is low and bushy. In addition to being known for its southern songs, the humpback is renowned for its powerful acrobatics which are emphasized by the white fins. Humpbacks commonly breach, roll on the water, surface, and engage in finning or holding one or both flippers out of the water while swimming along, lobtailing or slapping the water with a fin or with the flukes, and back somersaulting in midair. In addition, during mating season, they often give each other what look like love pats with their flukes.

Humpback baleen is coarse and stiff and suitable only for larger plankton, such as krill and fish, especially mackerel, capelin and herring. In addition to pelagic species, the humpback also takes benthic food, especially the northern shrimp, *Pandalus borealis*.

Though the humpback is an endangered species, signs of recovery are evident in Boreal populations. These hump-

132. A female humpback stays close to her calf for about a year.

backs winter in the Caribbean where the females bear a single 15 foot (4.5 m) calf every two or three years. The young nurse for up to a year and are 25 to 28 feet (7.6 to 8.5 m) long when they are weaned, growing more than a foot (30 cm) per month during this time.

Blue Whale. The largest animal to live on the earth is the great blue whale, *Balaenoptera muculus*. Reaching almost 100 feet (30 m) in length and over 120 tons in weight these animals are even larger in bulk than the giant dinosaurs of the Mesozoic era.

The large blue whales, which are actually a slate gray in color, were the first rorquals to be hunted commercially and are now severely threatened with extinction. Blues were hunted mercilessly, for a single blue yielded much more oil than a single whale of any other species. Like many other whales, the blue has been protected since 1967 by the International Whaling Commission, but whale specialists fear that the decimated populations are so small that the whales can not find each other to mate.

Since the blue eats only euphausiids, and since a medium sized blue (70 tons) eats several tons of krill a day, the blue whale is found in waters with high krill production. Definite populations of blue whales are known in Boreal waters in the Gulf of St. Lawrence, on the Grand Banks of Newfoundland and possibly on the outer Gulf of Maine banks.

Female blues calve every two or three years, producing little gaffers weighing in at 5000 pounds (2273 kg) and 23 feet (7 m) at birth. During the nursing period which lasts about a year, baby blues gain about 200 pounds (91 kg) a day. They reach sexual maturity when they are five to ten years old and may live about a hundred years.

The Toothed Whales or Odontocetes

There are many more species of Odontocetes, or toothed whales, in world oceans than there are baleen whales. The southern hemisphere is probably the major evolutionary center for the toothed whales, and early differentiation occurred in those unglaciated seas before fossil evidence for toothed whales appeared in northern waters. Three toothed whales, the beluga, the narwhal and the Atlantic bottlenose are northern, though, and were probably trapped in the Arctic basin during one of the cold periods of the Tertiary. This resulted in very rapid selection of those whales that carried out their whole life cycles, including calving, in cool water. The only one of these whales to venture into more temperate Boreal waters is the beluga or white whale.

The toothed whales also include dolphins and porpoises. Though technically the terms "dolphin" and "porpoise" refer to different families, common interchange of the terms has led to looser use of the words. The origins of the two names actually reveal the present-day differences in attitude towards whales in large.

"Dolphin" comes from the Greek "delphys" which means "womb" and which has sacred connotations. Aristotle noted long ago that dolphins were born from a womb, were nursed by their mothers and could utter sounds. Sacred and auspicious associations were thus developed and are revealed on a wall of the palace of Knossus on Crete where a panel of dolphins leaps across the royal room.

In contrast, "porpoise" comes from the Latin "porcus," meaning pig, and "pisces," meaning fish. This "sea pig" was prized only for its succulence, and today's technical classification of porpoises does include those small cetaceans that are considered more delectable. Like the Greeks, most North Americans feel that whales are creatures of intelligence and should be dealt with carefully and be protected. Like the Romans, the Russians and Japanese feel that whales provide an excellent source of protein for mankind and should be used as such. The gap between these attitudes is great.

Most Odontocetes exhibit at least seasonal oscillation in movement while others, like killer whales, have distinct migrations as they follow winter herring. In addition, few of the small Odontocetes can survive the cold winter waters of the Boreal region and they move south like the larger whales, which must breed in warmer temperatures.

Killer Whale. The killer whale, *Orcinus orca*, is one of the most beautiful of the whales, jet black on the back and glistening white on the belly with an additional white oval behind the eye. These medium sized whales reach about 30

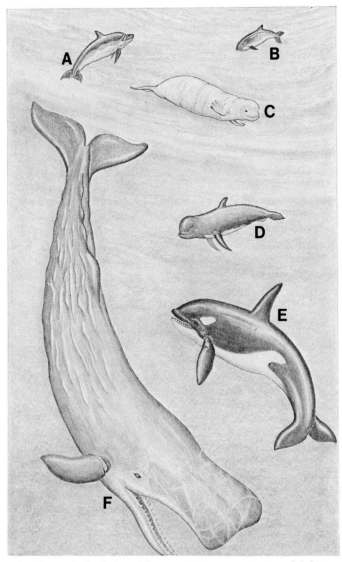

133. The toothed whales of the Boreal coast. A. common dolphin B. harbor porpoise C. beluga whale D. pilot or pothead whale E. killer whale F. sperm whales

feet (9 m) in length with mature females weighing about five tons and mature males as much as nine tons.

Killer whales are accomplished predators and often cooperate in an effort to secure prey. Instances of such group hunting abound in both polar regions where they are known to tip edges of ice floes, forcing seals or, in the Antarctic, penguins to slide off the floe and into the water where they are quickly caught by other killer whales in the group. Likewise, individual minke and sei whales are occasionally attacked by pods of killer whales. As many as ten individuals are common in a hunting pod.

Though they are the only flesh-eating whale, killer whales also eat many fish and squid, which actually make up the largest portion of their diet. However, in Boreal waters the harbor porpoise is a favorite item of food in addition to cod and squid.

Though reproductive information is known about killer whales in other oceans, little is known about the North Atlantic population. Calves are 8 to 9 feet (2.4 to 2.7 m) long at birth and nurse for a year before they are weaned. Females mature at four years of age and the lifespan of the killer whale is about 35 years.

Though killer whales are efficient predators, they have never threatened humans. People who have been closely associated with killer whales by training them in captivity find the animals to be gentle and affectionate as well as highly intelligent.

Harbor Porpoise. The most common whale in our waters is the harbor porpoise, *Phocoena phocoena*. The harbor porpoise has a well-developed melon which obscures the short beak line and continues the smooth line of the back all the way to the mouth. The harbor porpoise grows to a length of 6 feet (1.8 m) and a weight of 120 pounds (55 kg), reaching sexual maturity at three to four years of age. Calves are born from April to July after eleven months gestation, and they nurse for eight months.

Harbor porpoises are seen in groups of various sizes between July and September close to land or in shallow water. At these times they feed on squid and pelagic fish such as herring and mackerel, and groundfish, such as cod and redfish.

OTHER DOLPHINS. In addition to harbor porpoises, several other small cetaceans also occur in the Boreal region. The white-beaked dolphin, *Lagenorhynchus albirostris*, and the closely related white-sided dolphin, *L. acutus*, are sometimes seen in schools of 40 to 50 individuals off beaches in the spring.

134. The common dolphin, a classic omen of good luck, often porpoises in the wake of ships.

The common, or saddleback, dolphin, *Delphinus delphis*, is world-known as a good omen for boats, often playing the bow wake of ships, hitching a free ride in the frontal current and leaping clear of the water in apparent sheer abandon. They are often seen in herds in offshore waters.

The common dolphin has a more slender and elongated beak and more sharply pointed as well as more numerous teeth than the other porpoises of the region. This adaptive quality enables the dolphin to easily grasp relatively small pelagic fish that make up the bulk of its diet.

Life cycle patterns of the common dolphin are similar to other dolphins. Sexual maturity is reached at three years and a single calf is born after eleven months gestation. The young are weaned after only four months of nursing, a short period for most cetaceans, and lifespan is 25 to 30 years.

Pothead or Pilot Whale. Both its Latin name, *Globicephala malaena*, and one of its common names, pothead, reflect a prominent feature of the pothead or pilot whale: its bulbous melon which is so large in older animals that it hangs over the snout. The pothead whale is entirely black and grows to 20 feet (6 m) and three tons in size.

The lifespan of the pothead is about 25 years. Females mature at six years and males at thirteen. After a year of gestation, a 5½ foot (1.65 m) calf is born and it nurses for a year. Potheads winter offshore in warmer waters and summer inshore where food is plentiful.

Like the sperm whale, the pothead whale exhibits a high preference for squid, and in fact, the pothead has a close relationship with *Ilex*, following the short-finned squid north in the summer. Since squid are slippery, the teeth of both the pothead and the sperm whale have been modified. There is a huge reduction of maxillary teeth and instead, the palate is strongly ribbed, which facilitates holding of the slippery squid.

Potheads are sometimes found stranded and dying in large groups on the shore, a fact which still puzzles whale experts. Besides having a strong tendency to follow a leader, it seems that these whales are highly susceptible to a parasite in the inner ear which wreaks havoc with orientation mechanisms.

Sperm Whale. The sperm whale, *Physeter catodon*, of Moby Dick fame has a large square head and grows to a length of 60 feet (18 m). The upper jaw has a ribbed palate and no visible teeth, but the teeth of the lower jaw were prized by whalers for the ivory needed for scrimshaw work. The sperm whale gets its name from the spermaceti found in its head. This liquid wax or sperm oil was especially valued as lamp oil and in chemical industries. A similar high quality oil has recently been extracted from the bean of the jojoba plant in southwestern United States, the harvesting of which endangers no species.

The social structure of sperm whales is highly developed. Different ages and different sexes congregate separately. During the spring and summer breeding season, males round up harems often of several hundred females. Battles over females with challenges by young males are probably common. Sperm whale hunting especially damaged these populations, for whalers removed most of the largest harem masters, the prime members of the male population. Mothers are very protective of their calves, which nurse for a year and which are born every 2 or 3 years after 12 to 16 months gestation.

Sperm whales feed on all kinds of squid, including *Arch-iteuthis*, the giant squid. They are active hunters, able to dive to depths of over 1500 feet (460 m) and to stay submerged for more than an hour on a single breath, chasing their prey. In addition to this active predation, sperm whales may have a passive strategem for luring squid into their mouths. It seems that the whale may rest motionless in the water, mouth agape, while squid and some fish are lured into the mouth by the light coloring of the buccal area and by luminescence left on the teeth from previously eaten squid.

Beluga or White Whale. The Gulf of St. Lawrence provides breeding grounds for a large population of the all white, cold-water beluga whale, *Delphinapterus leucas.* After 13 to 14 months of pregnancy, females bear calves in the summer which are brown at birth and which slowly change to a gray color. The calves are not fully weaned until two years of age, though they begin hunting in their second year of life. Though the females are sexually mature at five years and the males are mature at eight years, the young whales are not fully white until ten years of age.

Belugas congregate in groups of up to several hundred animals and are called sea canaries for their high pitched squeaks and whistles which can even be heard through the hull of a boat. Their greatly rounded melon probably attests to the use of echo-location and their sharply pointed teeth reflects their broad diet, which is largely composed of small and medium sized fish such as capelin and sand launce. They feed on the seabed as well, often diving to 125 feet for flatfish and crustaceans.

Belugas travel north for summer feeding and their white color is possibly an adaptation to life among the ice floes of arctic seas.

The Demersal Realm

The demersal, or sea bed, habitat is, of course, greatly affected by some of the same currents, water fronts, gyres, and temperature and salinity changes which affect the pelagic habitat. Although cooling winter temperatures may force many shallow-water demersal organisms further offshore, temperatures near the bottom are more stable than those in the upper layers of water. More crucial to many demersal organisms is the nature of the substrate.

Certain species prefer soft bottom substrates where they root for worms and mollusks. Other species are found exclusively on hard rocky substrates where they feed on crabs and other crustaceans. Yet others are not as particular about bottom substrate and feed both on demersal fish and on small pelagic fish such as herring. This last type of demersal species, which includes fish like cod, hake and pollock, is included in the demersal grouping because though the animals spend much time between the surface waters and the bottom, their dependency on the bottom is still evident. In contrast, true pelagic species spend the large proportion if not all of their lives totally independent of the bottom.

Benthic substrates are usually patchy. Pockets of soft sediment often exist in predominantly rocky areas and vice versa. Since certain fish are extremely fastidious in their choice of substrate, their grounds are often less extensive and may have abrupt edges to them, almost islands, as it were. In addition, juveniles of demersal species must be able to find proper substrates, for the substrate type determines the kind of available food.

Most demersal species start life as pelagic organisms, however, because there is little food sufficiently abundant near the bottom for larvae to prey on. Most eggs are buoyant and immediately join the plankton where the newly hatching larvae have ample food and are also dispersed by the surface currents. When the larvae have grown large enough to feed on the food which is available on or near the seabed, they metamorphose into fry and settle to the bottom.

Invertebrates

Northern Shrimp. An important invertebrate which lives primarily in the deeper demersal waters is the northern shrimp, *Pandalus borealis*. This translucent red shrimp is a temperate and subarctic animal, present in northern oceans around the world. The northern shrimp is one of the largest cold-water prawns, growing to a length of 5 inches (12.5 cm). The Gulf of Maine is this shrimp's southern limit and in years of milder temperatures than usual, even these waters are too warm for it. Preferring cold water, the northern shrimp migrate in the opposite direction to most other species. Since offshore waters are coldest in summer and warm as winter approaches, this shrimp summers offshore and winters in the cold inshore waters. The trawl fisheries for northern shrimp is therefore carried out in the winter, usually in March, when the animals may be plentiful in inshore waters and on the fishing banks.

Like a few other marine animals the northern shrimp spends the first years of its life as a male, with a sex reversal changing it to female in its later years. When this type of sex reversal occurs, female fecundity significantly increases, for a larger (older) shrimp can carry more eggs than a smaller one. Other hermaphroditic species undergoing a male to female sex reversal are shipworms and slipper limpets.

The large females carry their eggs for seven months on their pleopods under their tails. Since the eggs look like berries clinging together, the females are said to be "berried" or "in berry." The eggs hatch as larvae in the spring, floating with the plankton, eating phytoplankton and being eaten by herring. In May and June the larvae settle on soft bottom substrates and stay within a few miles of the coast for the next year and a half until they are about 2 inches (5 cm) in length.

These small males migrate offshore to deeper water in the winter of their second year and mature as functional males by the summer of their third year. It is during this summer period that they fertilize the larger females. The males stay offshore the following winter where the warmer temperatures are important in their sex reversal. By the following summer, they have become functional females and are ready to be fertilized by the new year class of smaller males.

In the fall of this fourth year, the berried females migrate inshore, arriving in February and March. The cooler inshore temperatures are crucial for egg development, for if the temperature exceeds 43° F (6° C) eggs are often shed prematurely and egg death increases rapidly. The inshore spring hatching also ensures a good planktonic food supply for the larvae. Some females migrate offshore to mate again and then migrate inshore for one last reproductive winter. Since only the females migrate inshore, they supply the total human catch and consumption.

A large part of the diet of the northern shrimp is made up of euphausiids, and the shrimp migrate nocturnally with them to upper water layers each night. However, since the shrimp cannot tolerate water warmer than about 41° F (5° C), they never penetrate the summer surface waters. Berried females stay on the bottom, eating small clams, snails and worms from the muddy substrate. In turn, larger crustacean-eating groundfish, such as flatfish, redfish, cod and pollock prey on the succulent shrimp.

Groundfish

It was the abundance of groundfish or demersal fish that established the economic importance of the New World three centuries ago. Demersal fisheries, which include fisheries for hake and cod families as well as for all flatfish, the butterfish and the redfish or ocean perch, are still the most important commercial fisheries of the region.

The degree of dependence on the seabed varies from species to species of groundfish, and mouth structure often reveals a fish's predatory habits at a glance.

Whiting or Silver Hake. Whiting, *Merluccius bilinearis*, is a long, slender fish, reaching 2½ feet (75 cm) in length with two well developed dorsal fins and, as its name implies, it is brightly iridescent though it fades quickly after being taken from the water.

The whiting is a fast swimming and strong-toothed predator, preying on schools of small fish such as herring, mackerel, menhaden and alewives. Smaller silver hake, in particular, feed heavily on the northern shrimp, *Pandalus borealis*. Though not bottom-dependent, whiting are trawled as deep as 400 fathoms (750 m) off the continental slope.

Whiting is the most important summer spawner of the Boreal region. It spawns over the outer fishing banks from

Nova Scotia to Cape Cod and a single female may lay up to two million buoyant eggs. These eggs and subsequent larvae circulate in the Gulf of Maine, which is one of the most important of whiting nursery grounds.

Whiting do not school, but huge congregations of them band together in their voracious pursuit of smaller fish. In their hunger after fasting during summer spawning, such bands of whiting often drive schools of smaller fish ashore, even beaching themselves in their relentless pursuit. That their most active hunting time is after sunset has been known since 1616 when Captain John Smith wrote, "Hake you may have when the cod failes in summer, if you will fish in the night." As surface waters cool in the fall, they seek deep water where temperatures are milder for the winter.

Whiting meat is sweet but it softens quickly. Rapid freezing devices aboard freezer ships have enabled trawlers to bring the fish to market with the flesh still in prime condition.

White Hake or Ling. White hake, *Urophycis tenuis,* is a true hake, distinguished from whiting by having a small chin barbel and ventral fins that are elongated and feeler-like. Likewise, the mouth has a shorter lower jaw than upper, and the teeth are not nearly as prominent as those of the whiting.

The barbel and very long ventral fins suggest the impor-

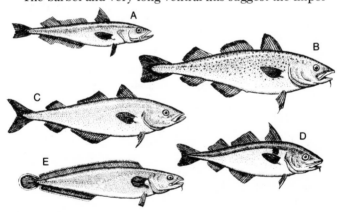

135. The cod family. A. whiting B. cod C. pollock D. haddock E. cusk.

tance of touch in white hake feeding behavior. And indeed, the white hake rarely travels to the surface, spending most of its time near the bottom, where it eats crustaceans such as the northern shrimp and amphipods as well as some small fish and squid.

The eggs and larvae drift in surface waters for several months until the fry are 2 to 4 inches (5 to 10 cm) in length. The early settling fry find good nurseries in inshore eel grass, Zostera, beds, and larger fry are often found living commensally inside the living shells of giant scallops. The young fish do not feed on the scallops; they only use the shells for refuge. White hake are rather inactive fish and except for seasonal inshore and offshore movements, they tend to remain in a particular area once they have taken to the bottom. Most of the white hake that are landed are taken with otter trawls.

Cod. The cod, Gadus callarias, fishery is one of the most important fisheries in the entire North Atlantic and certainly ranks as such in the Boreal region. In fact, in Newfoundland, "fish" is synonymous with "cod." Though bottom otter trawling is the most common way of catching the fish, they are still taken by gill nets as well. And on the Newfoundland Banks where the abundance has to be seen to be believed, cod are still jigged by unbaited hand lines.

The cod is a heavy-bodied and square-tailed fish. Like many groundfish, its color varies greatly, generally gray-green or reddish. Though the cod does pursue herring, capelin and mackerel, it spends most of its time on the bottom. The larger fish especially keep to the seabed, eating large mollusks including large clams, Mactra, and horse mussels, Modiolus modiolus. They also prey upon northern shrimp and rock crabs, Cancer species, and gorge on squid whenever possible.

In following small schooling fish, cod do wander into upper layers of water but their preference is for rocky and pebbly substrates, kelp areas, and deeper slopes of underwater ledges. The cod is a cold-water fish, always on the move over its chosen substrate. Though European cod populations show considerable migrational tendencies, North American populations seem to move only within specific regions where physical conditions are similar. The

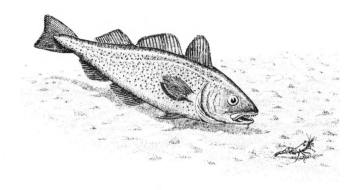

136. Favorite food of the cod is the northern shrimp *Pandalus borealis*.

only regular seasonal migrations known by cod in the Boreal region are concentrations over spawning grounds.

Though once reaching 200 pounds (91 kg) in weight and 6 feet (1.8 m) in length, the largest cod now caught are about 90 pounds (41 kg) with an average cod weighing only 10 to 25 pounds (11 kg). Cod are known for their high fecundity. A single 40 inch (1 m) female lays as many as 3 million eggs in a season. Cod spawn over locally well-known grounds beginning in late winter, though the breeding season is a prolonged one with Grand Banks populations spawning from April to June. Egg development takes from 10 to 40 days, dependent on temperature, and larvae spend about 2 months in their pelagic phase.

Small pollock devour and disperse huge numbers of cod fry and even medium-sized pollock are fierce predators on equally sized cod. Cod up to 7 or 8 inches (20 cm) are often eaten by larger cod as well, and spiny dogfish and sharks are the worst enemies of the adult fish.

Haddock. The haddock, *Melanogrammus aeglefinus*, is closely related to the cod though it is much more exclusively a groundfish and therefore more selective in its substrate. Though cod are sometimes found on haddock grounds, haddock are not found in rock or kelp areas, preferring only gravel, pebble, clay and sand areas, particularly those between rocky patches.

Though it resembles the cod very much, the haddock is a

137. The haddock snouts in the mud to capture its prey which includes worms and mollusks.

duskier colored fish with a dark, rather than a light, lateral line. It is a smaller fish than the cod, for the heaviest on record is still under 40 pounds (18 kg) and an average-sized haddock weighs between 14 and 23 pounds (6 to 10 kg).

Even when it is found in conjunction with cod, haddock have very different food preferences, as their small mouths and dull teeth reflect. Occasionally haddock eat small fish but they never pursue them into surface waters. Most often, haddock root in the bottom with their muscular lips for burrowing worms and small mollusks and crabs under 2 inches (5 cm) in length. They are known to congregate in masses to gorge on herring eggs which, unlike the eggs of most of the other fish, are not buoyant. In addition, they eat many brittle stars and small sea urchins.

The haddock is the most commercially important spring spawner of the region. It breeds from late January to July. Spawning peaks in March on Georges Bank, in April on the Scotian Banks and in June on the Grand Banks. Like the cod, it is a very prolific fish for its size; a single female will lay as many as 2 million eggs. The young hatch in fifteen days and spend three months in their pelagic phase, often finding refuge under the bell of the lion's mane jellyfish, *Cyanea*. Georges Bank, which is now of great interest to oil companies, is their biggest spawning grounds in the Boreal region and is the most productive haddock ground in the world.

Though it is a cold-water fish, haddock does not like water as cold as cod does and, in fact, cold deep-water channels like the Laurentian Channel act as a barrier to their movements, keeping populations distinct. Otter trawls are the main fishing gear used to capture this delicous table fish. Haddock has good keeping qualities as a fresh fish and is also treasured by finnan haddie lovers, who savour the lightly smoked flavor.

American Pollock or Boston Bluefish. Another member of the cod family, the American pollock, *Pollachius virens*, differs in general appearance from cod by its forked tail, its olive green color and its white lateral line which shows up in great contrast along its sides. Whereas haddock are strictly bottom-dwelling fish and cod are both bottom dwellers and semi-pelagic, pollock are the most active of this family, swimming often at the surface as they pursue pelagic euphausiids and small fish. They destroy great quantities of small herring, cod, haddock and sand launce, as well as chasing schools of whiting. In the fall they even pursue smelt into the estuaries. In reference to their appetities, it has been said that "ravenous" is only mildly descriptive, as a 9 inch (23 cm) pollock has been seen to eat 77 herring of 2 inches (5 cm) at one meal.

The pollock is the most important autumn spawner of the region, needing water several degrees warmer than that of haddock for spawning. Massachusetts Bay is an especially important spawning ground where a quarter of a million eggs are deposited by an average sized female. Young pollock are found more often in inshore coastal waters while older pollock prefer deeper waters. Being a cool- but not cold-water fish, pollock range as far north as southern Newfoundland and they may winter as far south as Cape Cod.

Most pollock are landed with otter trawls though gill nets and some long lines are also used. In addition, pollock is a good sport fish, rising fiercely to the fly and giving as long and strong a run as a salmon of equal size.

Cusk or Tusk. The cusk, *Brosme brosme*, looks quite different from the others of the cod and hake families for it has only a single dorsal fin which runs along much of its back, emphasizing its slimmer body shape. Older cusk are quite plain colored but younger ones are barred with yellow and blue bands. Their chin barbel is much longer than that of most of their relatives as well.

Cusk are sluggish fish and are exclusively groundfish of moderately deep water. They are only found where the substrate is rough with boulders or gravel and pebbles. Cusk do not seem to migrate with the seasons; due to its depth, the water they inhabit is quite stable in temperature. Shrimp and crabs seem to make up the bulk of their diet.

Like other members of their family, cusk are prolific fish, an average-sized female spawning more than two million eggs in spring and early summer. Since cusk inhabit rough bottoms and are relatively solitary fish, they are not suitable for trawling. So, despite the fact that at least 75 percent of all fish are taken by otter trawls, cusk are still caught mostly by long-line fishing.

The Flatfish

The flatfish are highly adapted to living on the bottom. Flatfish do not lie on their bellies, but instead they lie on either their right or left side. Though flatfish larvae swim upright as do most fish, they metamorphose just before they take to the bottom. At metamorphosis, the skull twists, and the eye of the side that is destined to be the underneath side migrates around the head by means of differential growth rates, placing both eyes on the side that will become the top of the fish. The mouth more closely maintains its original position, causing the adult fish to look as if its mouth is opening sideways. Adults are truly flat.

The underneath side of flatfish is usually white or very light colored while the top side is mottled grays or browns. All flatfish are capable of changing their color pattern to blend in with the substrate on which they live. This excellent camouflaging combined with the ability of flatfish to bury themselves in the sand makes them almost impossible to see.

Atlantic Halibut. Only swordfish, tuna and the larger

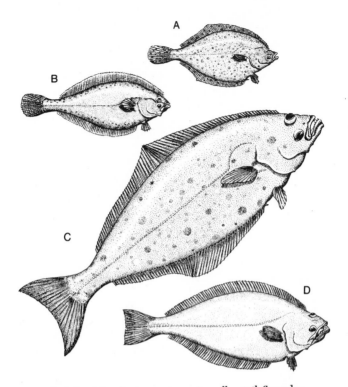

138. Flatfish of the deeper waters. A. yellowtail flounder
B. Canadian plaice or American dab C. Atlantic halibut
D. turbot

sharks are bigger fish than the Atlantic halibut, *Hippoglos-sus hippoglossus*, which grows to over 8 feet (2.4 m) in length and 700 pounds (318 kg), though most halibut taken now are much smaller, rarely weighing over 200 pounds (91 kg). The halibut is a right-eyed fish (its left side is underneath), narrower than most flatfish but thicker through the body.

Halibut are cool- but not cold-water fish; they are found at depths of 350 to 500 fathoms (635 to 900 m) on sand or gravel substrates at places where the icy Labrador Current does not reach. The halibut work their way in over the shallower banks in the summer in search of food. As temperatures cool in the fall, they work out again to deeper water.

Halibut are voracious fish, preying upon other groundfish and especially other flatfish, with diet somewhat dependent on which groundfish are available in a given locality. Like other flatfish, they lie almost invisible on the substrate, rushing suddenly at any prey which passes by within reach. They rarely follow their prey to surface waters.

Though halibut have been overfished in the North Atlantic, they were not always in demand. In 1634, writing about New England's Prospect, William Wood wrote, "the plenty of better fish makes these of little esteem, except the head and finnes, which stewed or baked is very good; these halibuts be little set by while basse is in season." But before the turn of the 20th century, overfishing had greatly depleted halibut stocks which have only maintained their numbers on the deeper continental slopes where fishing is less intense. Today otter trawls take the bulk of the catch though formerly long liners used to land many of the large fish.

Turbot or Greenland Halibut. Turbot, *Reinhardtius hippoglossoides*, closely resemble halibut, though they are much smaller and their fins give a more ovoid shape to the fish's body. Turbot grow to 25 pounds (11 kg) and about 40 inches (1 m) in length, and their jaws are large with stronger teeth than those of the halibut.

The turbot is a cold-water fish, found in the Arctic and subarctic as well as deep offshore the Boreal zone.

American Dab or Canadian Plaice. The dab, or Canadian plaice, *Hippoglossoides platessoides*, is a right-handed and large-mouthed flatfish, like the halibut, but it grows only to a maximum of about 30 inches (75 cm) and 14 pounds (6 kg). In addition, its tail is rounded instead of being concave.

The dab prefers a sandy mud or oozy mud substrate between rocky patches. Though many are caught in gill nets and trawls, indicating a certain activity, the dab is quite a sluggish fish and it eats slow-moving prey such as sea urchins, sand dollars and brittle stars.

Dabs are spring spawners in the southern and middle areas of the Boreal zone; spawning is delayed further north and east until temperatures warm sufficiently. A female lays from 30,000 to 60,000 buoyant eggs which hatch within two weeks. By its first winter, the young flatfish will be 2 or 3 inches (5 to 7.5 cm) in length and thereafter growth rate is related to temperature as well as to food.

Though halibut used to eat many dab in former years, the main dab predators left now are spiny dogfish and large cod. Though the dab is in good supply and is an excellent table fish, the demand for it is still relatively low.

FLOUNDERS. Three flounders, the yellowtail flounder, the winter flounder and the witch flounder are also of economic importance in this region. The winter flounder, *Pseudopleuronectes americanus*, is also a shallow- and brackish-water fish and is discussed in chapter 5.

Yellowtail Flounder. Like the other flatfish described here, the yellowtail flounder, *Limanda ferruginea*, is right handed with its eyes on its right side. It is relatively wide and though its snout is somewhat pointed, its mouth is

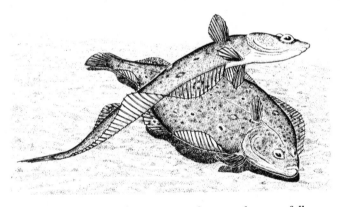

139. The undulating fins of the flounder propel it gracefully through the water.

small. As its name states, its fins and tail are yellow while the rest of the body is brownish and marked with rusty spots. The largest yellowtails grow to about 22 inches (55 cm) and 2½ pounds (1 kg).

The yellowtail makes up a large part of the fillet of sole that is sold and is caught by bottom trawl nets and gill nets over sand or mixed sand and mud substrates. They avoid rocky substrates as do most flatfish and are usually taken in less than 50 fathoms (90 m) of water. Their small mouths and sluggish habits allow yellowtails to prey only on small crustaceans such as amphipods and small shrimp, and on small mollusks and worms.

Yellowtails breed over a long period, beginning in March and continuing to mid-summer. By the end of its first year of growth, the young yellowtail is about 5 inches (12.5 cm) in length. It is a cool-water fish and breeds as far east as the Grand Banks.

Gray Sole or Witch Flounder.   The gray sole or witch flounder, *Glyptocephalus cynoglossus*, is a brownish or grayish flatfish which grows to 25 inches (63 cm) and 4 pounds (1.8 kg). It is a very thin fish, with a body shape that is over twice as long as it is wide and with a very small mouth. The gray sole is commonest between 50 and 150 fathoms (90 to 270 m) and survives impressive temperature ranges, from 30° to 48° F (−1° to 9° C). It does not migrate in either cold or warm seasons. Once it has taken to the bottom it rarely moves very far away. It prefers muddy sand and clay.

Like the yellowtail, the gray sole eats mostly small crustaceans, small mollusks, starfish and worms. It breeds from July to mid-October with peak spawning in July and August. Also like the yellowtail, the gray sole is caught by otter trawl.

Other Demersal Fish

Butterfish or Dollarfish.   Another very flat fish but one that swims vertically on its edge like most fish is the butterfish or dollarfish, *Poronotus triacanthus*. Grayish blue above and silver below, the butterfish shape and color combine to give it a silver-dollar appearance, hence its other common name. The dollarfish is relatively small, growing to 12 inches (30 cm) in length and about a pound (.45 kg) in weight. The snout is blunt and its mouth is small with weak teeth.

Butterfish prefer sandy bottoms where they feed on small fish, squid, small crustaceans and annelid worms. Though they winter in depths to 100 fathoms (180 m), in the summer they move into more shallow water, swimming in loose schools in upper layers of water where they are caught by trawls or in pound nets. During the summer they are also caught by draggers or bottom trawlers at night, indicating that they are less active during darkness.

Butterfish spawn in the summer a few miles out to sea. The young fry sometimes live under the bell of the lion's mane jellyfish, *Cyanea*, as do haddock fry. The young are eaten by seabirds as well as by larger fish. Though butterfish were used for fertilizer in the 19th century, the oily fish has now found favor at the table.

Porgy or Scup. Porgy, *Stenotomus versicolor*, are related to the sea basses though they aren't as elongated a fish, and the deep and sidewise-flattened body shape is accentuated by a prominently-spined dorsal fin and deeply concave tail, or caudal fin. The porgy reaches a length of 18 inches (45 cm) and a weight of up to 4 pounds (1.8 kg).

Though the porgy is small-mouthed, its teeth are strong and well adapted to feeding on crustaceans and shellfish. It prefers smooth, sandy to rocky bottoms where it remains most of the time feeding in schools. Porgy avoid cold water and are known to die in sudden cold spells. They winter offshore in depths of 50 to 70 fathoms (90 to 130 m) and come inshore with spring warming temperatures. Spawning occurs mostly in June, during which time the adults cease feeding as do most fish. When available, the young are heavily preyed upon by cod.

Porgy fisheries are irregular in the Boreal region, possibly due to variation in annual temperature. Porgy are taken by traps and otter trawls and are a good sport fish as well, favored for their fight as well as their flavor.

Redfish, Rosefish or Ocean Perch. Redfish or rosefish, *Sebastes marinus*, is very perch-like in shape, giving it its other common name of ocean perch, though its brilliant orange to bright red color makes it unmistakable. Like the sea basses and porgy, the forward spiny portion of its dorsal fin is continuous with the posterior soft portions of the fin. However, the mouth and eyes are much larger and the head itself is more spiny.

A fish of recent economic importance, the redfish grows slowly, reaching a maximum of 2 feet (60 cm) and 5 pounds (2.3 kg), though 18 inches (40 cm) and 3 pounds (1.4 kg) is

140. The redfish or ocean perch prefers cool deep water.

considered large. Redfish mature at 9 to 10 inches (23 to 25 cm) length at about 10 years of age, and the female retains her eggs internally until the fry are born anytime from May through August. Though redfish are not as prolific as other fish, a female producing only 25,000 to 40,000 eggs per year, the young have greater chance for survival as they are protected by their mothers through the egg stage.

The redfish is a cool-water fish, preferring rocky or hard ground in depths greater than 50 fathoms (90 m). Though it remains on the bottom during the day, the redfish often migrates to surface waters at night. It does move seasonally to greater and lesser depths, though many inhabit great enough depths to avoid extremely warm or cold temperatures without much migration. The Gulf of St. Lawrence populations, for instance, inhabit deep troughs, avoiding the icy intermediate layer which acts as an effective barrier and keeps the fish from any upward migration.

Redfish eat many crustaceans, including the pelagic mysids, euphausiids and northern shrimp at night, as well as mollusks and small fish. In turn, it is eaten by all larger predaceous fish, and its fry are devoured by cod and halibut as well as by older redfish, re-emphasizing how the young of a species are usually not recognized by the adults except as prey.

Fishing year round, otter trawls take most of the commercial catch of this excellent table fish. Redfish are usually marketed as frozen fillets of ocean perch.

Appendices

USEFUL ADDRESSES

Parks and Reserves

Massachusetts Department of Commerce
and Development
Box 1775,
Boston, Massachusetts 02195

New Hampshire Division of Parks
Concord, New Hampshire 03301

Maine Bureau of Parks and Recreation
State House
Augusta, Maine 04333

New Brunswick Tourism
P.O. Box 12345, Fredericton,
New Brunswick, Canada E3B 5C3

Tourisme—Québec
Casier Postal 20,000
Québec, Canada G1K 7X2

Nova Scotia Communications and Information Centre
1650 Bedford Row, P.O. Box 2206
Halifax, Nova Scotia, Canada B3J 3C4

Prince Edward Island Department of Tourism
P.O. Box 2000, Charlottetown,
Prince Edward Island, Canada C1A 7N8

Newfoundland and Labrador Department of Tourism
P.O. Box 4750, St. John's,
Newfoundland, Canada A1C 5T7

United States National Parks Service
North Atlantic Regional Office,
15 State Street
Boston, Massachusetts 02109

Rachel Carson National Wildlife Refuge
U.S. Fish and Wildlife Service
Washington, D.C. 20240

Parks Canada
Department of Indian and Northern Affairs,
400 Laurier Avenue West
Ottawa, Ontario, Canada K1A 0H4

Cape Cod National Seashore
South Wellfleet,
Massachusetts 02663

Acadia National Park
Bar Harbor,
Maine 04609

Parker River National Wildlife Refuge
Plum Island, Newburyport,
Massachusetts 01950

Scarborough Marsh
Maine Audubon Society, 118 Old Rte. 1
Falmouth, Maine 04105

Fundy National Park
Alma,
New Brunswick, Canada E0A 1B0

Kouchibouguac National Park
Kouchibouguac,
New Brunswick, Canada E0A 2A0

Bowdoin Scientific Station Seabird Sanctuary
Kent Island, Grand Manan,
New Brunswick, Canada E0G 2C0

Forillon National Park
P.O. Box 1220, Gaspé,
Québec, Canada G0C 1R0

Bonaventure Island Bird Sanctuary
Percé, Gaspé,
Québec, Canada G0C 2L0

Cape Breton Highlands National Park
Ingonish Beach,
Nova Scotia, Canada B0C 1L0

Prince Edward Island National Park
P.O. Box 487, Charlottetown,
Prince Edward Island,
Canada C1A 7L1

Gros Morne National Park
P.O. Box 130, Rocky Harbor,
Newfoundland, Canada A0K 4N0

Terra Nova National Park
Gloverton,
Newfoundland, Canada A0G 2L0

Witless Bay Island Seabird Sanctuary
Office of Director of Wildlife
Department of Tourism, Bldg. 810,
Pleasantville, St. John's,
Newfoundland, Canada A1C 5T7

Organizations

Association For Preservation of Cape Cod
Box 636
Orleans, Massachusetts 02653

Audubon Society—Northeast U.S. Regional Office
44 Exchange Street
Portland, Maine 04101

Massachusetts Audubon Society
South Great Road
Lincoln, Massachusetts 10773

Maine Audubon Society
118 Old Route 1
Falmouth, Maine 04105

Friends of the Earth
Anne Wickham, 620C Street SE
Washington, D.C. 20003

Greenpeace (Canada)
2007 West 4th Avenue, Vancouver,
British Columbia, Canada

Greenpeace (U.S.)
Box 4793
Santa Barbara, California 93103

The Nature Conservancy—New England Regional Office
294 Washington Street, Rm 850
Boston, Massachusetts 02108

Nature Conservancy Canada
2180 Yonge Street
Toronto, Canada M4S 2E7

Rare Animal Relief Effort
David Hill, National Audubon
950 Third Avenue
New York, New York 10022

Sierra Club
3 Joy Street
Boston, Massachusetts 02108

World Wildlife Fund
1319 18th Street NW
Washington, D.C.

New Brunswick Wildlife Federation
Box 30, Grand Bay P.O.
Kings Co.
New Brunswick, Canada E0G 1W0

Nova Scotia Wildlife Federation
P.O. Box 654, Halifax,
Nova Scotia, Canada B3J 2T3

Québec Wildlife Federation
6420 Saint Denis Street
Montreal, Canada H2S 2R7

Newfoundland-Labrador Wildlife Federation
Mr. George Spence
49 Midland Row, Pasadena,
Newfoundland, Canada

Whales and Whale Trips

Allied Whale
College of the Atlantic
Bar Harbor, Maine 04609

Friends of the Museum of Comparative Zoology
Harvard University
Cambridge, Massachusetts 02138

Zoological Society of Montreal
2055 Peel Street
Montreal, Canada H3A 1V4

National Museum of Natural Sciences
Ottawa, Ontario
Canada K1A 0M8

Aquaria

New England Aquarium
Central Wharf
Boston, Massachusetts 02110

Seaquarium (summer only)
Department of Marine Resources
Boothbay Harbor, Maine 04538

Huntsman Laboratory Aquarium (summer only)
St. Andrews, New Brunswick, Canada

Gulf of Maine Aquarium (summer only)
Long Wharf
Portland, Maine

USEFUL ADDRESSES

CLASSIFICATION OF MARINE
PLANTS AND ANIMALS

The terminology used in classification schemes is important only in that it identifies the degree of similarity or evolutionary closeness of different species. Extremely closely related species are members of the same genus; less closely related ones will belong to different genera but perhaps the same family or superfamily; extremely different species may belong to different orders, classes, phyla (or divisions), or even subkingdoms or kingdoms.

This classification follows that of W.T. Keeton in *Biological Science*, 3rd ed., W.W. Norton & Co., Inc., 1980. For historical reasons, the level of organization called a phylum in the animal kingdom is called a division in the plant kingdom.

Kingdom Monera

Division Schizomycetes: Bacteria
Division Cyanophyta: Blue-green algae. *Calothrix*

Kingdom Protista

    Section Protophyta: Algal protists

Division Chrysophyta: Diatoms.
Division Pyrrophyta: Dinoflagellates. *Noctiluca, Gonyaulax*

    Section Protozoa

Phylum Mastigophora: Flagellated protozoans.
Phylum Sarcodina: Pseudopodial or ameboid protozoans.
Phylum Ciliata: Ciliated protozoans.

Kingdom Plantae

Division Chlorophyta: Green algae. *Ulva, Enteromorpha, Spongomorpha.*
Division Phaeophyta: Brown algae. *Fucus, Ascophyllum, Laminaria.*
Division Rhodophyta: Red algae. *Porphyra, Rhodymenia, Chondrus.*
Division Tracheophyta: Vascular plants
  Subdivision Spermopsida: Seed plants.
   Class Angiospermae: Flowering plants. *Spartina, Hudsonia.*

Kingdom Animalia
    Subkingdom Parazoa

Phylum Porifera: Sponges.
  Class Calcarea: Calcareous sponges.
  Class Hexactinellida: Glass sponges.
  Class Desmospongiae: *Halichondria, Haliclona, Cliona.*

    Subkingdom Metazoa

    Section Radiata

Phylum Coelenterata: Stinging organisms.
  Class Hydrozoa: Hydroids. *Obelia, Tubularia, Hydractinia.*
  Class Scyphozoa: Jellyfish. *Aurelia, Cyanea.*
  Class Anthozoa: Sea anemones and corals. *Metridium, Astrangia.*
Phylum Ctenophora: Comb jellies. *Pleurobrachia, Mnemiopsis.*

    Section Protostomia

Phylum Platyhelminthes: Flatworms.
Phylum Nemertina: Ribbon worms. *Cerebratulus.*
Phylum Aschelminthes.
  Class Rotifera.
  Class Gastrotricha.
  Class Kinorhyncha.
  Class Nematoda: Round worms.
Phylum Bryozoa (or Ectoprocta): Bryozoans or moss animals.
    Bugula, Membranoptera.
Phylum Brachiopoda: Lamp shells.
Phylum Mollusca: Mollusks.
  Class Amphineura: Chitons. *Ischnochiton.*
  Class Gastropoda: Snails and their allies. *Littorina, Lacuna,
    Thais, Crepidula, Acmaea.*
  Class Pelecypoda: Bivalves. *Mytilus, Mya, Aequipecten.*
  Class Cephalopoda: Squid, octopus. *Loligo, Ilex.*
Phylum Annelida: Segmented worms.
  Class Polychaeta: Sandworms, tubeworms. *Nereis, Nephtys,
    Amphitrite, Arenicola, Spirorbis.*
  Class Oligochaeta: Earthworms and allies. Marine tubificids.
Phylum Tardigrada: Water bears.
Phylum Arthropoda.
  Subphylum Chelicerata.
    Class Xiphosura: Horseshoe crabs. *Limulus.*
    Class Arachnida: Spiders, ticks, mites.
    Class Pycnogonida: Sea spiders.
  Subphylum Mendibulata.
    Class Crustacea
      Subclass Ostracoda.
      Subclass Copepoda. Copepods.
        Order Calanoida. *Calanus.*

Order Harpacticoida. Harpacticoids.
Subclass Cirripedia: Barnacles. *Balanus, Lepas.*
Subclass Malacostraca: Crabs, Lobsters, Shrimp.
  Superorder Peracarida.
    Order Mysidacea. *Praunus, Neomysis, Mysis.*
    Order Isopoda. *Ligia.*
    Order Amphipoda.
      Suborder Gammaridea: *Gammarus, Orchestia, Coro-phium.*
      Suborder Caprellidea: Skeleton shrimp. *Caprella.*
    Superorder Eucarida.
      Order Euphausiacea. Euphausiids or krill. *Meganyc-tiphanes, Thysanoessa.*
      Order Decapoda.
        Suborder Natantia: Swimmers.
          Section Caridea: Shrimp. *Crangon, Pandalus.*
        Suborder Reptantia: Crawlers.
          Section Macrura: Lobsters and crayfish. *Homarus.*
          Section Anomura: Crab-like crustaceans.
            Superfamily Paguridea: Hermit crabs. *Pagurus.*
            Superfamily Hippidea: Mole crabs. *Emerita.*
          Section Brachyura: True crabs.
            Superfamily Brachyrhyncha: *Cancer, Carcinus.*
            Superfamily Oxyrhyncha: Spider crabs. *Hyas, Libinia.*
  Class Insecta.
    Order Collembola: Springtales. *Anurida.*
    Order Diptera: Mosquitos and true flies. *Aedes.*

    Section Deuterostomia

Phylum Chaetognatha: Arrow worms. *Sagitta.*
Phylum Echinodermata.
  Class Asteroidea: Starfish. *Asterias, Henricia, Solaster.*
  Class Ophiuroidea: Brittle stars. *Ophiopholus.*
  Class Echinoidea: Sand dollars and sea urchins. *Echinarachnius, Strongylocentrotus.*
  Class Holothuroidea: Sea cucumbers. *Cucumaria, Psolus, Syn-apta.*
Phylum Hemichordata.
  Class Enteropneusta. Acorn worms.
Phylum Chordata.
  Subphylum Tunicata (or Urochordata): Tunicates.
  Class Ascidiacea. Sea squirts or ascidians. *Molgula, Botryllus, Boltenia.*
  Subphylum Cephalochordata. *Amphioxius.*

Subphylum Vertebrata.
  Class Agnatha: Jawless fish. *Petromyzon*.
  Class Chondrichthyes: Cartilaginous fish. Sharks and skates.
  Class Osteichthyes: Bony fish.
  Class Aves: Birds.
  Class Mammalia: Mammals.

Glossary

ABIOTIC: physical aspects of the environment such as wind, currents, wave action.

ALGIN: a gelatinous extract of certain seaweeds used in many types of industries.

ALTRICIAL BIRD: a bird which is born naked, blind and helpless.

ANADROMOUS: the ability of fish to go from salt water to fresh water, usually to breed.

ANAEROBIC: without air; some animals are able to respire for at least brief periods without the use of atmospheric oxygen.

ANNUAL PLANTS: plants which live only for a single year or season.

AUTOTROPHS: organisms capable of manufacturing organic nutrients from inorganic raw materials. Most plants are autotrophs.

BALEEN: the fringed mouth plates of certain whales, used in a sieve-like manner during feeding; whalebone.

BENTHIC: bottom-dwelling.

BIOMASS: the total amount of all living things.

BIOTIC: biological aspects of the environment, such as competition and predation.

BIVALVE: a two-shelled mollusk.

BOREAL: northern, cold-temperate.

BYSSAL THREADS: horny threads secreted by some bivalves, used to secure the animals to a substrate.

CARAPACE: a hard, bony or chitinous covering or shell.

CARNIVORE: an animal which is exclusively a meat-eater.

CATADROMOUS: the ability of certain fish to go from fresh to salt water, especially to breed.

CHELIPED: large claw of a crustacean.

CHLOROPHYLL: the green pigment of plants necessary for photosynthesis.

COMPETITION: an attempt by two or more individuals to use the same limited resource such as food or space.

Glossary

435

CONSUMERS: organisms which feed on other plants or animals.

DEMERSAL: living on or near the sea-bed.

DEPOSIT FEEDER: an animal that feeds on detritus and loose sediment that has settled on the substrate.

DESICCATION: drying-out.

DETRITUS: bits of decaying plant and animal material.

DIATOMS: microscopic unicellular plants.

DINOFLAGELLATES: microscopic unicellular organisms which have two flagella, or whip-like appendages.

DIVERSITY: the variety of species of organisms in an area.

DORSAL SIDE: the upper side or back of an animal; opposite to ventral.

DRUMLIN: a streamlined mound of earth formed by a glacier riding up over soft bedrock.

ECOSYSTEM: a community of plants and animals and its physical environment considered altogether.

ENDEMIC: restricted to a given locality.

EXOSKELETON: a hard supporting or protective covering on the outside of an animal's body, like the shell of a crustacean.

FILTER-FEEDER: an organism which feeds by filtering microscopic food particles out of the water.

FOOD WEB: the sequence of organisms, including producers, consumers and decomposers through which energy and materials may move in a community.

FROND: the blade or leaf-like part of marine algae.

GAMETOPHYTE: the stage of a plant's life cycle which produces sexual reproductive cells called gametes or eggs and sperm.

GRAZERS: animals which eat plants; herbivores.

GYRES: localized columns of rising or sinking water. A cyclonic gyre rotates in a counter-clockwise direction and its water rises. An anti-cyclonic gyre rotates in a clockwise direction and its water sinks.

HABITAT: the kind of place a plant or animal usually lives.

HERBIVORE: an animal that eats plants.

HERMAPHRODITE: an animal that has both male and female reproductive organs.

HOLDFAST: the part of a marine plant that secures it to the substrate.

IGNEOUS: rock formed by the cooling and solidification of magma.

INTERSTITIAL: the spaces in between sand and mud particles.

INTERTIDAL: the shore area between the highest spring tides and the lowest spring tides.

INVERTEBRATE: an animal lacking a backbone.

KRILL: small shrimp-like animals, known also as euphausiids.

LARVA: the early development stage of most marine animals. A larva looks quite unlike its adult form and is often planktonic.

MACROALGAE: marine plants which commonly have holdfasts and fronds, and which are considerably larger than unicellular algae.

MACROFAUNA: animals which are larger than 2 mm.

MAXIMUM SUSTAINED YIELD (MSY): a fisheries management approach whereby a certain number of tons of fish remain in a population to ensure adequate propagation of the species. This management approach considers each species of fish in a given area as an isolated unit.

METAMORPHOSIS: radical reorganization of an immature animal, often a larval stage, into the adult form.

MICROALGAE: microscopic plants.

MICROHABITAT: a subdivision of a standard habitat.

MOLT: the shedded exoskeleton of certain animals, allowing the animal to grow larger.

MORAINE: rock material brought forward to the outer edge of glacial ice and deposited in ridges.

MULTISPECIES MANAGEMENT: the management of fisheries through recognition of inter-relationships of species, holding that if one species' population is altered by human predation, at least several other populations of different species are likely to be affected.

OMNIVORE: an animal that eats both plants and animals.

OPERCULUM: a horny plate attached to the foot of many gastropods, which closes the aperture of the shell when the foot is withdrawn.

ORGANIC COMPOUNDS: chemical compounds that contain carbon and usually hydrogen, oxygen and/or nitrogen, forming the carbohydrates, lipids, proteins and nucleic acids, which are the basic constituents of living organisms.

OVIDUCT: the tube down which eggs must pass before being liberated.

PARABOLIC DUNE: U-shaped sand dune which gradually moves downwind.

PELAGIC SPECIES: those organisms that swim or drift in the water above the ocean bottom, in contrast to benthic or demersal species.

PERENNIAL PLANTS: plants that live for years, reproducing annually.

PERIOSTRACUM: the layer of horny material covering the outer surface of the shells of mollusks.

pH: measurement of acidity or alkalinity; negative log of the hydrogen ion concentration; pH of 7 is neutral, below pH of 7 is acid, above pH of 7 is basic or alkaline.

PHOTIC ZONE: the depth of surface waters to which light penetrates sufficiently to permit photosynthesis.

PHOTOSYNTHESIS: production of organic materials by plants, using light as the source of energy.

PHYTOPLANKTON: microscopic plants that drift with the ocean currents.

PLANKTON: plants or animals that drift with the ocean currents.

POLYP: the sedentary hydroid or anemone-like stage in the life cycle of a coelenterate.

PRECOCIAL BIRD: a bird that is born capable of caring for itself, independently of its parents.

PROBOSCIS: in invertebrates, an elongate, sometimes eversible organ situated in or near the mouth and usually used in feeding.

PRODUCERS: plants and other autotrophs which are the food source of herbivores or primary consumers, forming the base of every food web.

PRODUCTIVITY: the energy bound into new plant or animal material by growth.

PROMISCUOUS MATING: mating in species which form no pair bonds at all, though the choice of mates is random.

PROTANDROUS SPECIES: species in which individuals develop first as males and then become females when they are older and usually larger.

RADULA: rasp-like organ used by many gastropods in feeding.

RESPIRATION: the taking in of oxygen and releasing of carbon dioxide by breathing; the release of energy by the oxidation of organic molecules.

SCAVENGER: an animal that eats decaying plants or animals.

SEDIMENTARY ROCK: rock such as sandstone formed from accumulations of sediment, characterized by stratification.

SEICHE: rhythmic rocking movement of water back and forth within an enclosed basin.

SEMIPRECOCIAL BIRD: a bird that is born neither helpless nor independent.

SESSILE: fastened to a substrate.

SPAWN: to shed eggs or sperm.

SPOROPHYTE: the stage of a plant's life cycle which produces asexual reproductive cells called spores.

SUBSTRATE: the base on which an organism lives, such as mud, sand or rock.

SUCCESSION: progressive change in the plant or animal life of an area.

SUSPENSION FEEDER: an animal that feeds by filtering suspended plankton or detritus from the water.

TECTONIC: relating to the deformation of the earth's crust.

TIDES: ebb—the dropping or falling tide.
flow—the rising tide.
neap—tides of minimum range occurring at first and third quarters of the moon.
spring—tides of maximum range occurring at the times of new and full moon.

TURBIDITY: degree of cloudiness of water due to presence of suspended particles.

VENTRAL SIDE: usually the under or abdominal side of an animal; opposite to dorsal.

ZONATION: subdivision of the organisms of a habitat into zones or regions experiencing different degrees of exposure to critical biotic or abiotic factors.

ZOOPLANKTON: animals that drift with the ocean currents.

Bibliography

Geology and Geography

Apollonio, S. *The Gulf of Maine*. Rockland: Courier of Maine Books, 1979. A good, brief account of the geological and oceanographic processes that have determined the nature of the Gulf of Maine.

Chapman, C. A. *The Geology of Acadia National Park*. Chatham, Mass.: The Chatham Press, Inc., 1970. An account of a representative part of Maine's rocky coast.

Farb, Peter. *The Face of North America*. New York: Harper Colophon Books, 1968. A broad inclusive description of the geology and geography of the continent.

Strahler, A. N. *A Geologist's View of Cape Cod*. Garden City, N.Y.: Natural History Press, 1966. A good introduction to the geological past and present of the Cape.

Wilson, J. Tuzo. *Continents Adrift and Aground, Readings from Scientific American*. San Francisco: W.H. Freeman & Co., 1976. A collection of some excellent discussions of the evidence supporting the theory of continental drift.

Marine Science Texts

Barnes, Robert D. *Invertebrate Zoology*. Philadelphia: W. B. Saunders, 1974. A detailed, sophisticated introduction to the biology of marine invertebrates.

Briggs, John C. *Marine Zoogeography*. New York: McGraw-Hill Book Co., 1974. A well-documented analysis of the world's marine geographical regions.

Cushing, D. H. and J. J. Walsh, eds. *The Ecology of the Seas*. Philadelphia: W. B. Saunders, 1976. A discussion of many of the major concepts of marine ecology.

Dawson, E. Yale. *Marine Botany, An Introduction*. New York: Holt, Rinehart, Winston, 1966. A valuable text, introducing marine algae to both the novice and experienced botanist.

Green, J. *The Biology of Estuarine Animals*. Seattle: Univ. of Washington Press, 1968. A detailed introduction to the plants and animals in estuaries around the planet.

Hedgpeth, J. W., ed. *Treatise on Marine Ecology and Paleoecology. Vol. 1, Ecology.* Memoirs of the Geological Society of America, 1957. An extraordinary and immense book, with a wealth of information about marine habitats from all parts of the world.

Keeton, William T. *Biological Science 3rd Edition.* New York: W. W. Norton & Co., 1980. A general introductory textbook in biology which is up-to-date, challenging, and one of the best.

Menard, H. W. *Ocean Science: Readings from Scientific American.* San Francisco: W. H. Freeman & Co., 1977. A wide selection of articles on oceanography, marine geology and marine ecology.

Newell, R. C. *Biology of Intertidal Organisms.* New York: American Elsevier Publishing Co., 1970. Emphasizes the various physiological adaptations of organisms, especially invertebrates, to intertidal existence.

Nybakken, J. W., ed. *Readings in Marine Ecology.* New York: Harper & Row, 1971. A collection of some of the most important articles on marine ecology published in the biological periodicals prior to 1970.

Zottoli, Robert. *Introduction to Marine Environments.* St. Louis, Mo.: C. V. Mosby, 1976. A detailed text which has some emphasis on the northeast coast and which contains many useful references.

General Seashore

Amos, William H. *Life of the Seashore.* New York: McGraw Hill, 1966. Contains many fine photographs as it introduces the various seashore habitats.

The Audubon Society Book of Marine Wildlife. New York: Harry Abrams, 1980. A magnificent collection of some of the best photographs of marine life.

Berrill, N. J. *The Living Tide.* New York: Dodd Mead, 1953. An evocative exploration of marine life along parts of the U.S. east coast.

Berrill, N. J. and Jacquelyn Berrill. *One Thousand and One Questions Answered About the Seashore.* New York: Dover Publ., 1976. As informative as its title implies.

Carson, Rachel. *The Edge of the Sea.* Boston: Houghton Mifflin Co., 1979. Beautifully written description of marine life and habitats along the U.S. east coast. Originally published in 1955.

Culliney, J. L. *The Forests of the Sea.* San Francisco: Sierra Club Books, 1976. A selective presentation of marine habitats and their organisms and the degrees to which they are threatened.

Edey, Maitland A. and the Editors of Time-Life Books. *The Northeast Coast.* New York: Time-Life Books, 1972. General account with fine photographs of the geology and marine life of the Boreal coast.

Gibbons, Euell. *Stalking the Blue-eyed Scallop.* New York: David McKay Co., 1964. A famous introduction to what is most edible among the plants and animals of the seashore.

MacGinitie, G. E., and Nettie MacGinitie. *Natural History of Marine Animals 2nd Edition.* New York: McGraw Hill, 1968. A relatively non-technical account of a broad diversity of marine invertebrates.

Miller, Dorcas. *The Maine Coast: A Nature Lover's Guide.* Charlotte, N.C.: East Woods Press Books, 1979. A concise and valuable guide to the marine habitats and organisms to look for along the coast of Maine.

Yonge, C. M. *The Sea Shore.* London: Collins-World, 1963. Despite its emphasis on the British coast, still an excellent introduction to seashore life.

Beaches, Sand Dunes and Salt Marshes

Bascom, Willard. *Waves and Beaches.* Garden City, N.Y.: Anchor Books, Doubleday, 1980. An updated edition of a clear account of the dynamics of beaches, first published in 1964.

Giese, G. S. and R. B. Giese. *The Eroding Shores of Outer Cape Cod.* Orleans, Mass: Association for the Preservation of Cape Cod, Information Bull. #5, 1974. A brief but disturbing warning.

Hay, John. *The Great Beach.* New York: W. W. Norton & Co., 1980. A naturalist's celebration of Cape Cod.

Kopper, P. *The Wild Edge: Life and Lore of the Great Atlantic Beaches.* Times Books, 1979. Fine evocation of much of the life and feeling of the beaches.

Sterling, Dorothy. *Our Cape Cod Salt Marshes.* Orleans, Mass: Association for the Preservation of Cape Cod, 1976. A concise review of the biology and importance of salt marshes on the Cape.

Teal, J. and M. Teal. *Life and Death of the Salt Marsh.* New York: Ballantine Books, 1969. An excellent tale of the historical use of salt marshes along the Atlantic coast as well as of the adaptations of the marsh plants and animals.

Townsend, Charles Wendell. *Sand Dunes and Salt Marshes*. Boston: Dana Estes & Co., 1913. A book worth looking for, written by a fine naturalist and illustrated with remarkable black and white photographs.

Higher Plants

Gleason, Harry A. *Illustrated Flora of the Northeastern United States and Adjacent Canada*. 3 Vols. Lancaster, Penn: Lancaster Press, Inc., 1952. An excellent and complete identification guide.

Hinds, H. R. and W. A. Hathaway. *Wildflowers of Cape Cod*. Chatham, Mass: Chatham Press, 1968. Useful for identification of salt marsh and sand dune plants.

Peterson, Roger Tory and Margaret McKenny. *A Field Guide to Wildflowers of Northeastern and North Central North America*. Boston: Houghton Mifflin Co., 1968. Good for rapid identification.

Ryan, A. G. *Native Trees and Shrubs of Newfoundland and Labrador*. St. John's, Nfld: Government of Newfoundland and Labrador, 1978. Identification guide for shrubs along the northern part of the Boreal coast.

Algae and Invertebrates

Arnold, Augusta. *The Sea-beach at Ebb-tide*. New York: Dover, 1968. A republication of a 1901 guide to intertidal seaweeds and invertebrates.

Crowder, William. *Seashore Life Between the Tides*. New York: Dover Publications, 1975. A republication of a 1931 guide to the invertebrates of the Atlantic coast.

Gosner, Kenneth L. *Guide to Identification of Marine and Estuarine Invertebrates*. New York: Wiley, 1971. A detailed guide, particularly useful to specialists.

Gosner, Kenneth L. *A Field Guide to the Atlantic Seashore*. Boston: Houghton Mifflin Co., 1979. An excellent guide for identifying the marine algae and invertebrates on the coast from the Bay of Fundy to Cape Hatteras.

Miner, R. W. *Field Book of Seashore Life*. New York: G.P. Putnam's Sons, 1950. A very useful guide to the marine invertebrates along the U.S. east coast.

Morris, Percy A. *A Field Guide to Shells of the Atlantic and Gulf Coasts and the West Indies.* Boston: Houghton Mifflin Co., 1973. Clear photographs for rapid identification.

Ricketts, Edward F. and Jack Calvin. *Between Pacific Tides.* Stanford, California: Stanford University Press, 1968. Though it describes the invertebrates of the Pacific Boreal coast, it remains a treasure of information.

Robbins, Sarah F. and Clarice M. Yentsch. *The Sea is All About Us.* Salem, Mass: Peabody Museum of Salem and Cape Ann Society of Marine Science, 1973. A selective guide to the algae, marine invertebrates and fish of the Cape Ann region.

Taylor, W. R. *Marine Algae of the North East Coast of North America.* Ann Arbor: University of Michigan Press, 1966. A detailed account of boreal seaweeds.

Fish and Fisheries

Bigelow, Henry B. and William C. Shroeder. *Fishes of the Gulf of Maine.* Washington: U.S. Government Printing Office, 1953. This is the best, most detailed description of the fish found in Atlantic boreal waters.

Clifford, Harold B. *Charlie York, Marine Coast Fisherman.* Camden, Maine: International Marine Publishing Co., 1974. In the words of Charlie York, a delightful account of fishing along Maine's coast from the 1880's to 1960's.

Hardy, Alister. *The Open Sea,* 2 Vols. Boston: Houghton Mifflin Co., 1971. An excellent introduction to the plankton and fish of the sea away from shore.

McClane, A. J. *McClane's Field Guide to Saltwater Fishes of North America.* New York: Holt, Rinehart & Winston, 1978. A well-illustrated and informative identification guide to both cold and warm water fish.

Noel, H. S. *Fisherman's Manual.* London: Riverside House, 1976. Good description of commercial fishing gear.

Birds

The Audubon Society Field Guide to North American Birds, Eastern Region. Westminster, Maryland: Alfred A. Knopf, 1977. Identification guide, with photographs instead of drawings.

Bent, Arthur Cleveland. *Life Histories of North American Shore Birds*, 2 Vols. 1962. *Life Histories of North American Diving Birds*, 1963. *Life Histories of North American Gulls and Terns*, 1963. *Life Histories of North American Marsh Birds*, 1963. *Life Histories of North American Petrels and Pelicans and their Allies*, 1964. New York: Dover Publications. Originally published between 1919 and 1927, Bent's descriptions are detailed and fascinating, and give us a clear picture of the bird populations at the beginning of the century and as long ago as the 1830's.

Nelson, Bryan. *Seabirds: Their Biology and Ecology*. New York: A & W Publishers, 1979. An authoritative and well illustrated account of the biology of seabirds around the world.

Peterson, Roger Tory. *A Field Guide to the Birds*. Boston: Houghton Mifflin Co., 1980. Still the best guide for rapid identification of birds.

Pough, Richard H. *Audubon Water Bird Guide*. Garden City, New York: Doubleday & Co., 1951. Still in print and more than just an identification guide.

Robbins, Chandler S., Bertel Bruin and Herbert Zim. *Birds of North America*. New York: Golden Press, 1966. Another good identification guide.

Tinbergen, N. *The Herring Gull's World*. New York and San Francisco: Harper & Row, 1960. A fine, detailed account of the social life of the herring gull.

Marine Mammals

Coffey, David J. *Dolphins, Whales and Porpoises: An Encyclopedia of Sea Mammals*. New York: Collier Books, 1978. Good photographs and accounts of the habits and other aspects of the biology of the world's cetaceans and seals.

Friends of the Earth. *The Whale Manual*. San Francisco: Friends of the Earth Books, 1978. Lots of valuable information about whales, whaling and the present national and international laws.

Katona, Steven, David Richardson, and Robin Hazard. *A Field Guide to the Whales and Seals of the Gulf of Maine*. Published by the authors, 1975. A short, informative guide to the marine mammals of the Northeast coast.

Scammon, Charles, M. *The Marine Mammals of the Northwestern Coast of North America*. New York: Dover Publications, 1968.

A republication of Scammon's remarkable 1874 account of the whales, seals and fishing methods of his times.

Scheffer, Victor B. *The Year of the Whale*. New York: Charles Scribner's Sons, 1969. A lyrical and fact-filled tale of the life of the sperm whale.

Periodicals

Ecological Monographs: available in most university libraries; publishes a surprising number of articles on marine ecology.

Journal of the Fisheries Research Board of Canada: a more technical journal also available in most university libraries; a source of a great many articles on the east coast marine flora and fauna, with an emphasis on species of commercial interest.

Oceans: available at good bookstores; contains excellent articles and photographs on all aspects of marine life and history.

Oceanus: available in most libraries; contains good reviews of coastal and offshore topics in marine science.

INDEX

Index   457

FIELD NOTES

FIELD NOTES

FIELD NOTES

FIELD NOTES

1
2
3
4
5
6
7
8
9
10
11
12
13
14
15
16
17
18

MEASURING SCALE IN CENTIMETERS AND MILLIMETERS

MEASURING SCALE IN INCHES

1

2

3

4

5

6

7